CASTLES *of* SCOTLAND
IRELAND & WALES

CASTLES *of* SCOTLAND
IRELAND & WALES

MARTIN J. DOUGHERTY

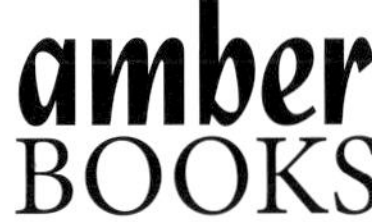

First published as *Celtic Castles* in 2018

This edition published in 2025

Published by Amber Books Ltd
United House
North Road
London
N7 9DP
United Kingdom

www.amberbooks.co.uk
Facebook: amberbooks
YouTube: amberbooksltd
Instagram: amberbooksltd
X(Twitter): @amberbooks

ISBN: 978-1-83886-618-1

Project Editor: Michael Spilling
Designer: Keren Harragan
Picture Research: Terry Forshaw

Printed in China

Contents

Introduction

The word 'Celt' comes from the ancient Greek *Keltoi*, for 'barbarian', but there was nothing uncivilized about Celtic culture. The ancient Celts were fearsome warriors, but they were also excellent metalsmiths, hard-working farmers and well-travelled traders. Celtic tribes inhabited much of Europe, from the fringes of Asia to Spain and the British Isles. Their culture varied from place to place and from time to time over their long history, and even after they were eclipsed or absorbed into changing societies their legacy still lives on. Celtic languages are still spoken in some areas and elements of their art and culture are intertwined into modern society. The early Celts built fortified places to protect themselves against their enemies, and later on the warrior heritage of the Celtic people caused those who opposed them to fortify themselves wherever they could. The Celtic legacy can be seen today, in hill forts built by the ancient tribes and in castles meant to secure control over post-Celtic people.

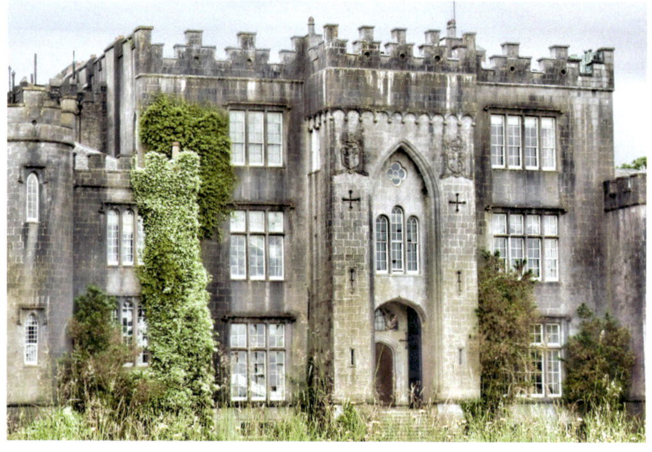

ABOVE:
There has been a castle at Birr since 1170, the era of the Norman invasion of Ireland. The modern castle was built in 1620 and was besieged during the Irish Rebellion of 1641.

RIGHT:
Ogmore Castle in South Wales was built by the Normans to control the nearby river crossing. The original fortification was a motte-and-bailey design begun in 1116; it gradually evolved into a stone castle.

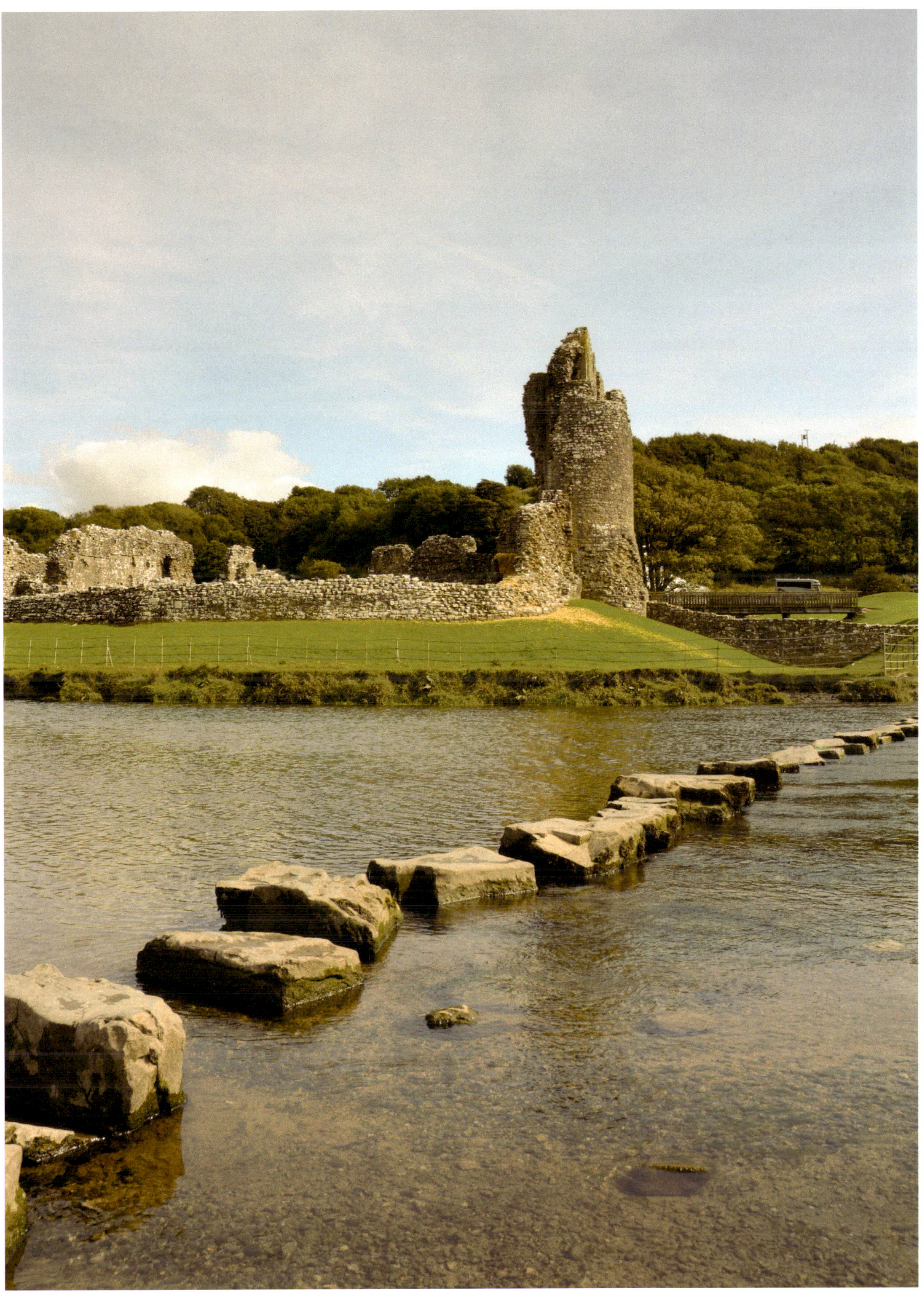

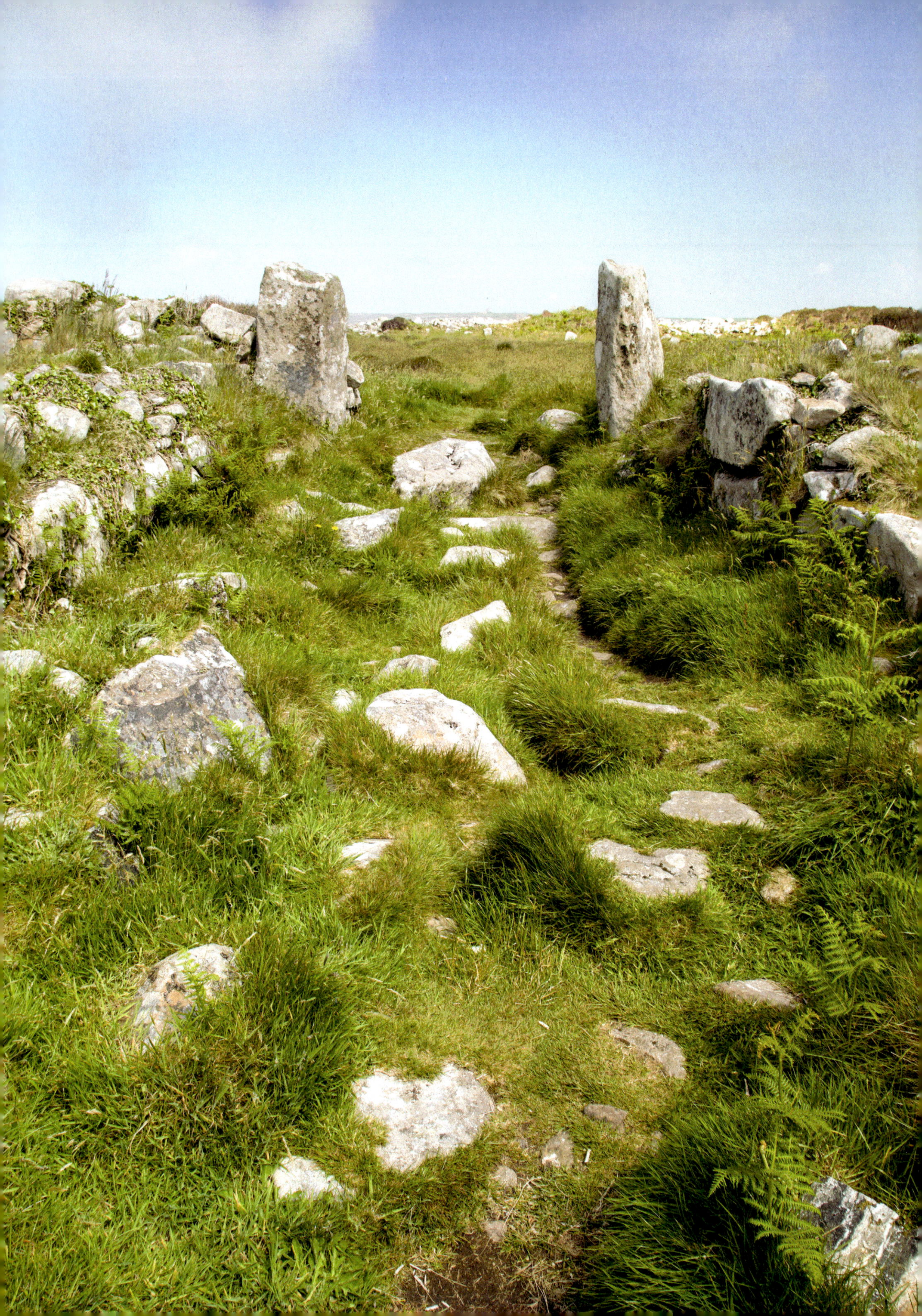

Hill Forts

Hill forts were common across the Celtic world, from Russia to Iberia, though their form varied according to local conditions and customs. Although not as sophisticated as a stone castle, they offered impressive defensive advantages yet required far less time and effort to construct and maintain.

Hill forts took advantage of natural defensive features, creating an effective defensive position with a minimum of materials and effort. Some hill forts had complete and even multi-layered defences, with rings of ditches, earthworks or wooden palisades surrounding a settlement atop a hill with sufficient space at the top. Others had only partial defences, which was still very effective where the terrain made approach from some directions impractical.

Some forts backed onto a cliff or river. Others used artificial defences to cut off part of a ridge or promontory. Even a steep grassy slope more than a couple of metres in height would make a concerted assault from that direction all but impossible, especially in wet conditions. Defences could thus be concentrated on easier approaches, such as a winding path up the side of a steep hill, or the gentler slopes. Natural obstacles such as boulders were often incorporated into the defensive arrangements.

LEFT:
Chun Hill Fort, Cornwall, England
Chun Hill Fort was constructed some time in the 3rd century BC, well into the Iron Age. Its impressive defences took the form of two concentric stone walls, each with a ditch in front of it. The original entrances were in line, but later reconstruction offset the inner entry point and improved its defences. This would be a significant undertaking which would only be worthwhile if there was a real need for enhanced security.

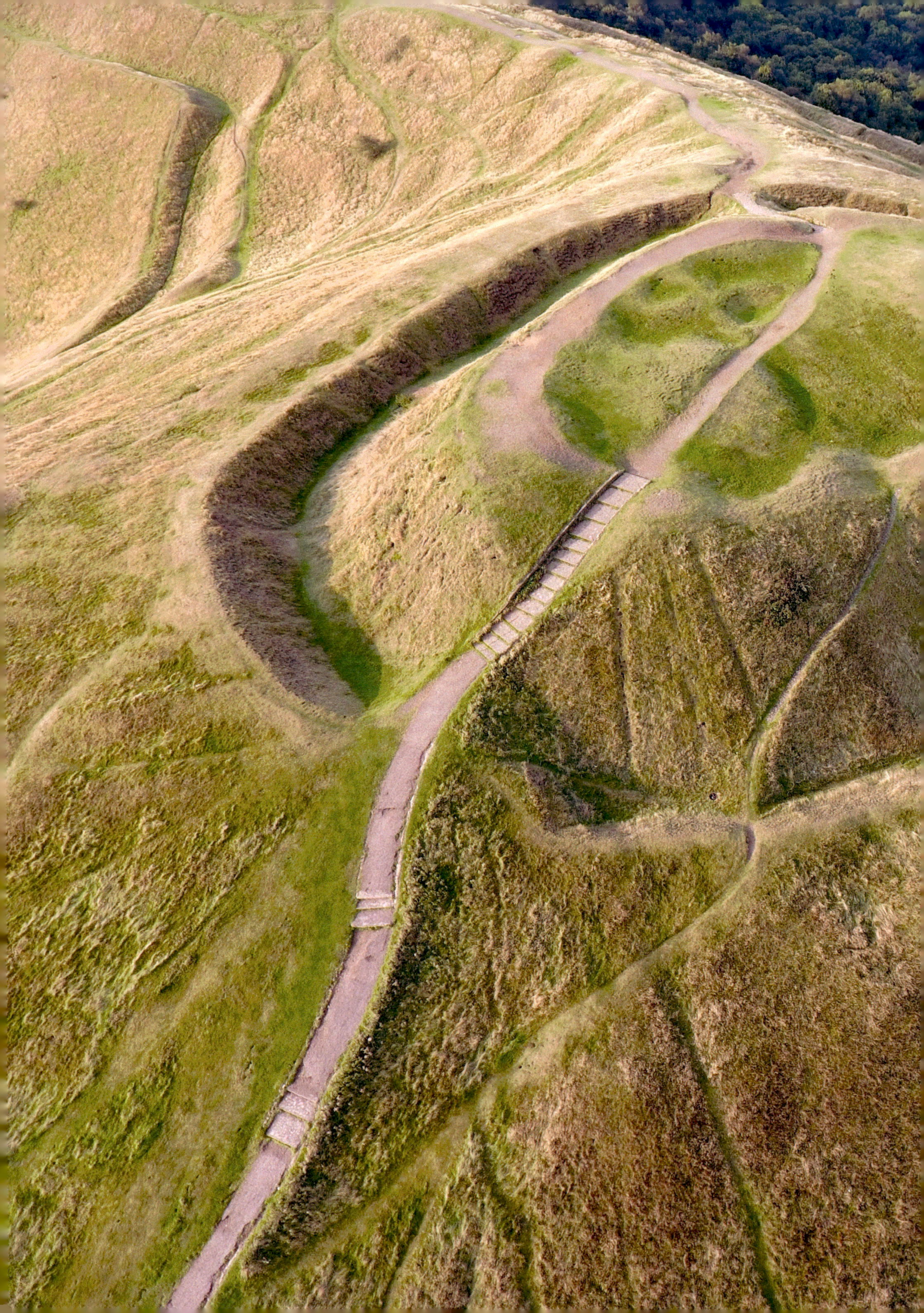

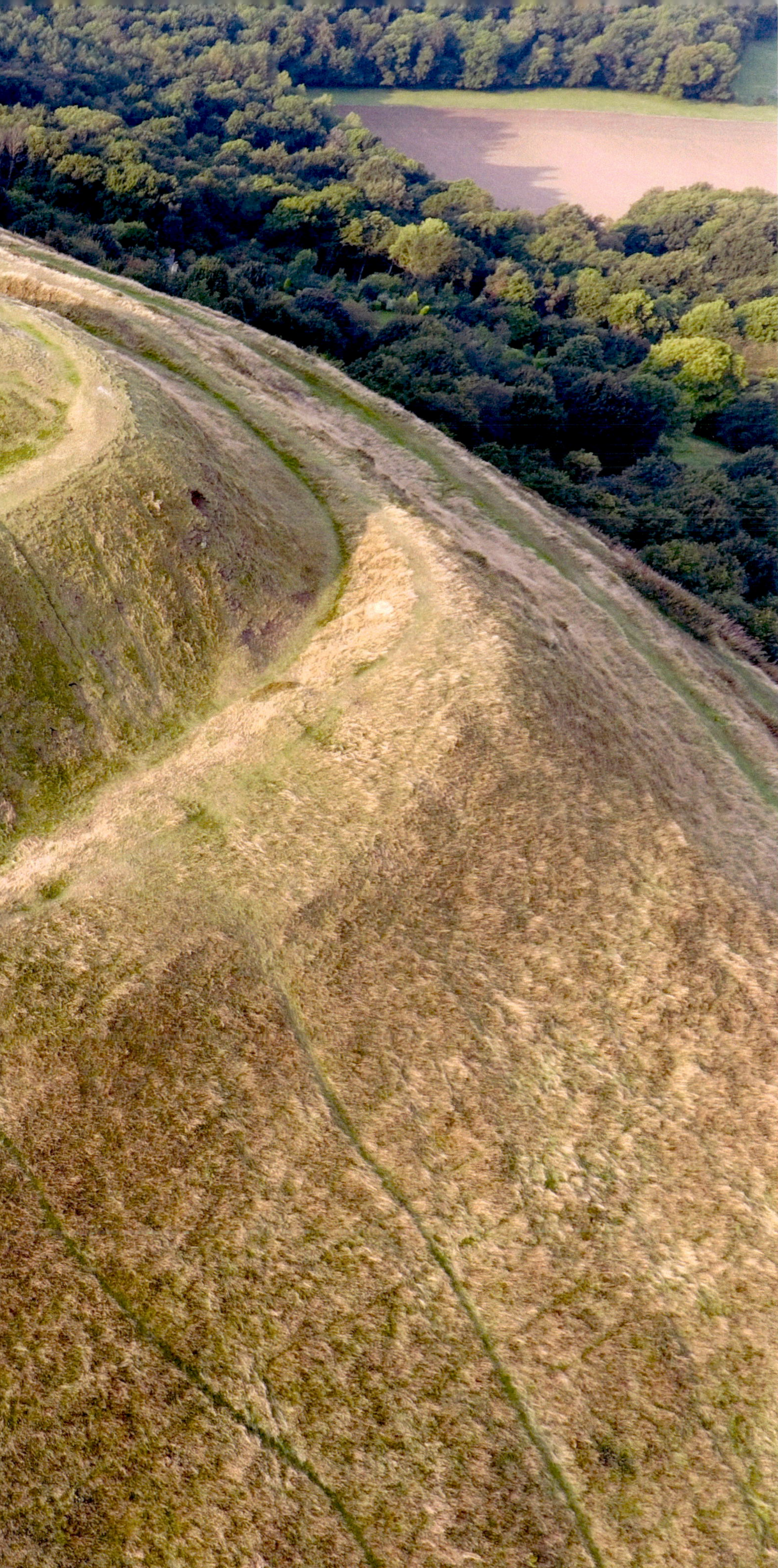

British Camp, Herefordshire, England
British Camp in the Malvern Hills uses a system of concentric ditches and earthworks. The original work was carried out in the 2nd century BC, creating a fortified hilltop that was probably inhabited on a full-time basis. According to local legend the great Celtic king Caratacus fought his last battle against the invading Romans here, but this is unlikely to be true. Later fortifications were built on the same site at the beginning of the Norman era, and were used well into the Middle Ages.

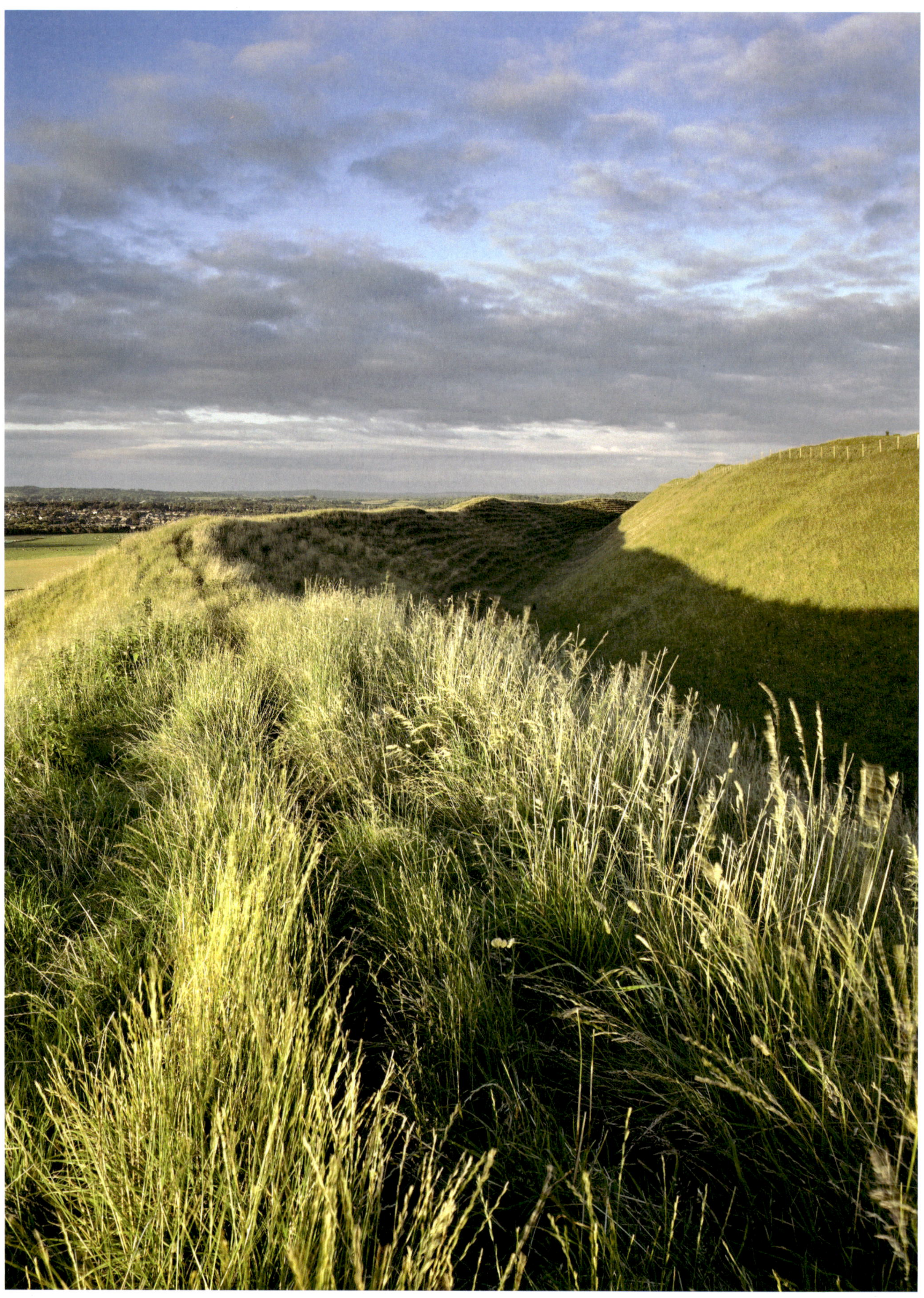

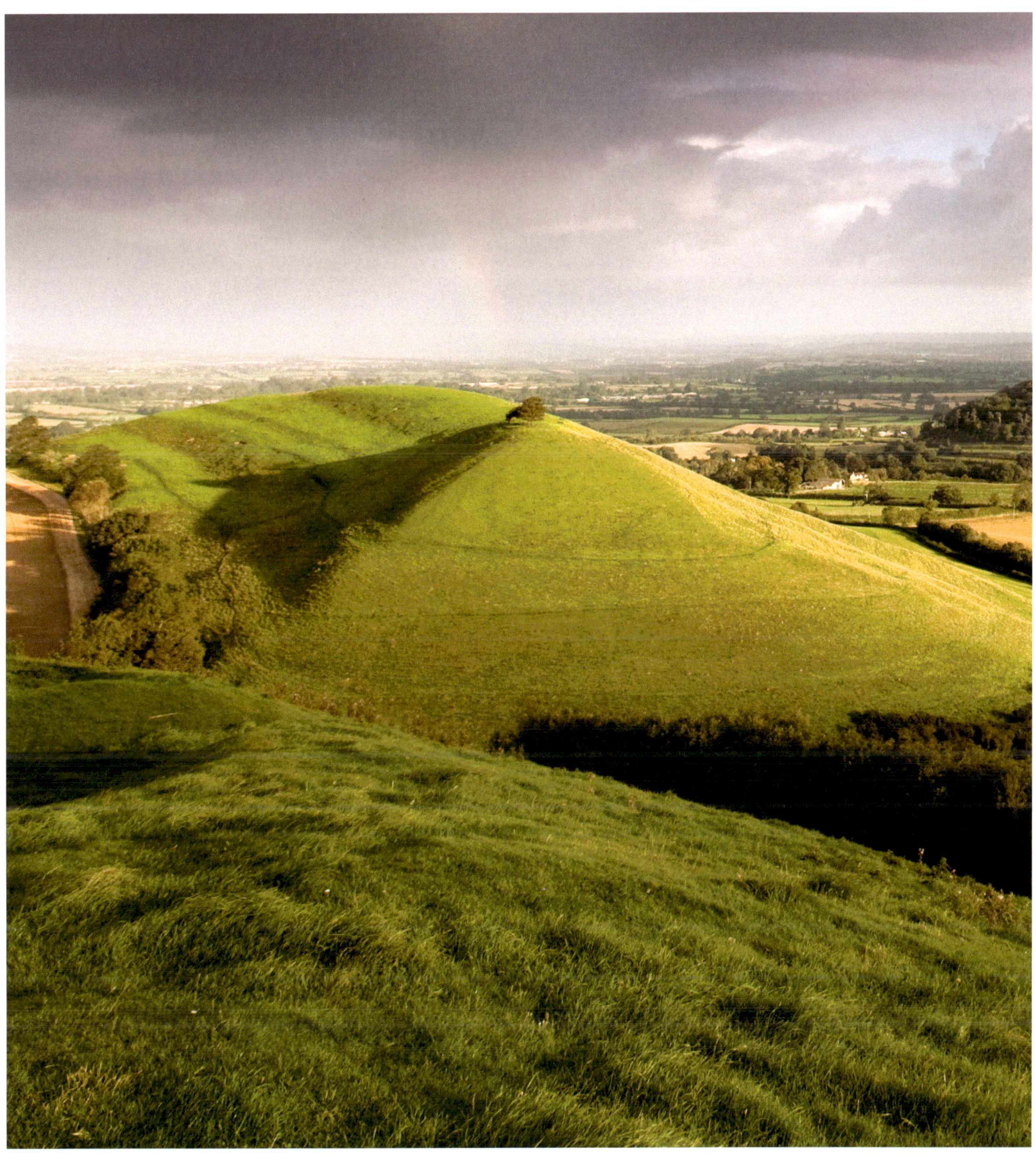

LEFT:

Maiden Castle, Dorset, England

Maiden Castle is one of the largest and most extensive hill forts ever discovered. The site was used and may have been fortified in Neolithic times, around 3000–3500 BC. By the height of the Celtic era, Mai Dun (Great Hill, eventually corrupted to Maiden) was a major stronghold capable of housing a large population. The concentric defences of three earthworks, each with a ditch, enabled the Durotriges tribe to inflict heavy casualties on an attacking Roman army, though the fort eventually fell to assault.

ABOVE:

Cadbury Castle, Somerset, England

Like many hill fort sites, Cadbury Castle was inhabited during Neolithic times. Habitation may have been continuous throughout the Bronze Age and into the Iron Age, and by the first century BC the site possessed sophisticated earthwork defences with concentric layers. The fort was stormed by Roman forces around 43 AD, and later was used by the Romans and Romano–Britons. Cadbury Castle has become associated with the legends of King Arthur, and is a strong contender for the site of his castle, Camelot.

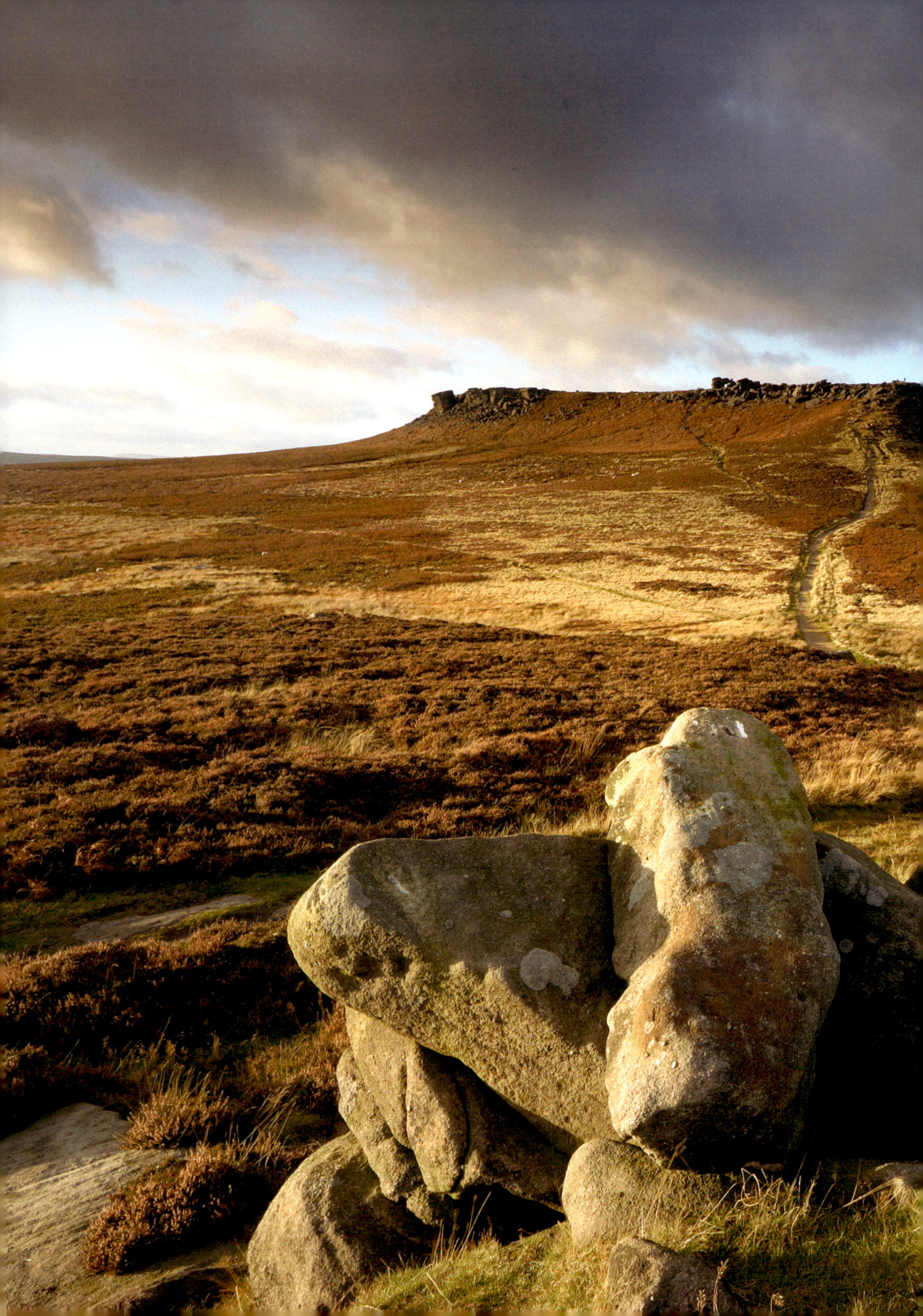

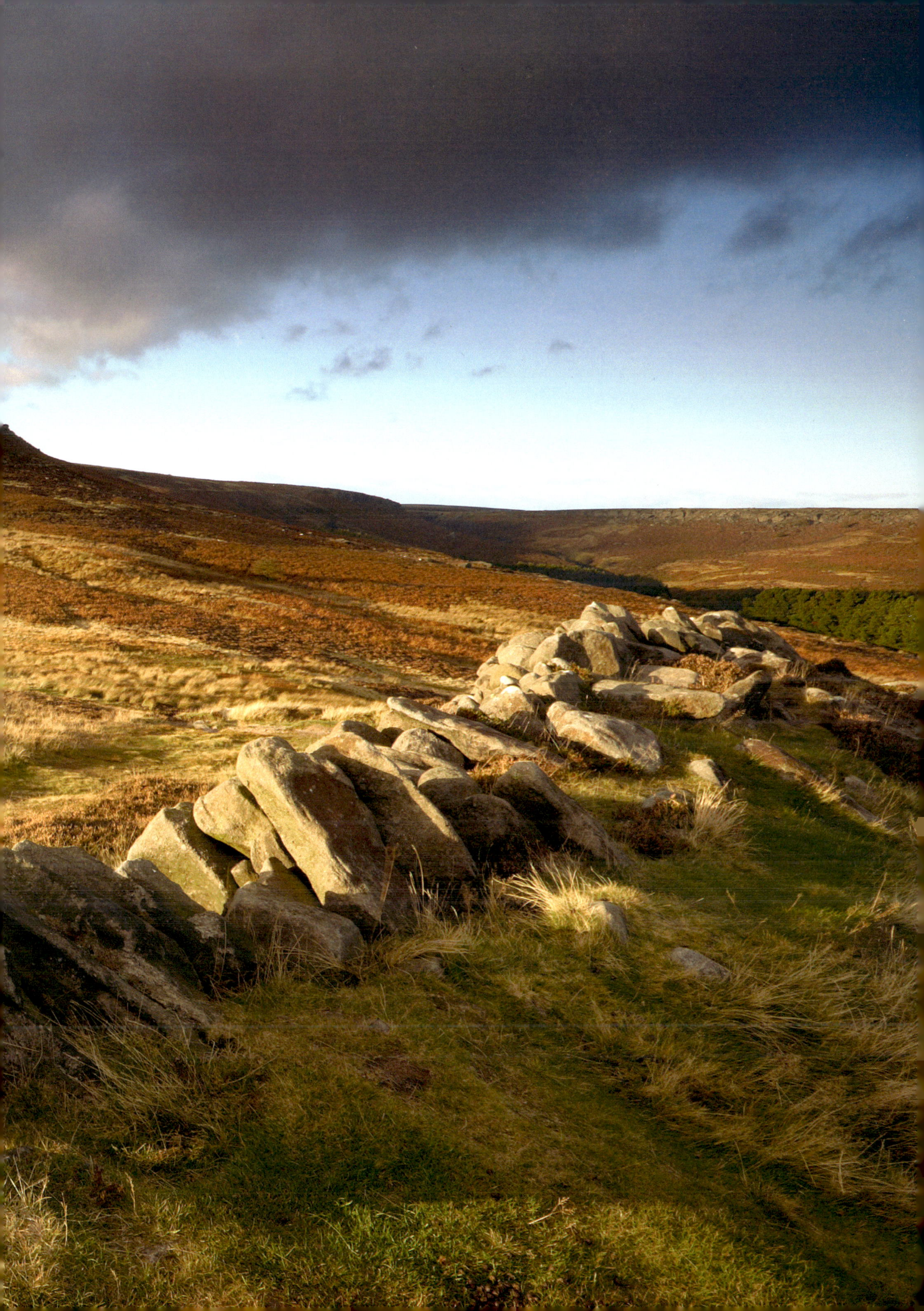

PREVIOUS PAGES:

Carl Wark Hill Fort, Peak District National Park, England

Carl Wark Hill Fort is built on a promontory of millstone grit on Hathersage Moor in the Peak District, and is protected on three sides by cliffs. The enclosure is fortified with a stone wall, taking advantage of locally occurring boulders. The date of this fortification work is open to some debate, especially since the site is different to other hill forts in England. It is possible that Carl Wark was fortified as early as 1300 BC, though there is evidence that the current defences might date from around 500 AD, after the departure of Roman troops from the British Isles. The enclosure does not seem to have been permanently occupied, suggesting it was a refuge or ceremonial area rather than a habitation.

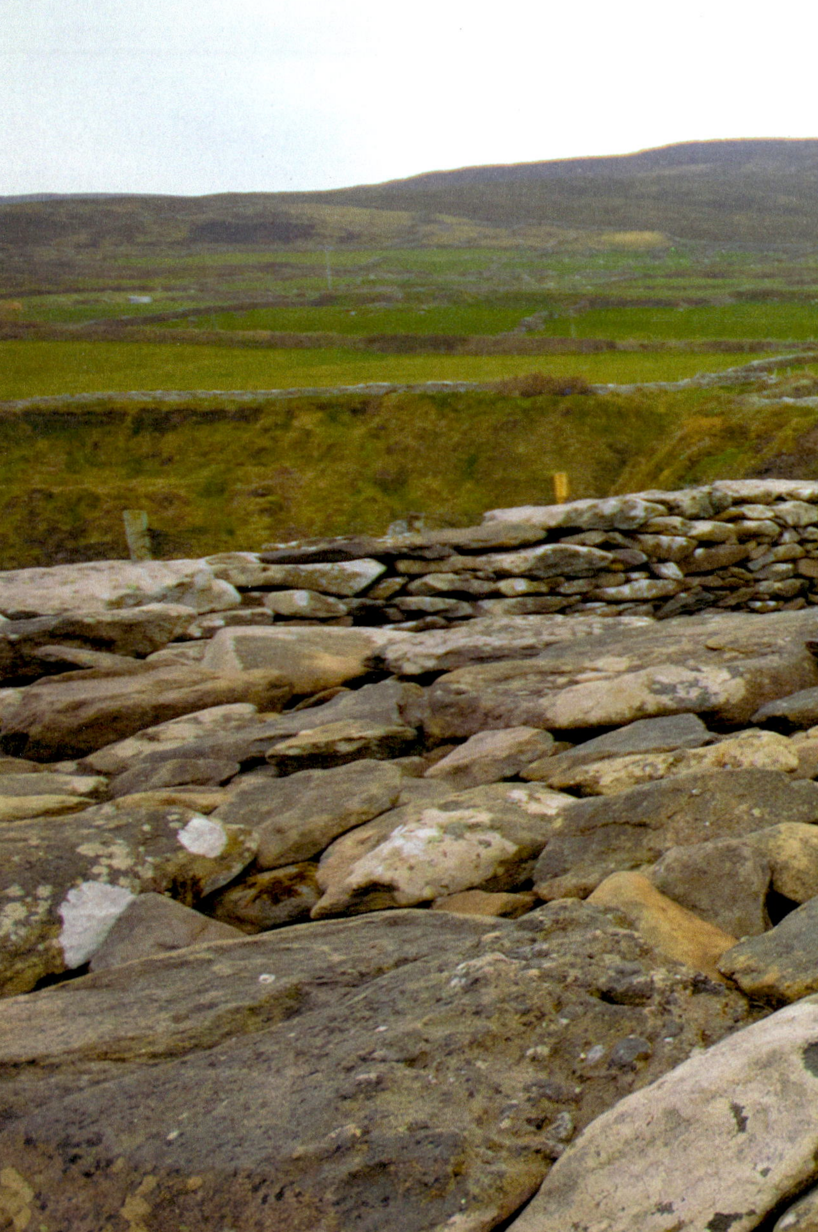

RIGHT:

Dunbeg Fort, County Kerry, Ireland

Dunbeg Fort stands atop sea cliffs on the west coast of Ireland. The site may have been inhabited in the 8th century BC or even earlier, and was in use as late as 1000 AD. The only approach is from the landward side, which is protected by four concentric earthworks and five ditches. Beyond this is the inner stone wall, protecting an enclosure that can only be reached through a narrow passage. Chambers flanking the passage allowed spear-armed defenders to strike anyone passing through. A tunnel was built into the defences, perhaps for escape and perhaps to allow warriors or messengers to slip out of the fort unobserved.

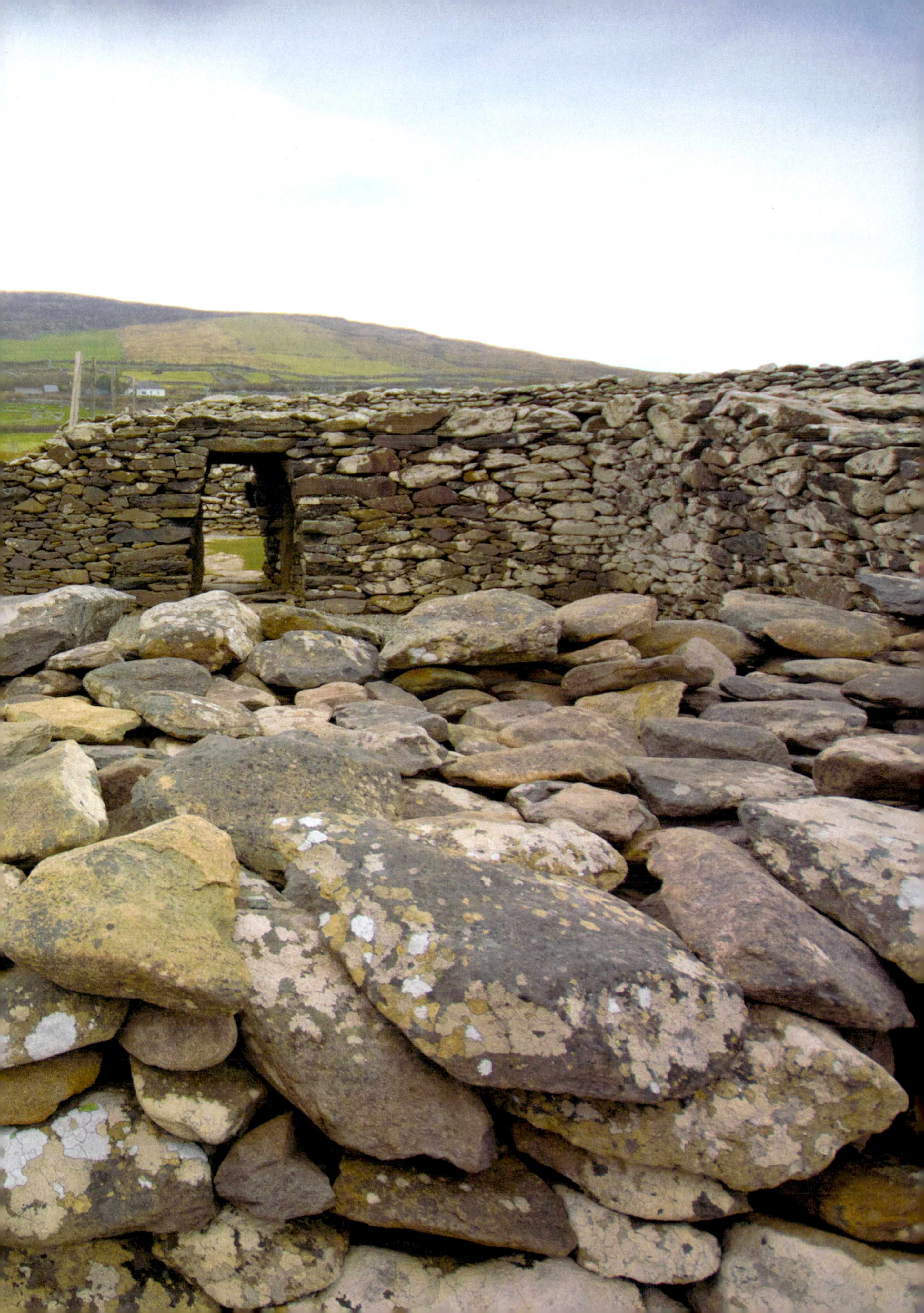

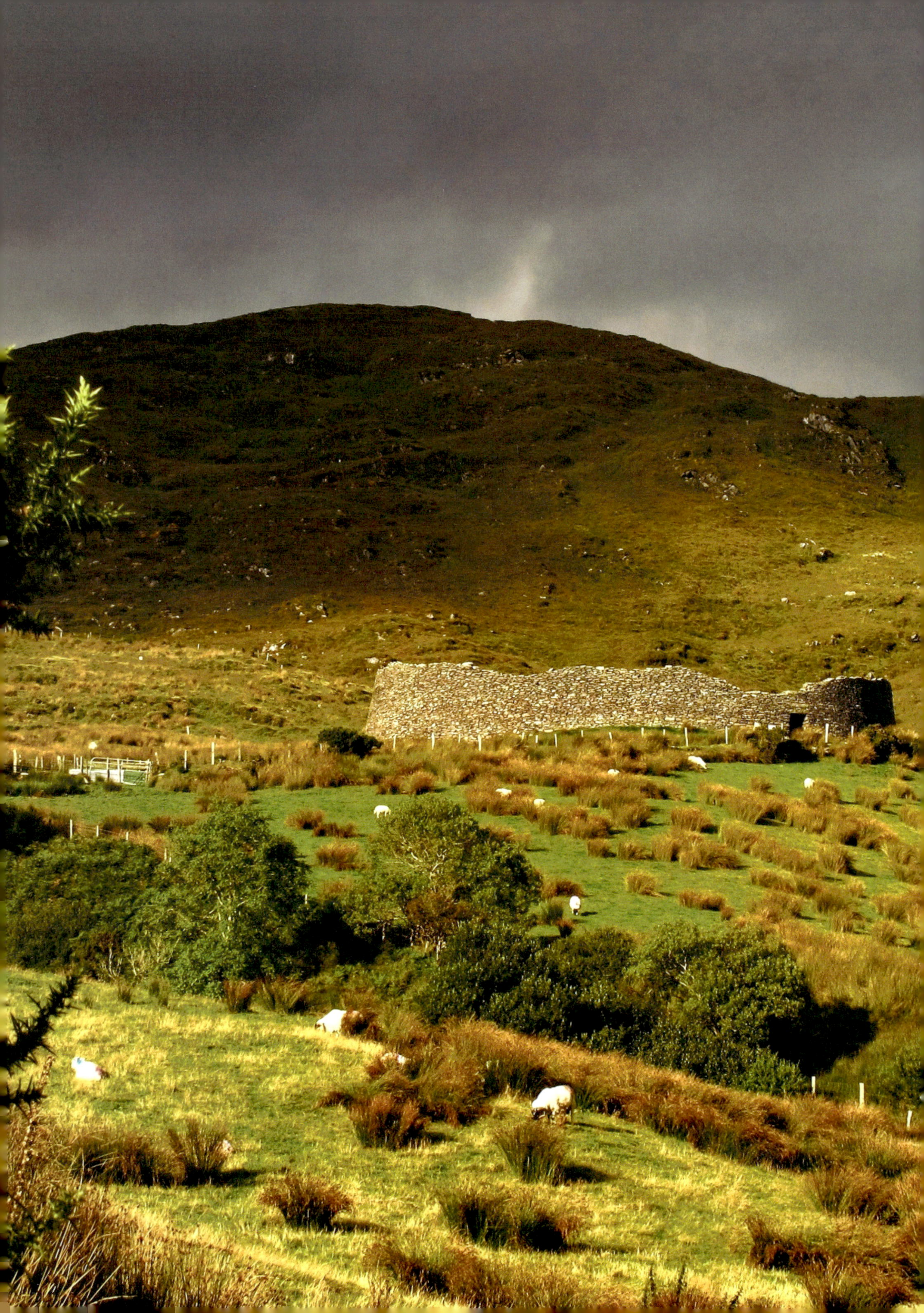

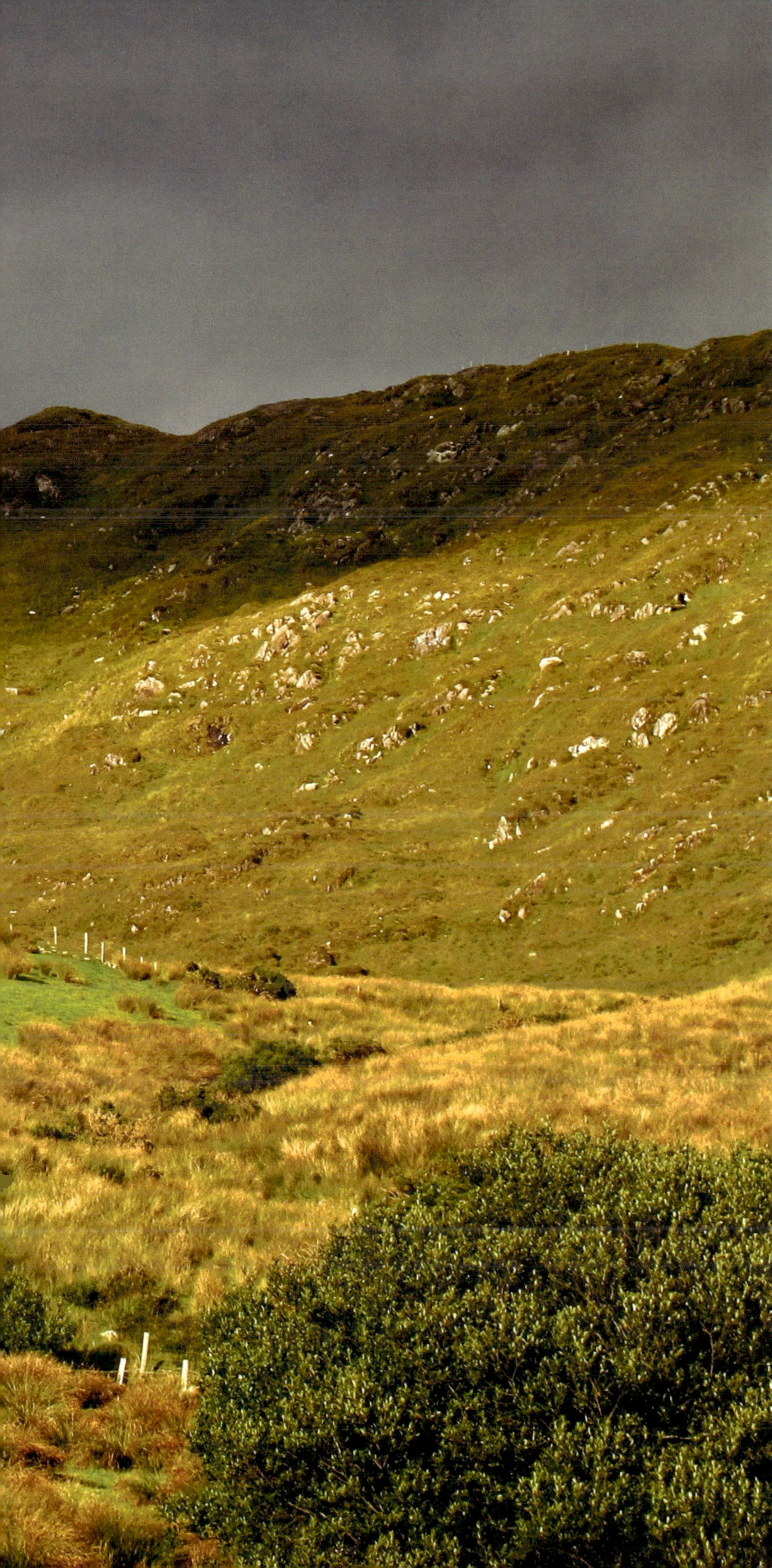

Staigue Stone Fort, County Kerry, Ireland

Staigue Stone Fort is built atop a low hill, but its defences take the form of a thick drystone wall rather than earthworks making use of natural contours. The walls are about four metres (13 feet) thick at the base, and half that at the top, and are faced with a ditch. Ring forts of this sort exist across Europe, though their origins are open to debate. There is some evidence to suggest that construction may have begun in the Iron Age, though many date from the Medieval period.

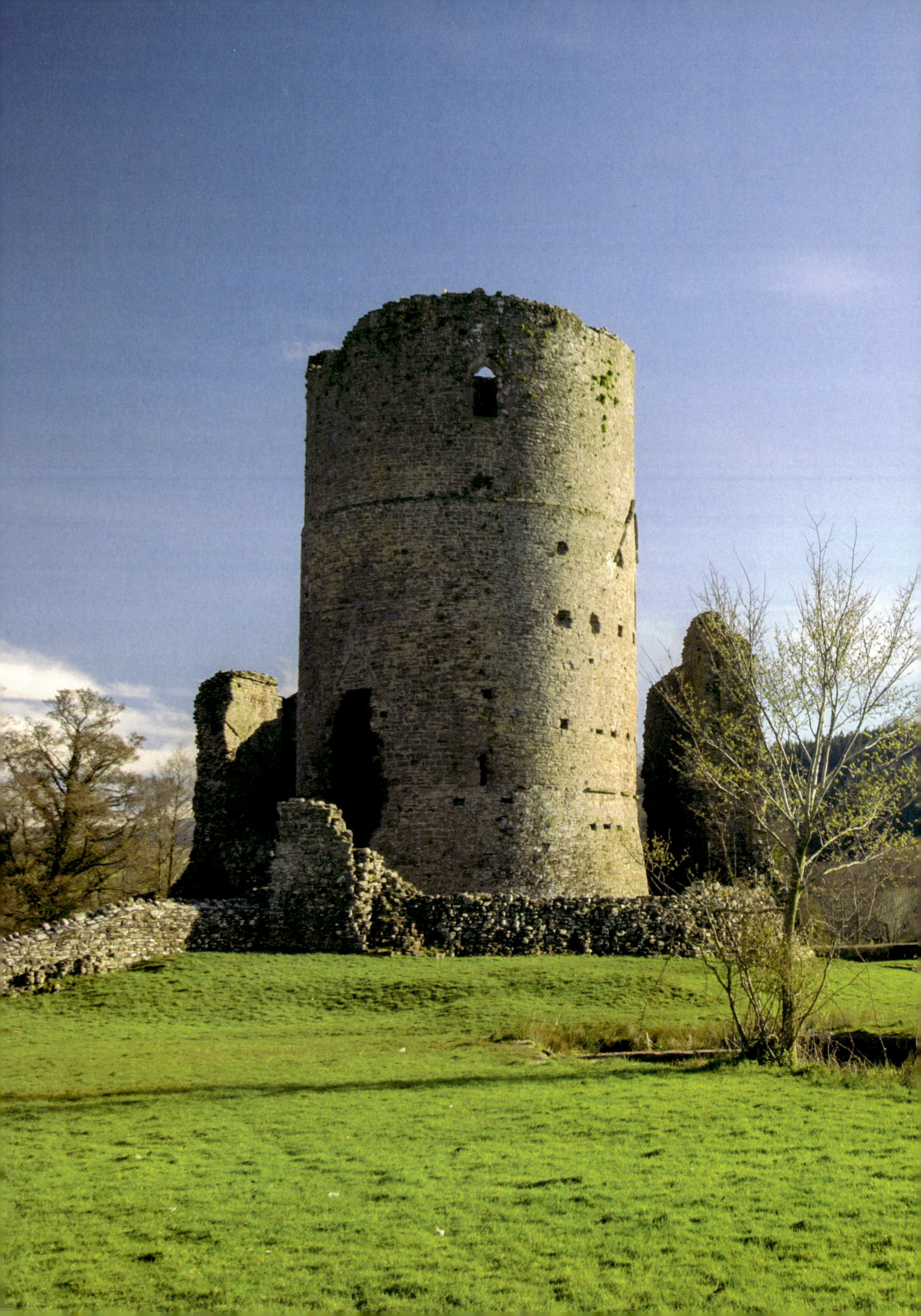

Early Middle Ages

The first permanent settlements began to appear in the Middle East in the Neolithic era, starting around 10,000 BC. Some form of defence against wild animals and rival tribes was desirable, so fortification began almost as soon as people ceased to wander as hunter-gatherers. Widespread use of metal tools probably began around 3200 BC, with the Bronze Age giving way to the Iron Age as metal-working techniques advanced. This was a gradual process, beginning around 1000–800 BC in some areas and later elsewhere.

The technology required to create a hill fort with earthworks, ditches and a wooden palisade was not very advanced, but by the time good iron tools were available other technologies had been developed that enabled stone to be shaped and supported by sophisticated frameworks of timber. Large and strong structures could be built, and a need for them certainly existed.

The Early Middle Ages are generally considered to have begun after the fall of Rome (in AD 476), at a time when whole tribes were on the march as a result of the Hunnish invasion of Europe. Wood and stone fortifications helped secure the lands of those who resisted invasion or those who successfully wrested control from another tribe. Just as the Celtic people of Europe were absorbing an influx of outsiders, causing their culture to evolve into a post-Celtic form, the art of fortification took a great leap forward as a result of the same troubled times.

LEFT:

Tretower Castle, Powys, Wales

Tretower Castle was built during the Norman invasion of Wales, in an effort to control the countryside. It began as a motte-and-bailey castle; a simple wooden structure protected by an earth mound, ditches and a wooden palisade. The castle was rebuilt in stone and later updated, remaining in use throughout the Middle Ages. Welsh castles controlling major roads and river crossings became strategic assets in the early 1400s, during the Welsh Rebellion against the English led by Owen Glendower.

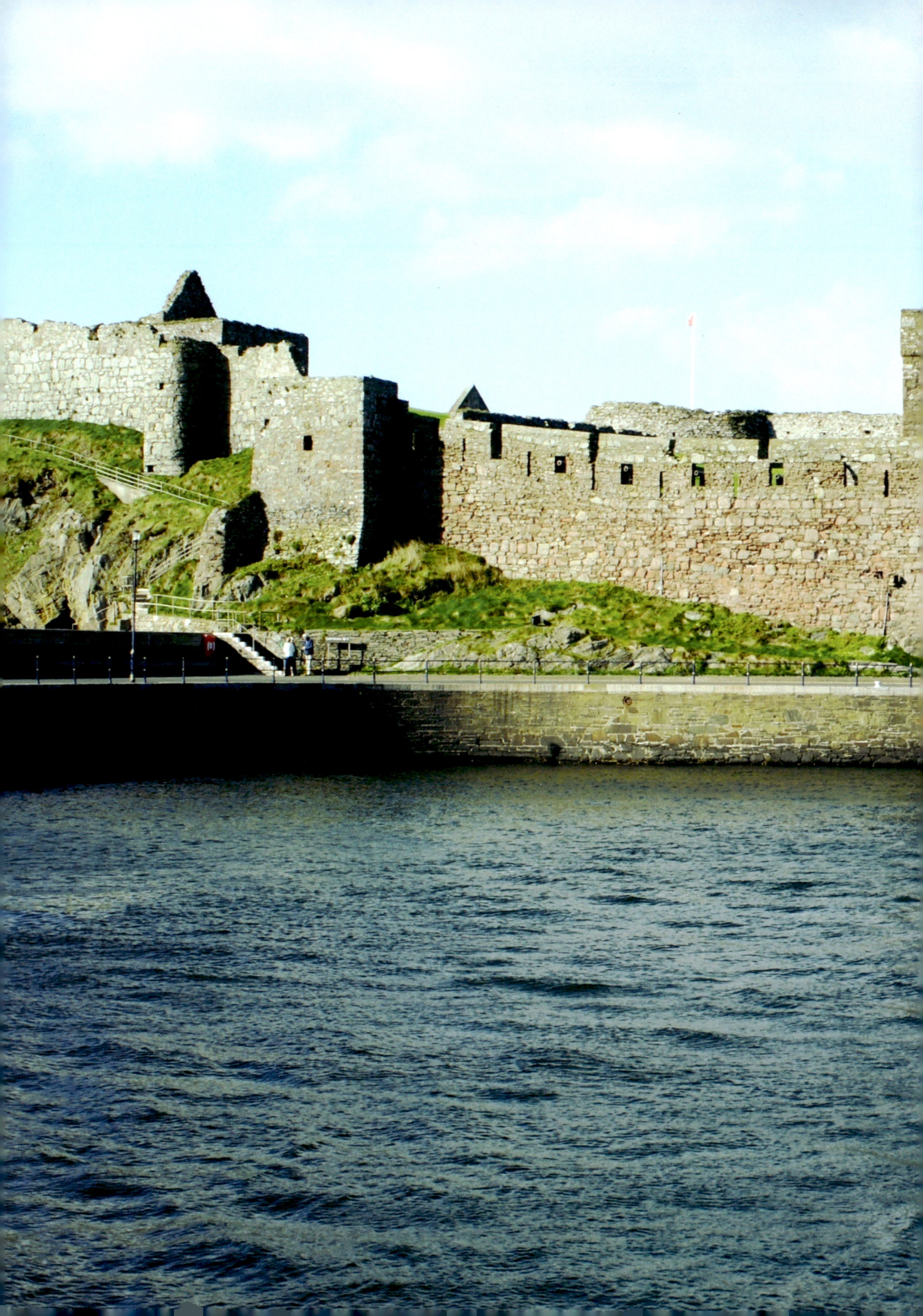

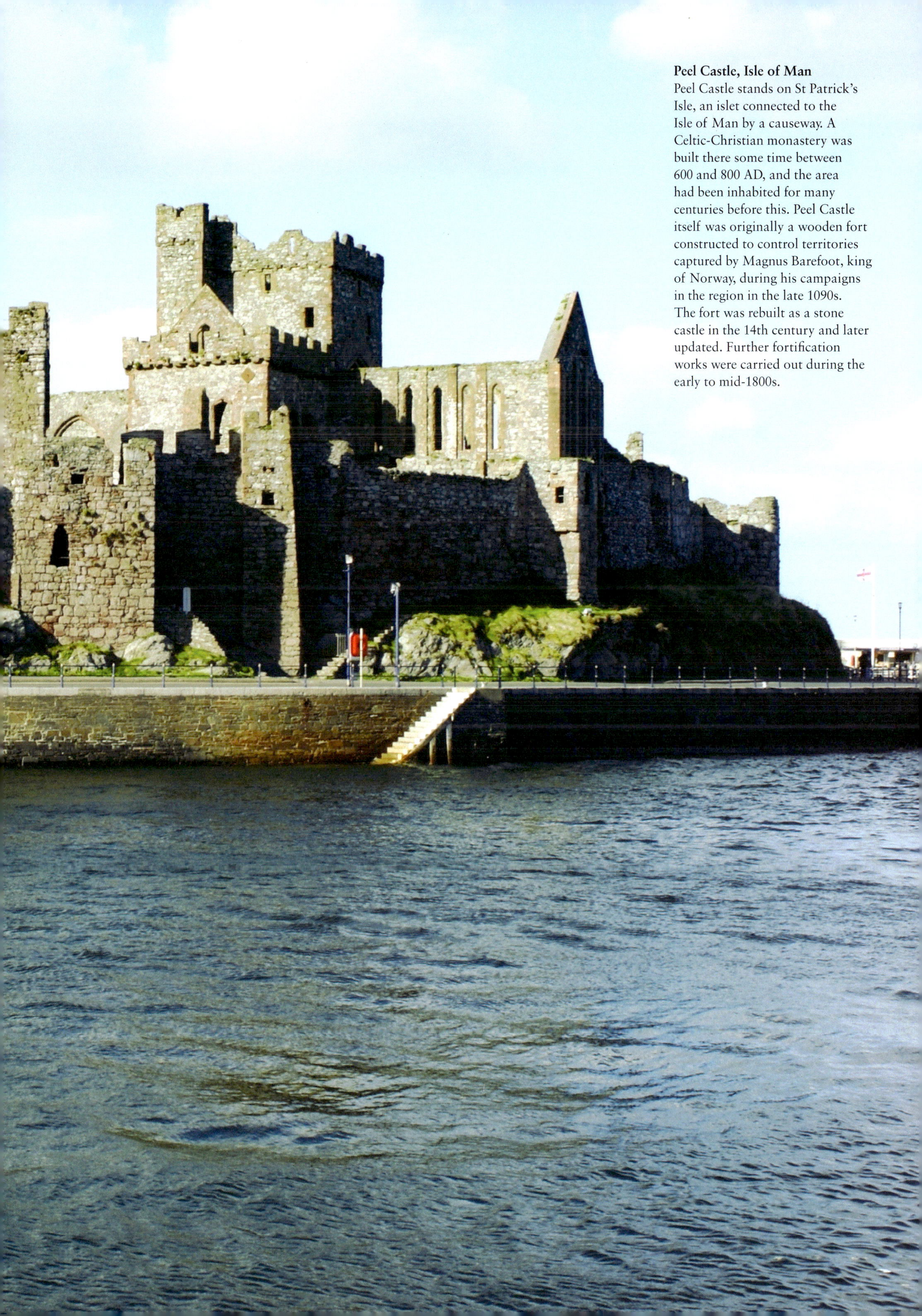

Peel Castle, Isle of Man
Peel Castle stands on St Patrick's Isle, an islet connected to the Isle of Man by a causeway. A Celtic-Christian monastery was built there some time between 600 and 800 AD, and the area had been inhabited for many centuries before this. Peel Castle itself was originally a wooden fort constructed to control territories captured by Magnus Barefoot, king of Norway, during his campaigns in the region in the late 1090s. The fort was rebuilt as a stone castle in the 14th century and later updated. Further fortification works were carried out during the early to mid-1800s.

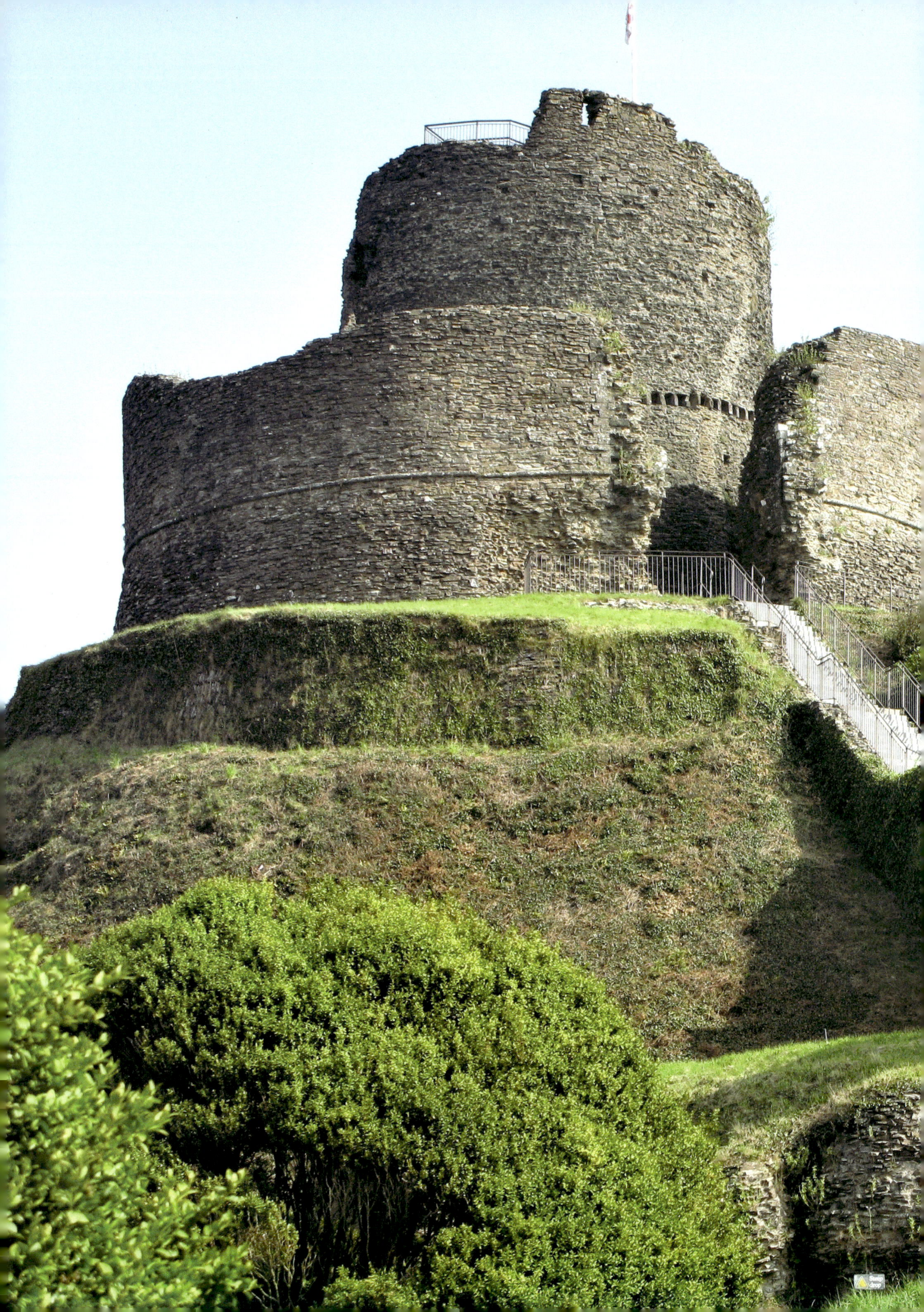

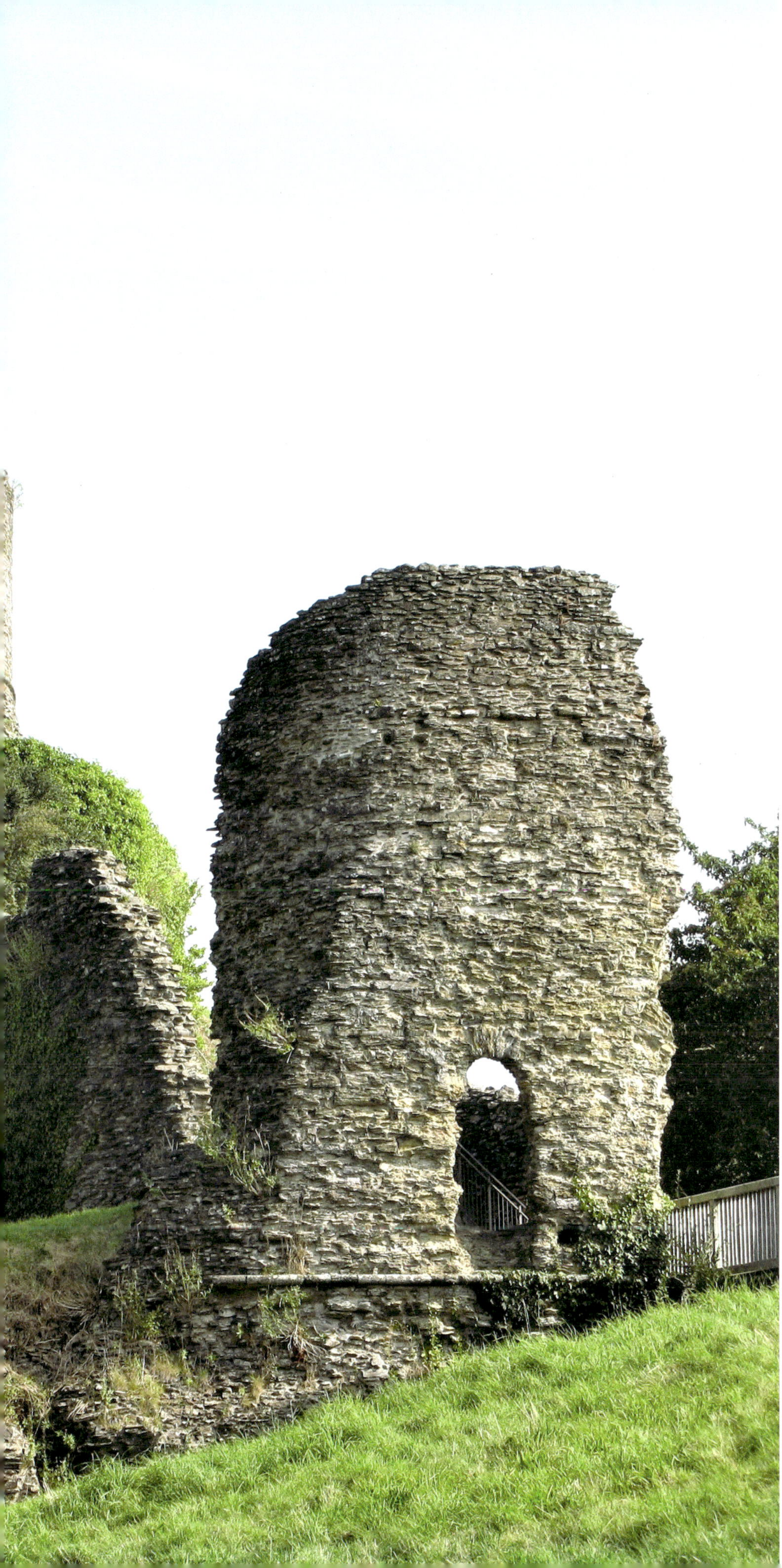

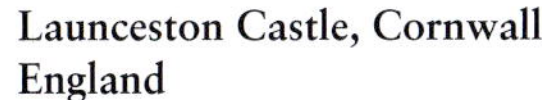

Launceston Castle, Cornwall, England

Launceston Castle was built as a wooden motte-and-bailey construction during the Norman conquest of Britain, probably in the late 1060s. Constructed atop a natural motte, or mound, the wooden fortification was rebuilt in stone in the early 13th century on the orders of Earl Richard of Cornwall. Further defences were added at this time in the form of stone curtain walls, but the importance of the castle declined when the Earls of Cornwall moved their seat elsewhere. Launceston Castle was later used as a prison; among those confined there was George Fox, founder of the Quakers.

Cardiff Castle, Cardiff, Wales
The region around Cardiff has been inhabited since Neolithic times, and some form of fortifications may have existed even before the extensive hill fort at Caerau was constructed around 500 BC. The modern castle was constructed as a Norman motte-and-bailey fortification intended, like many other castles all over England and Wales, to control newly conquered territories. It was rebuilt in stone in the 12th century and extended in the 13th century. Cardiff Castle was of strategic importance in the conflicts surrounding Welsh resistance to Norman rule, and again during the revolt of Owen Glendower in the early 1400s.

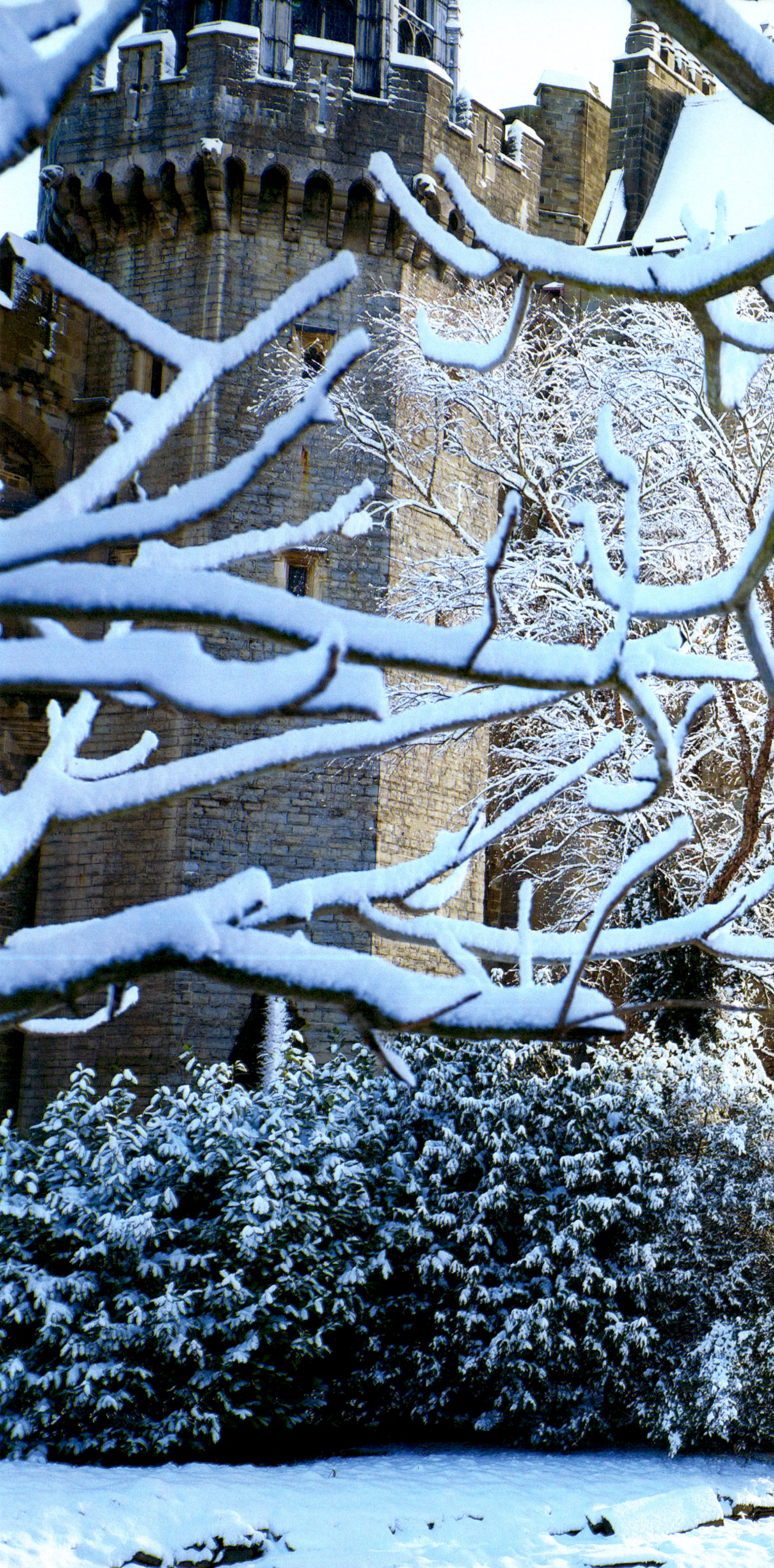

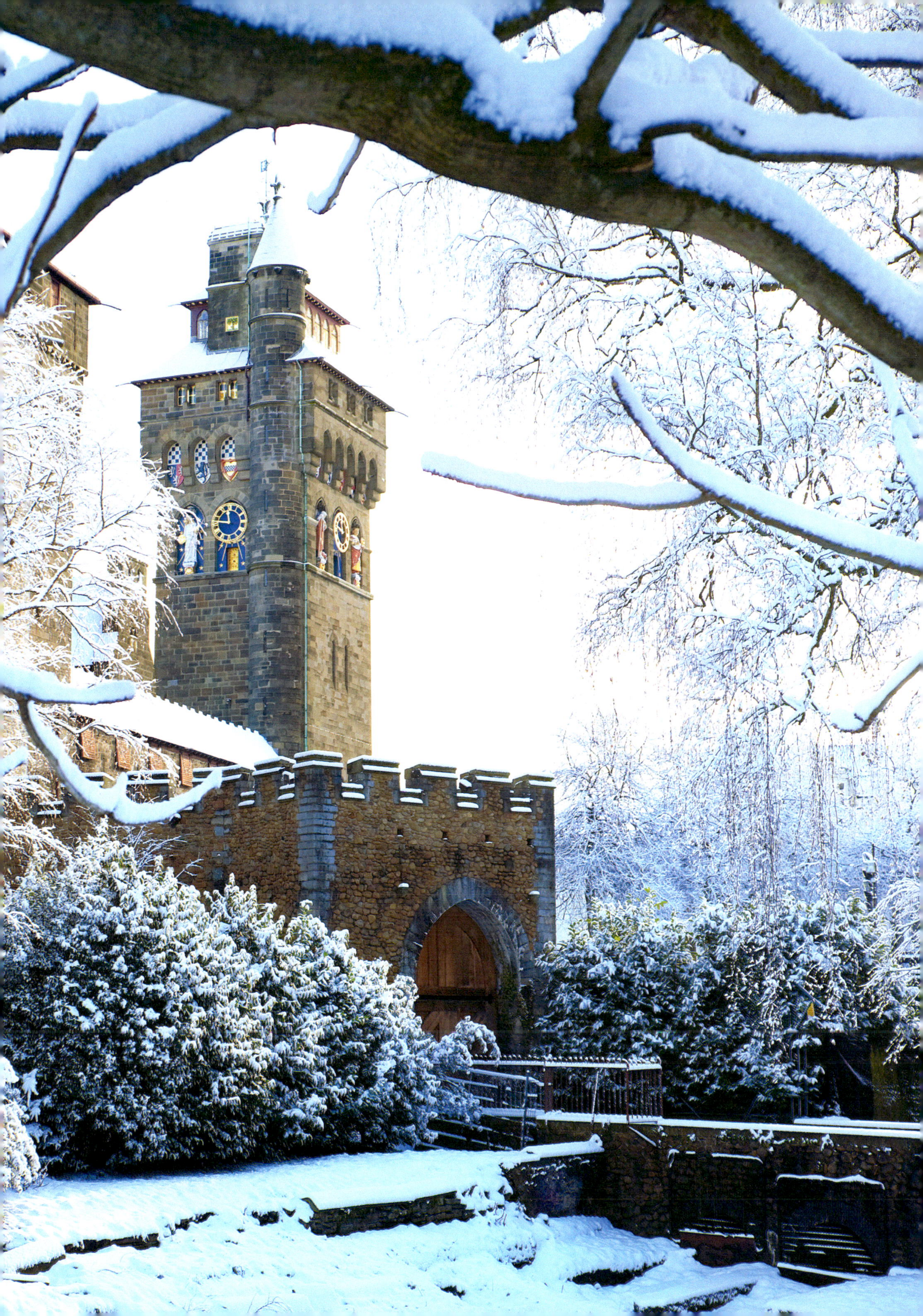

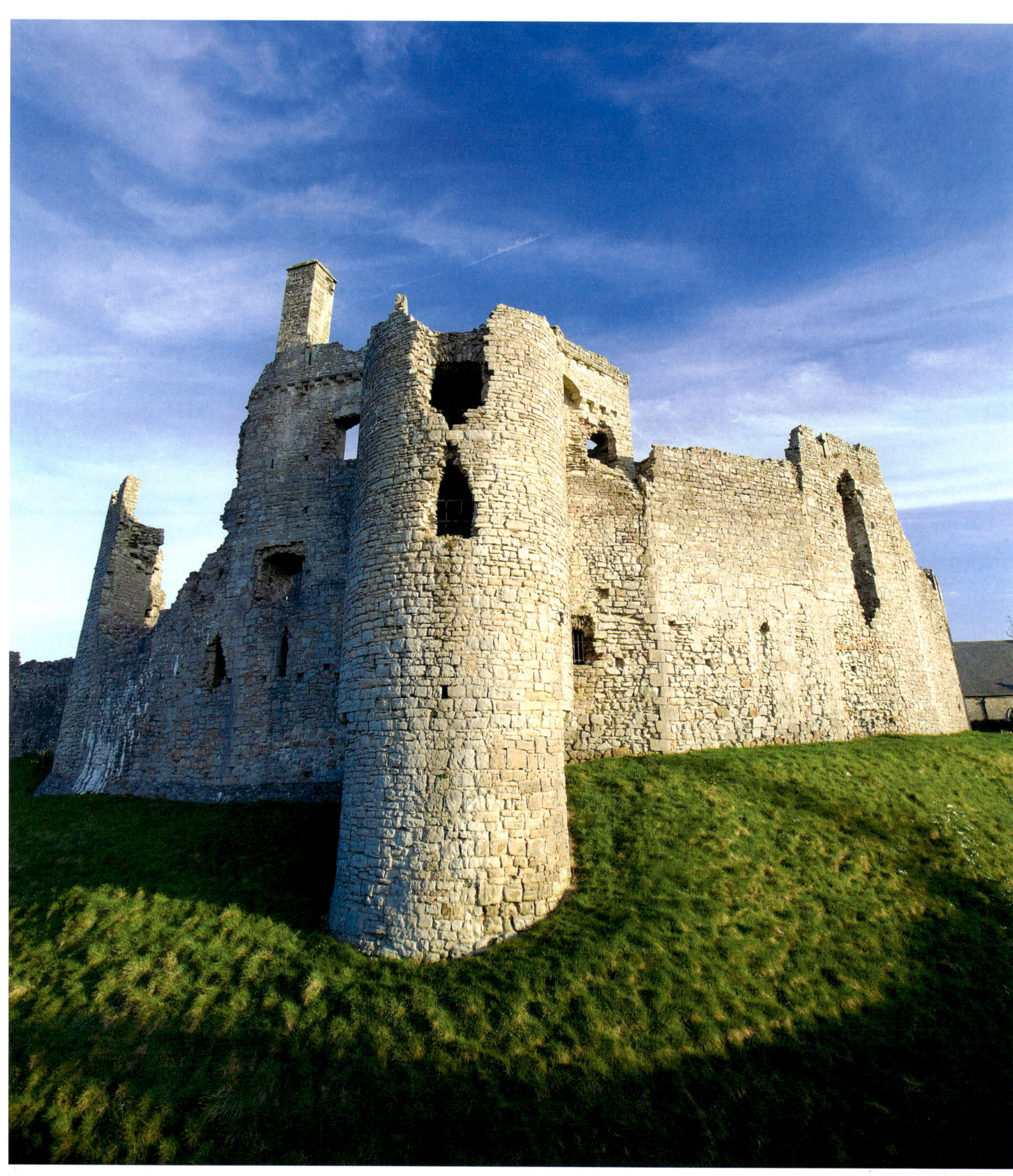

ABOVE, RIGHT AND OVERLEAF:
Coity Castle, Glamorgan, Wales
Coity Castle may have been originally constructed by Welsh lords, but was rebuilt after the Norman conquest. According to legend, the Welsh lord Morgan Gam was ordered to hand over his castle to the Norman knight Sir Payn de Turberville and offered him a choice between marriage to Morgan's daughter or fighting for the castle. Morgan Gam thus married his family into the new power structure and avoided being eclipsed. During the early 1400s, the castle was unsuccessfully besieged by Owen Glendower's forces.

The Norman castle was a ringwork of earth and timber. It was rebuilt in the 1080s in stone, retaining the original layout, and was extended in the next century with the addition of stone curtain walls and a keep.

Further modifications took place in the 1300s, and many of the castle's surviving features date from this era. A final set of modifications took place in the 1500s, with habitation continuing at least until the end of the 16th century.

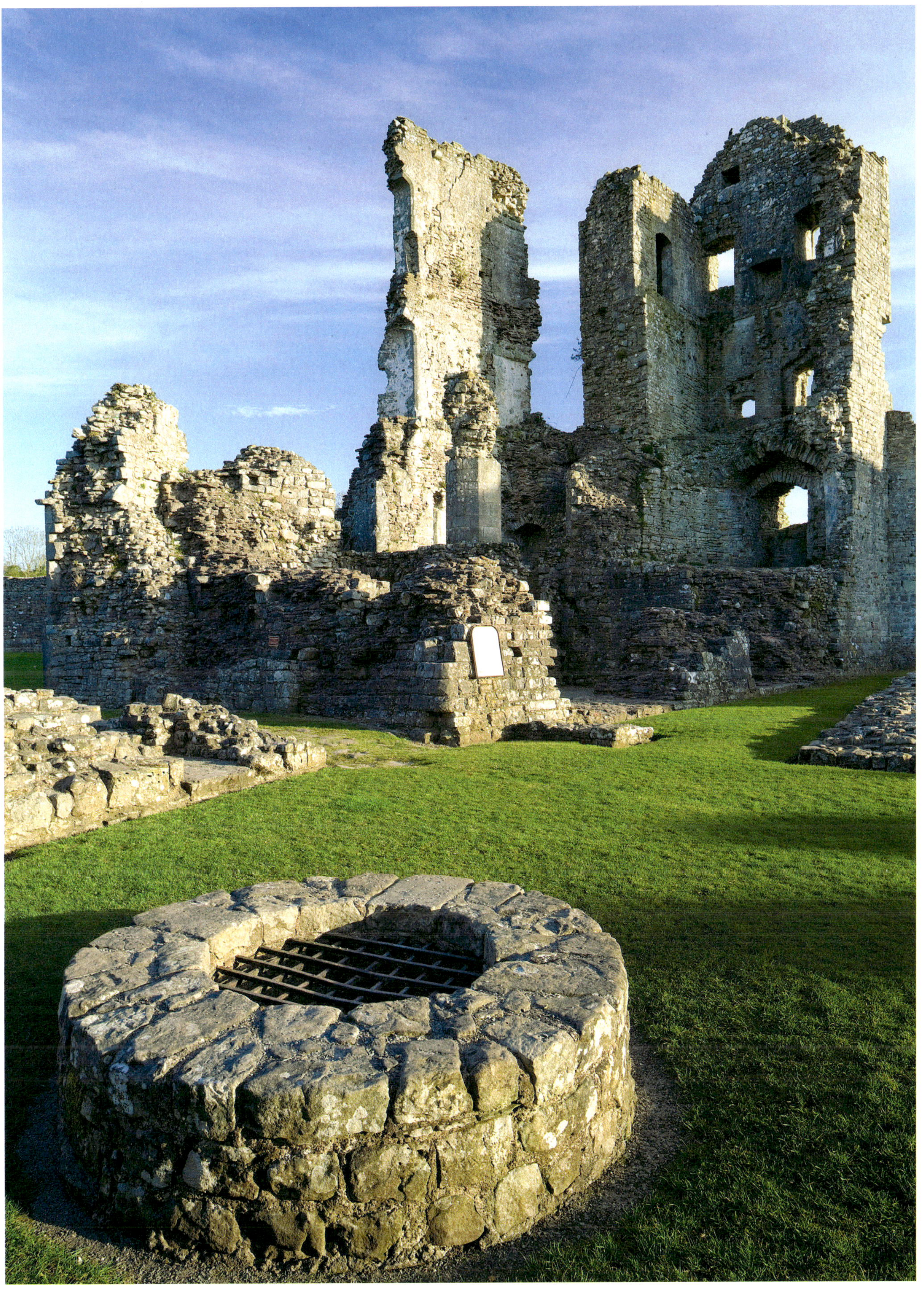

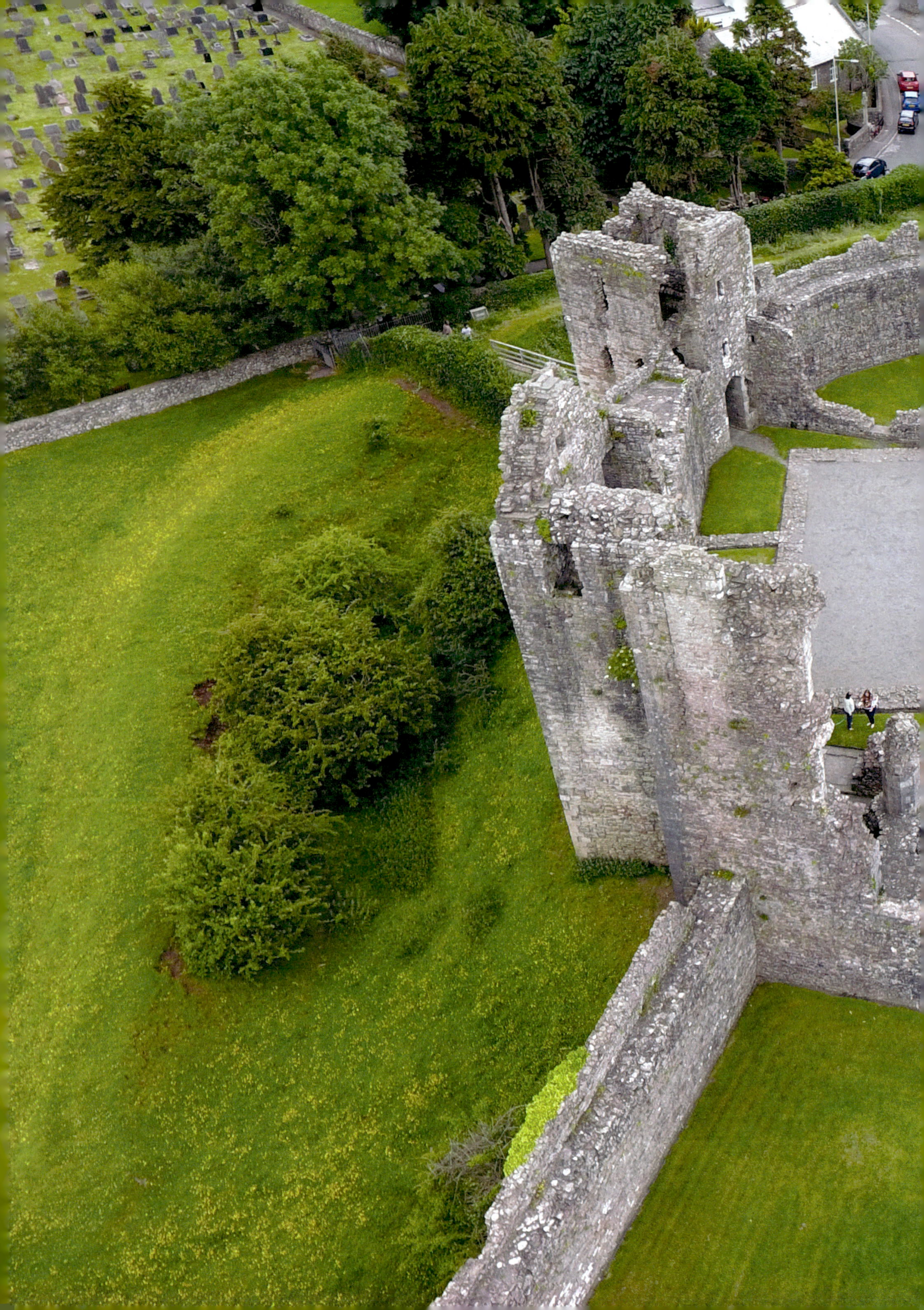

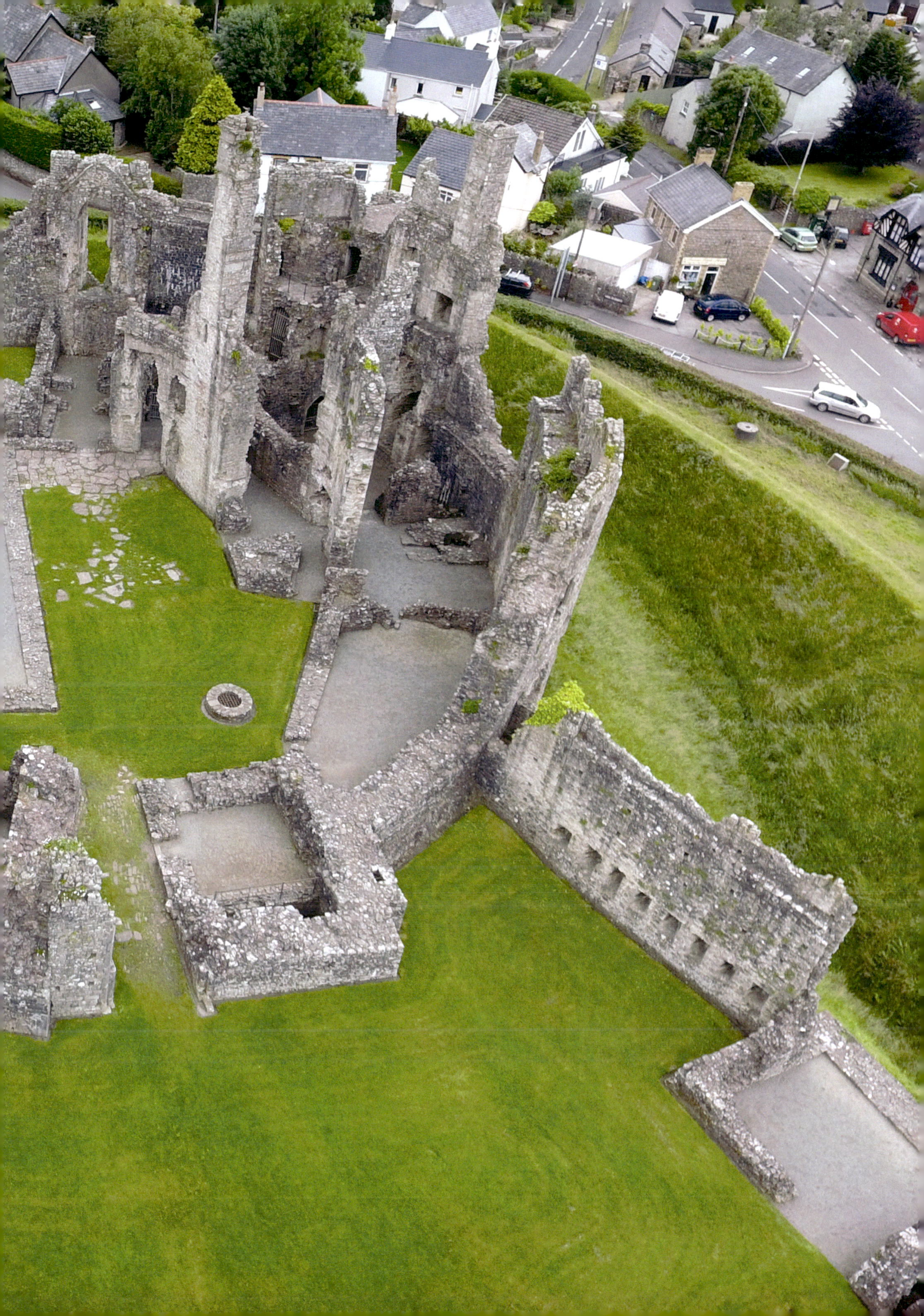

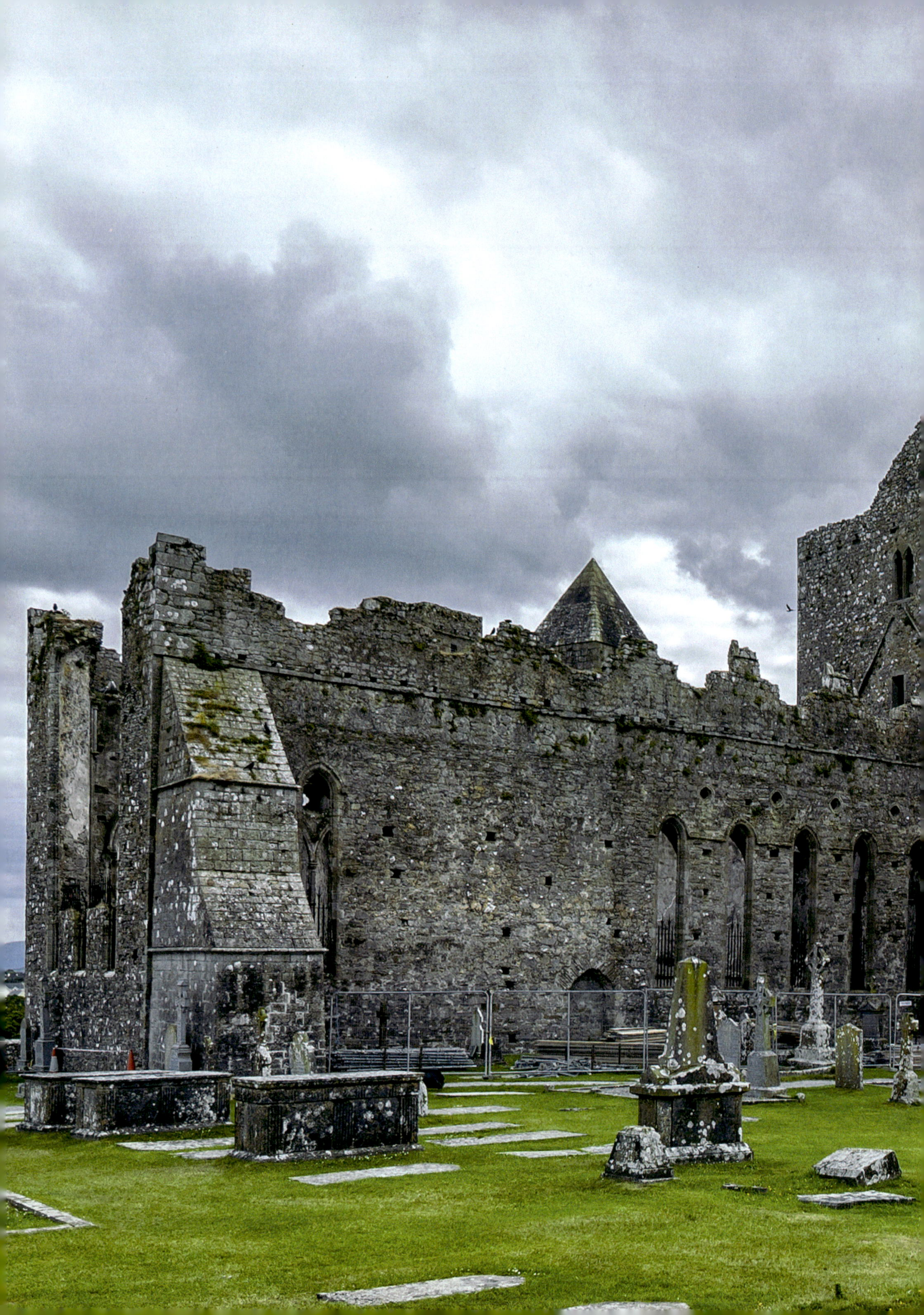

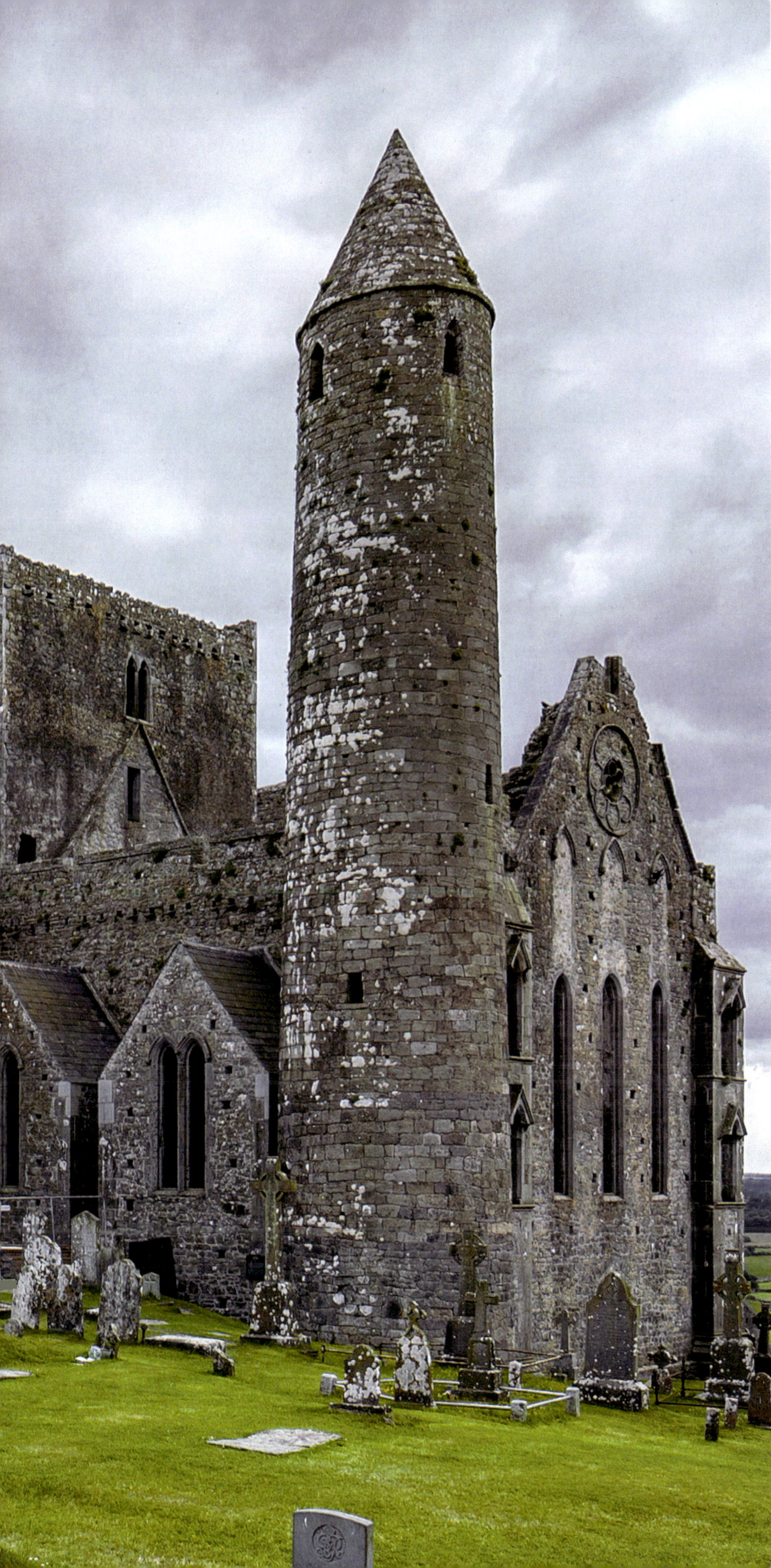

Rock of Cashel, County Tipperary, Ireland
The Rock of Cashel was fortified long before the modern castle was built. A seat of the kings of Munster, it was given to the Church in 1101 and was entirely rebuilt in the years that followed. The oldest surviving part of the castle, a round tower of drystone construction, was built around 1100, with most other features dating from the mid-1100s to the late 1200s.

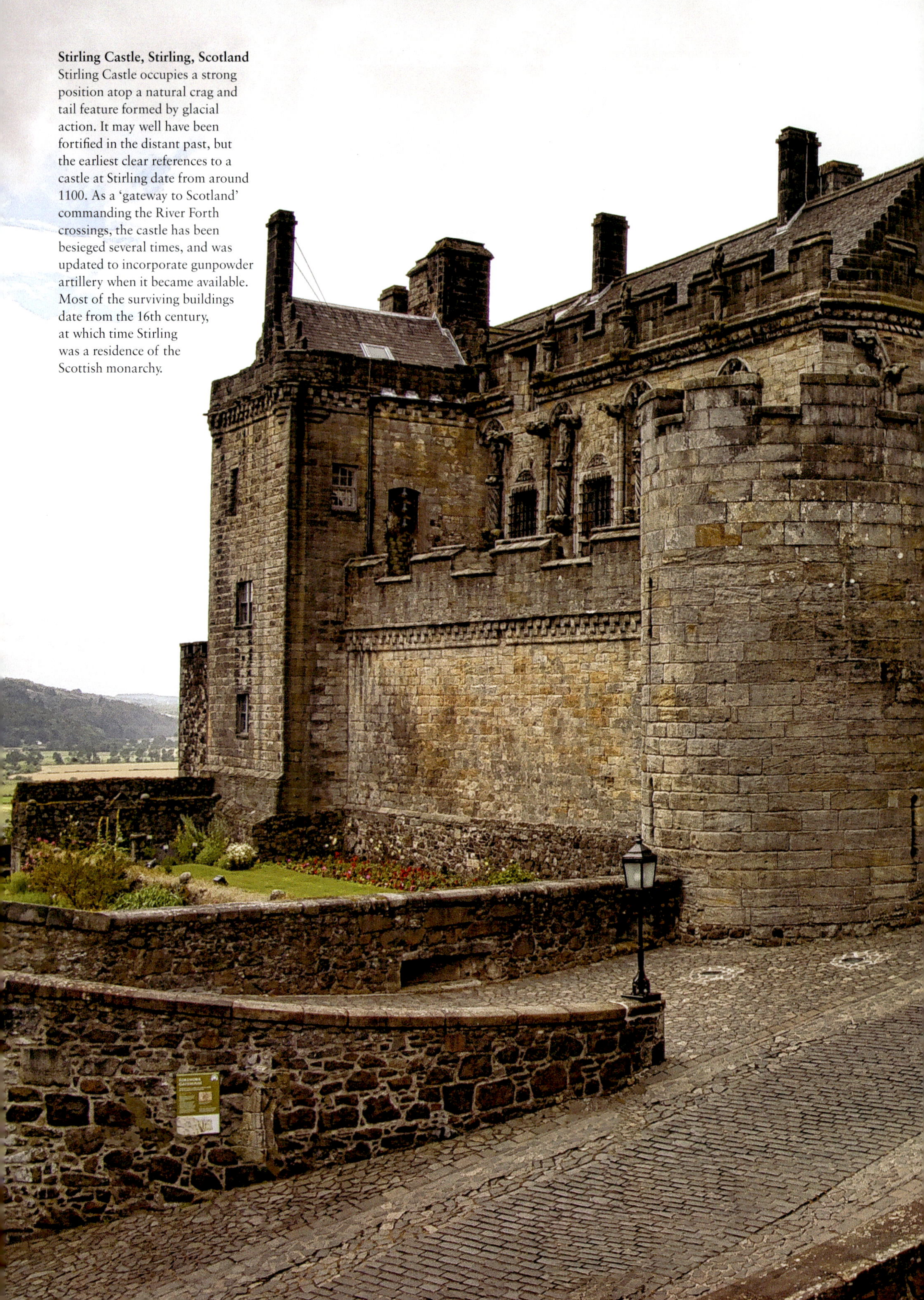

Stirling Castle, Stirling, Scotland
Stirling Castle occupies a strong position atop a natural crag and tail feature formed by glacial action. It may well have been fortified in the distant past, but the earliest clear references to a castle at Stirling date from around 1100. As a 'gateway to Scotland' commanding the River Forth crossings, the castle has been besieged several times, and was updated to incorporate gunpowder artillery when it became available. Most of the surviving buildings date from the 16th century, at which time Stirling was a residence of the Scottish monarchy.

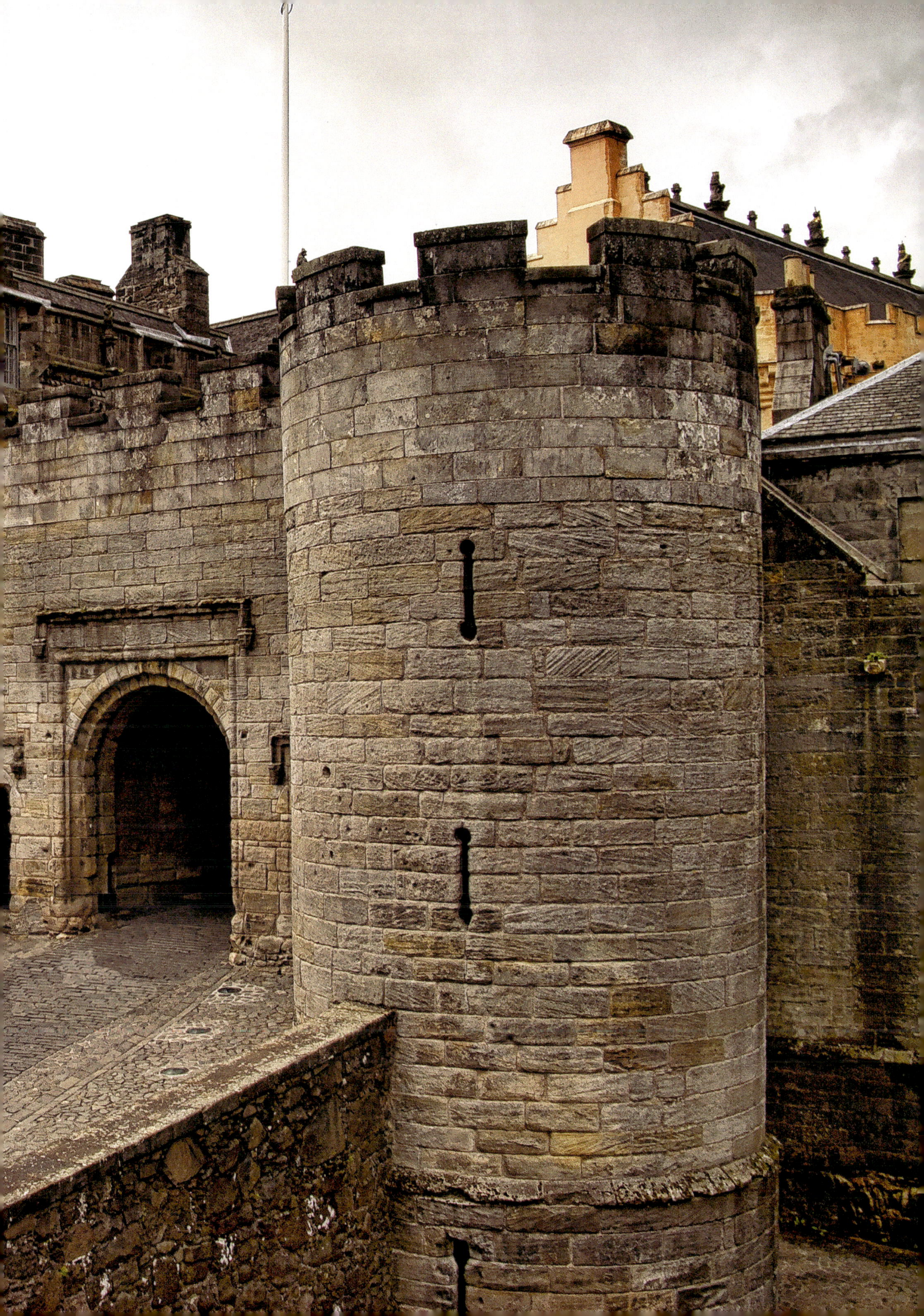

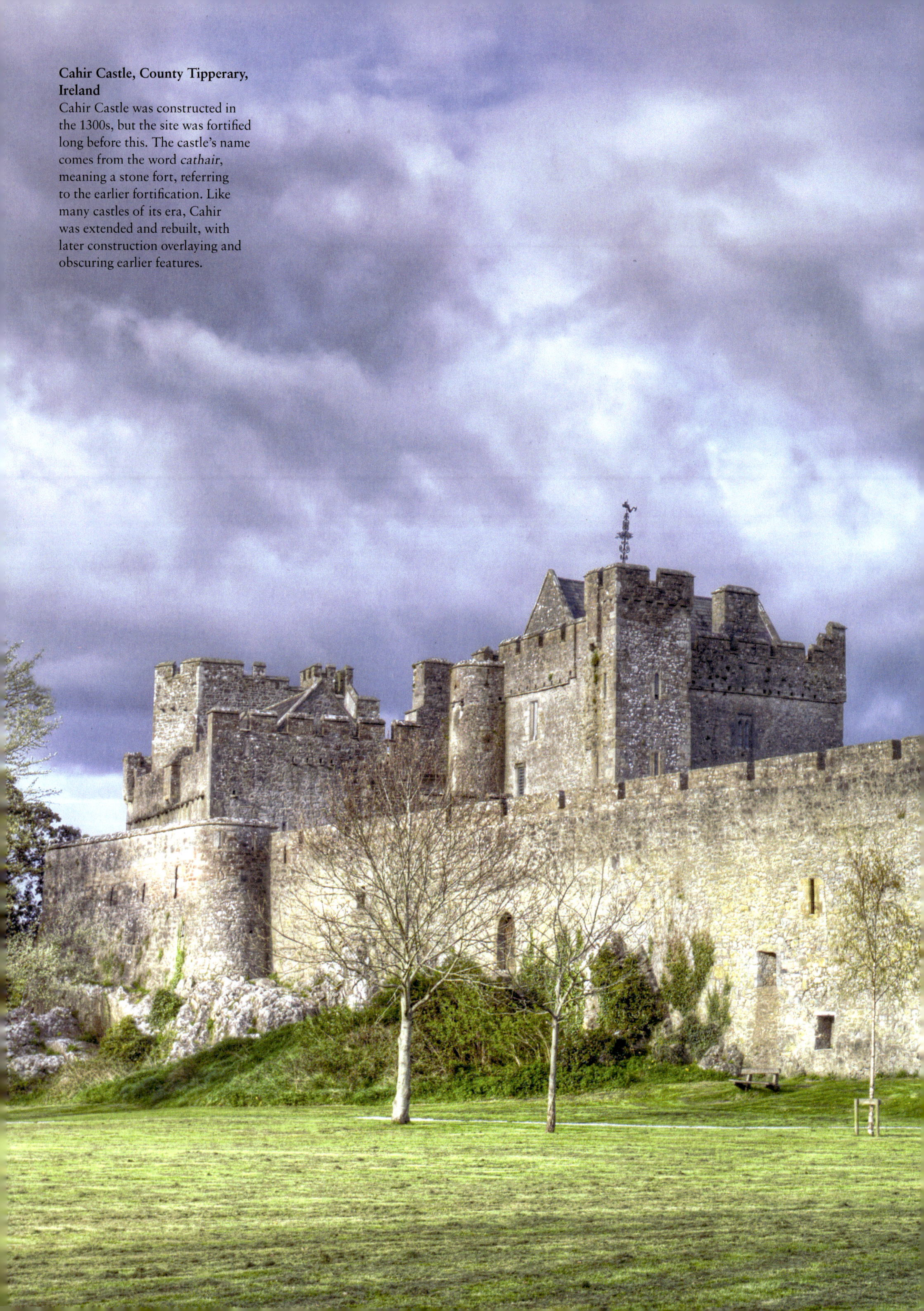

Cahir Castle, County Tipperary, Ireland
Cahir Castle was constructed in the 1300s, but the site was fortified long before this. The castle's name comes from the word *cathair*, meaning a stone fort, referring to the earlier fortification. Like many castles of its era, Cahir was extended and rebuilt, with later construction overlaying and obscuring earlier features.

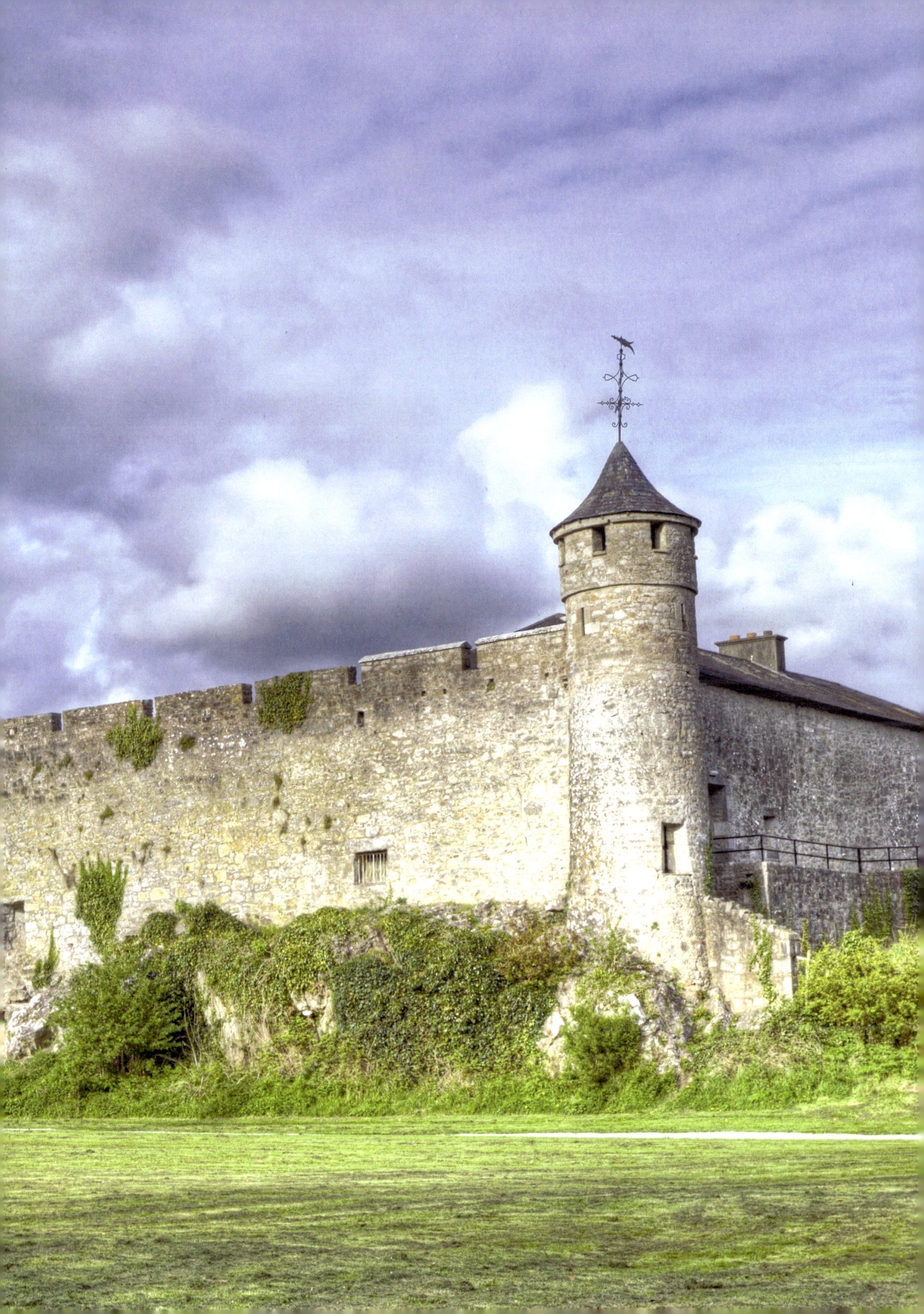

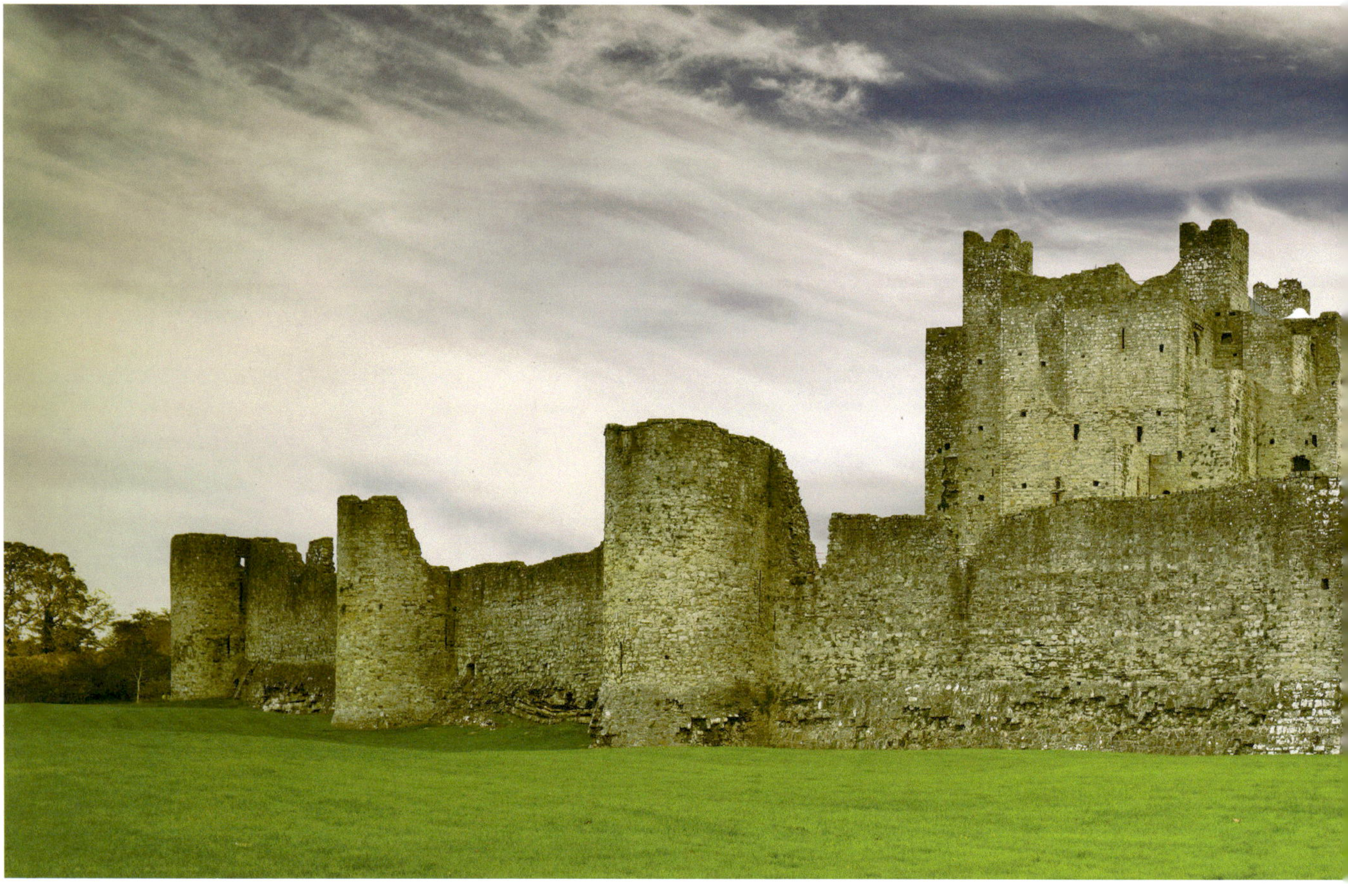

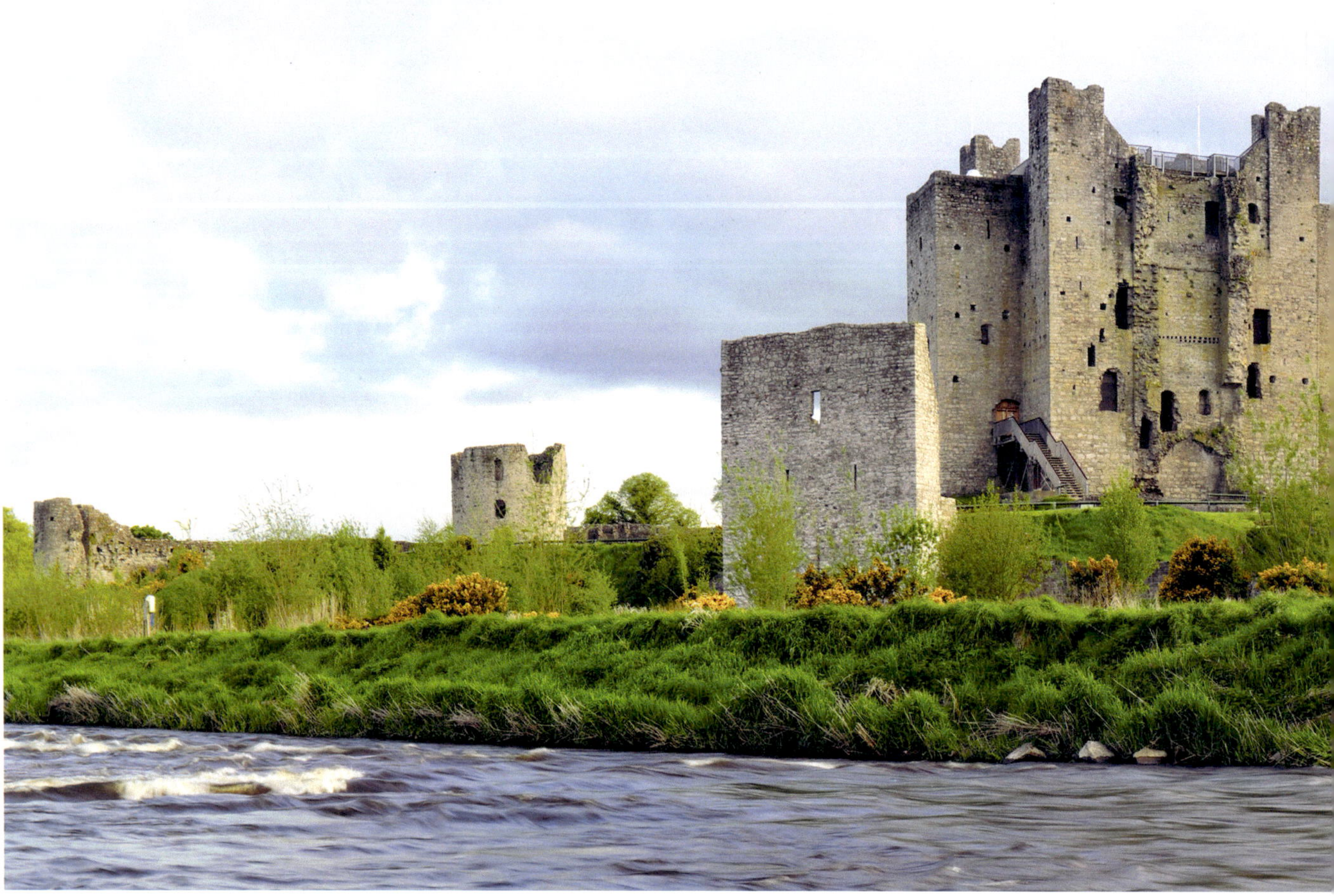

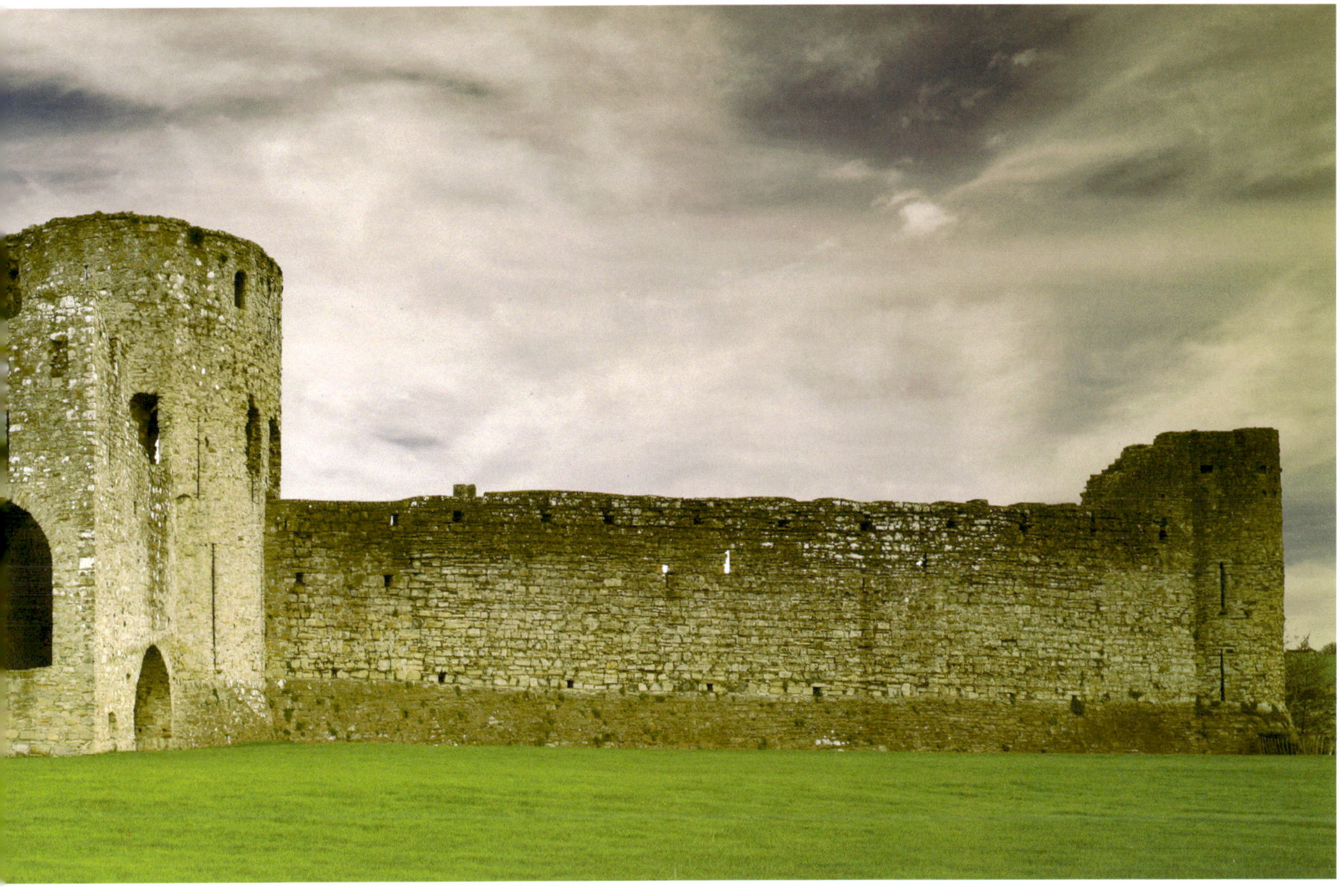

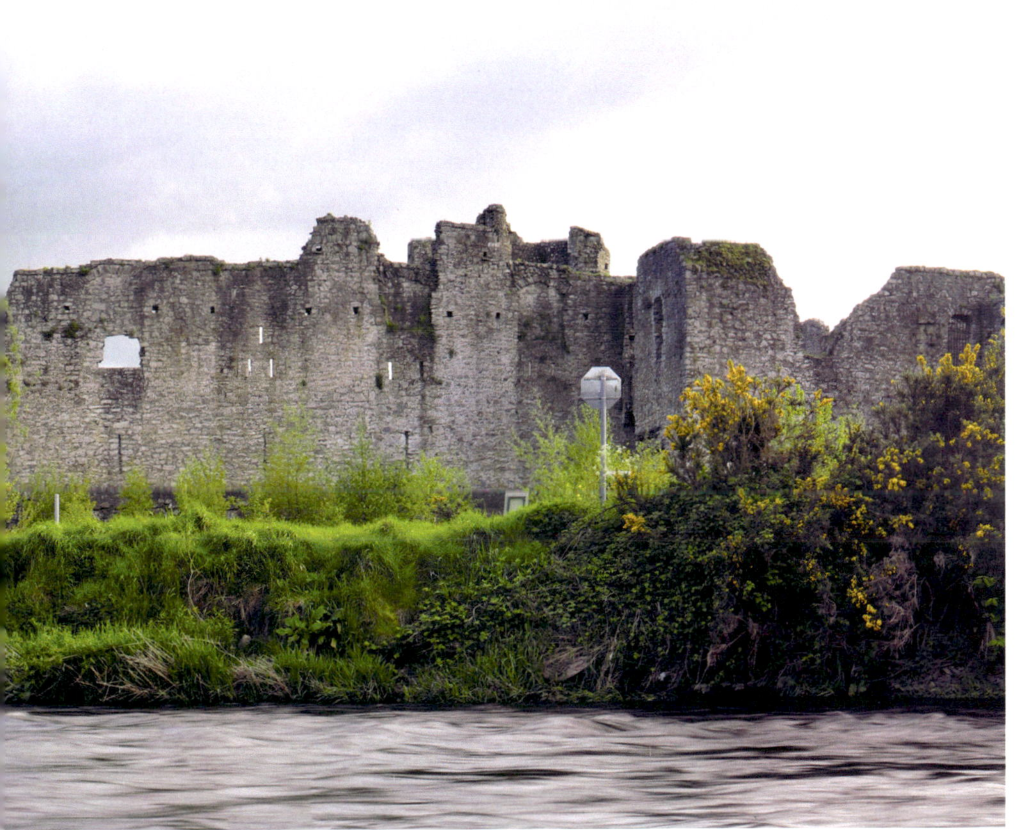

ABOVE AND LEFT:

Trim Castle, County Meath, Ireland

Construction of Trim Castle began in 1172 with a wooden fortification overlooking the River Boyne. Once the surrounding works of earth and timber were complete, rebuilding in stone commenced in 1176. Over the next decades Trim Castle was expanded to become the largest Norman fortification in Ireland.

Trim Castle's central keep is notable for its twenty-sided shape, with three of its four flanking towers still standing. The castle was inhabited for a relatively short time, so was not subject to the usual modifications and additions. As a result, the remains of Trim Castle are the original Anglo-Norman construction rather than a mix of styles and defensive features built to suit changing methods of siege warfare.

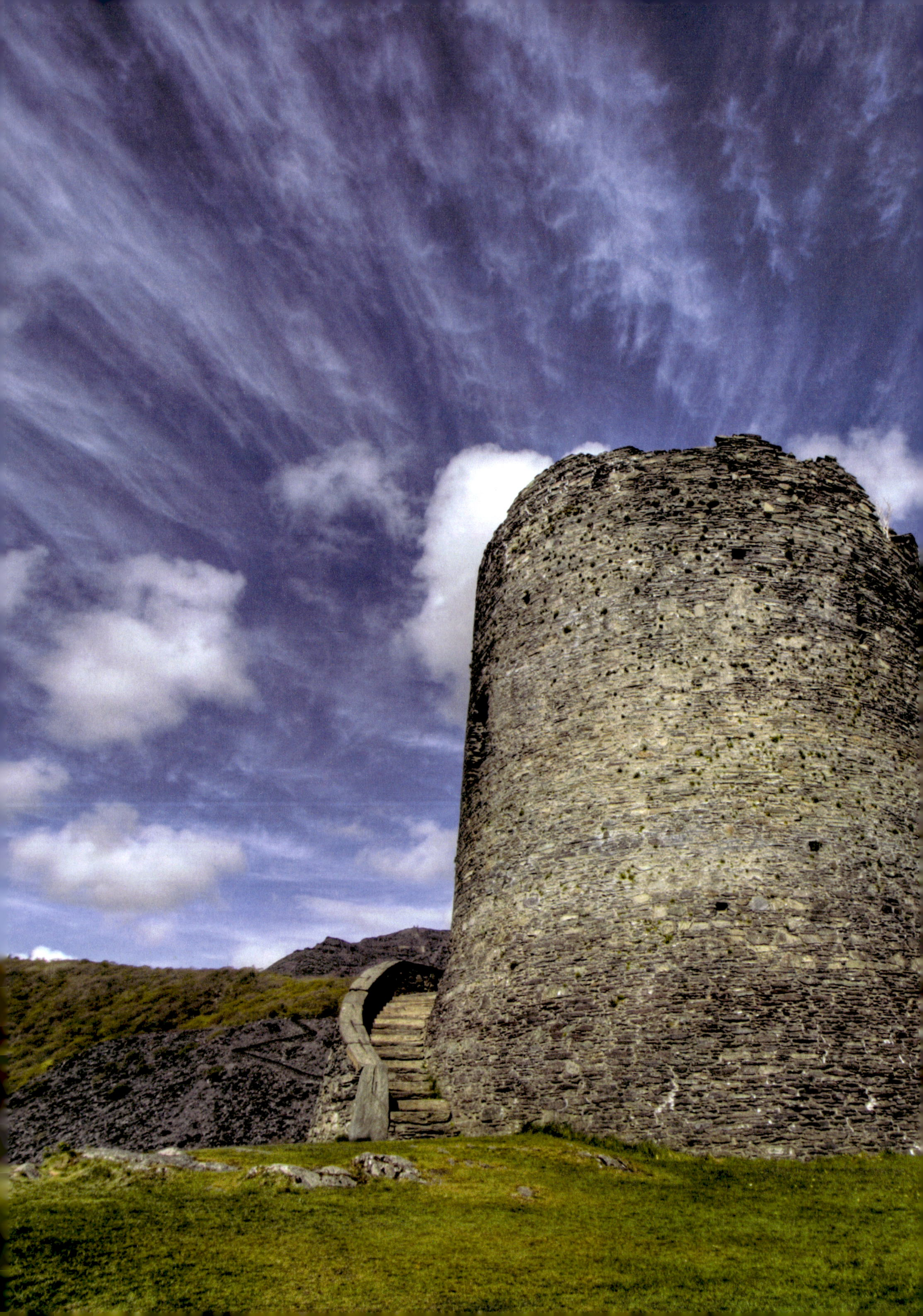

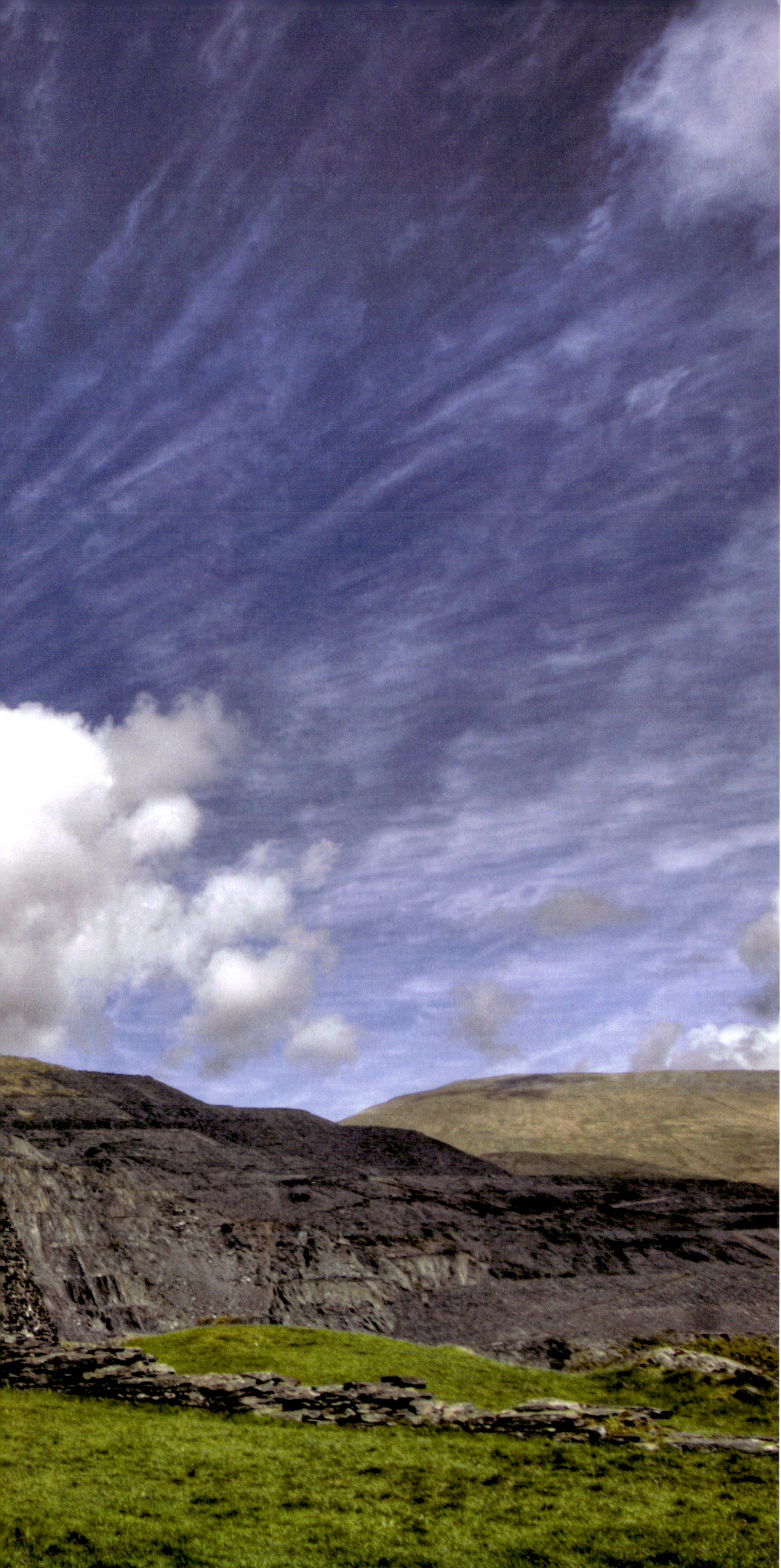

Dolbadarn Castle, Gwynedd, Wales

Dolbadarn Castle was built around 1220–1230 to control the Llanberis Pass in Gwynedd, Wales. The castle takes the form of a round tower with surrounding buildings, and predates the castles built by English kings attempting to control Wales. Dolbadarn Castle was briefly the centre of resistance against Edward I of England, and was garrisoned for a time after its capture. Edward I ordered timbers from the castle to be used in his own construction at Caernarfon, after which the remains of the castle were abandoned.

RIGHT:

Dolbadarn Castle, Gwynedd, Wales

Dolbadarn Castle at times served as a prison. During the power struggles of the 1250s, Owain Goch was imprisoned in a tower – more than likely it was Dolbadarn Castle – for twenty years by his brother, Llewellyn. There is also evidence that the castle was used to house prisoners taken by Owen Glendower during his rebellion in the early 1400s.

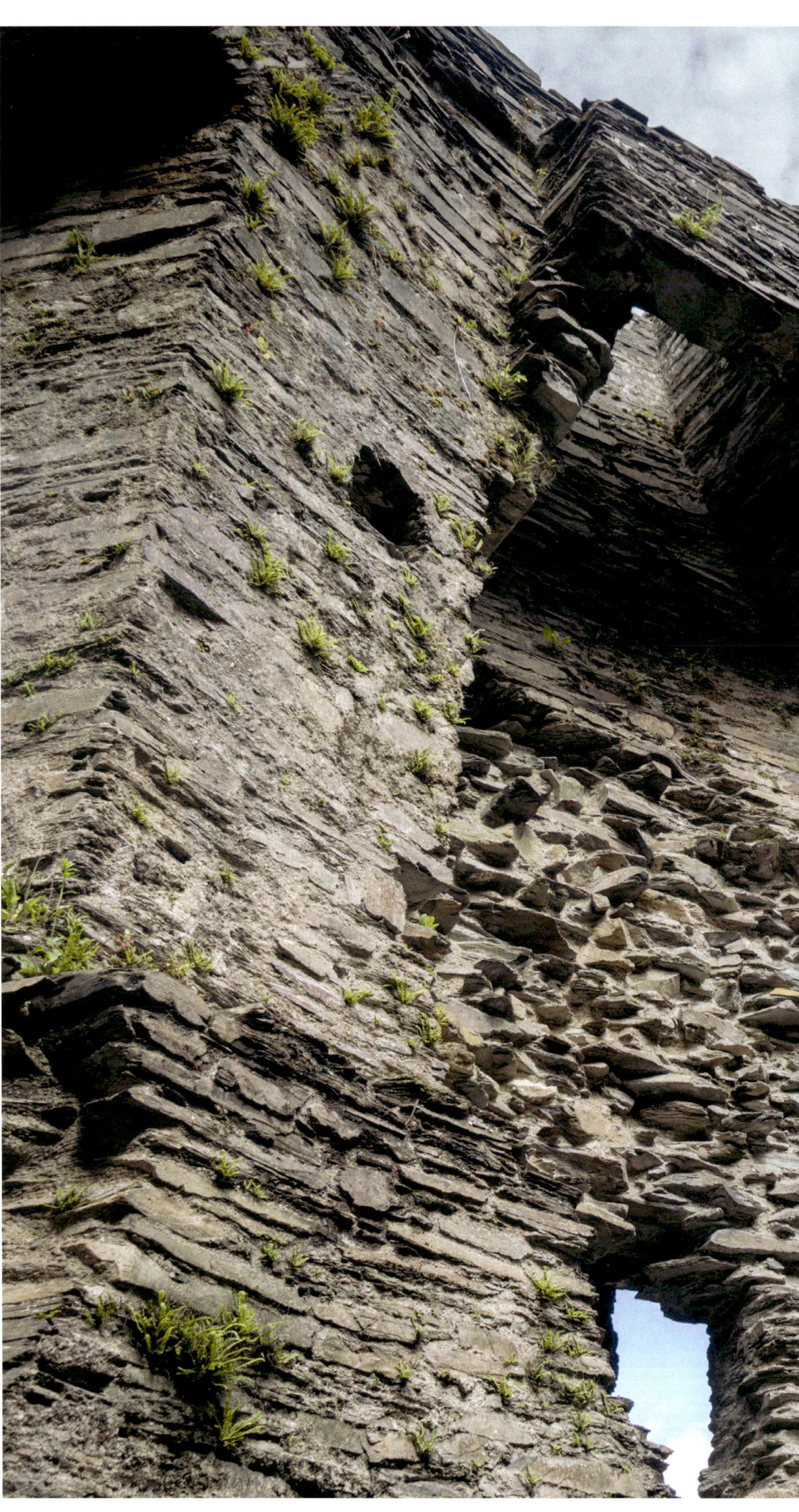

OVERLEAF:

Edinburgh Castle, Edinburgh, Scotland

Edinburgh Castle occupies an excellent defensive position atop Castle Rock, which was inhabited (and possibly fortified) since the Iron Age, or even much earlier. The modern castle was built by David I of Scotland in the 12th century and has been extensively rebuilt over the centuries.

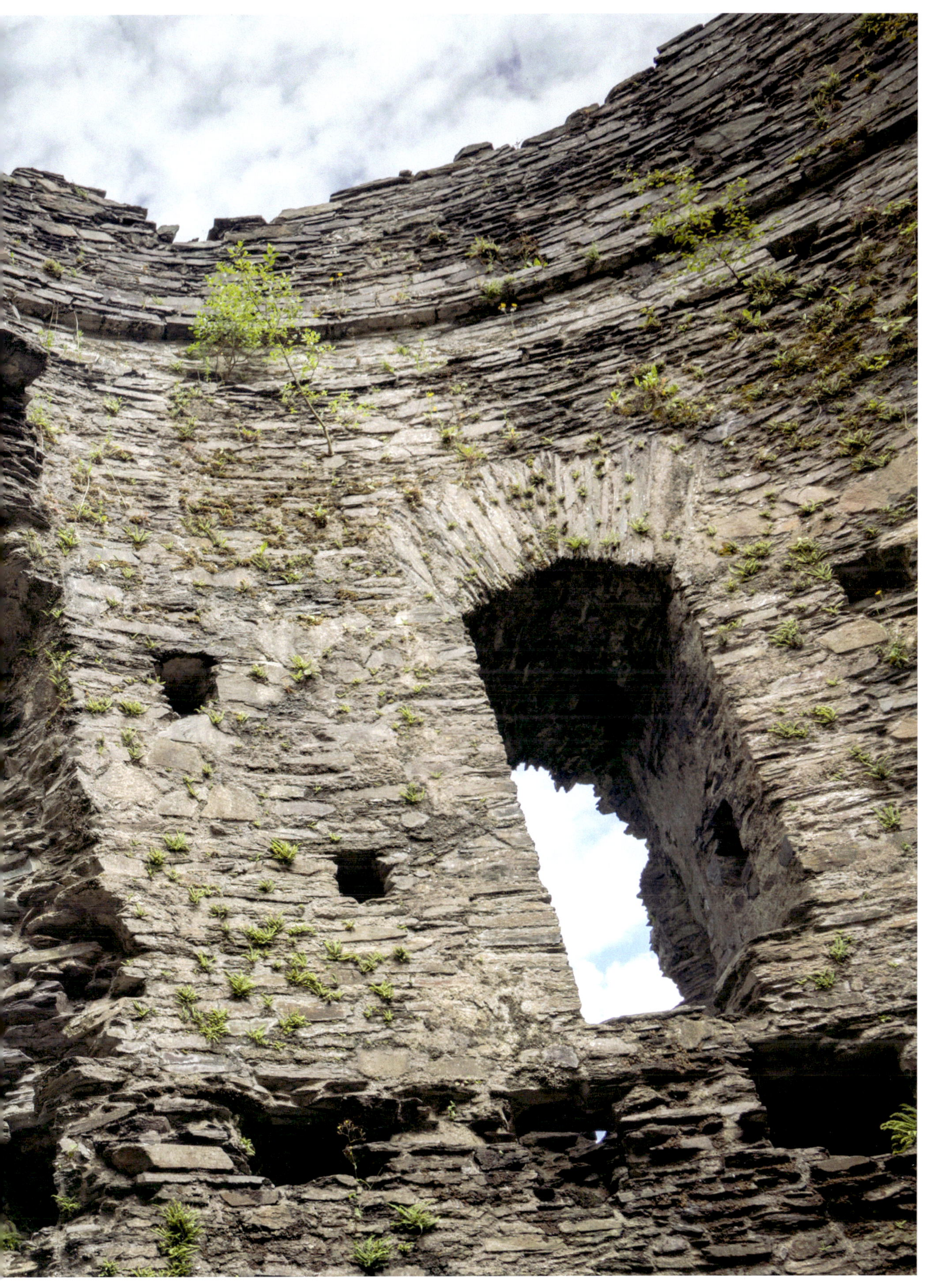

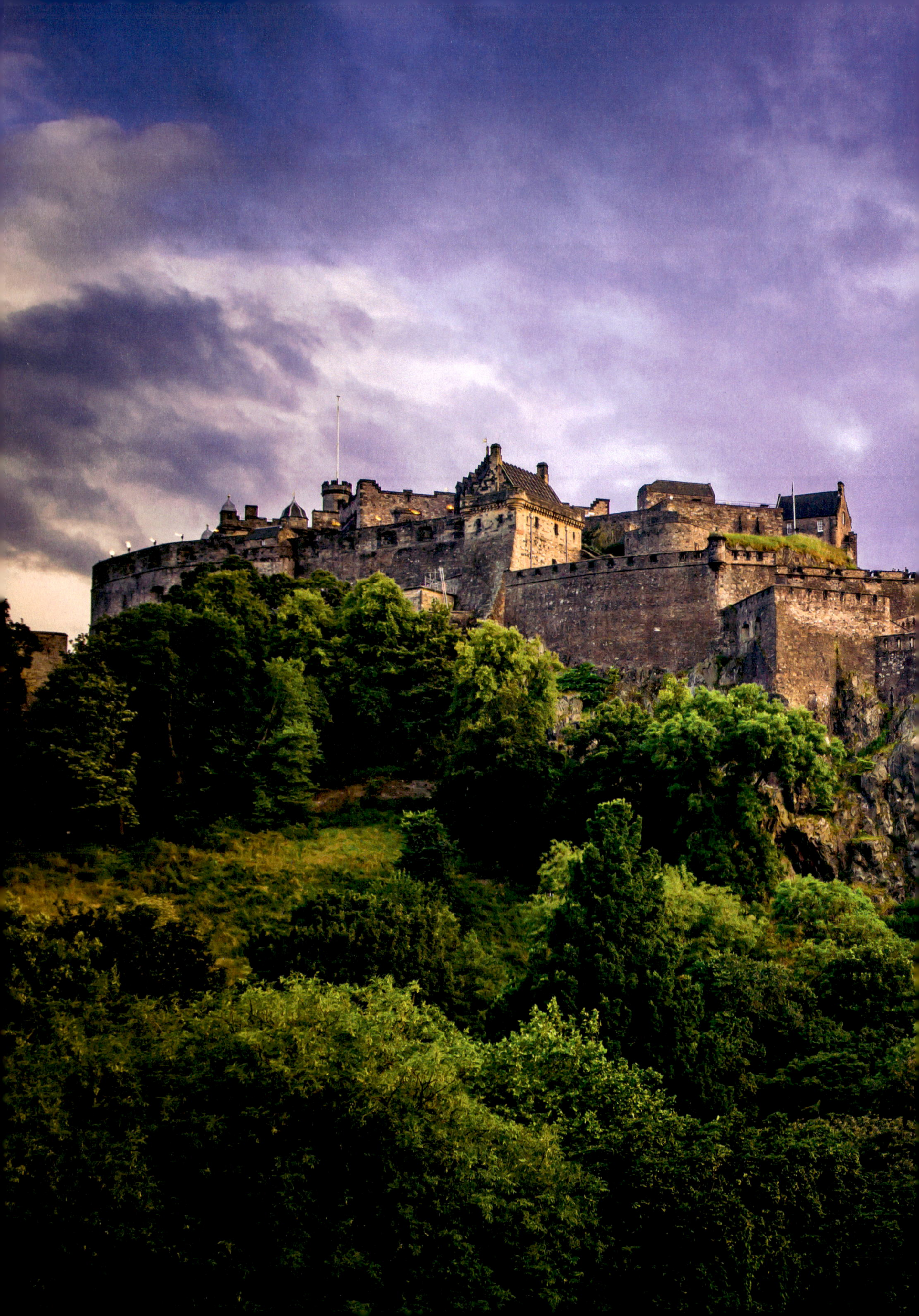

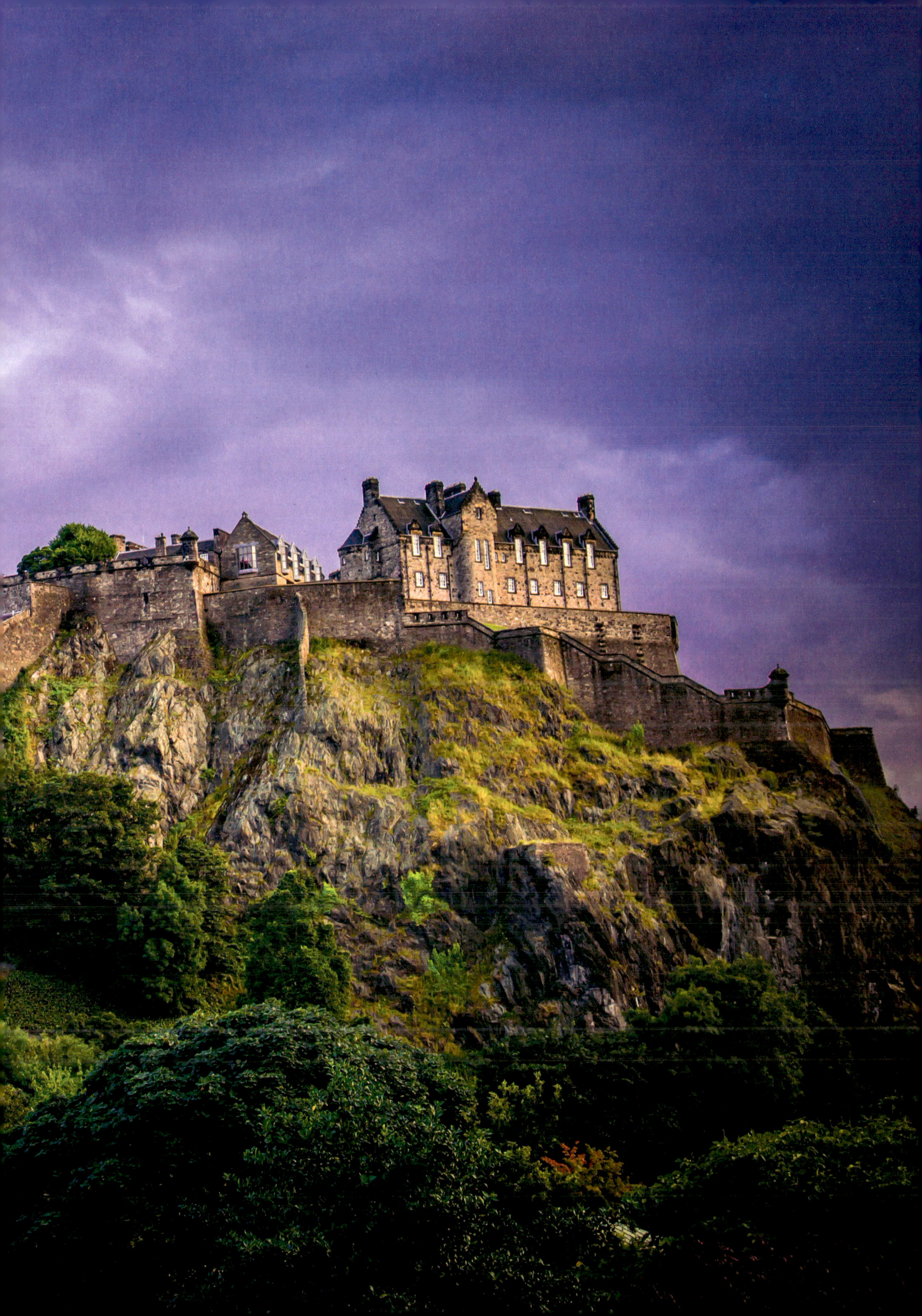

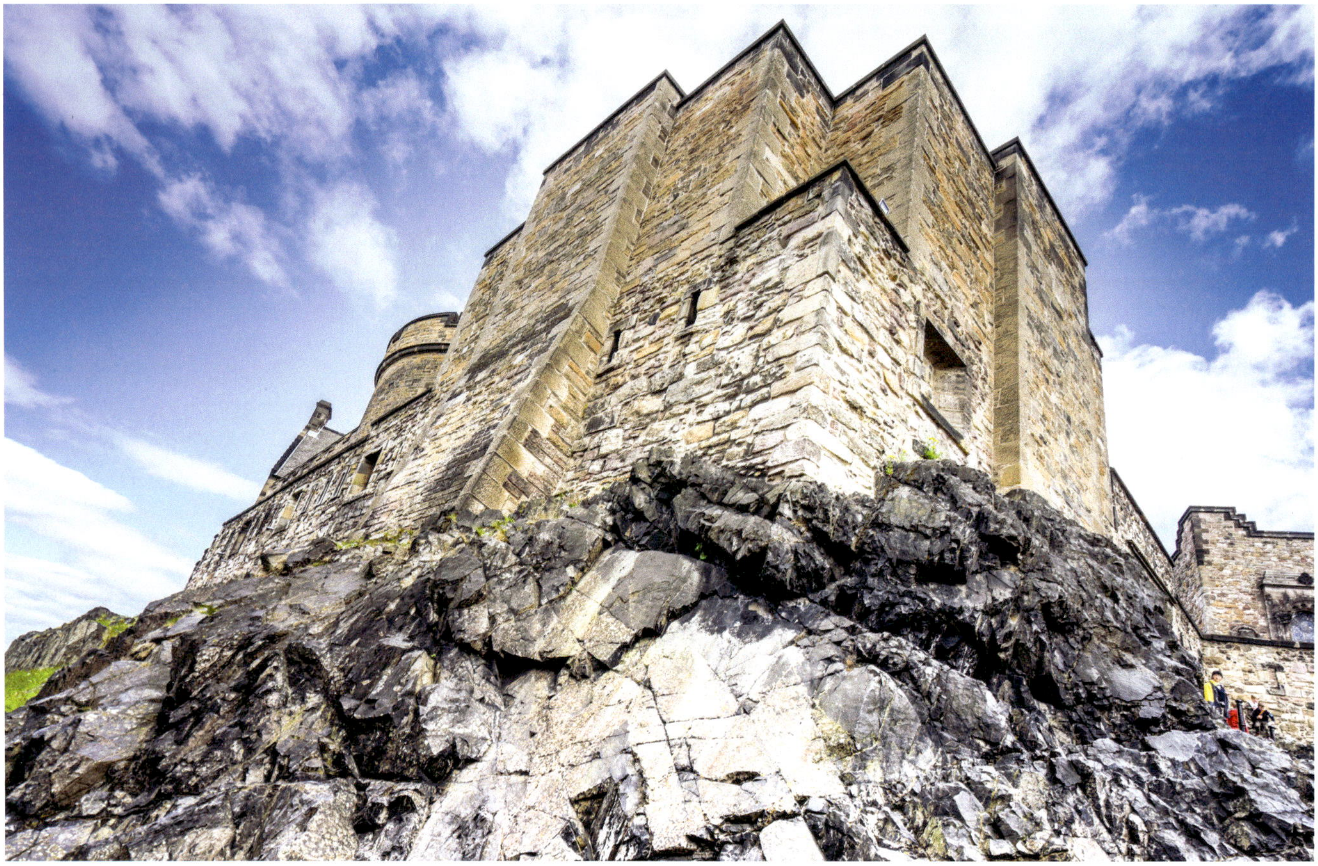

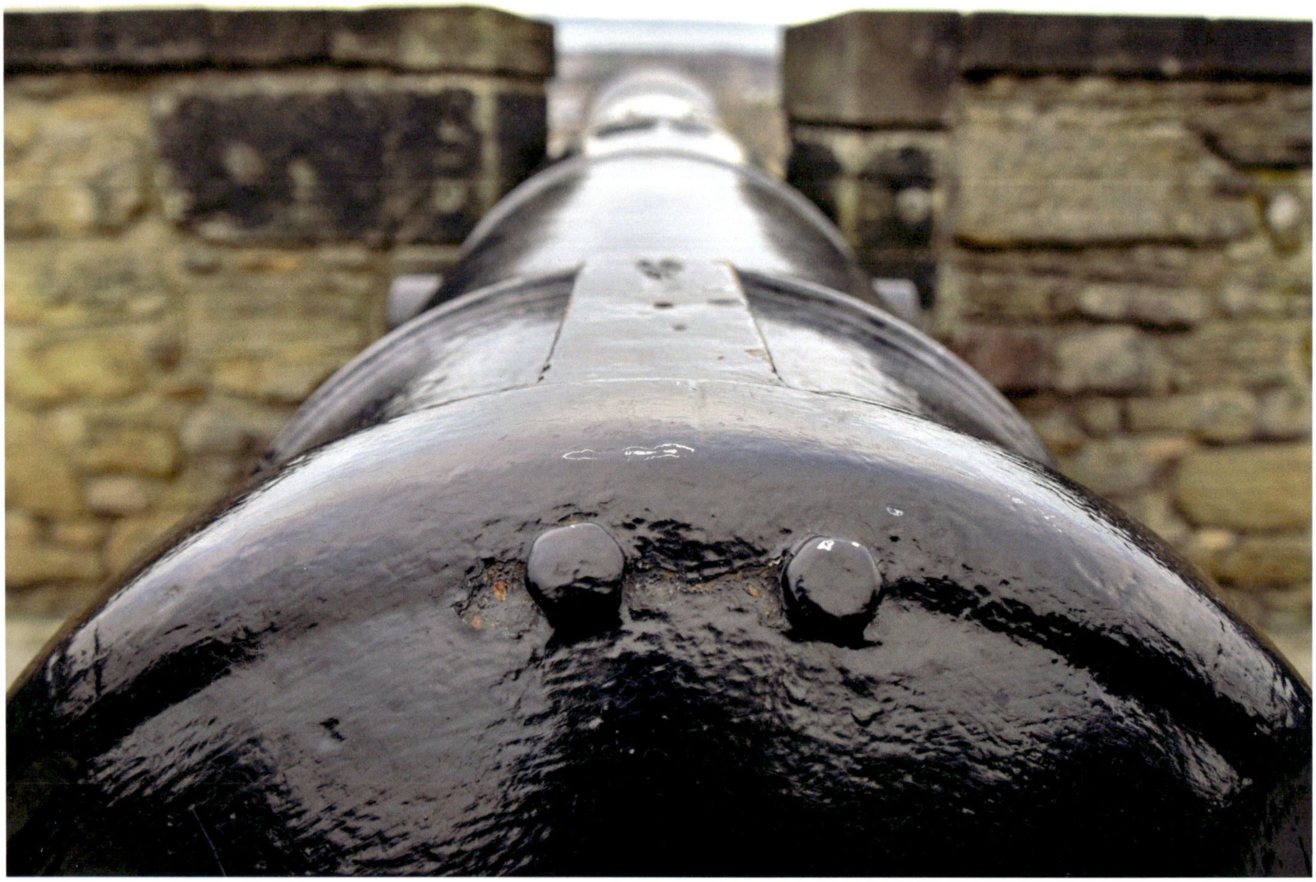

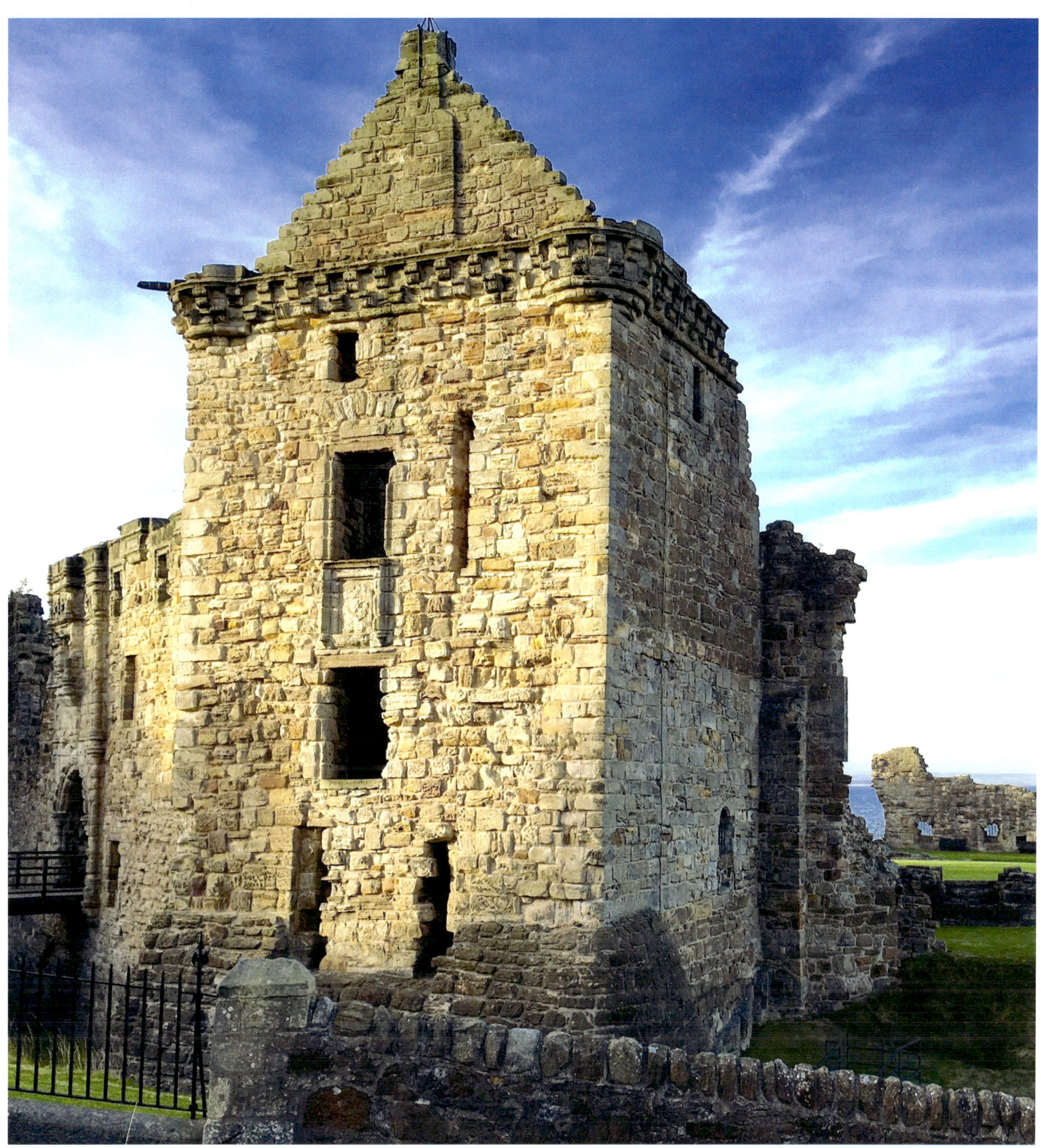

LEFT, TOP AND BOTTOM:
Edinburgh Castle, Edinburgh, Scotland
Edinburgh Castle was a strategic location in the wars between England and Scotland, and was repeatedly besieged during the Wars of Scottish Independence, in the late 13th and early 14th centuries. Most surviving structures date from the 1600s or later, when the defences were extended and updated after the Lang Siege of 1571–73. By this time, artillery was an important factor in both attack and defence.

ABOVE:
St Andrews Castle, Fife, Scotland
St Andrews Castle stands on a site fortified by the Scots since the 1100s, though little remains of it. The modern castle was built in the 1400s, with additional artillery defences added in the early 1500s. After suffering serious damage during the siege of 1546–47, the castle was rebuilt once again; most surviving features date from this era.

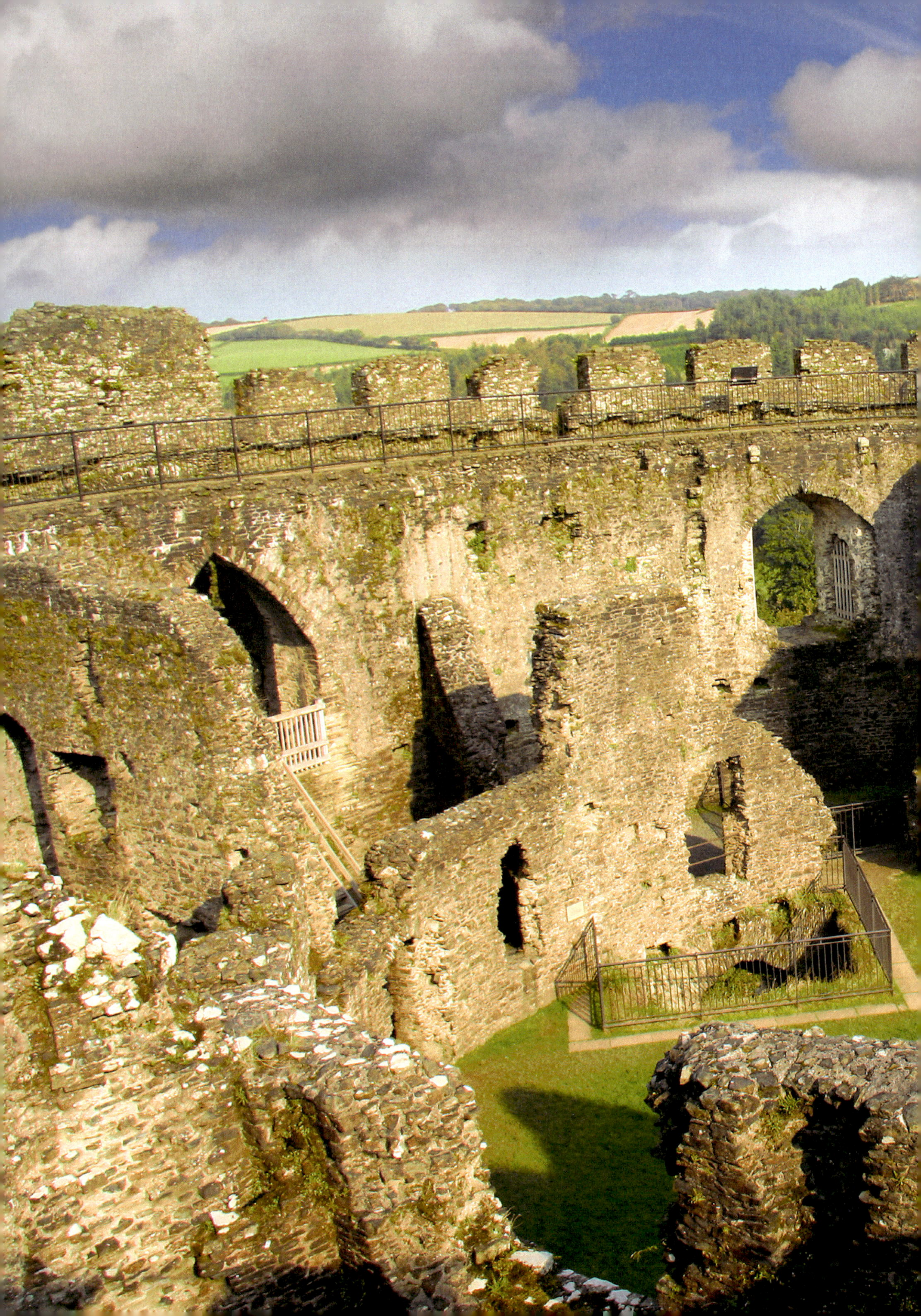

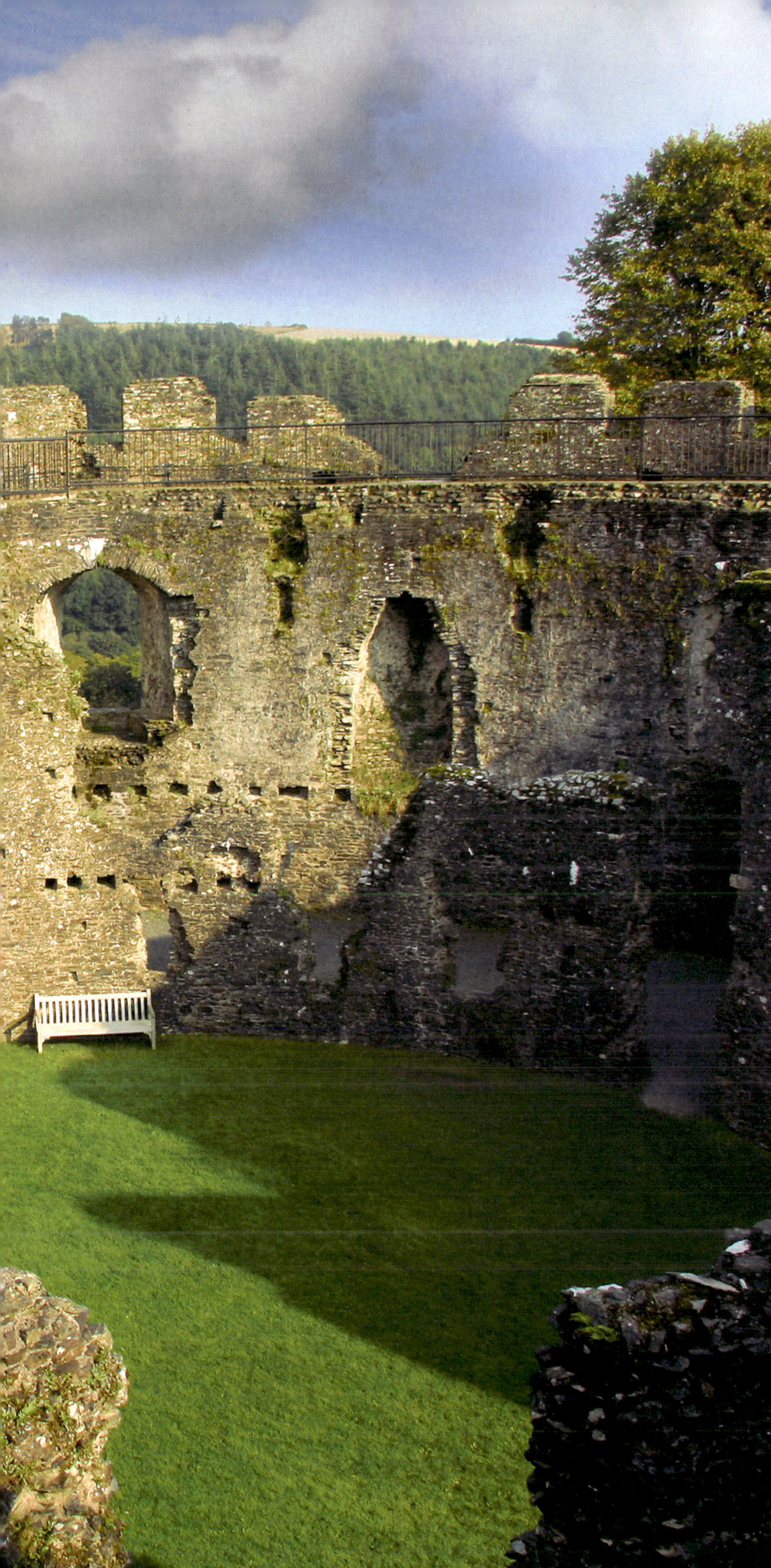

Restormel Castle, Cornwall, England
Restormel Castle was originally a Norman motte-and-bailey construction, converted into a shell keep by rebuilding the circular structure in stone. The original fortification dates from the 1100s, with rebuilding taking place around 1190–1225. The castle was renovated in the mid-1300s but was a ruin by the time of the English Civil War, when it was temporarily occupied by Parliamentarian forces.

Castle Rushen, Isle of Man

Castle Rushen on the Isle of Man was probably constructed in the mid- to late-12th century. The original keep was later expanded and additional defences in the form of a curtain wall and towers were added in the 14th century. The castle was originally built by the rulers of the Isle of Man but was at times held by the English and the Scots. It was held by Royalist forces in the English Civil War, falling to the Parliamentarians in 1651.

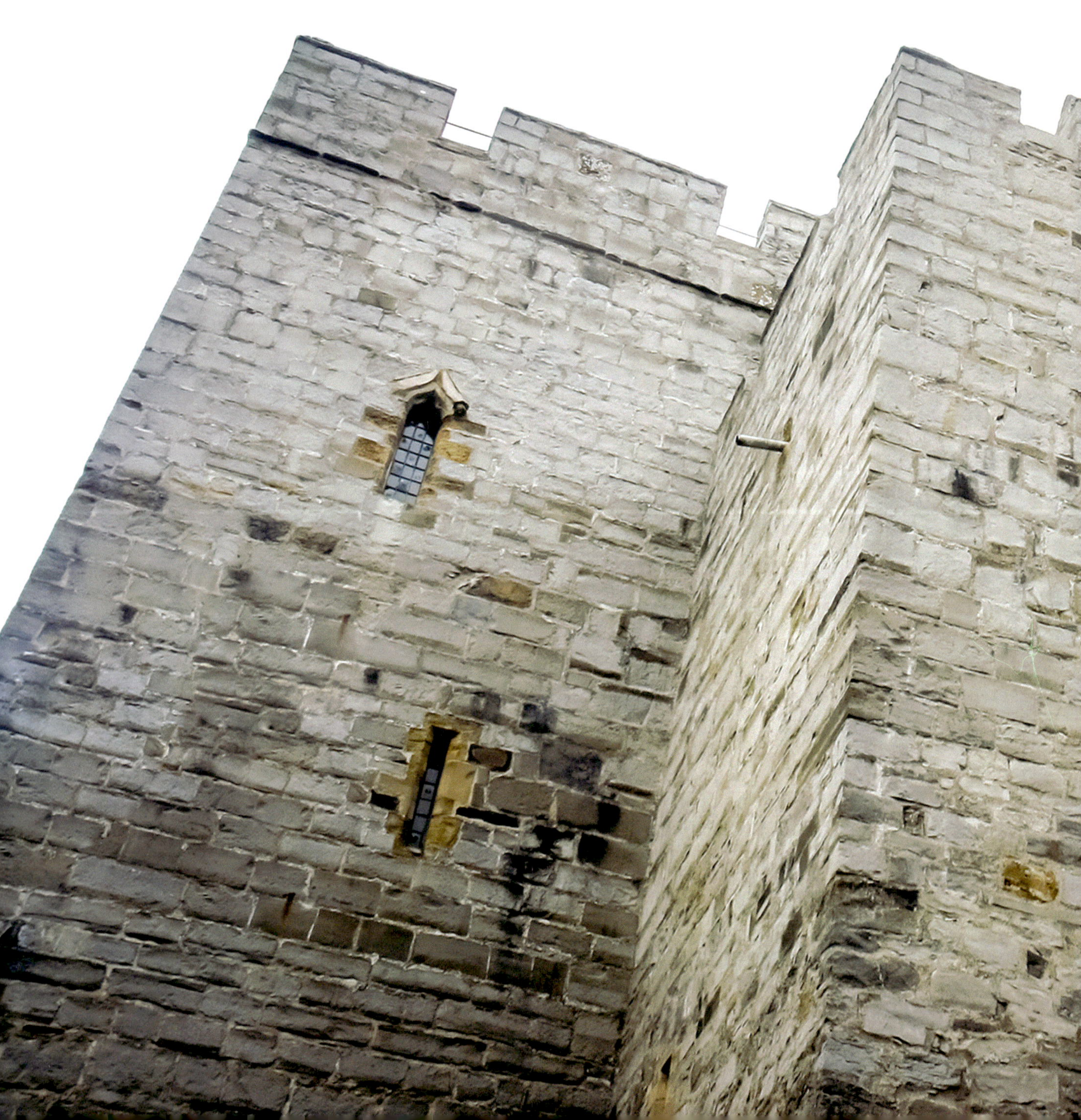

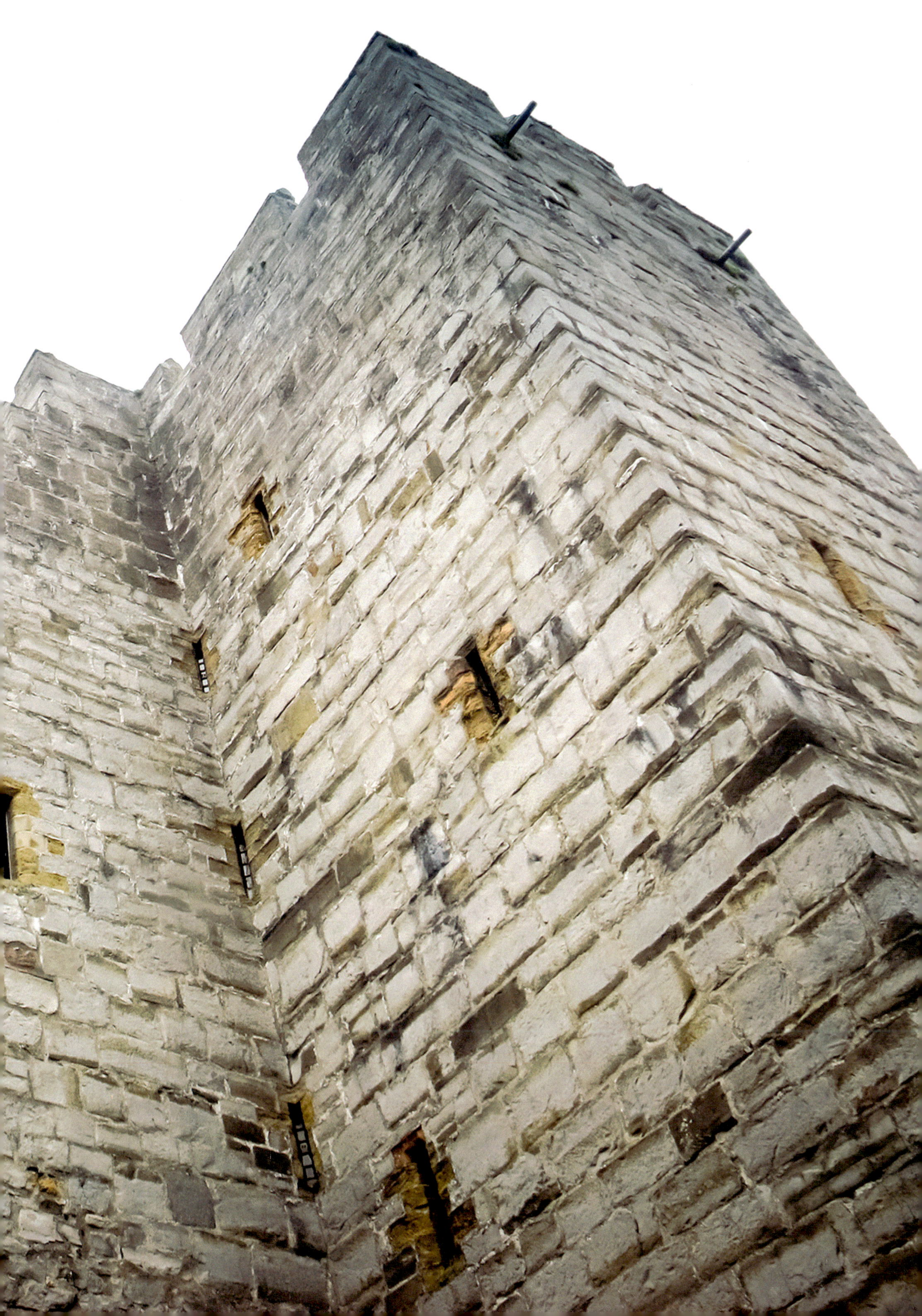

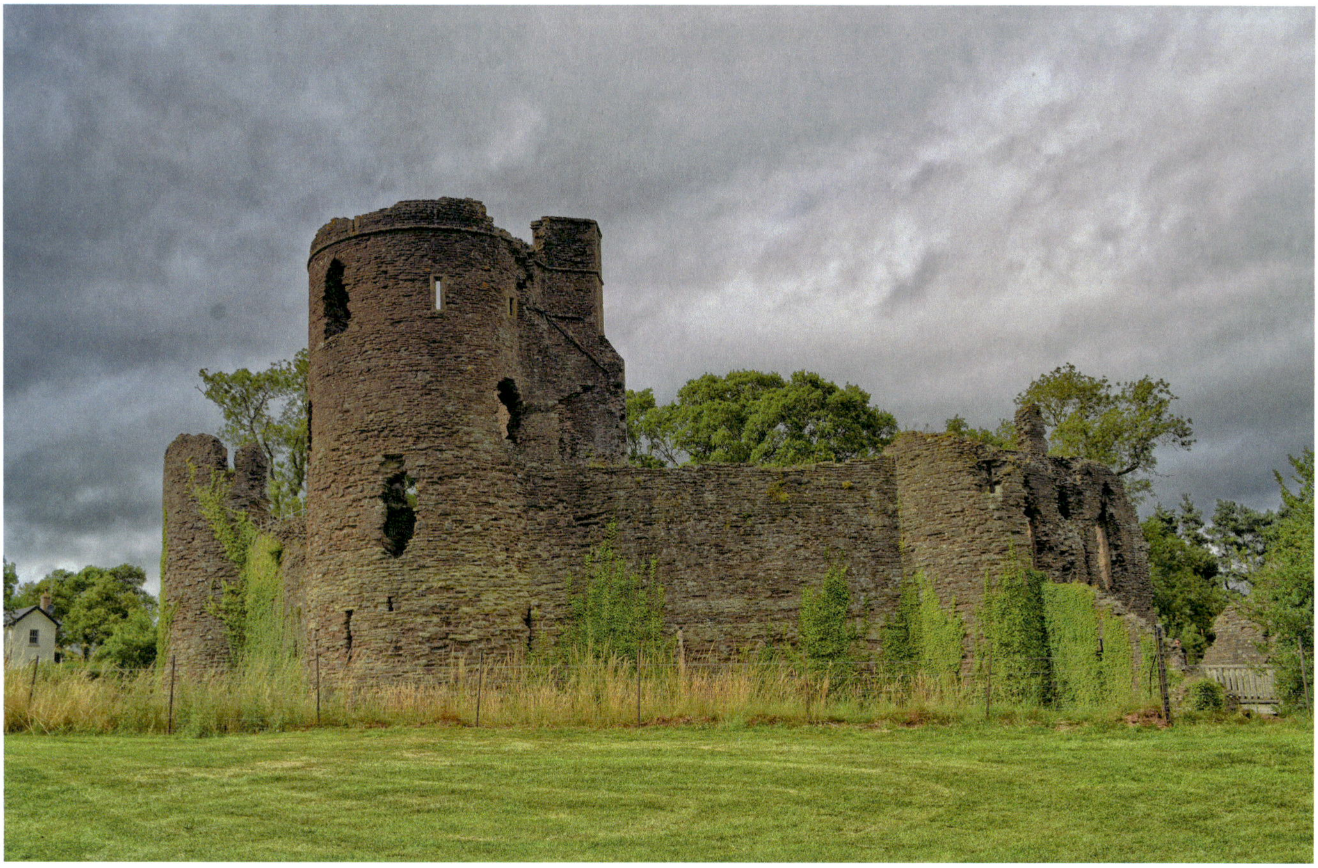

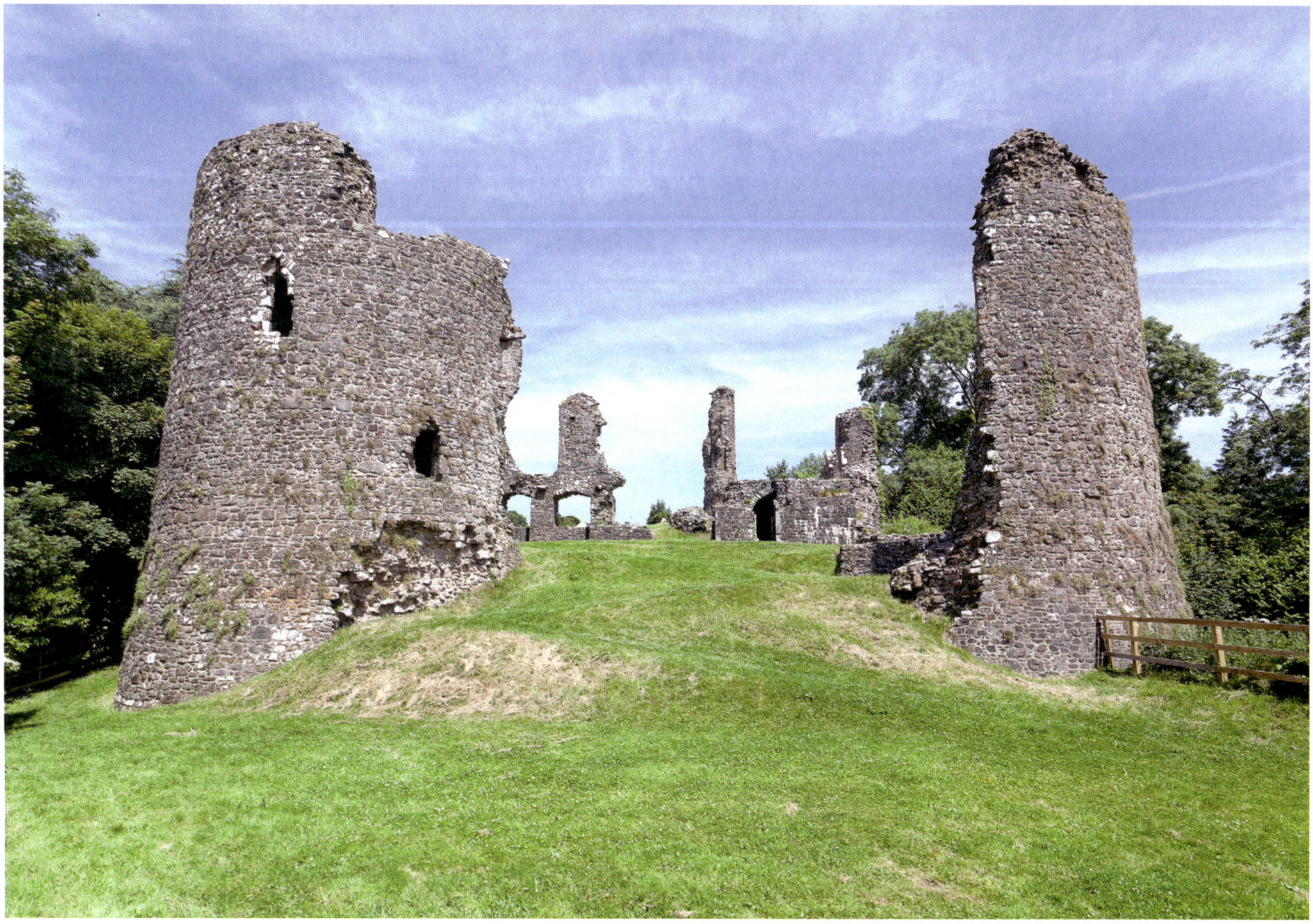

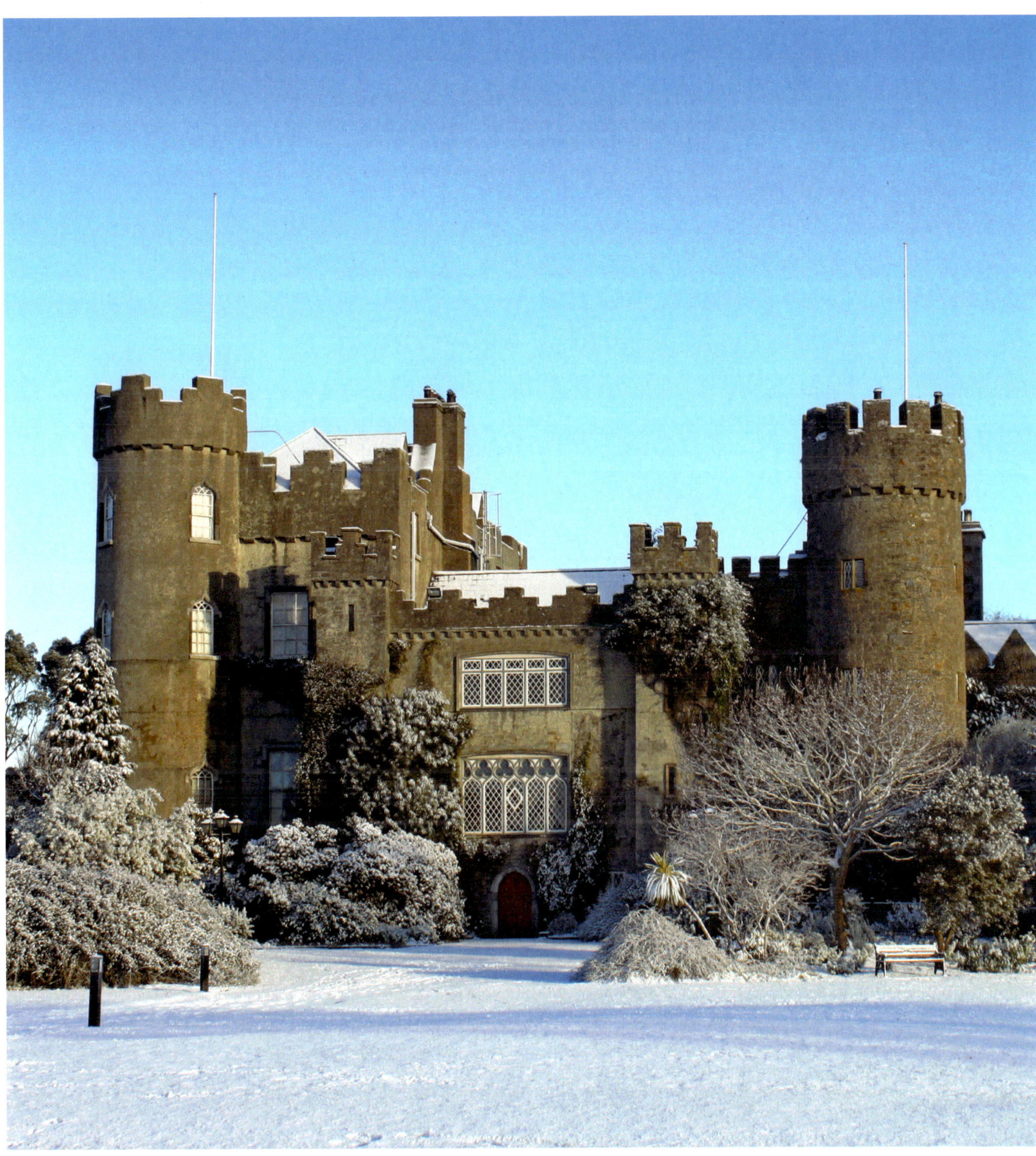

LEFT, TOP:
Grosmont Castle, Monmouthshire, Wales
Grosmont Castle was probably begun around 1070. There is evidence that the castle was built in stone from the outset rather than being a rebuilt wooden fort. The castle was expanded in the early 1200s and extensively rebuilt later that century. It was besieged in 1405, during the rebellion of Owen Glendower against English rule.

LEFT, BOTTOM:
Narberth Castle, West Wales
Narberth Castle was built by the Normans as a motte-and-bailey some time before 1116, and was reconstructed in stone in the 1200s. After serious damage, the castle was rebuilt and expanded by Roger Mortimer, 1st Earl of March, in the 1280s. During the English Civil War the castle was slighted (rendered indefensible) by Parliamentarian forces.

ABOVE AND OVERLEAF:
Malahide Castle, Dublin, Ireland
Work on Malahide Castle began in 1185 after the Norman invasion of Ireland. The castle was later expanded, with four towers around the original keep added during the reign of Edward IV of England. The castle was the home of the Talbot family for nearly eight centuries, apart from a short period where it was seized during Oliver Cromwell's invasion of Ireland (1649–53).

The main entrance to Malahide Castle reflects the changes the structure underwent during its long history. With the advent of gunpowder artillery, traditional castles became obsolete and those that remained inhabited were often modified to become comfortable stately homes.

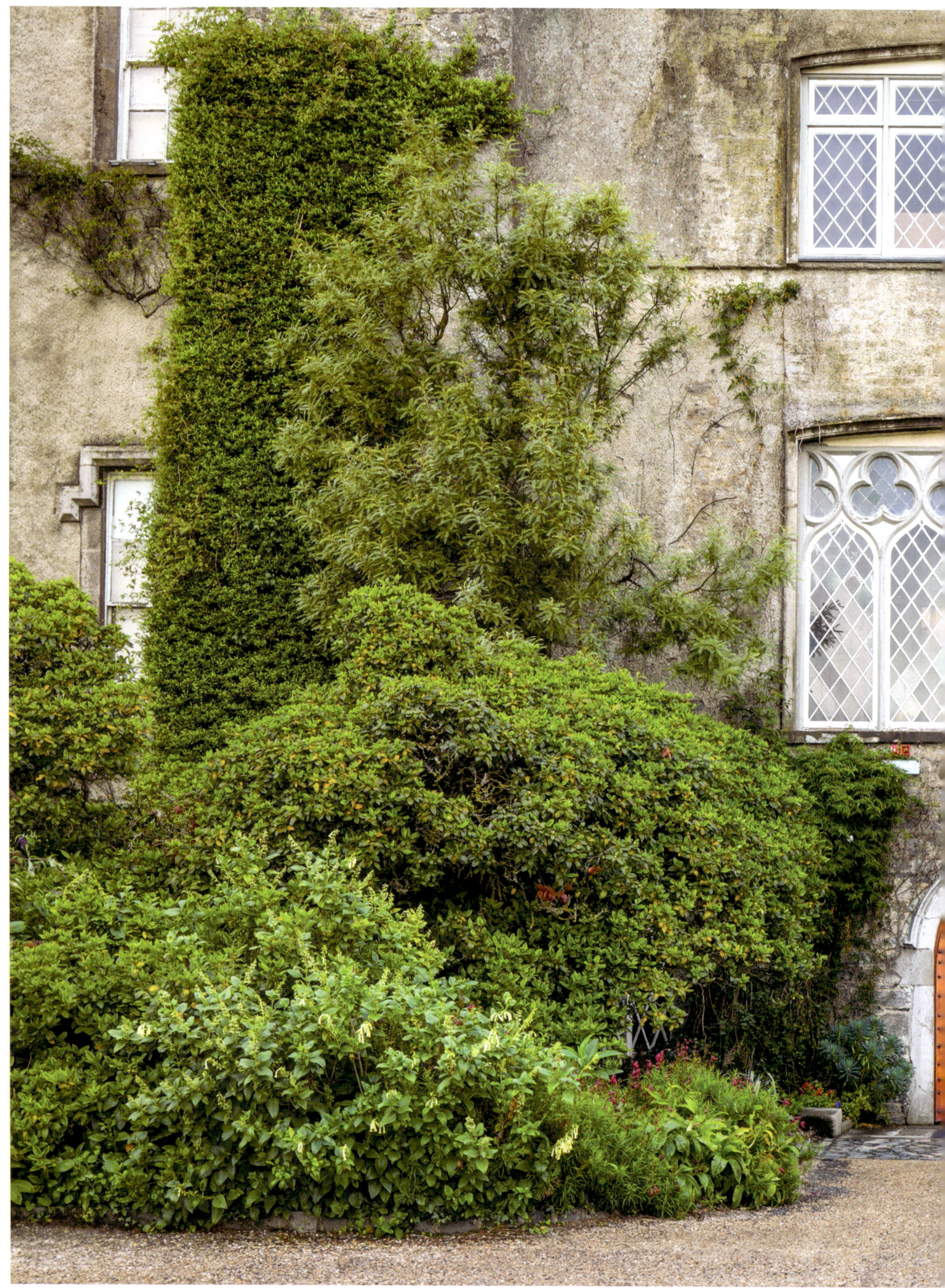

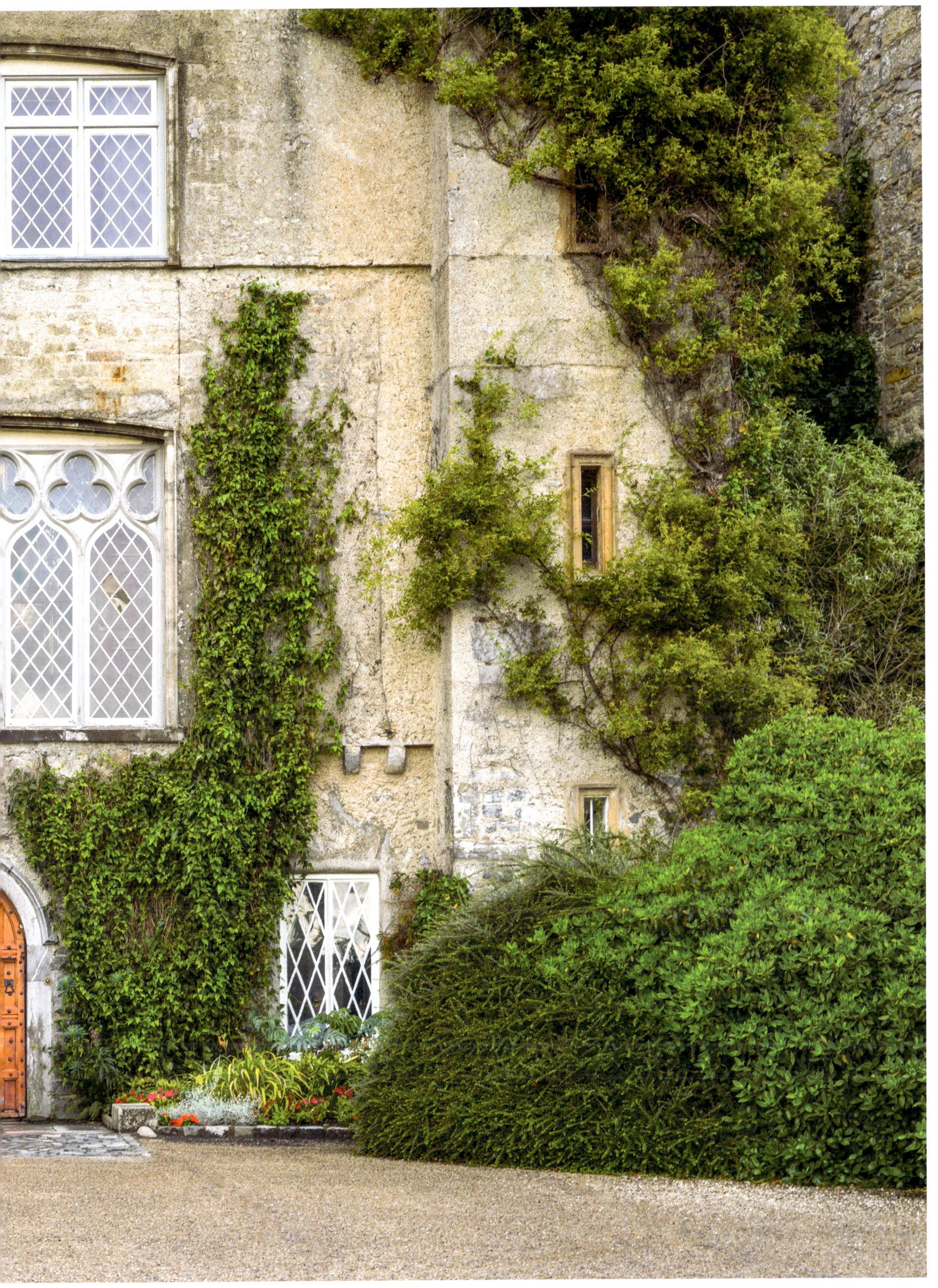

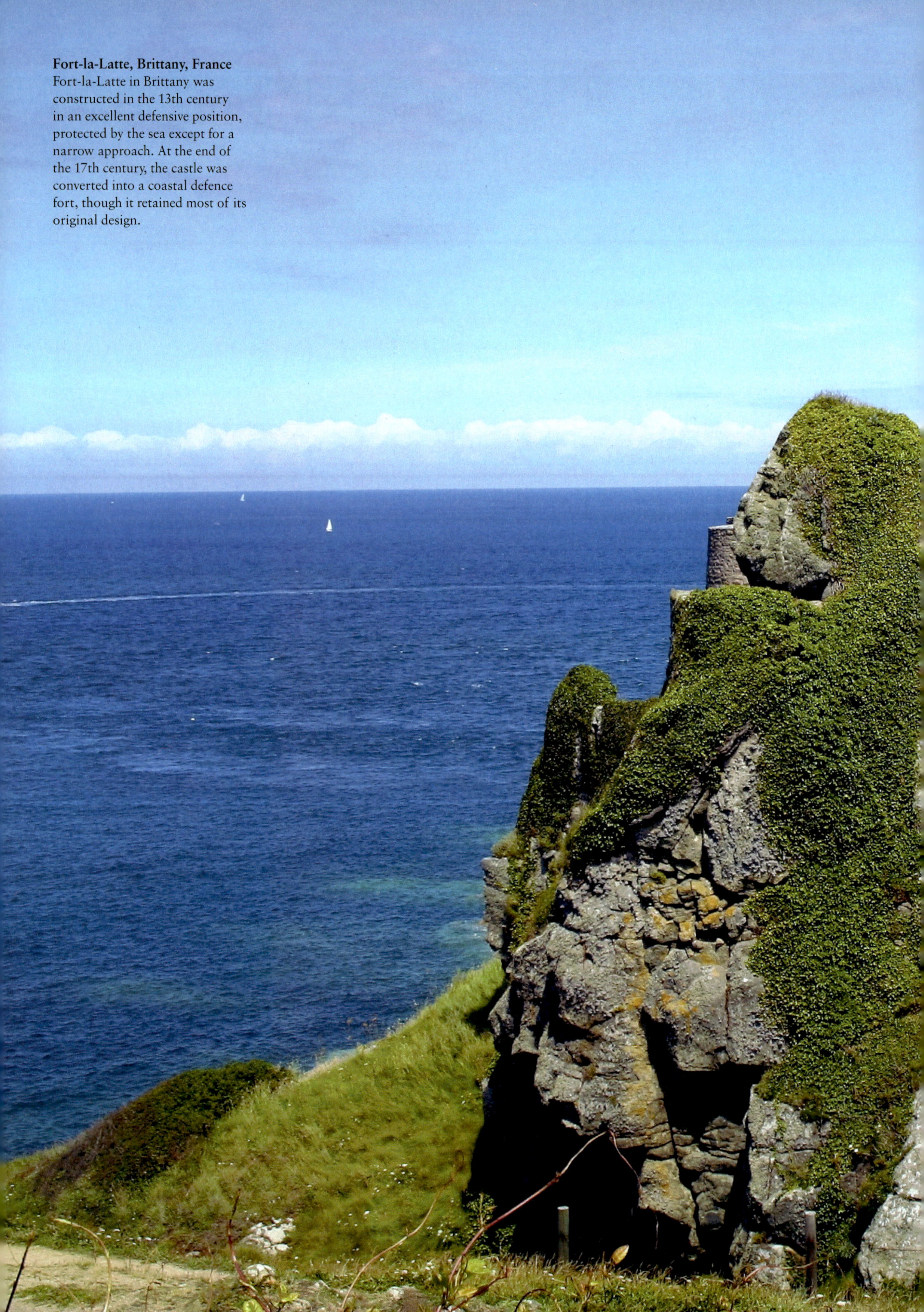

Fort-la-Latte, Brittany, France
Fort-la-Latte in Brittany was constructed in the 13th century in an excellent defensive position, protected by the sea except for a narrow approach. At the end of the 17th century, the castle was converted into a coastal defence fort, though it retained most of its original design.

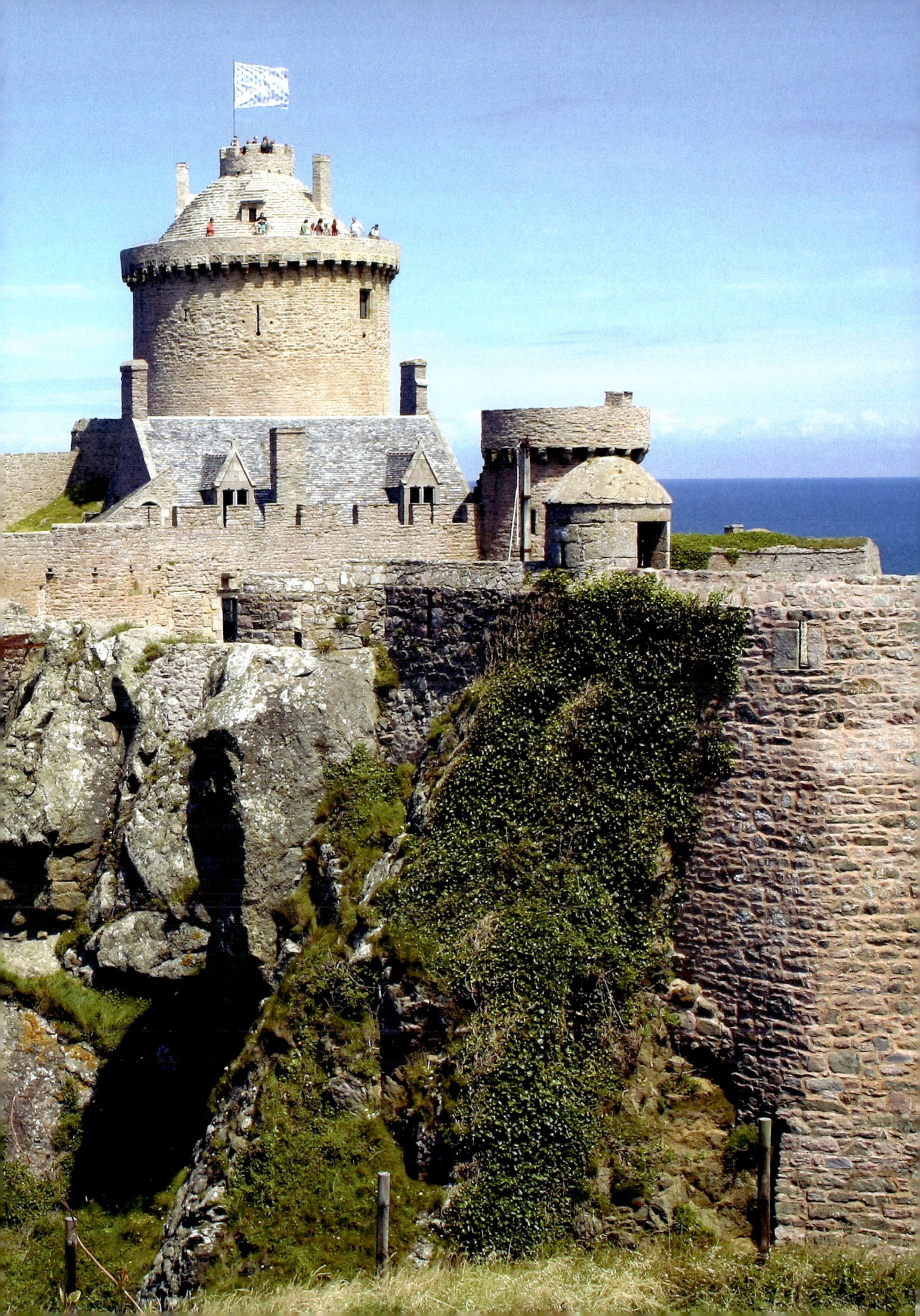

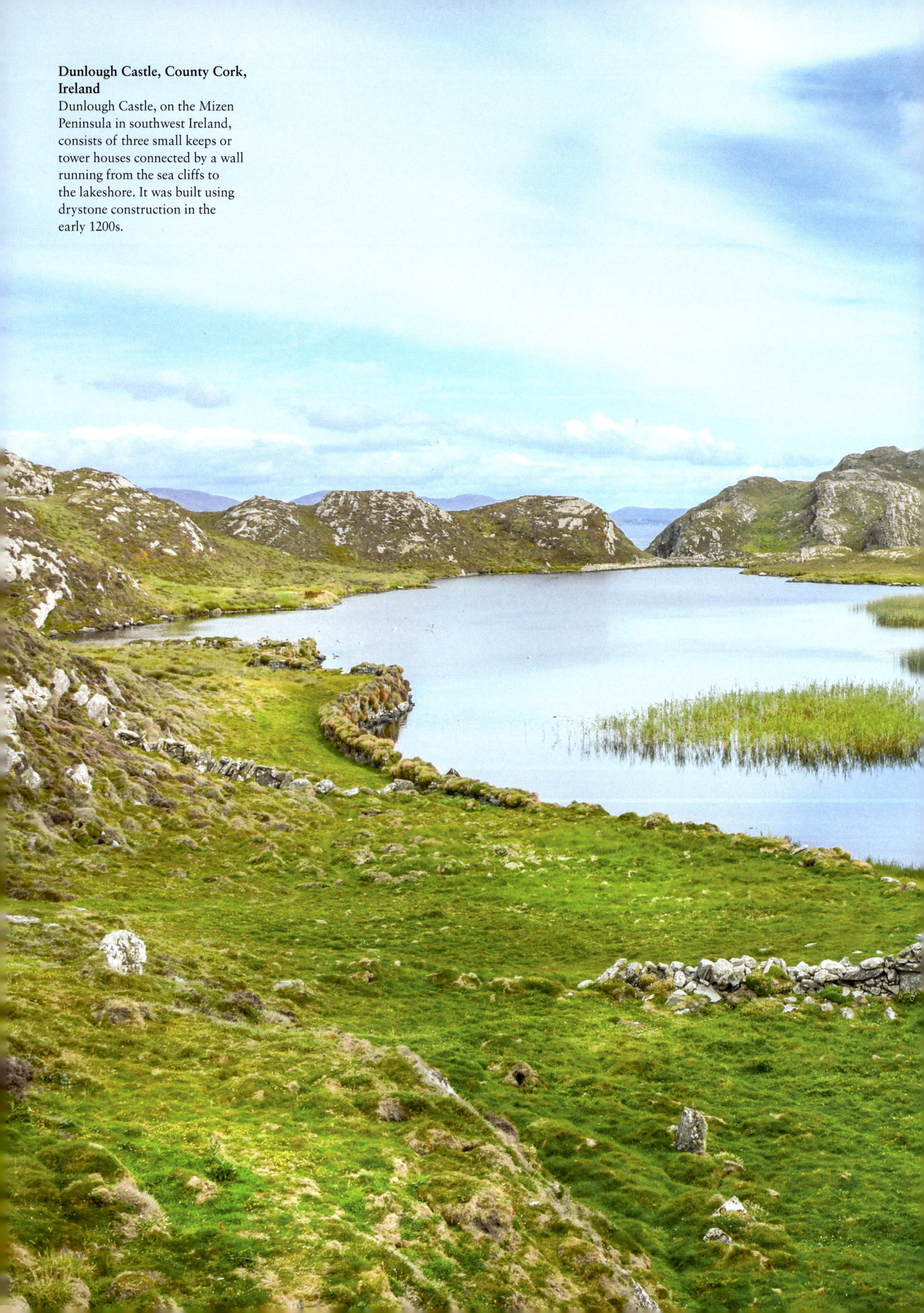

Dunlough Castle, County Cork, Ireland
Dunlough Castle, on the Mizen Peninsula in southwest Ireland, consists of three small keeps or tower houses connected by a wall running from the sea cliffs to the lakeshore. It was built using drystone construction in the early 1200s.

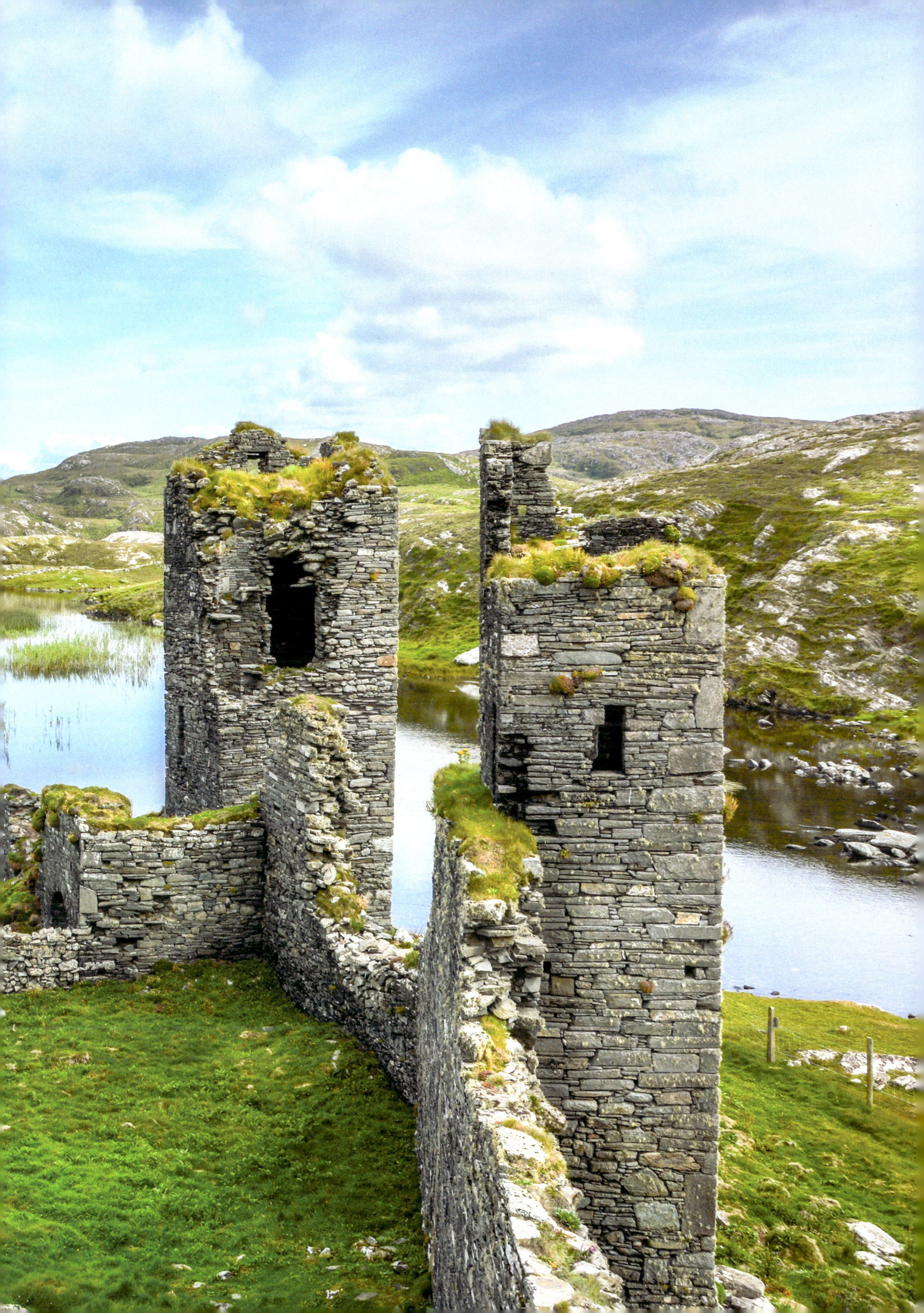

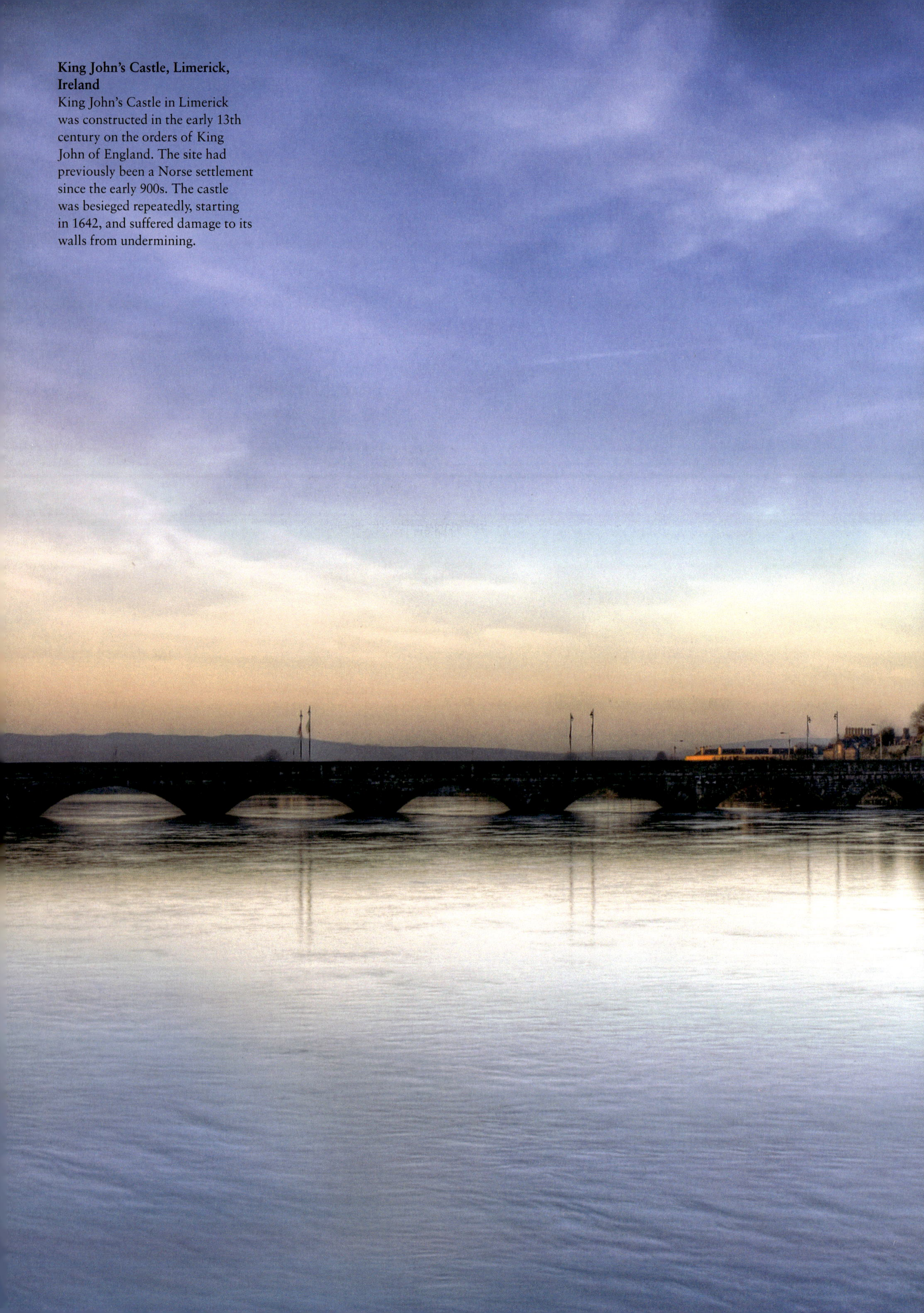

King John's Castle, Limerick, Ireland
King John's Castle in Limerick was constructed in the early 13th century on the orders of King John of England. The site had previously been a Norse settlement since the early 900s. The castle was besieged repeatedly, starting in 1642, and suffered damage to its walls from undermining.

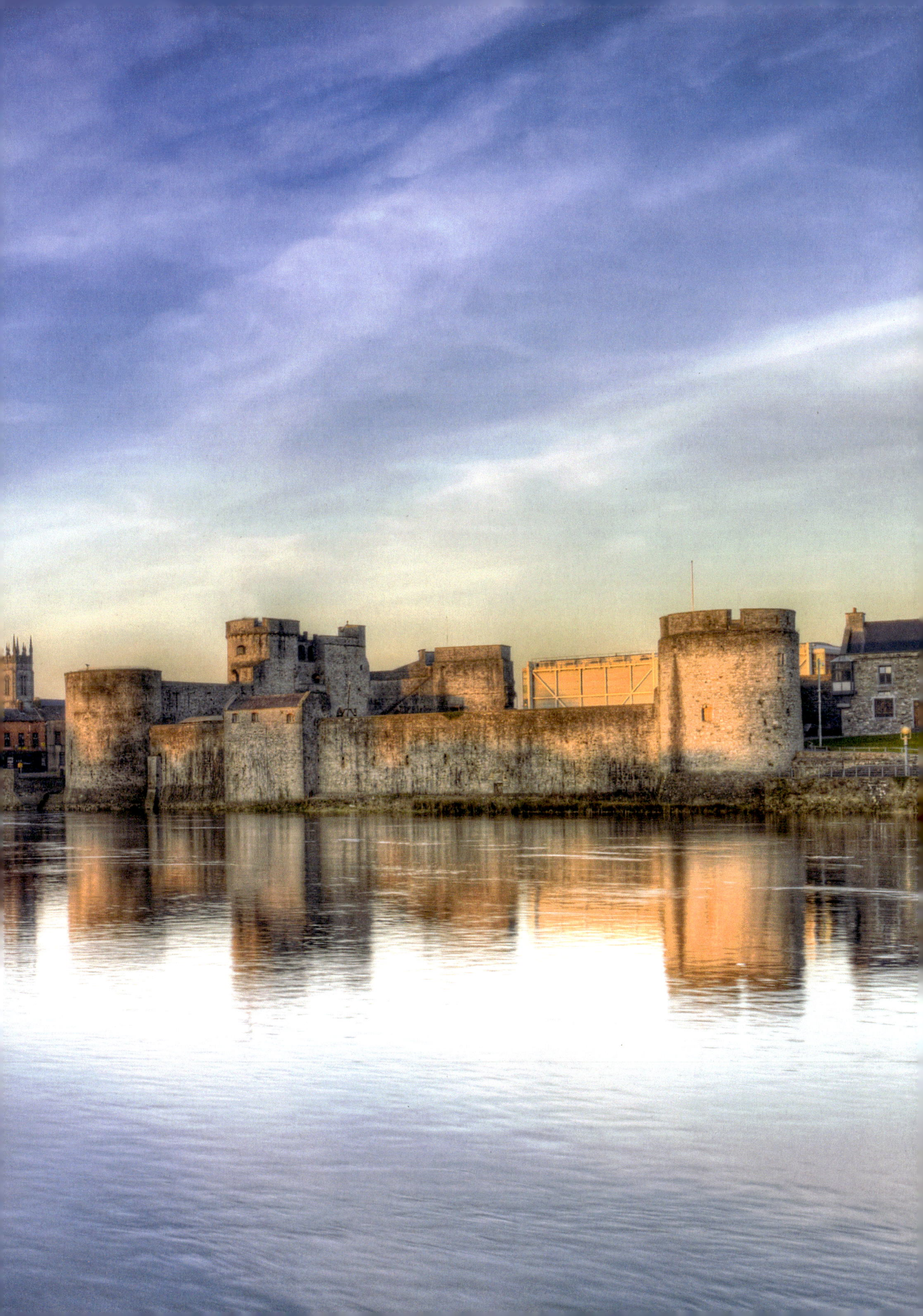

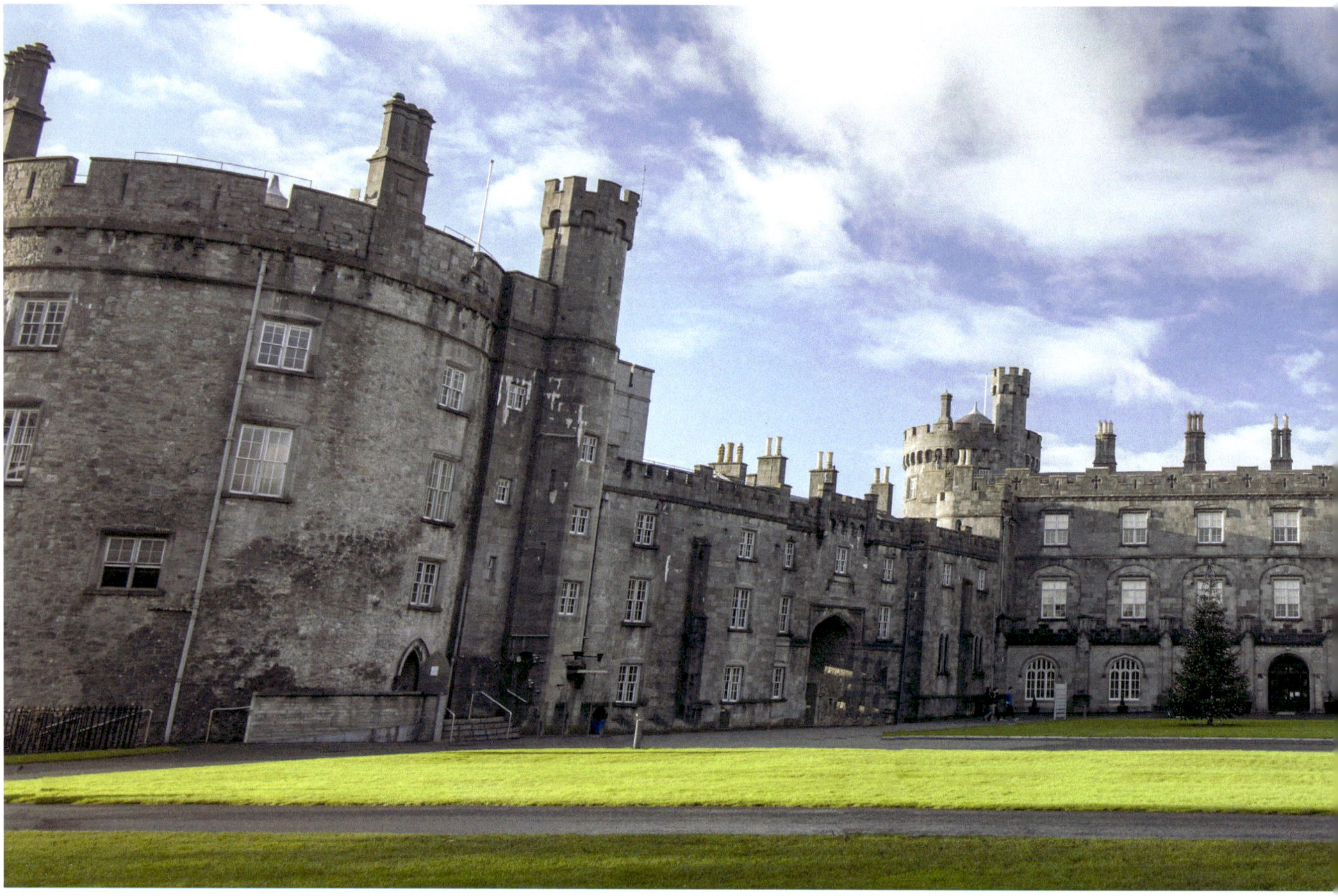

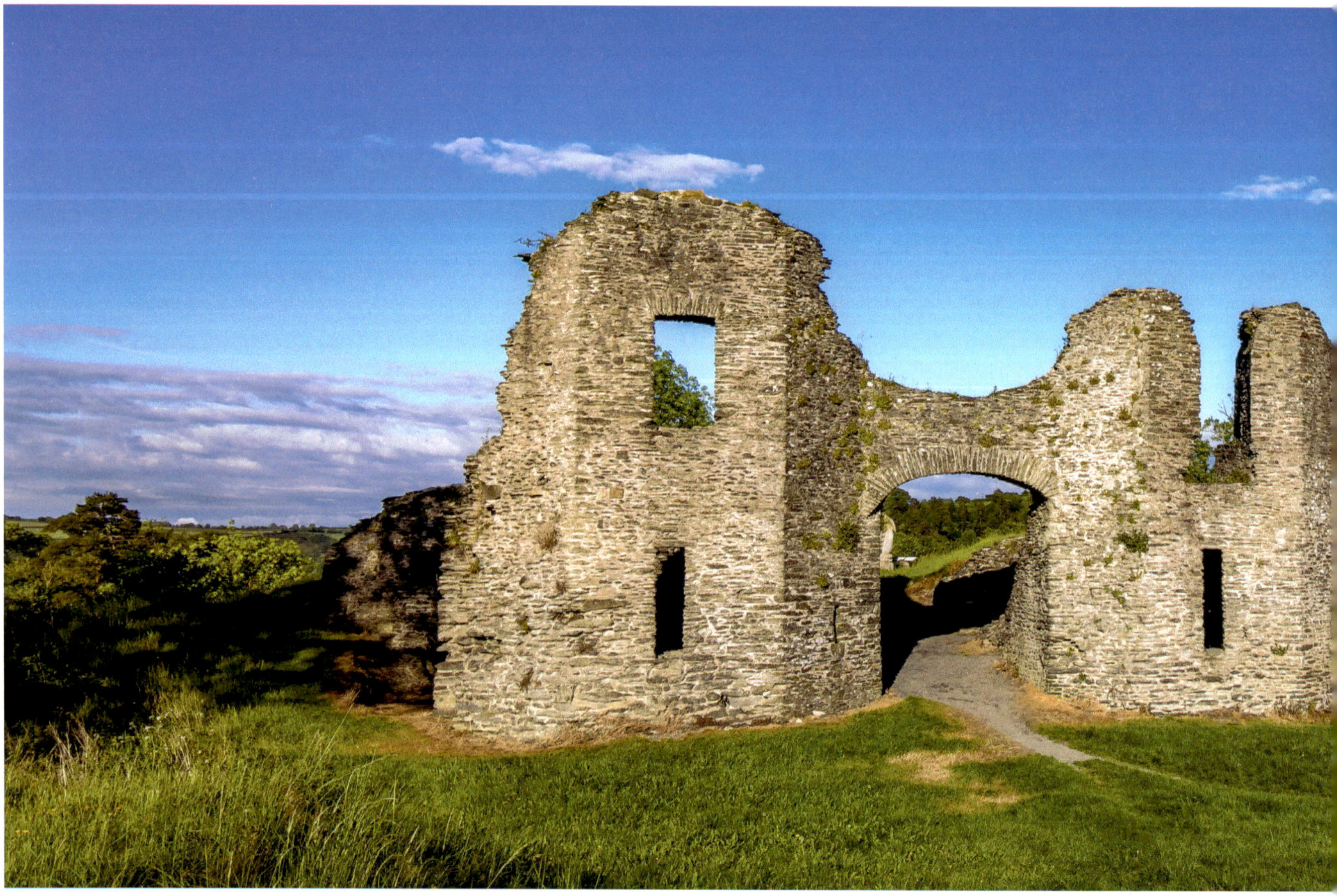

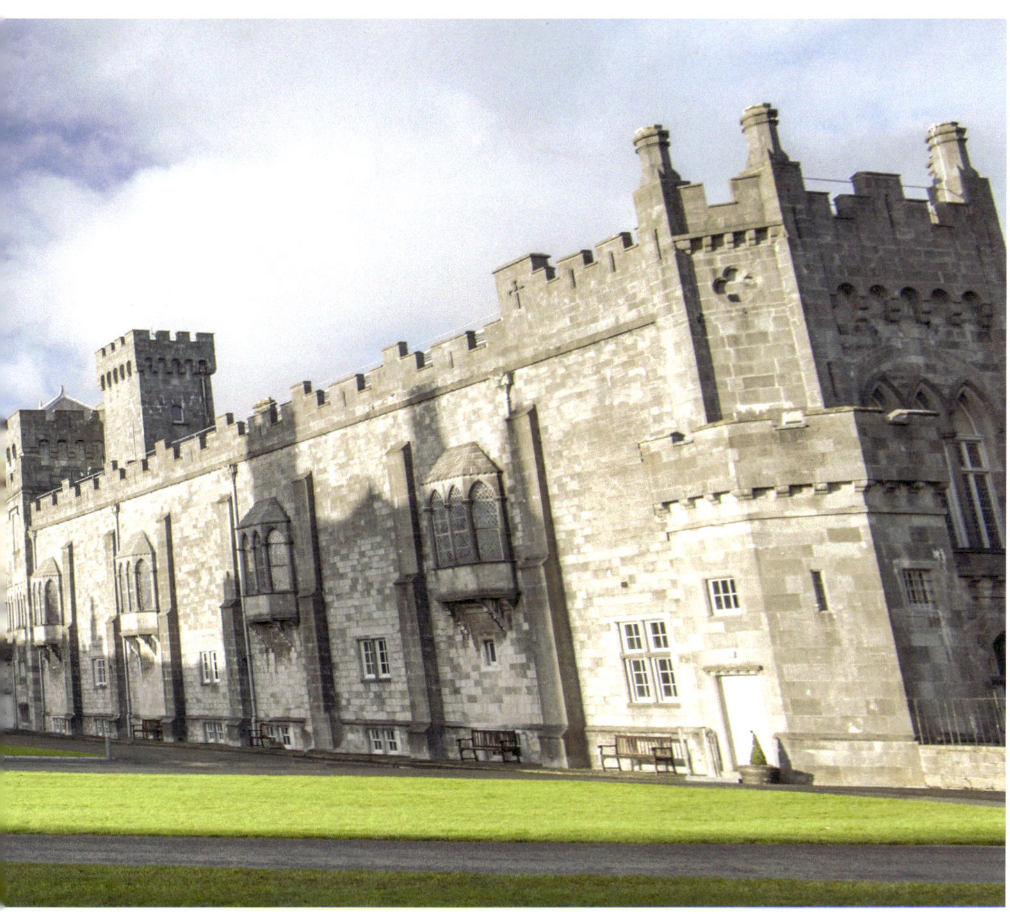

LEFT:

Kilkenny Castle, Kilkenny, Ireland

Kilkenny Castle was begun as a motte-and-bailey construction in the 1170s, and was rebuilt in stone and then expanded from 1209 onwards. Three of its four drum towers still exist; the other was destroyed by forces under Oliver Cromwell in 1650. Rebuilt in a fanciful mix of styles in the 19th century, the castle was besieged again in 1922 during the Irish Civil War.

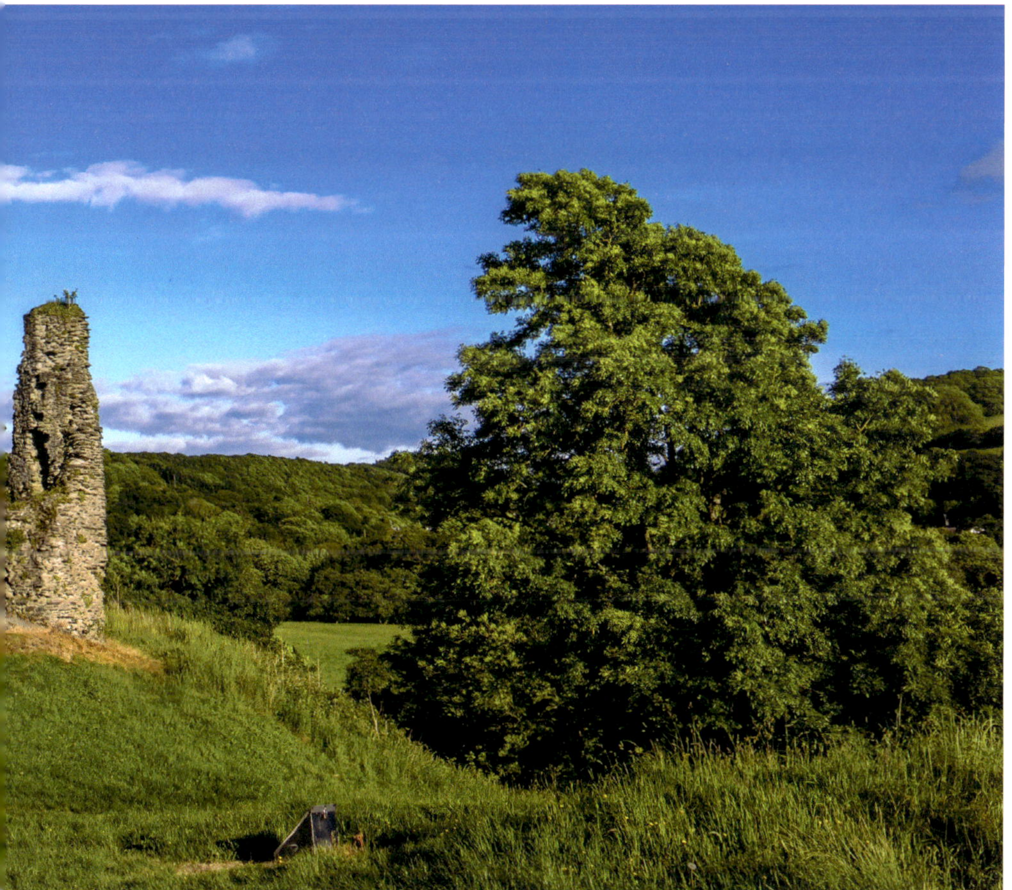

LEFT:

Newcastle Emlyn, Carmarthenshire, Wales

Newcastle Emlyn was constructed from around 1240. It was attacked on various occasions, notably during the Welsh revolt of 1287 and Owen Glendower's rebellion of the early 1400s. The castle was 'slighted' during the English Civil War, making it useless as a defensive position.

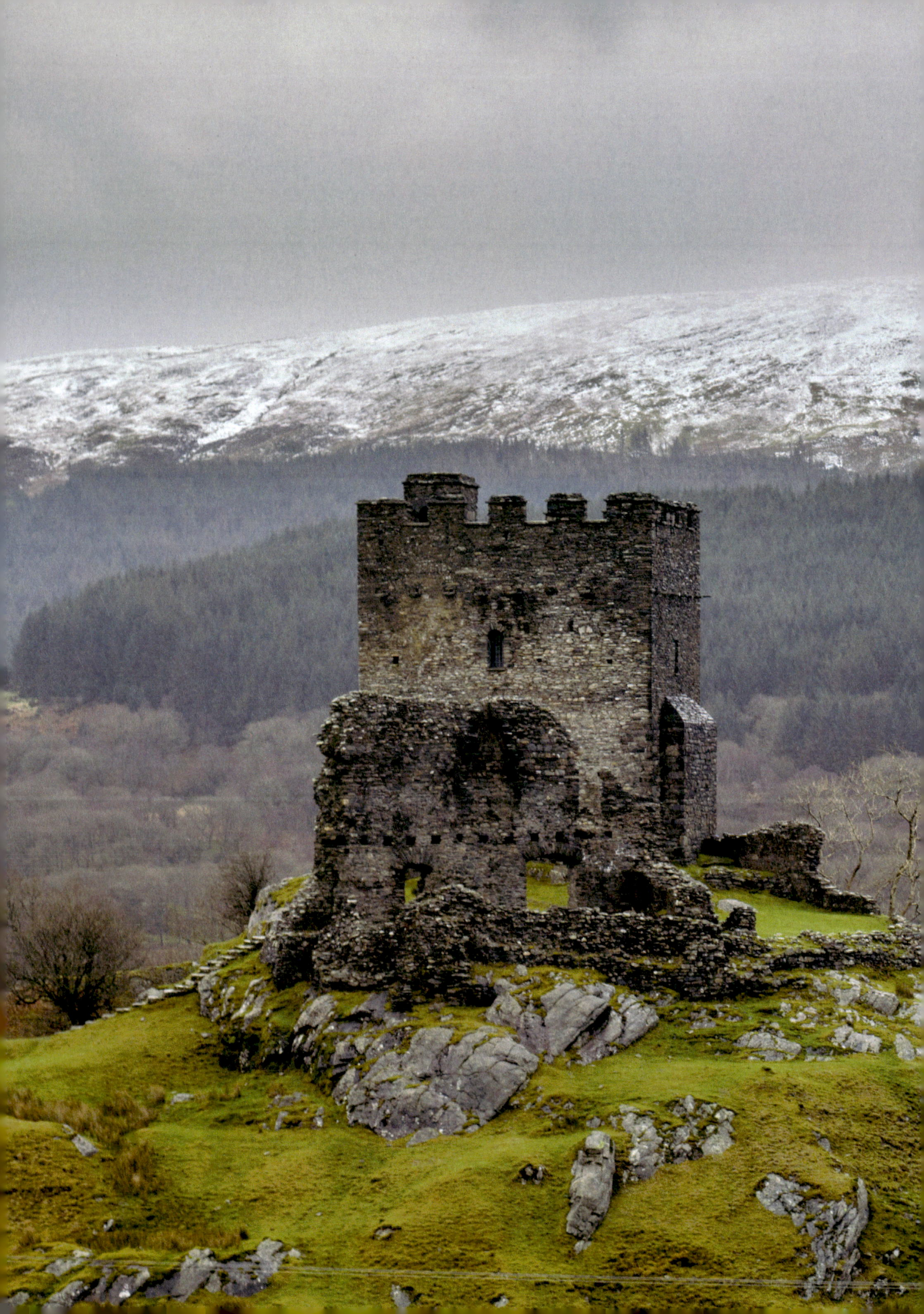

RIGHT AND OVERLEAF:

Tintagel Castle, Cornwall, England

Tintagel Castle in north Cornwall is associated with the legends of King Arthur, though there is no evidence of a castle there until Richard, 1st Earl of Cornwall, built one in 1233. The castle was deliberately constructed in an archaic style, playing to the legends surrounding the location.

The site of Tintagel Castle was a seat of the rulers of Cornwall after the departure of Roman forces from Britain. The headland previously was home to a Celtic-Christian monastery and was an important site for long-distance trade. Although it offered good defensive advantages, Tintagel had no real strategic value by the 1200s.

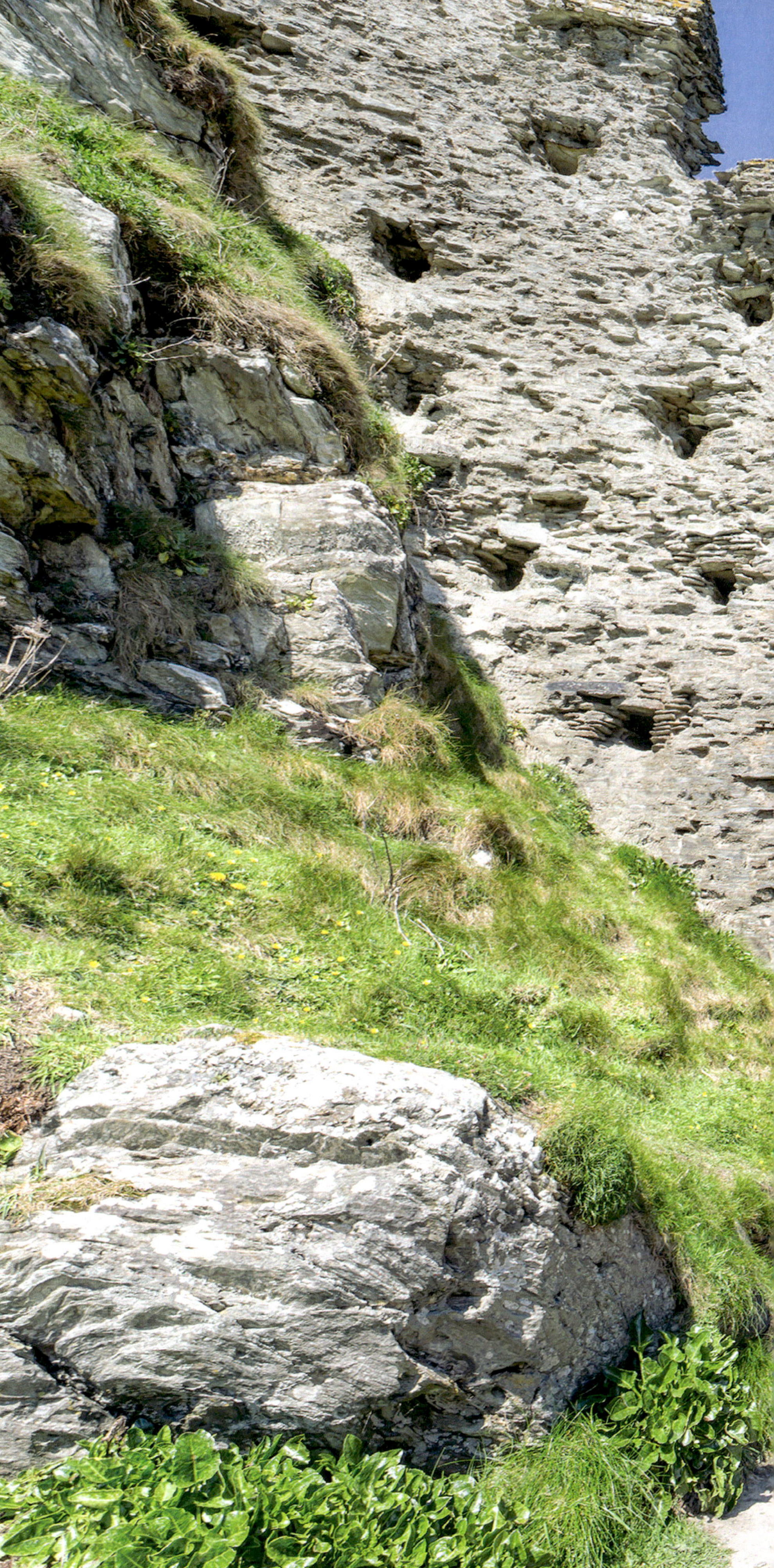

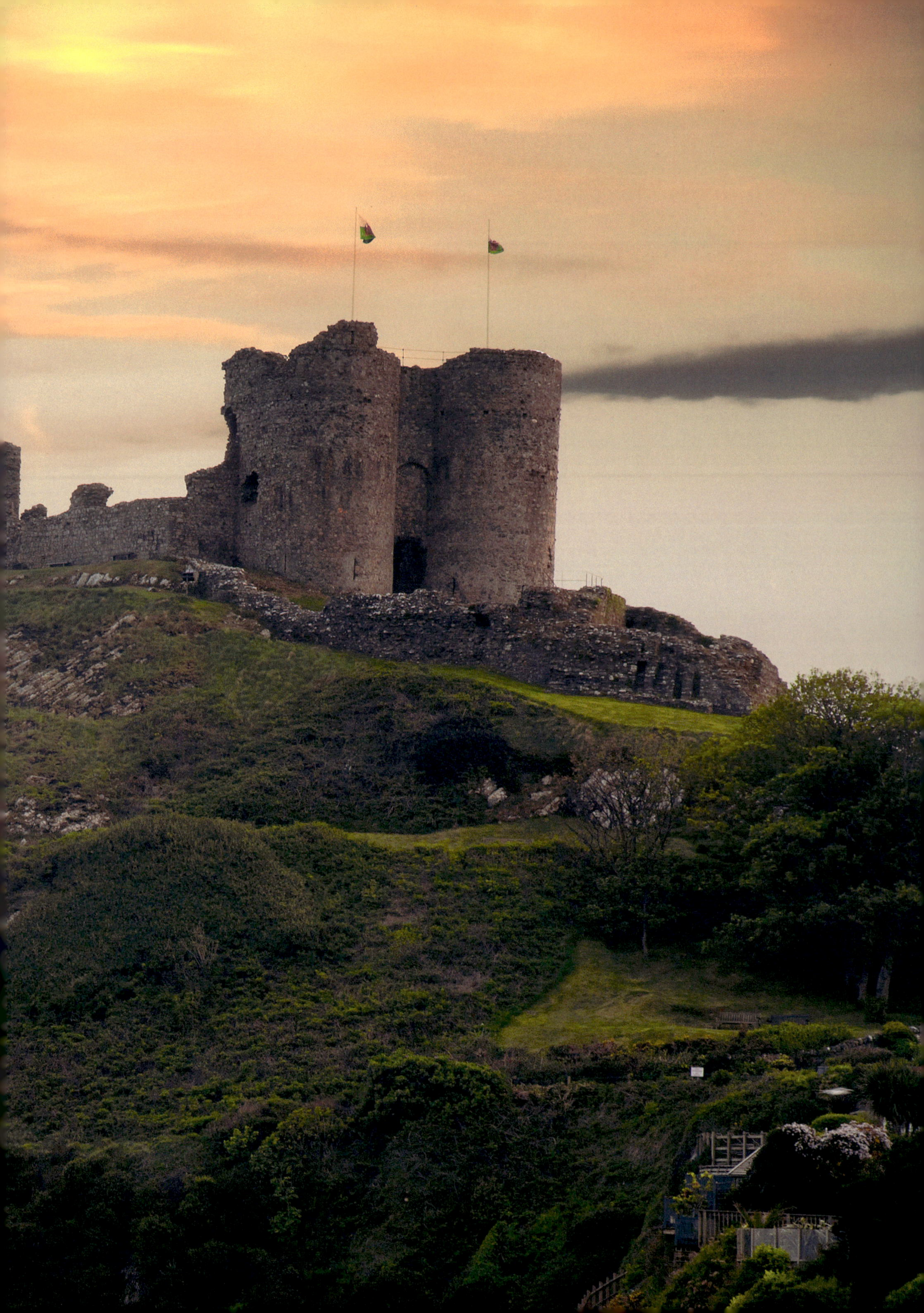

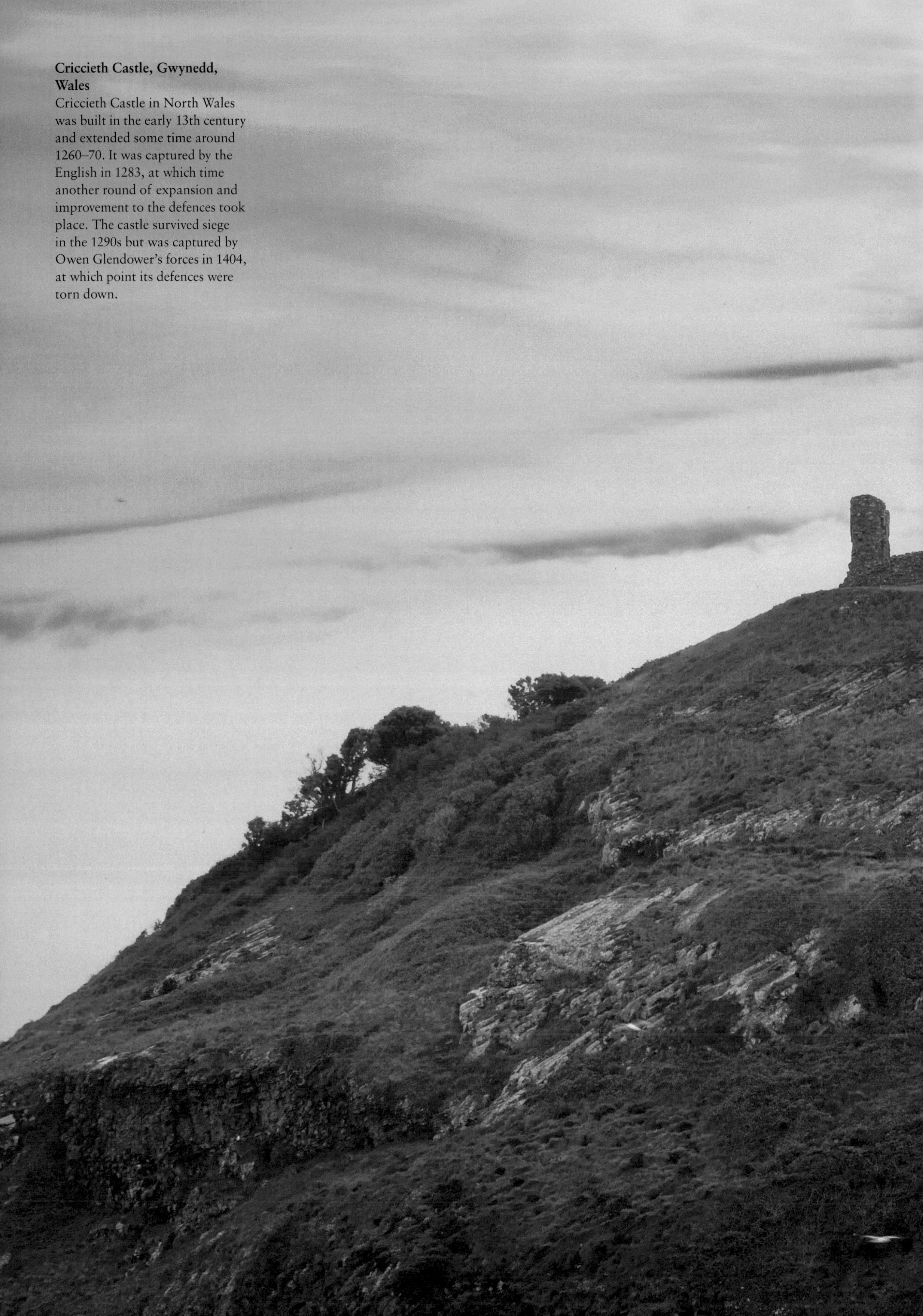

Criccieth Castle, Gwynedd, Wales
Criccieth Castle in North Wales was built in the early 13th century and extended some time around 1260–70. It was captured by the English in 1283, at which time another round of expansion and improvement to the defences took place. The castle survived siege in the 1290s but was captured by Owen Glendower's forces in 1404, at which point its defences were torn down.

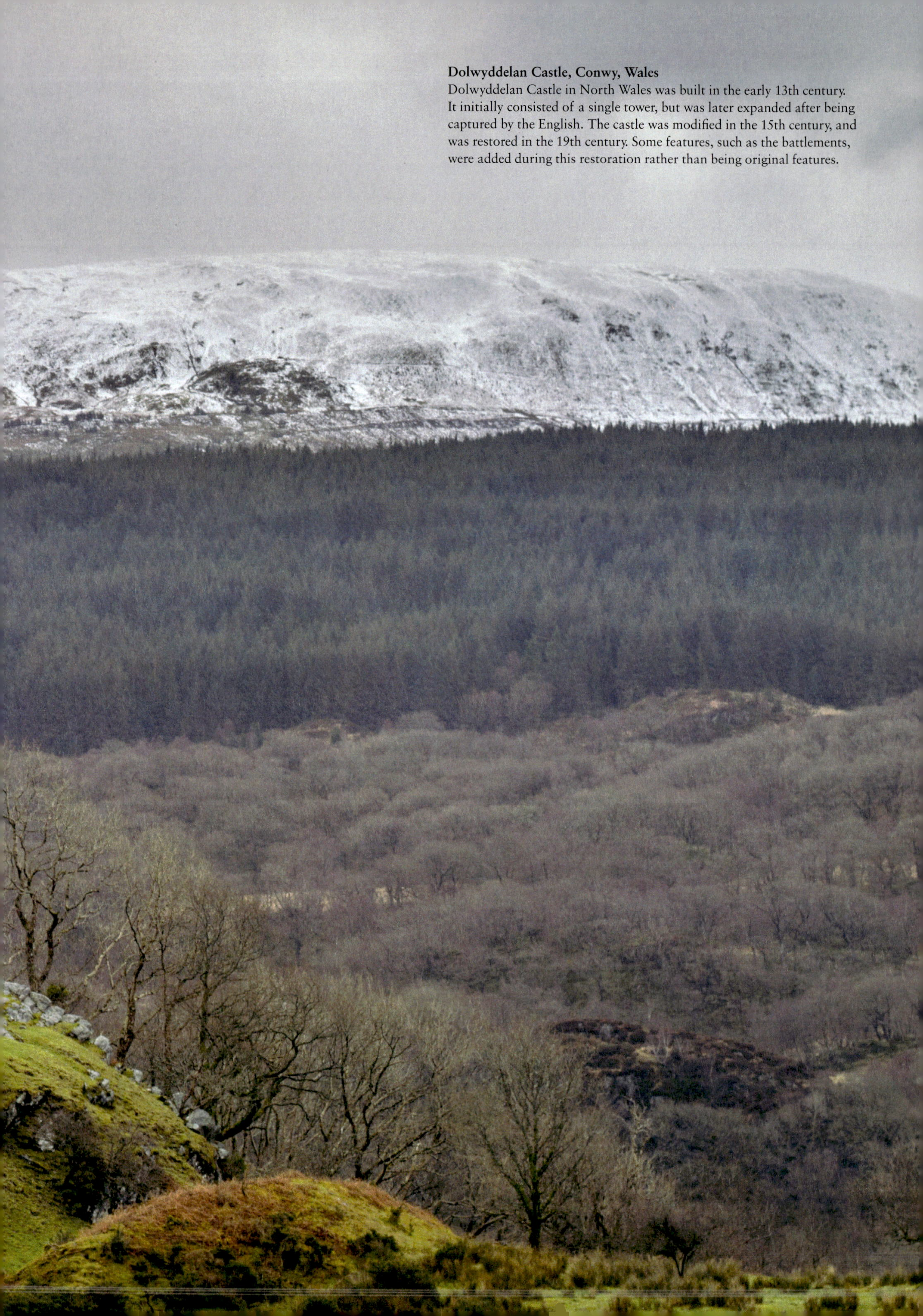

Dolwyddelan Castle, Conwy, Wales
Dolwyddelan Castle in North Wales was built in the early 13th century. It initially consisted of a single tower, but was later expanded after being captured by the English. The castle was modified in the 15th century, and was restored in the 19th century. Some features, such as the battlements, were added during this restoration rather than being original features.

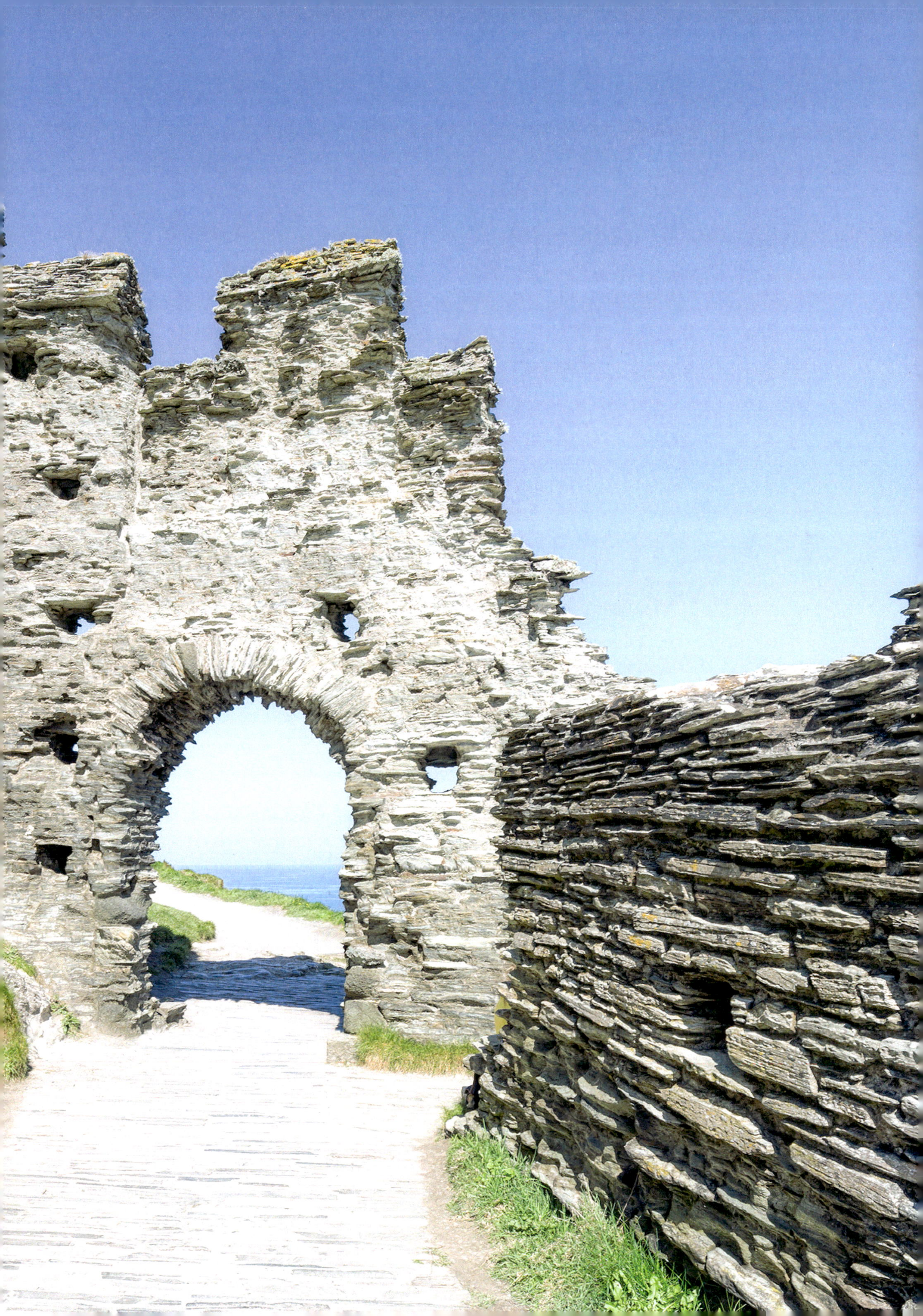

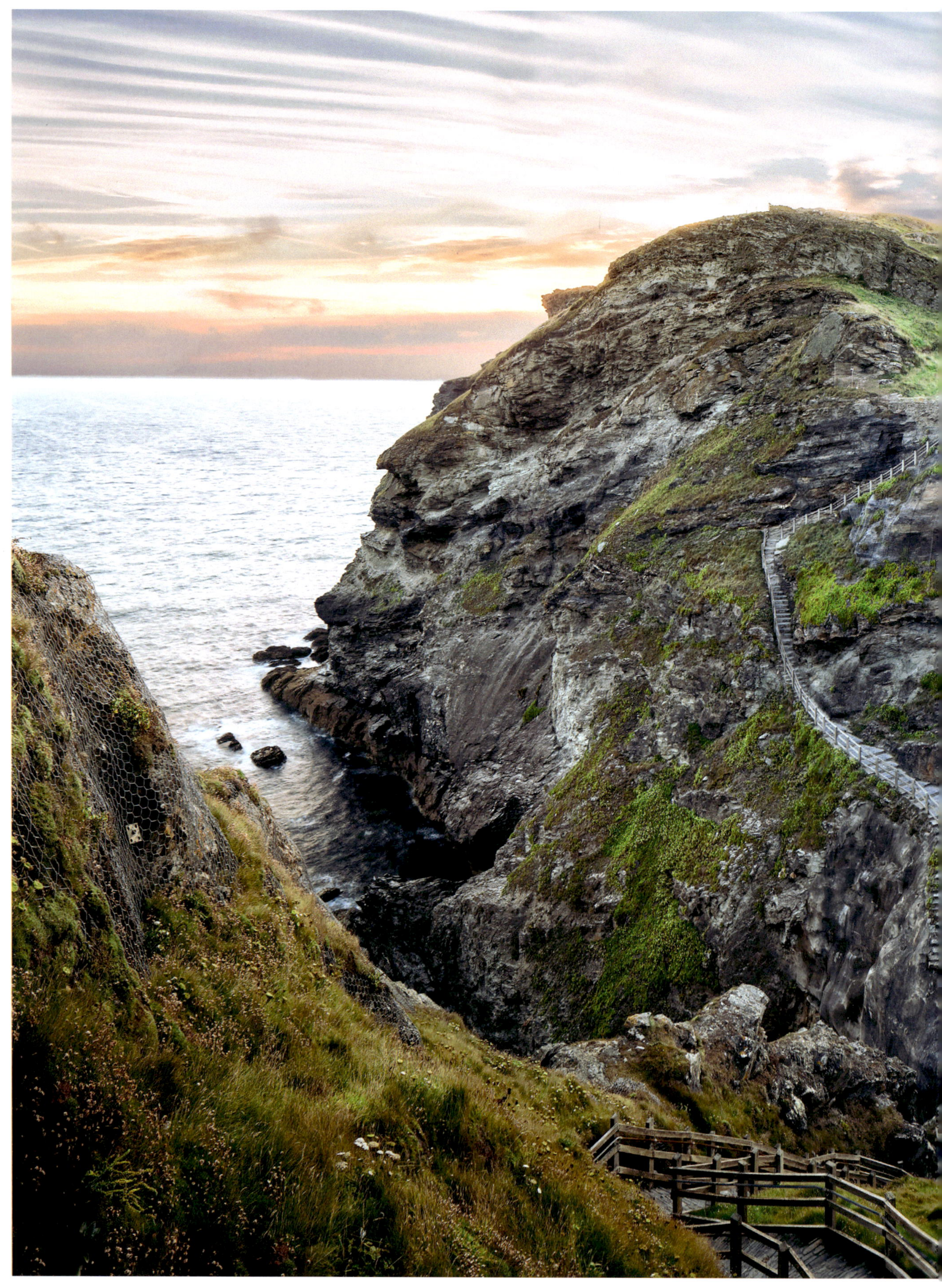

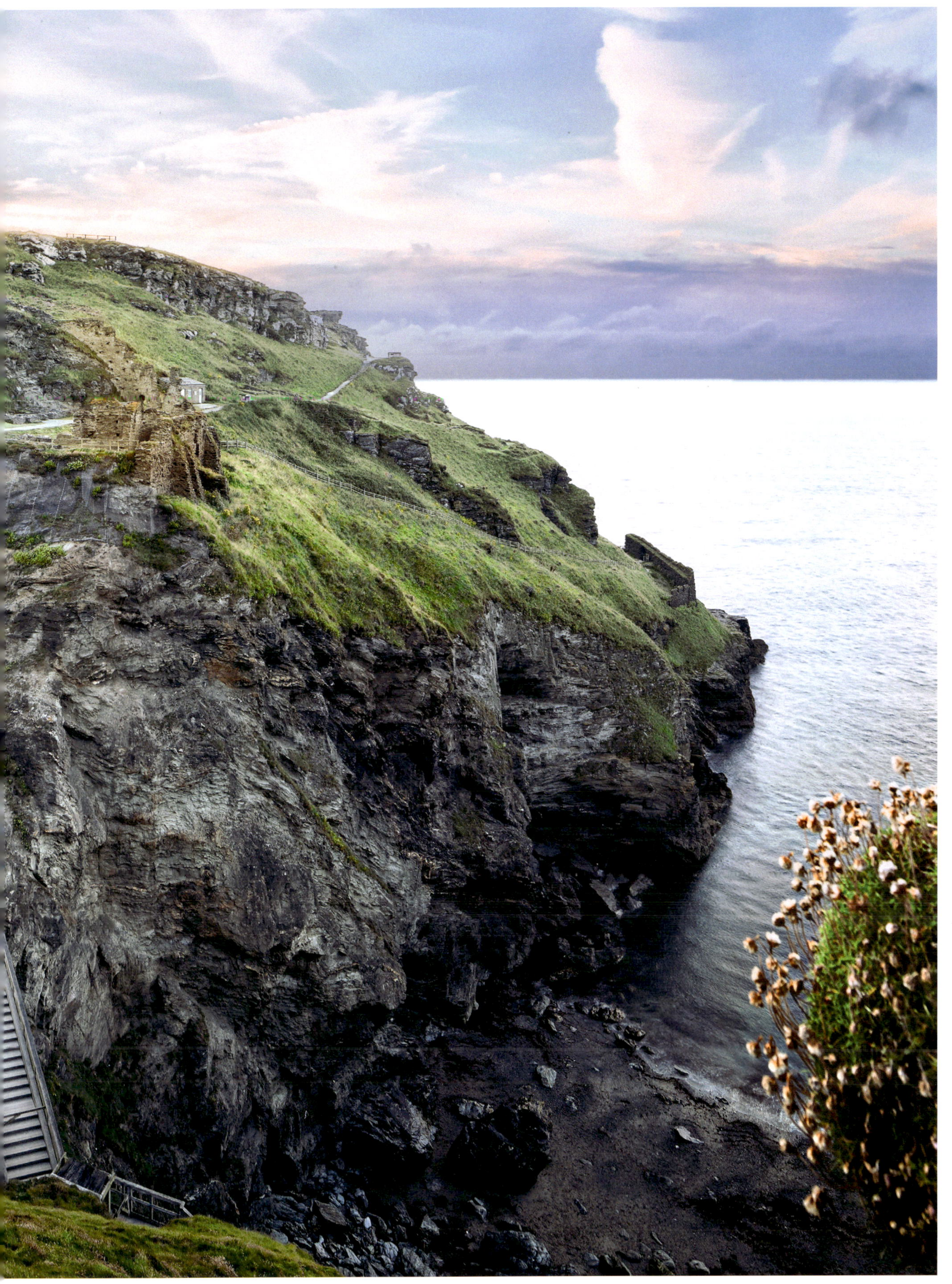

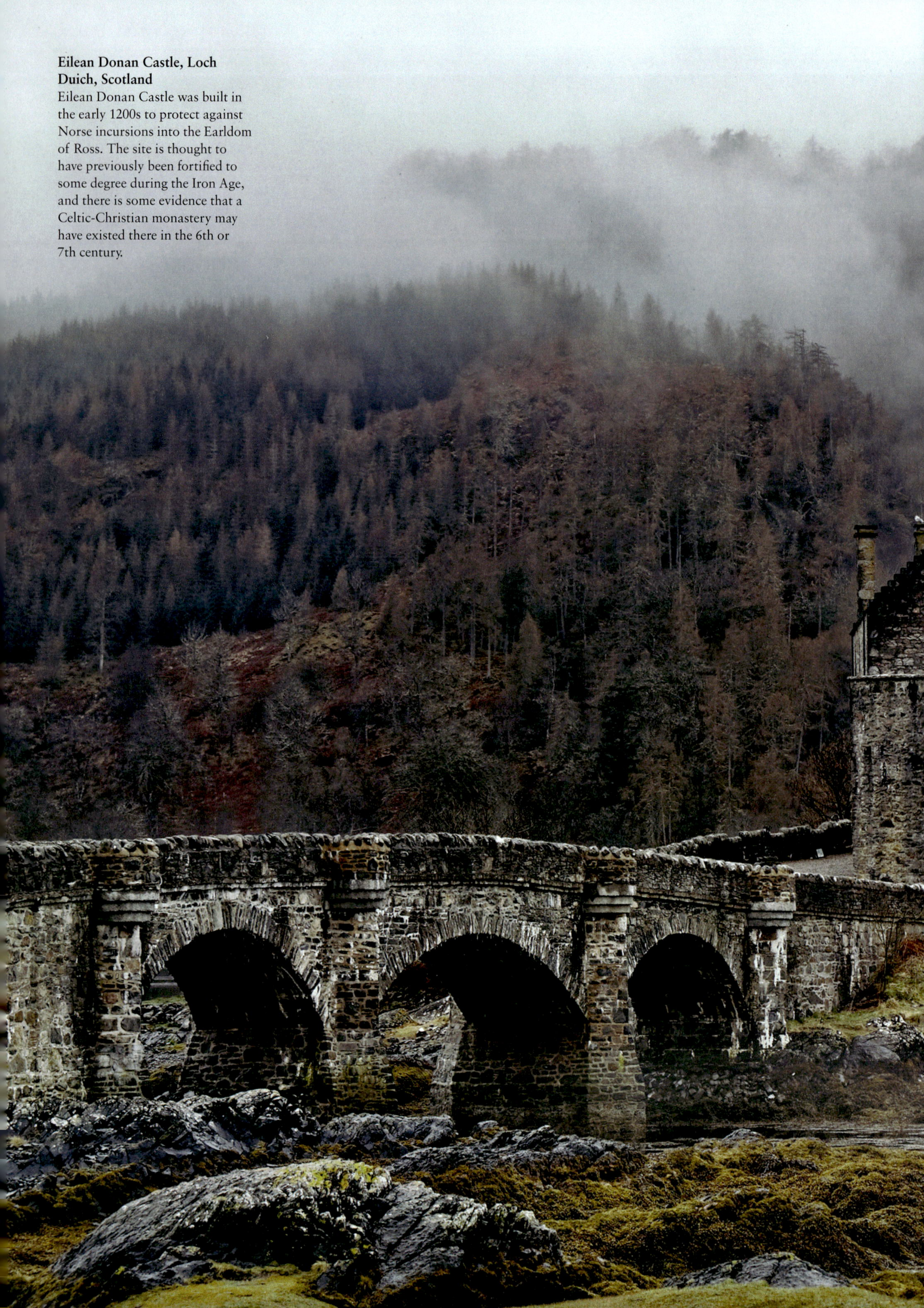

Eilean Donan Castle, Loch Duich, Scotland

Eilean Donan Castle was built in the early 1200s to protect against Norse incursions into the Earldom of Ross. The site is thought to have previously been fortified to some degree during the Iron Age, and there is some evidence that a Celtic-Christian monastery may have existed there in the 6th or 7th century.

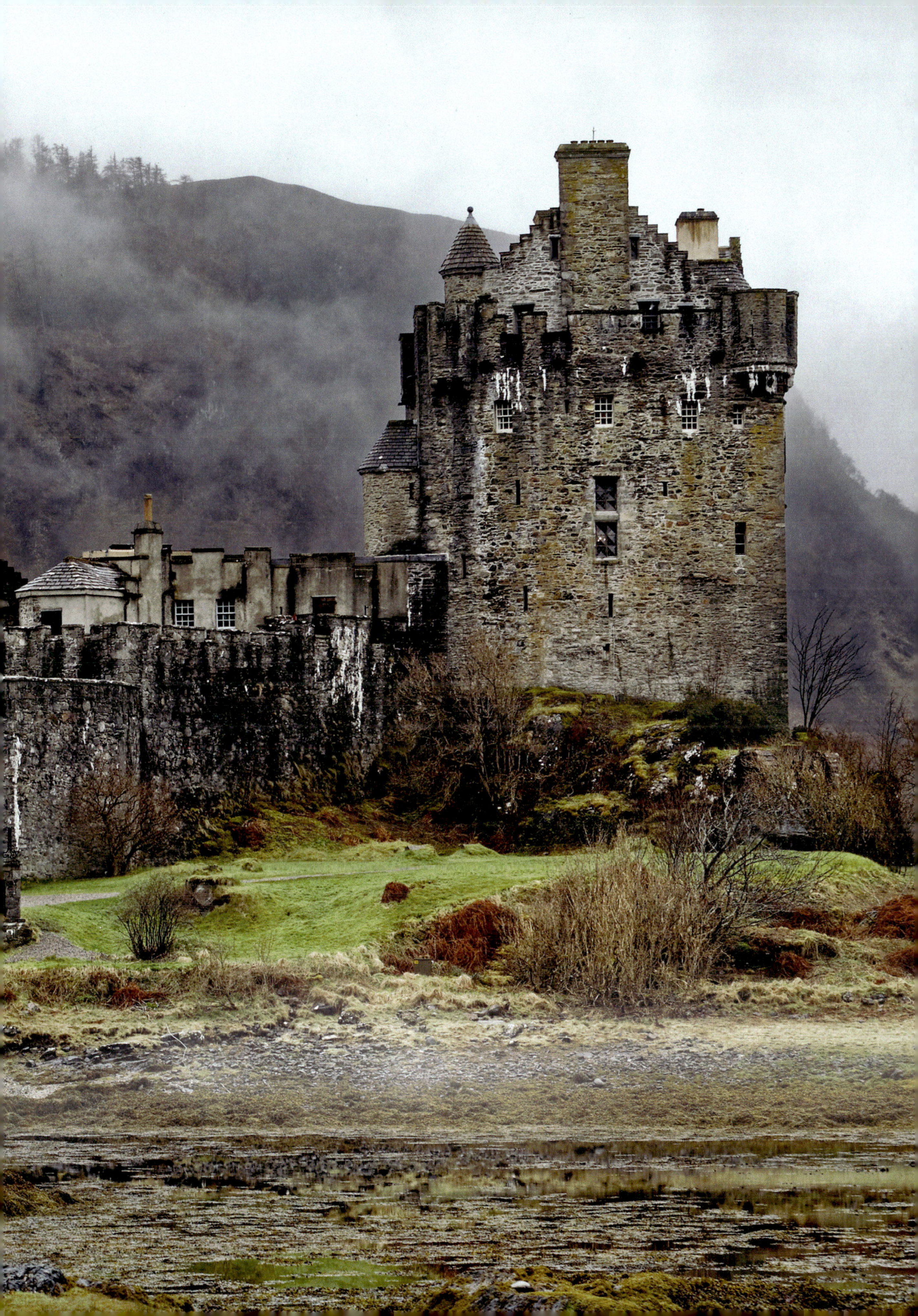

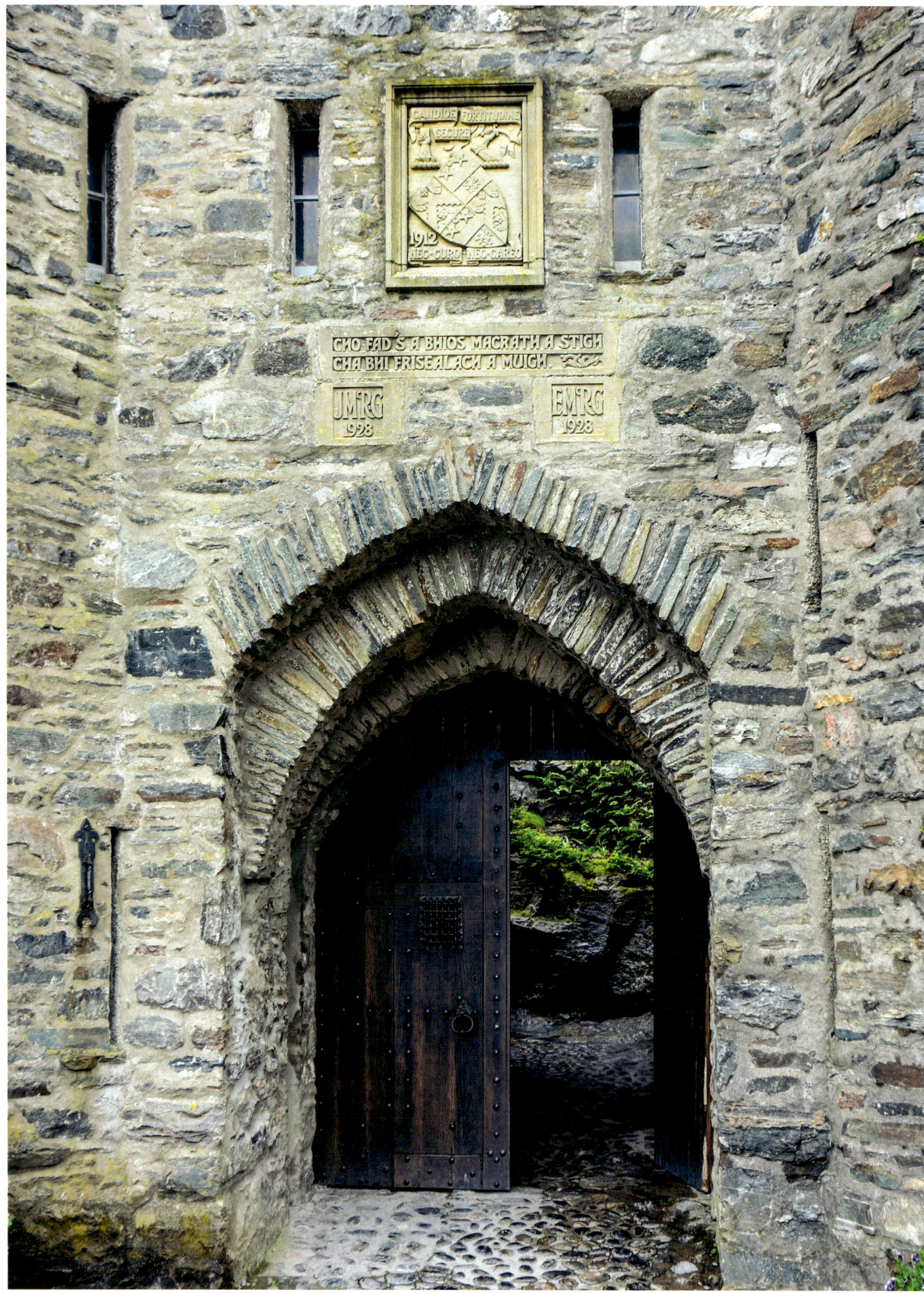
CANDIDE FORTITUDINE
SECURE
1912
NEC CURO NEC CAREO
CHO FAD'S A BHIOS MACRATH A STIGH
CHA BHI FRISEALACH A MUIGH.
JMRG
1928
EMRG
1928

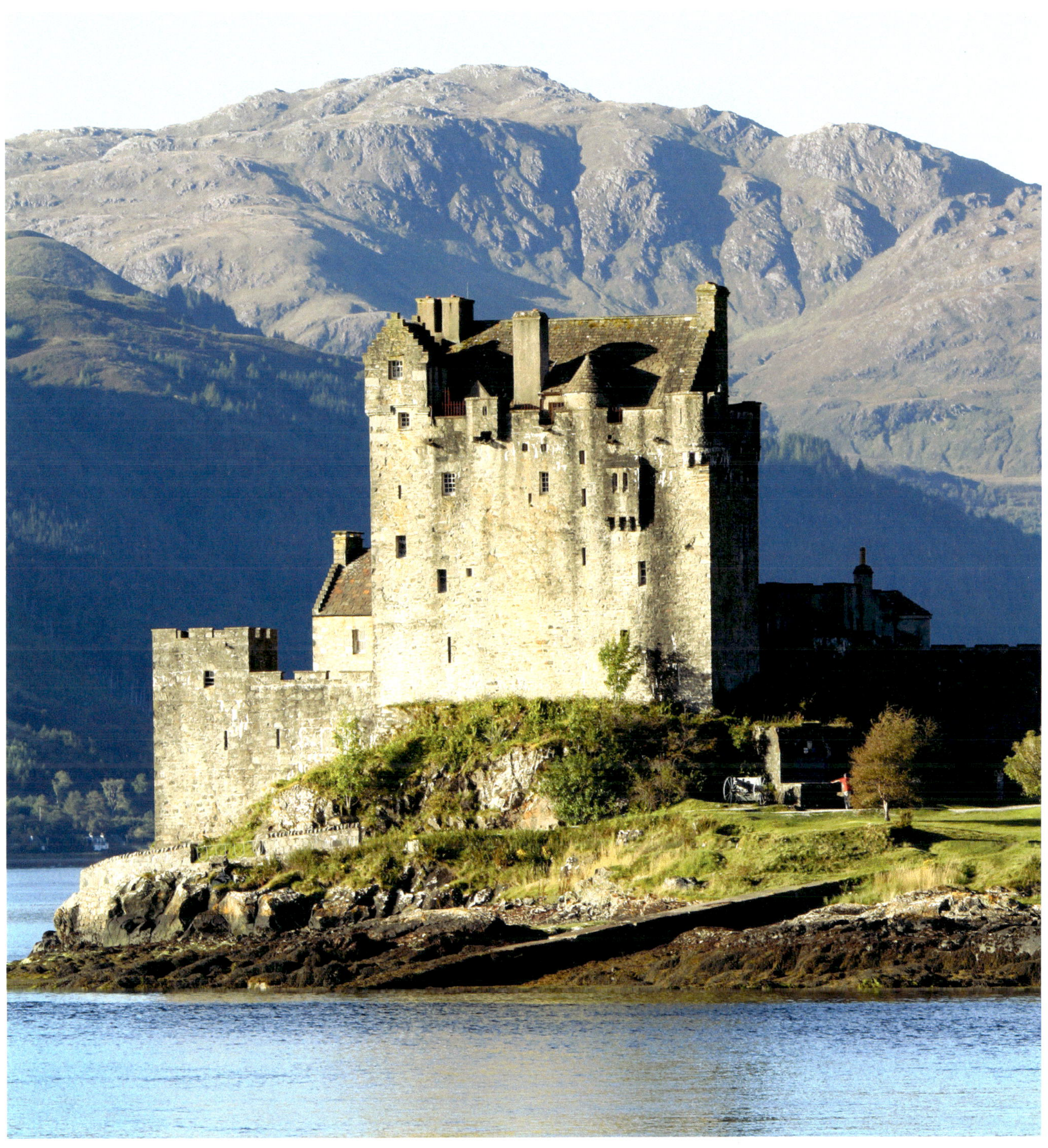

LEFT AND ABOVE:
Eilean Donan Castle, Loch Duich, Scotland
The modern castle at Eilean Donan is a result of rebuilding in the early 20th century, after the original castle was destroyed in 1719 by naval bombardment. It was occupied at the time by Spanish troops sent to support a Scottish uprising that failed to materialize.

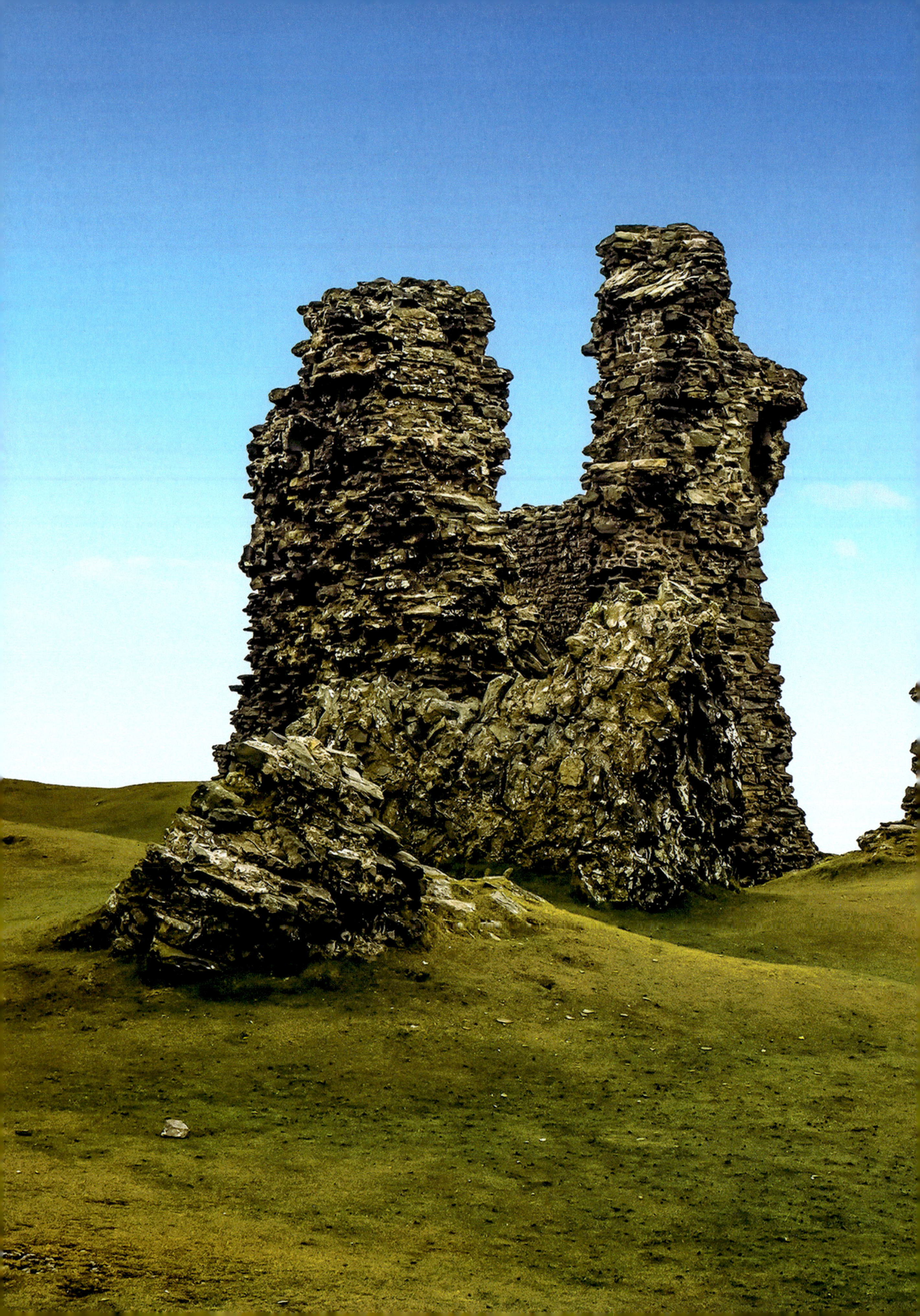

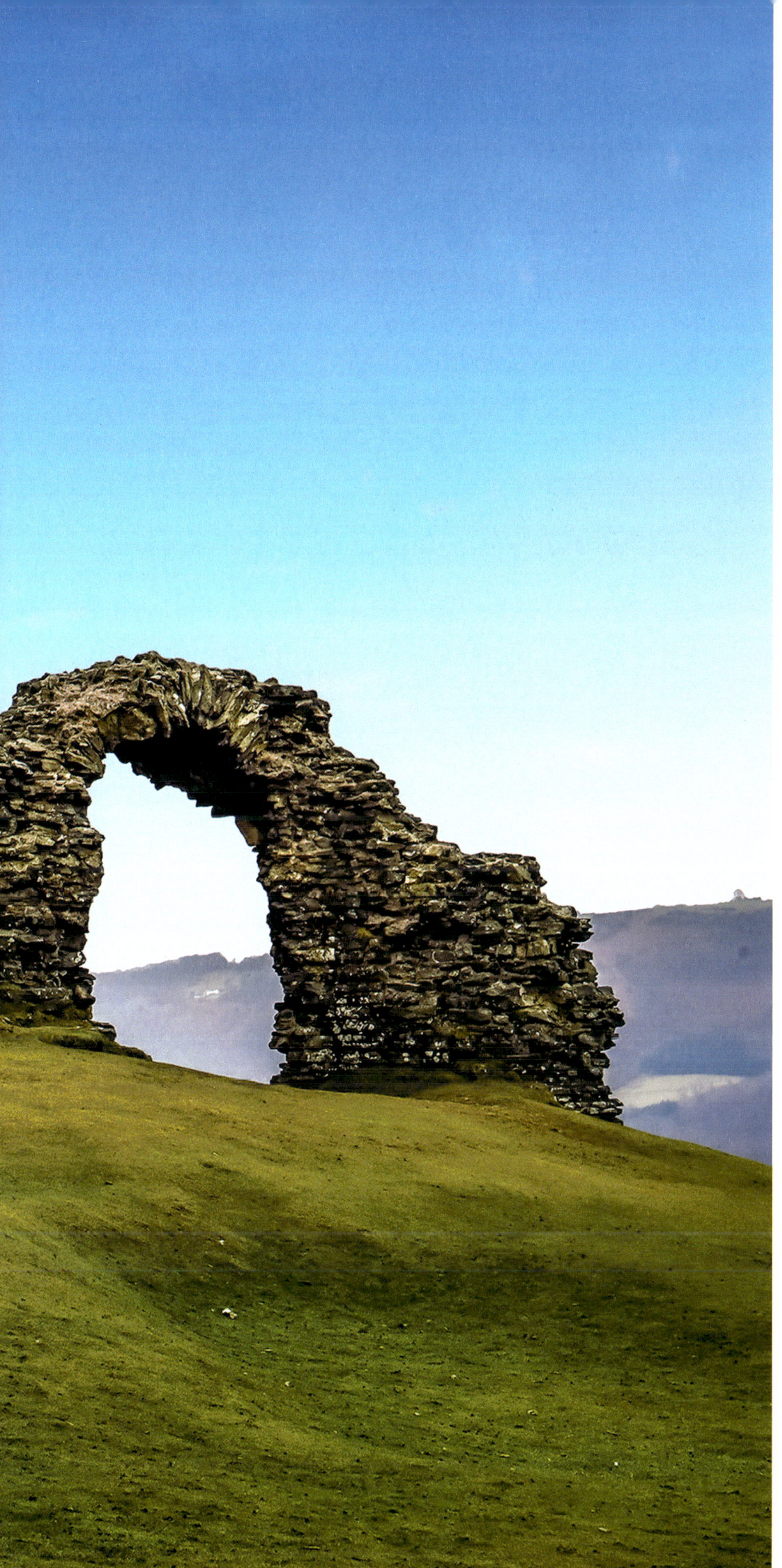

Castell Dinas Bran, Denbighshire, Wales
Castell Dinas Bran, located above the Dee Valley in Wales, was built in the mid-13th century, probably around 1260. The site is thought to have previously been an Iron Age hill fort, and there are some references to a more recent fortification – perhaps a wooden fort built by the Normans. The castle was destroyed in 1277 by invading English forces.

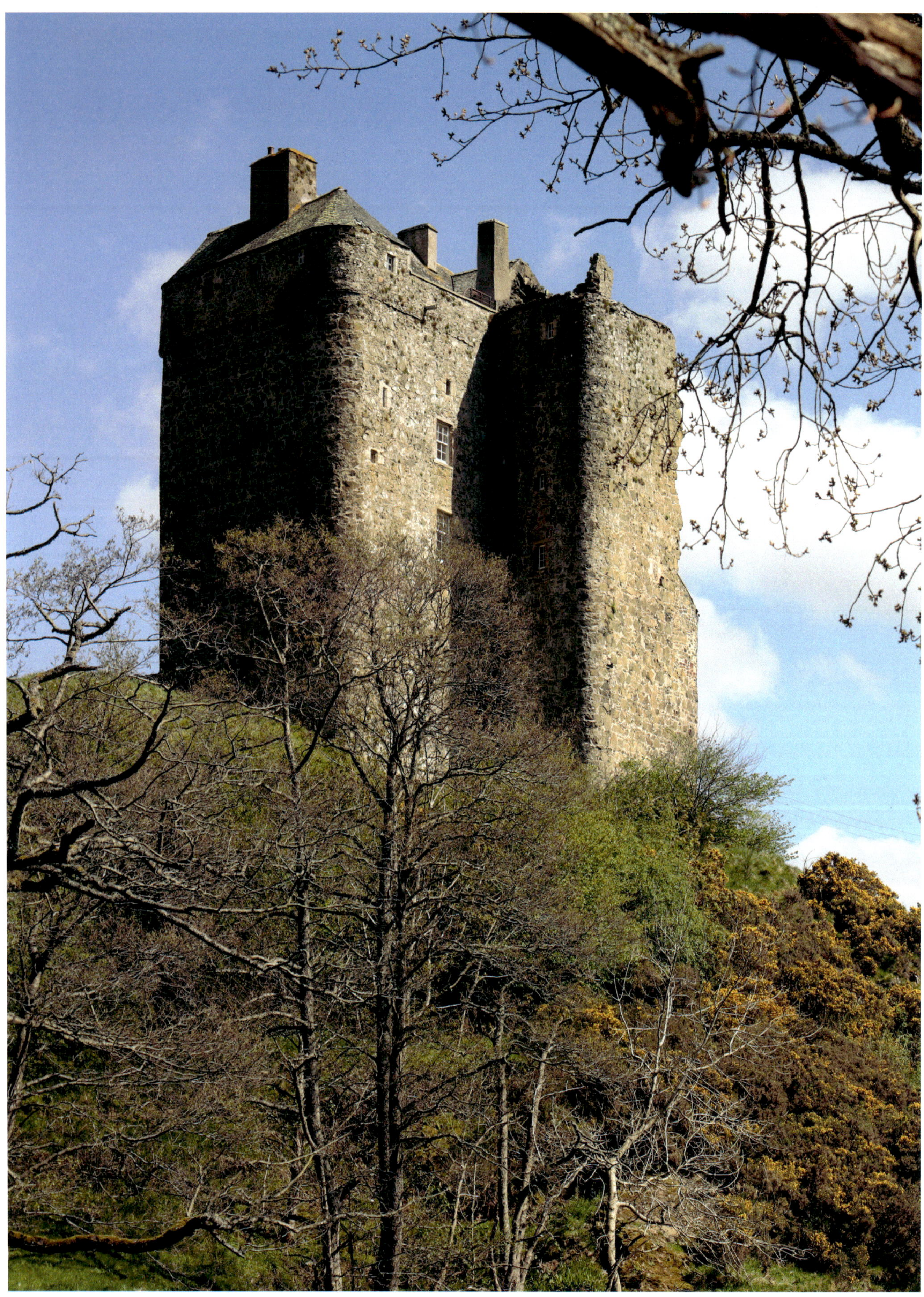

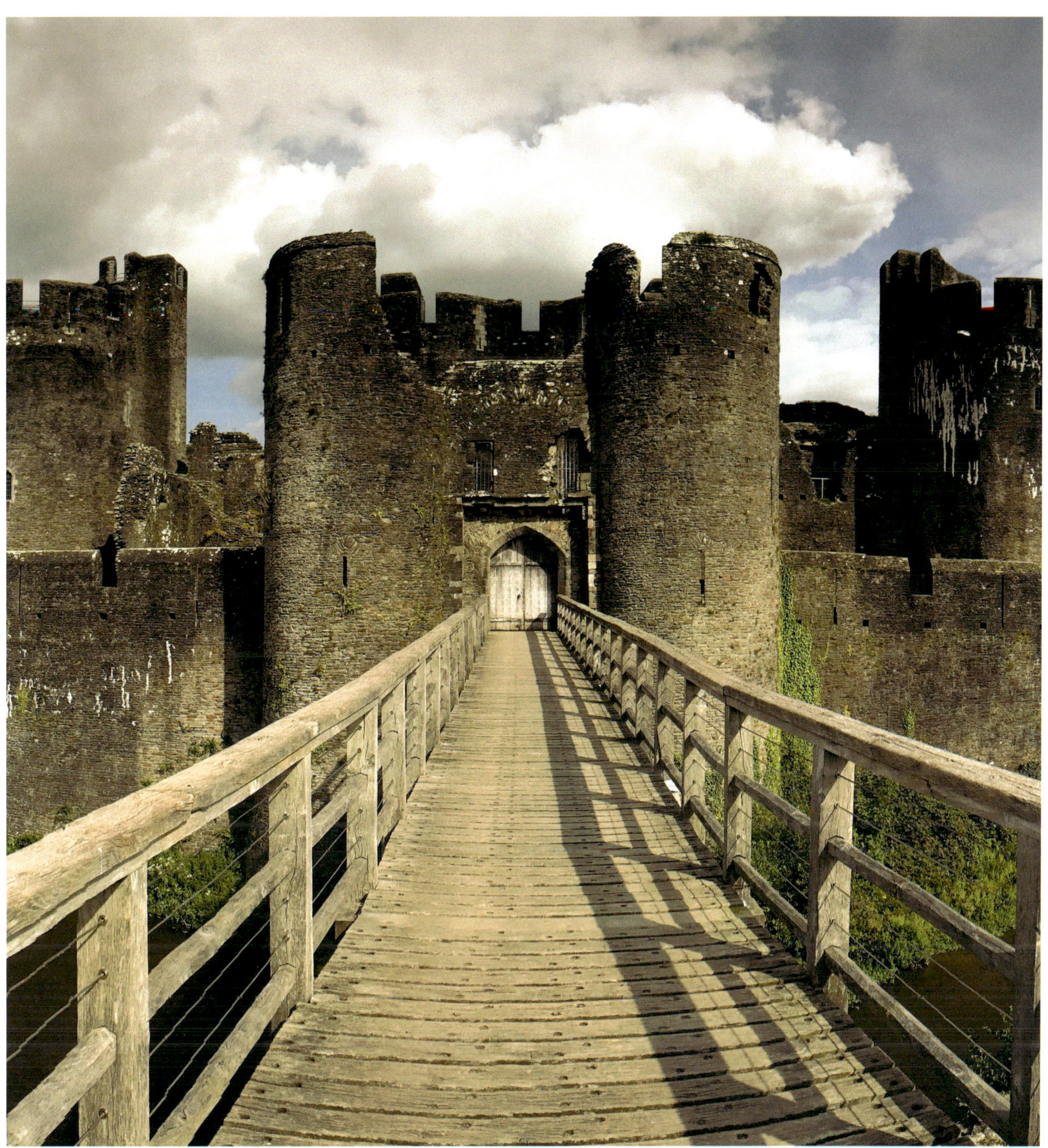

LEFT:

Neidpath Castle, Scottish Borders, Scotland

Neidpath Castle is a tower house constructed in the late 1300s. An earlier castle was built on the same site, starting around 1266. It was attacked during the English Civil War, though accounts of the event vary considerably.

ABOVE:

Caerphilly Castle, Glamorgan, Wales

Caerphilly Castle in South Wales was built with concentric rings of fortification that included artificial lakes and curtain walls. The large gatehouses (see above) built to protect entry points were comparable in size with the keeps of some small castles.

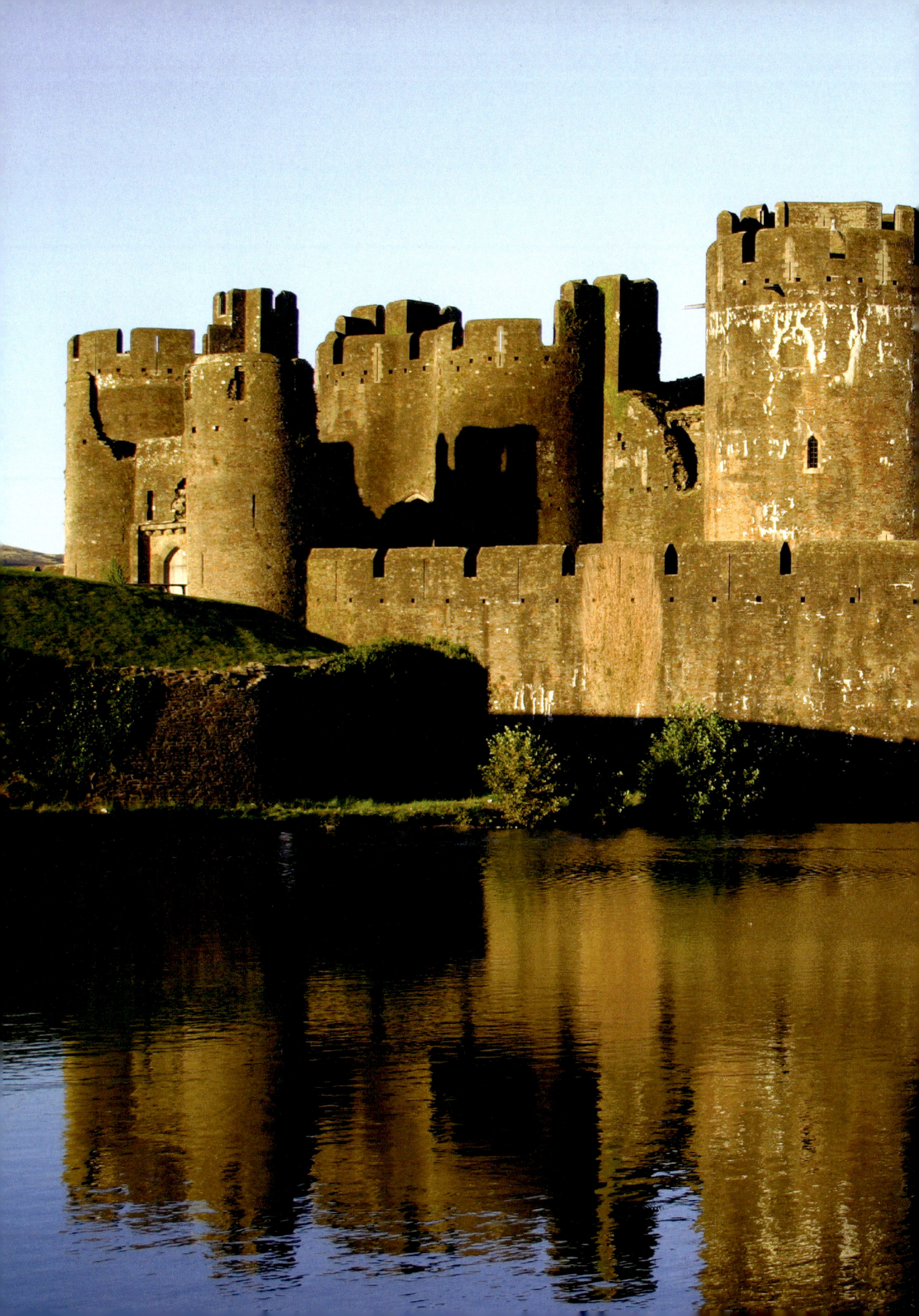

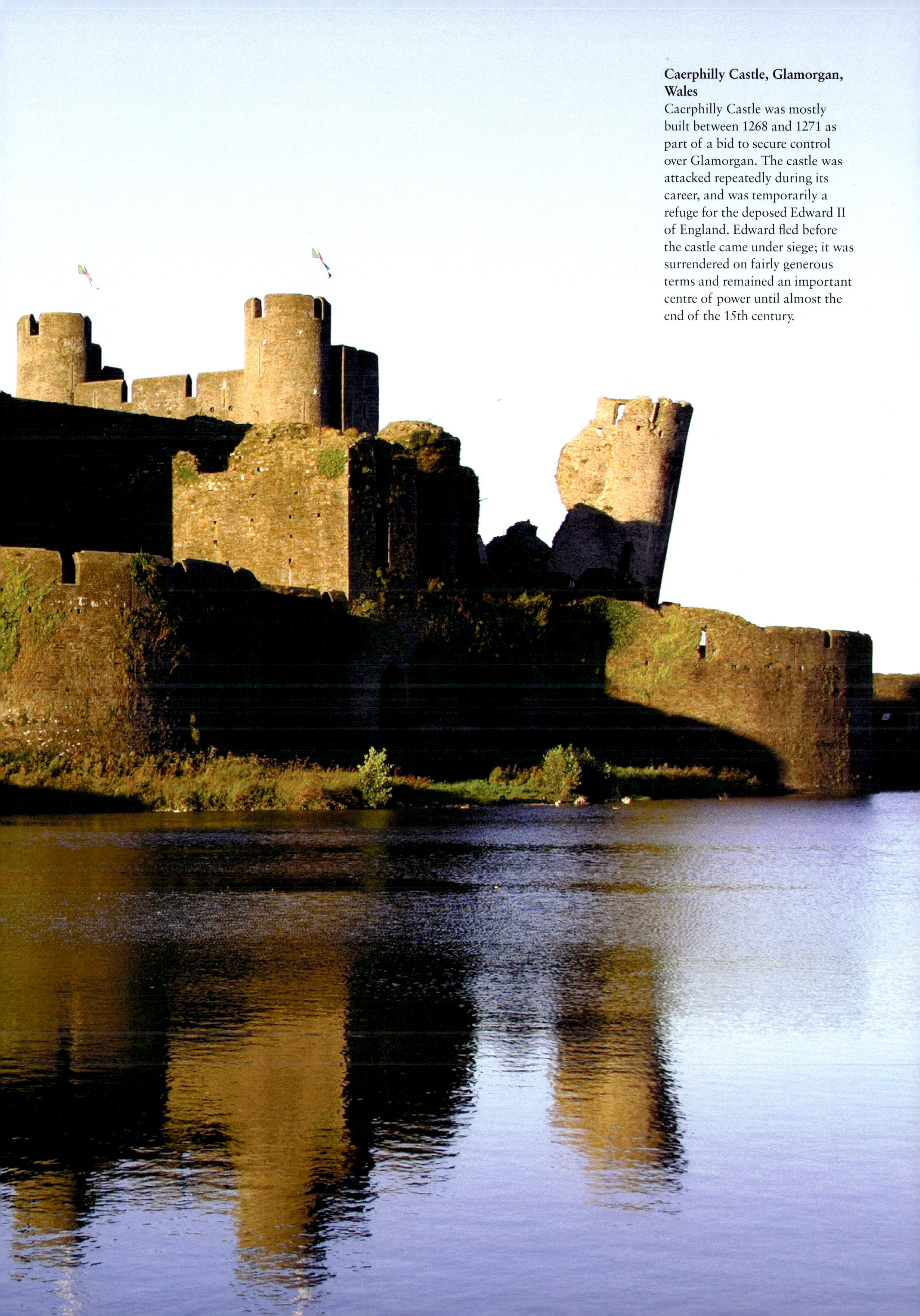

Caerphilly Castle, Glamorgan, Wales

Caerphilly Castle was mostly built between 1268 and 1271 as part of a bid to secure control over Glamorgan. The castle was attacked repeatedly during its career, and was temporarily a refuge for the deposed Edward II of England. Edward fled before the castle came under siege; it was surrendered on fairly generous terms and remained an important centre of power until almost the end of the 15th century.

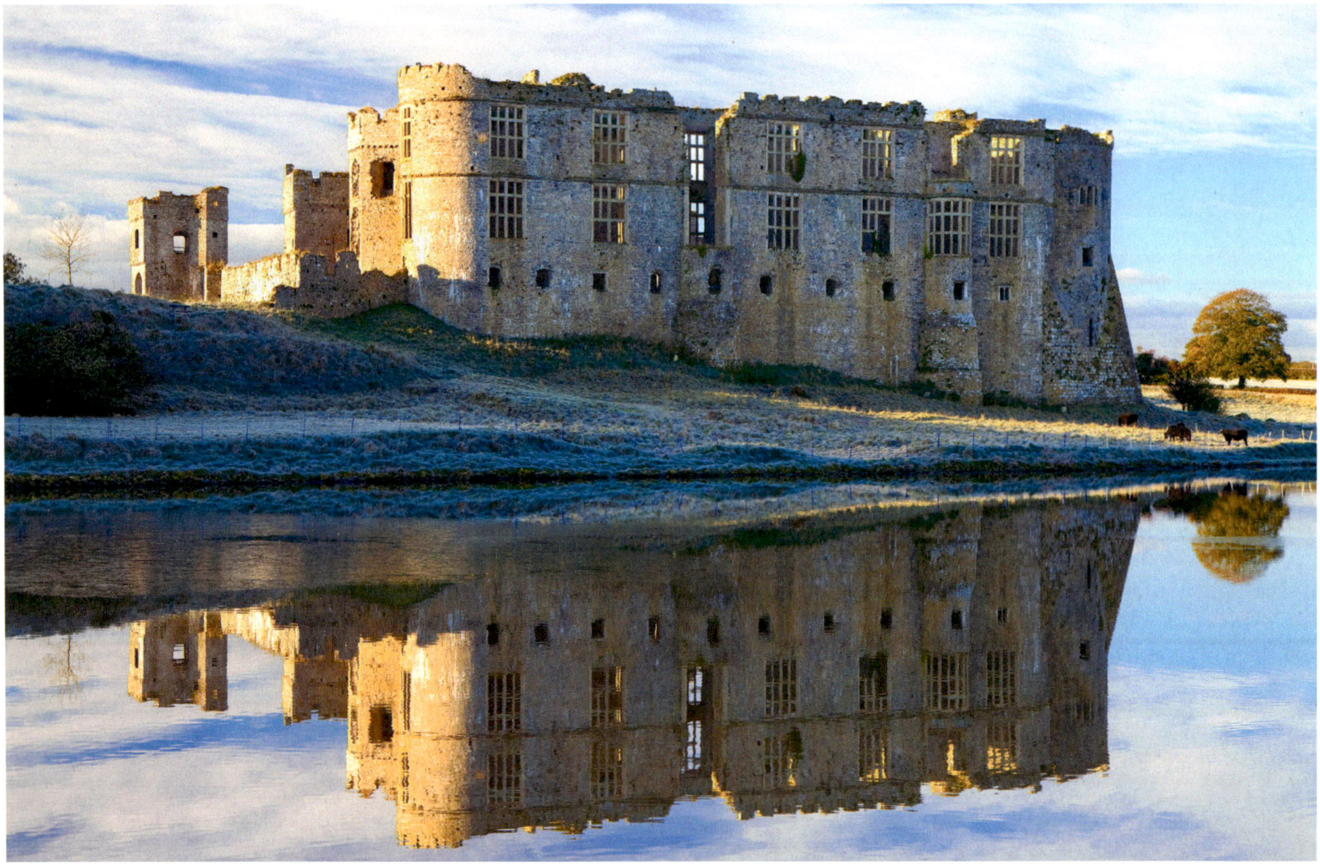

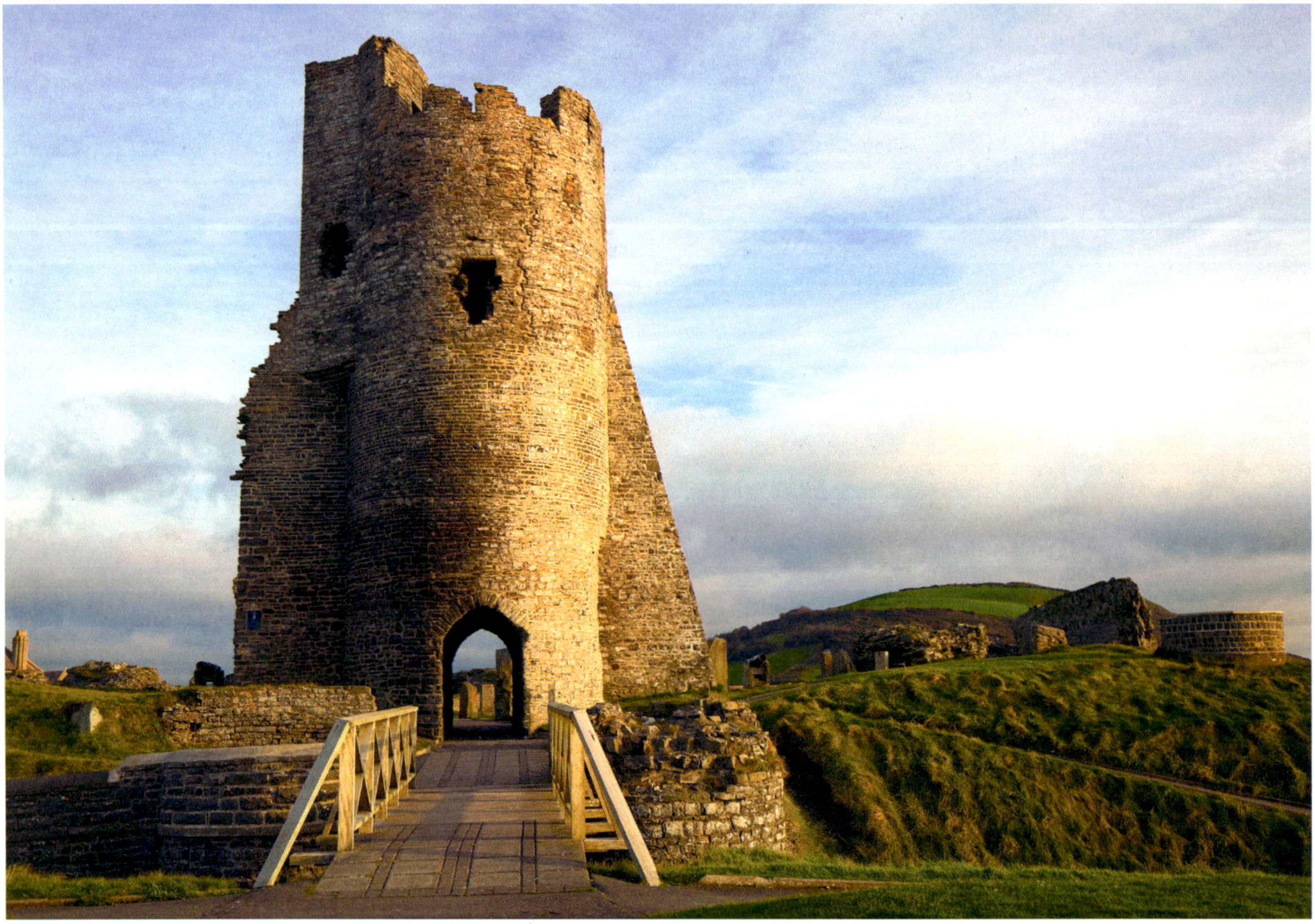

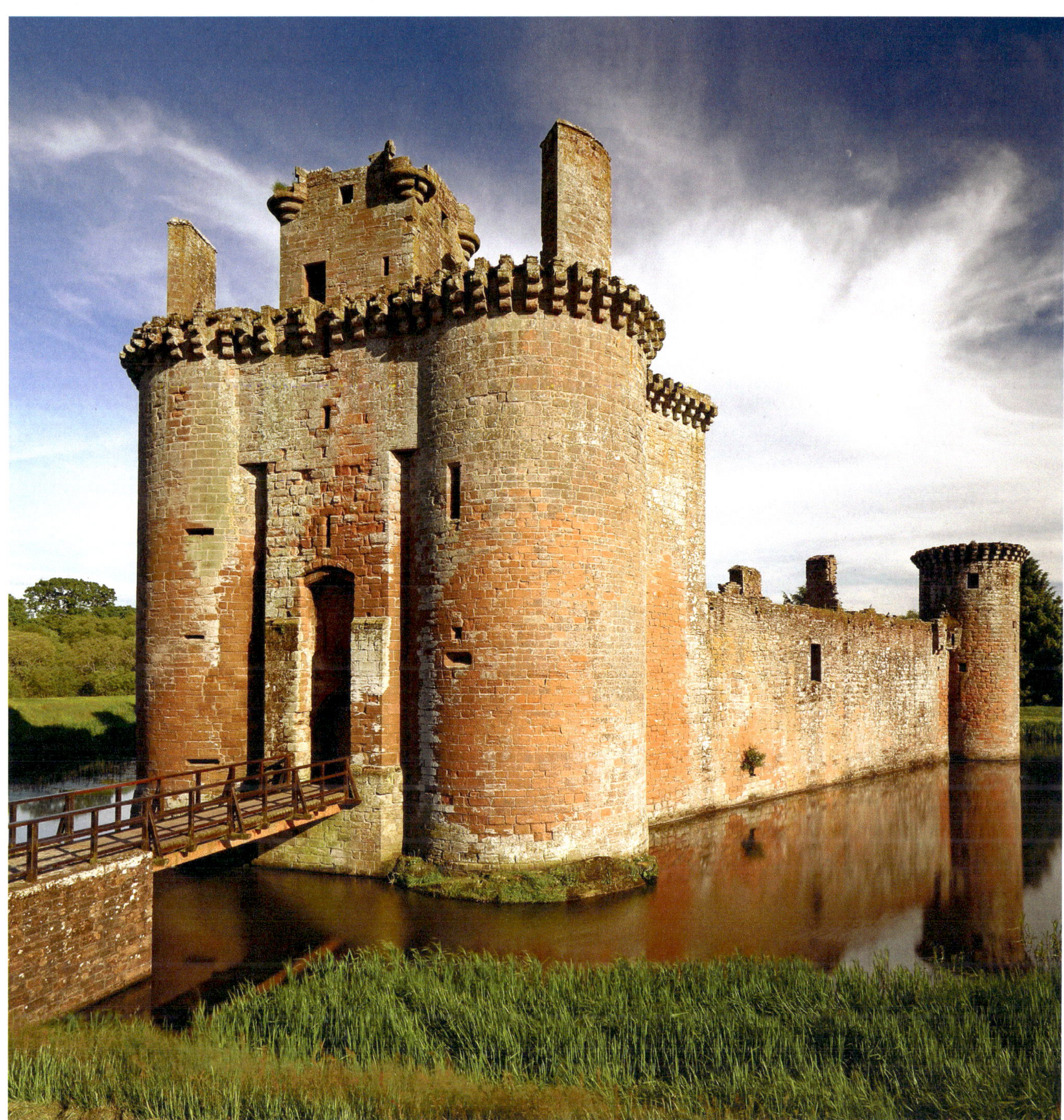

LEFT, TOP:
Carew Castle, Pembrokeshire, Wales
Carew Castle commanded a crossing of the Carew River. A wooden fort was built there around 1100 atop much older fortifications, probably dating from the Iron Age. The castle was gradually expanded in stone throughout the 13th and early 14th centuries. Additional grand accommodation was added in the mid-16th century.

LEFT, BOTTOM:
Aberystwyth Castle, Ceredigion, Wales
Aberystwyth Castle was built from 1277 to 1289 to secure English control over the region. During its construction the site was overrun and the work destroyed. It was again captured by the Welsh in 1404 during the rebellion of Owen Glendower, and was 'slighted' by Parliamentarian forces during the English Civil War. A previous fortification stood close to the site; this was a motte-and-bailey construction built around 1100.

ABOVE AND OVERLEAF:
Caerlaverock Castle, Dumfries, Scotland
Caerlaverock Castle on the Solway Firth was built on the site of Roman fortifications and later wooden defences. Work began on a stone castle around 1220 but the initial site was abandoned; only the foundations now remain. The second castle was built to an unusual triangular design with round towers at the corners. Caerlaverock Castle was completed around 1270 and was partially destroyed in 1640.

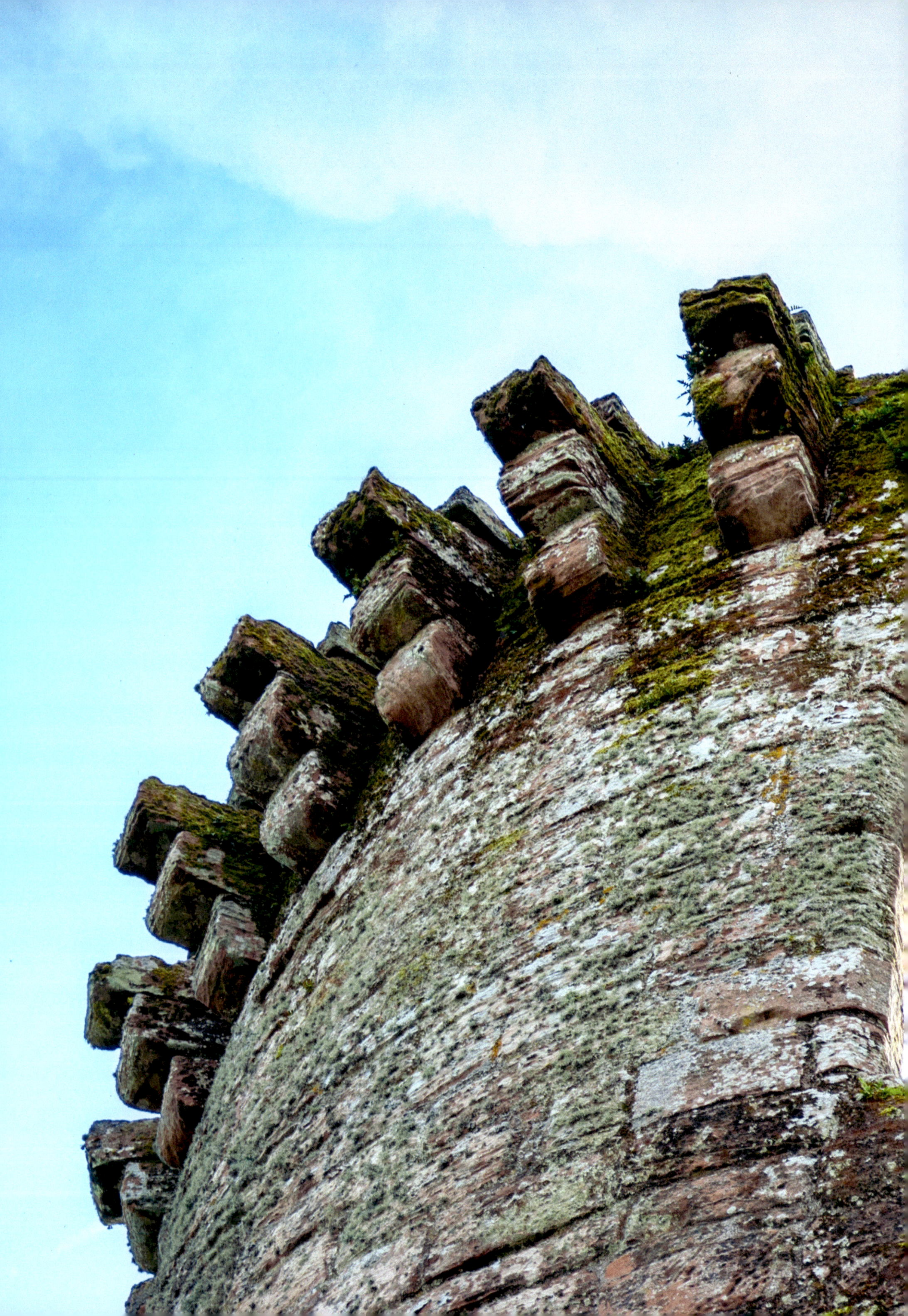

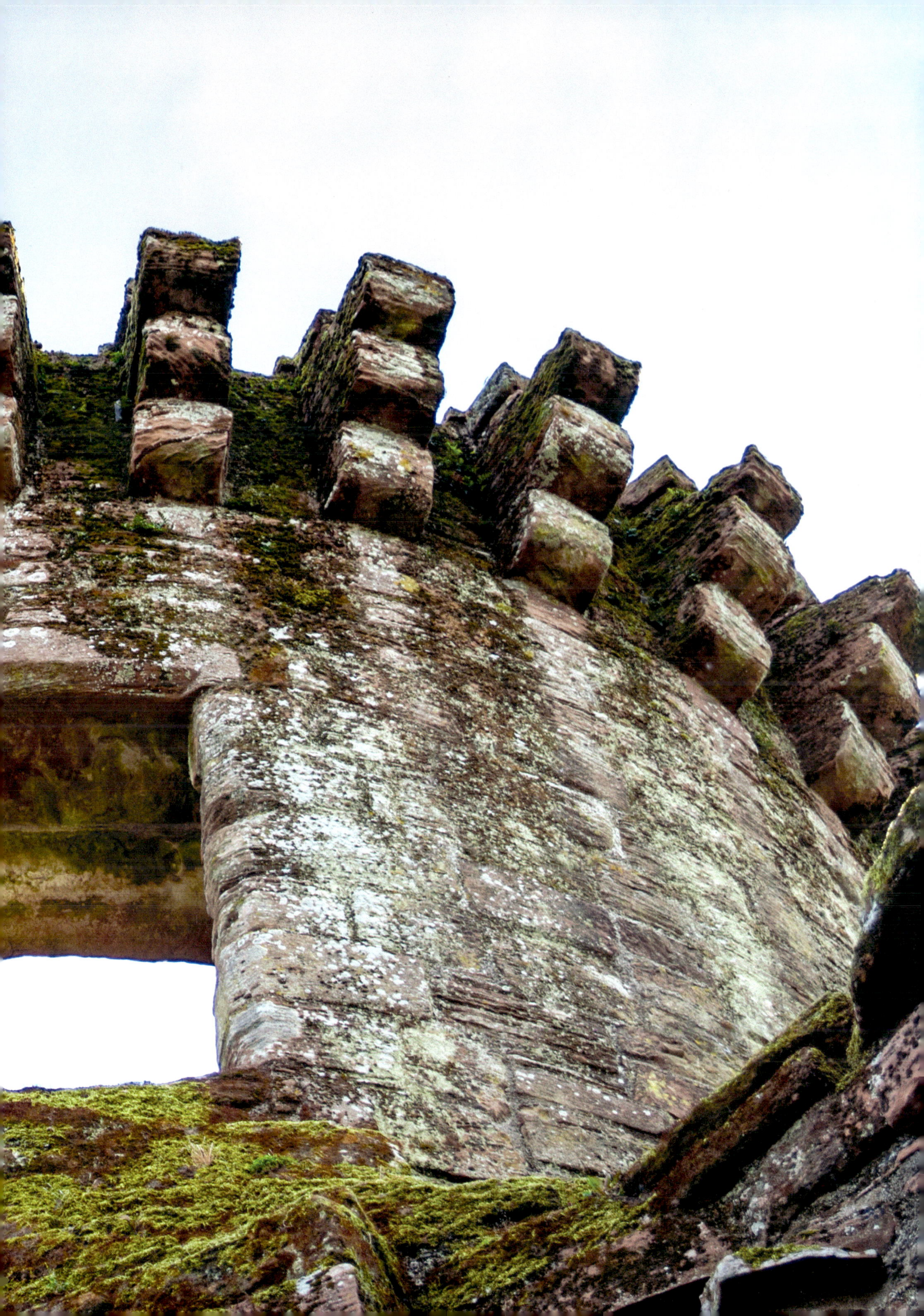

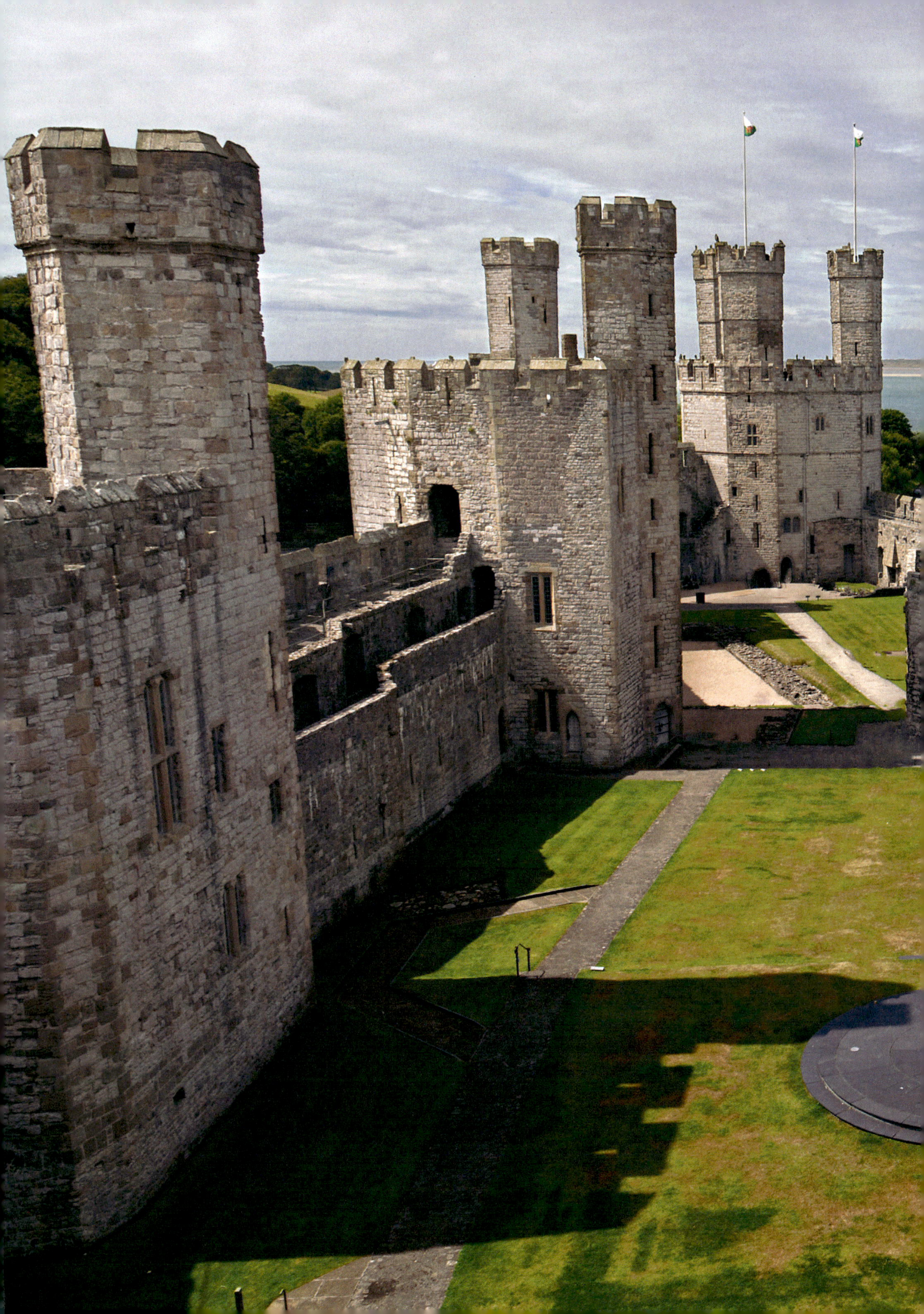

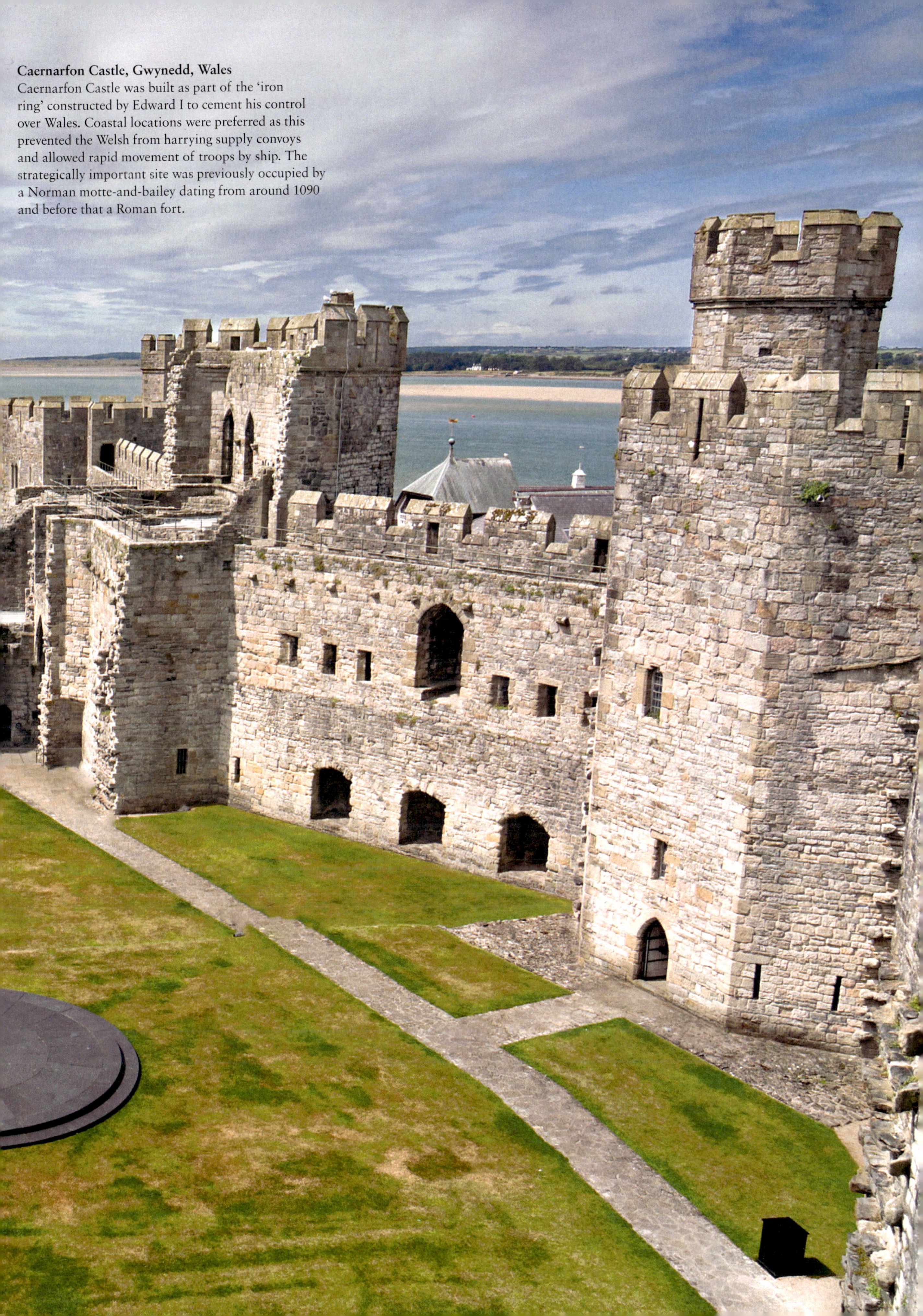

Caernarfon Castle, Gwynedd, Wales
Caernarfon Castle was built as part of the 'iron ring' constructed by Edward I to cement his control over Wales. Coastal locations were preferred as this prevented the Welsh from harrying supply convoys and allowed rapid movement of troops by ship. The strategically important site was previously occupied by a Norman motte-and-bailey dating from around 1090 and before that a Roman fort.

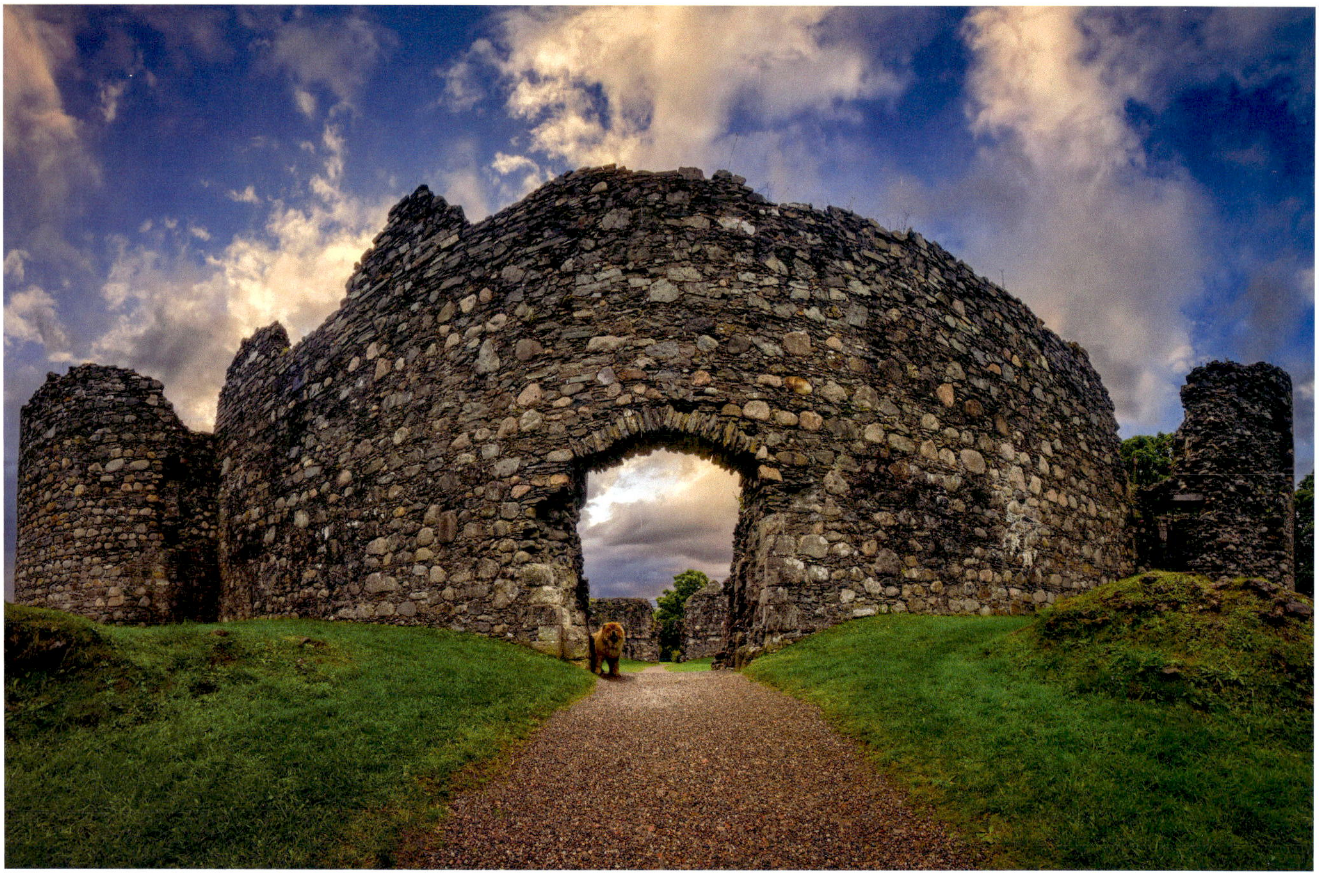

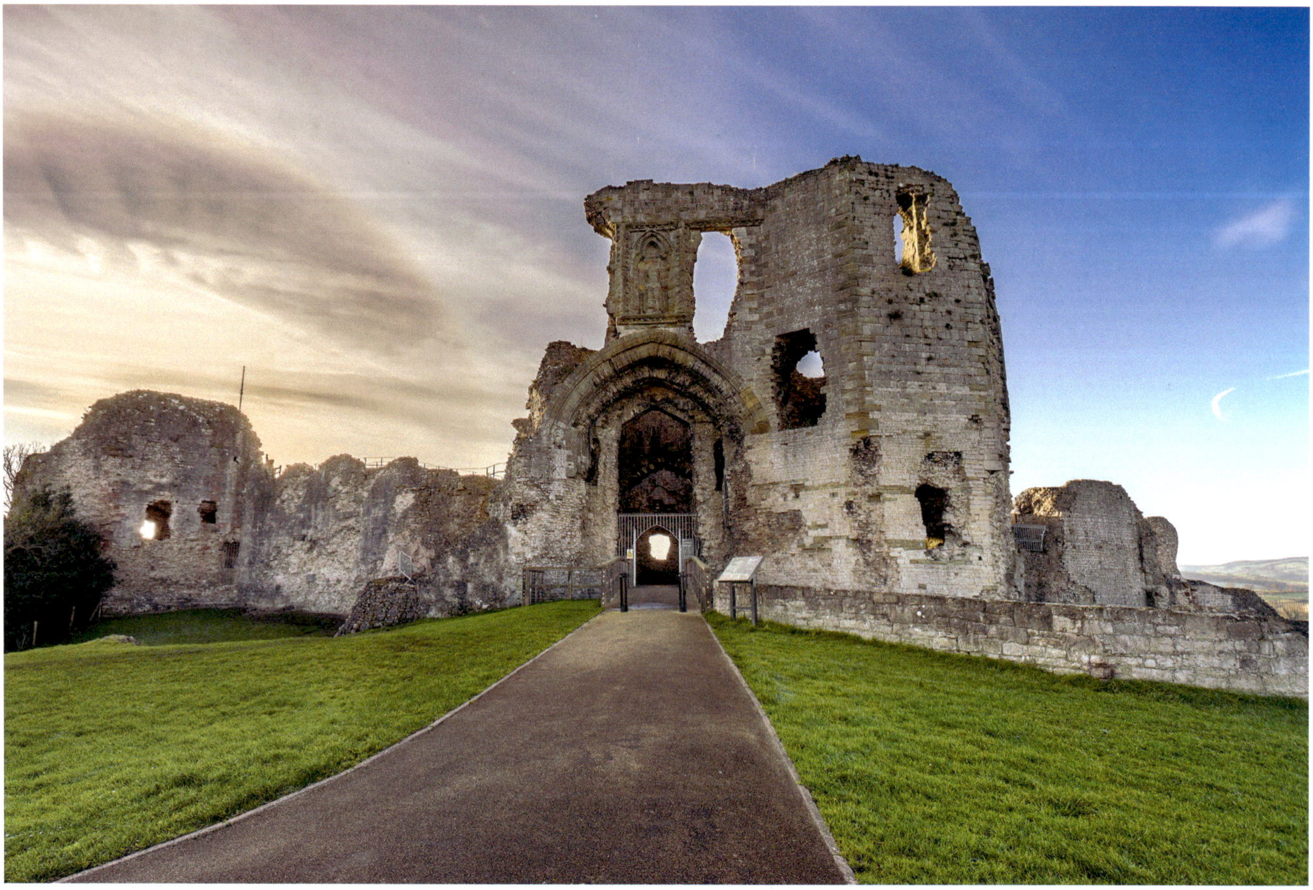

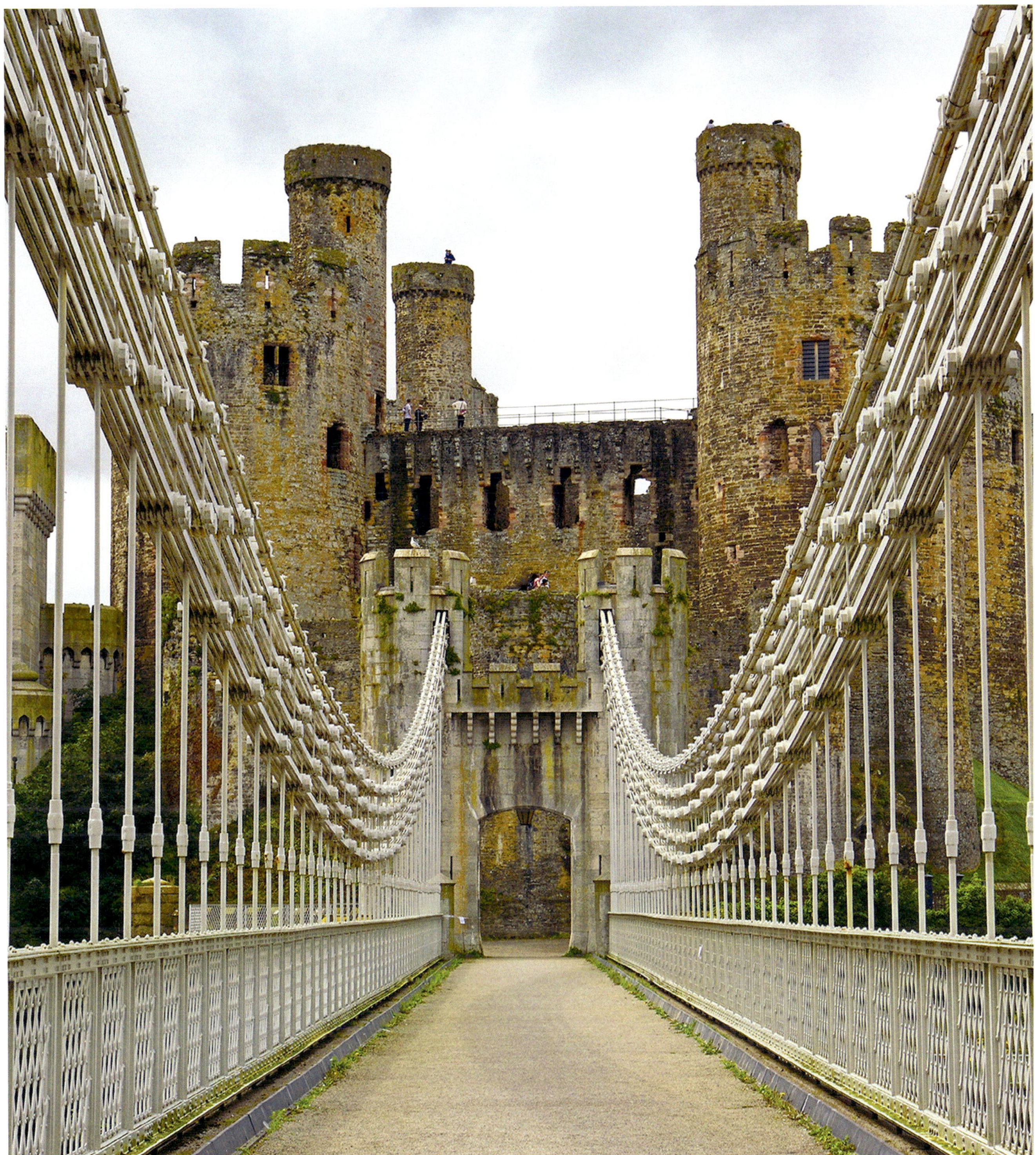

LEFT, TOP:

Inverlochy Castle, Highlands, Scotland

Inverlochy Castle stands at the western end of the Great Glen in Scotland. It was built in the 13th century and was the site of two major battles – in 1431 and 1645. During the 1650s, the castle was abandoned and fell into disrepair. A new Inverlochy Castle was built nearby in the 19th century.

LEFT, BOTTOM:

Denbigh Castle, Denbighshire, Wales

Denbigh Castle was one of several built on the site of a previous Welsh fortification as part of Edward I's castle-building programme. Work began in 1282, but was interrupted in 1294 by a rebellion in which the site was seized. Once the revolt was put down, the existing defences were strengthened.

ABOVE:

Conwy Castle, Conwy, Wales

The photograph shows the entrance and drawbridge to Conwy Castle. The castle was first constructed by Edward I between 1283 to 1289. The nearby Deganwy Castle was built on the site of an earlier Roman-era fortification but was destroyed in 1263. Conwy Castle took over the task of controlling the region. It was captured by Owen Glendower's forces, who gained entry by sending men into the castle disguised as carpenters undertaking repairs.

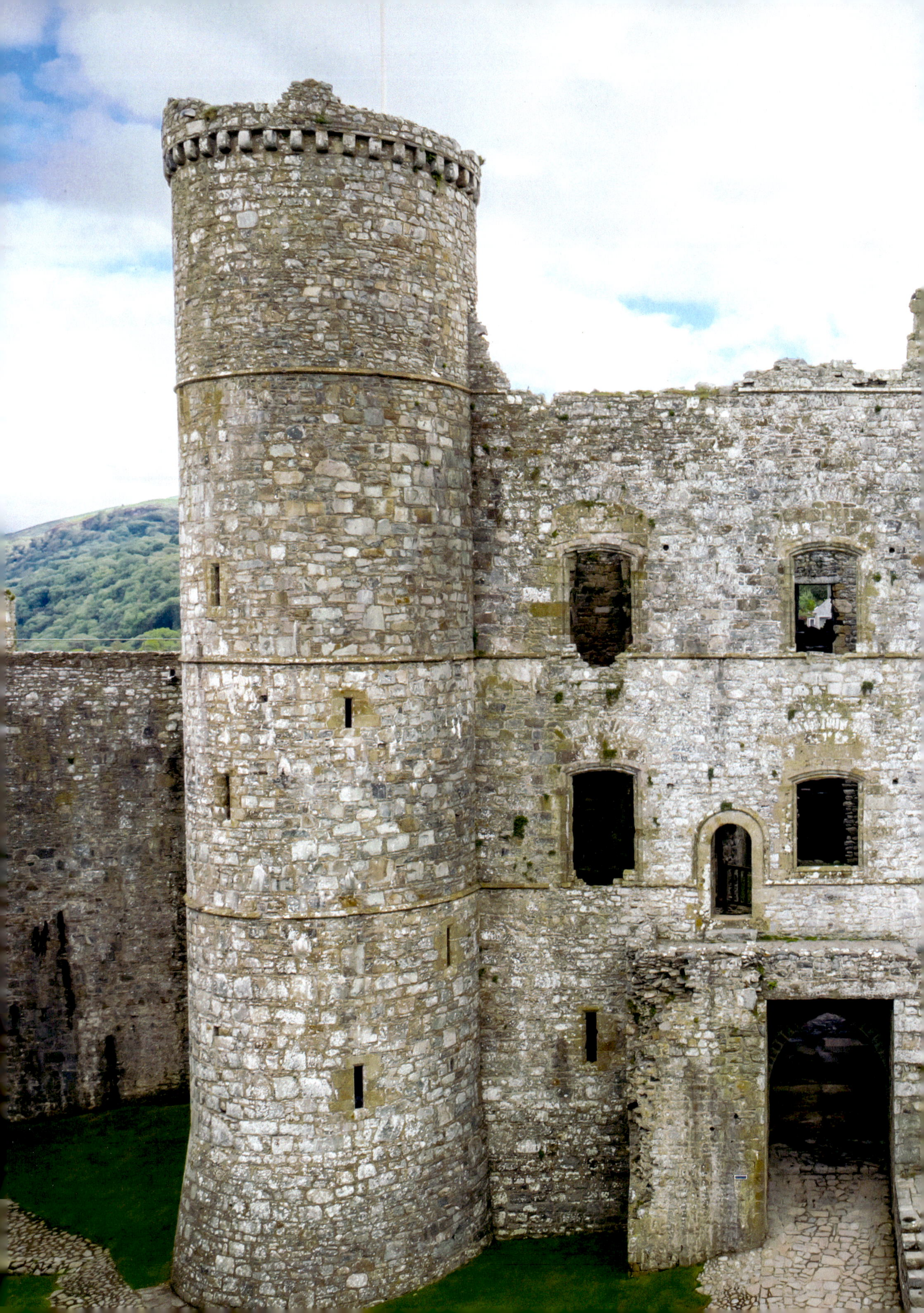

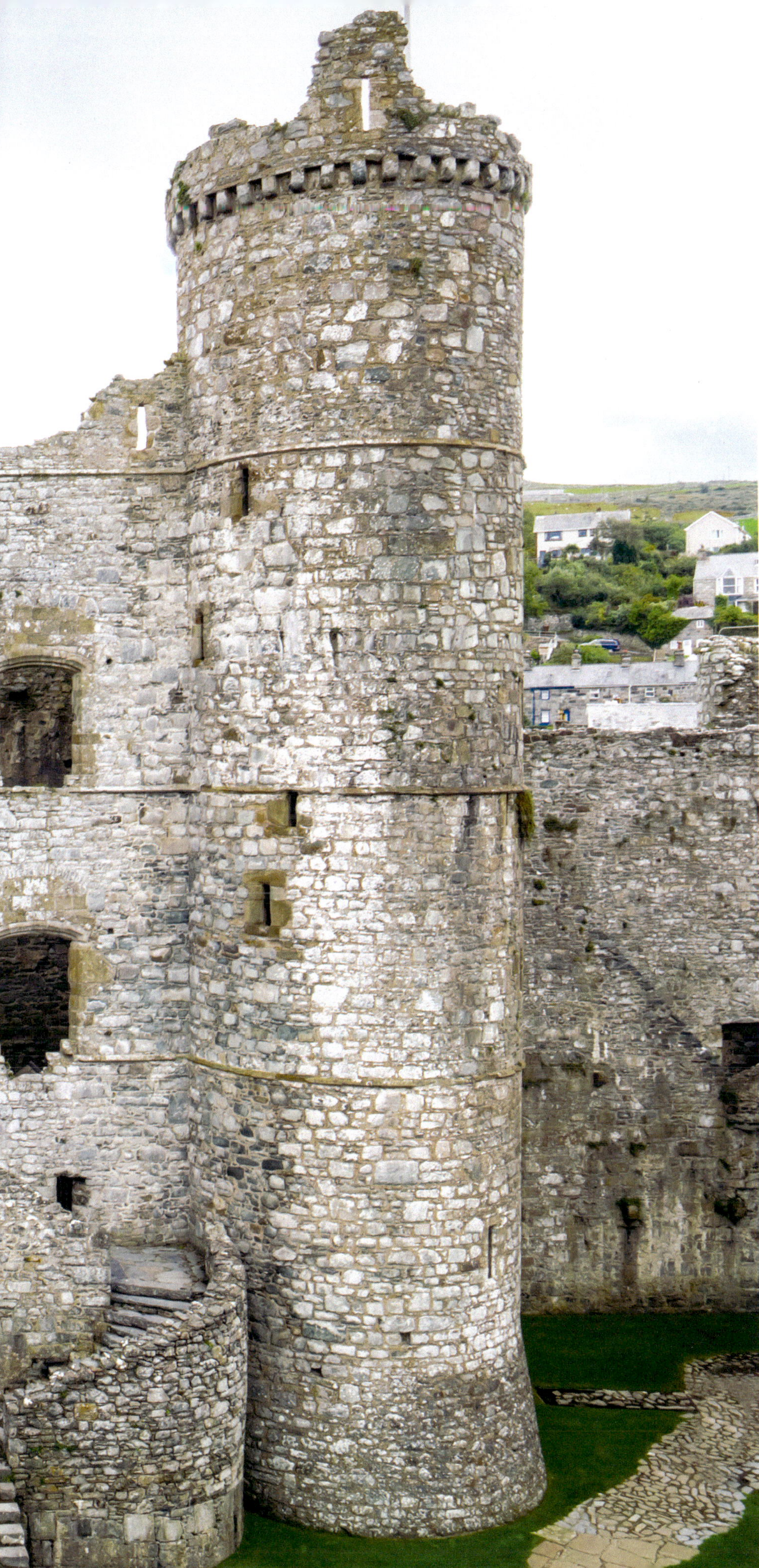

Harlech Castle, Gwynedd, Wales

Harlech Castle in West Wales was built in the 1280s as part of Edward I's 'iron ring' of castles. The defences used a concentric design, with an outer wall surrounding the keep, and took advantage of a naturally very strong position. The only feasible avenue of attack was against the eastern side of the castle, which was protected by a formidable gatehouse, as seen in this photograph.

Achadun Castle, Isle of Lismore, Scotland

Achadun Castle was probably built at the end of the 13th century. It was long supposed to have been built by the Bishop of Argyll, though it now seems more likely that it was constructed by the MacDougall clan. It has been abandoned since the early 15th century.

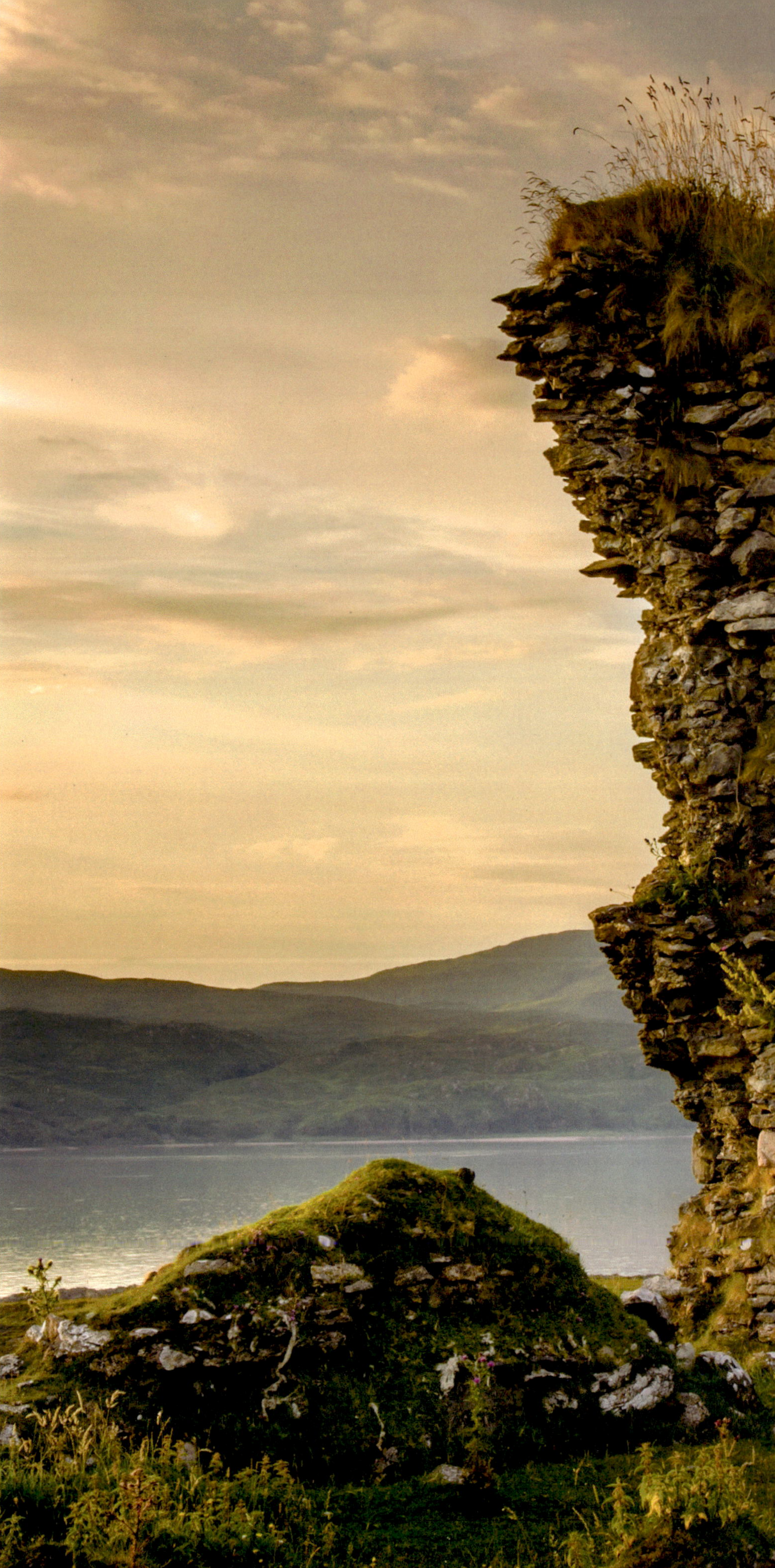

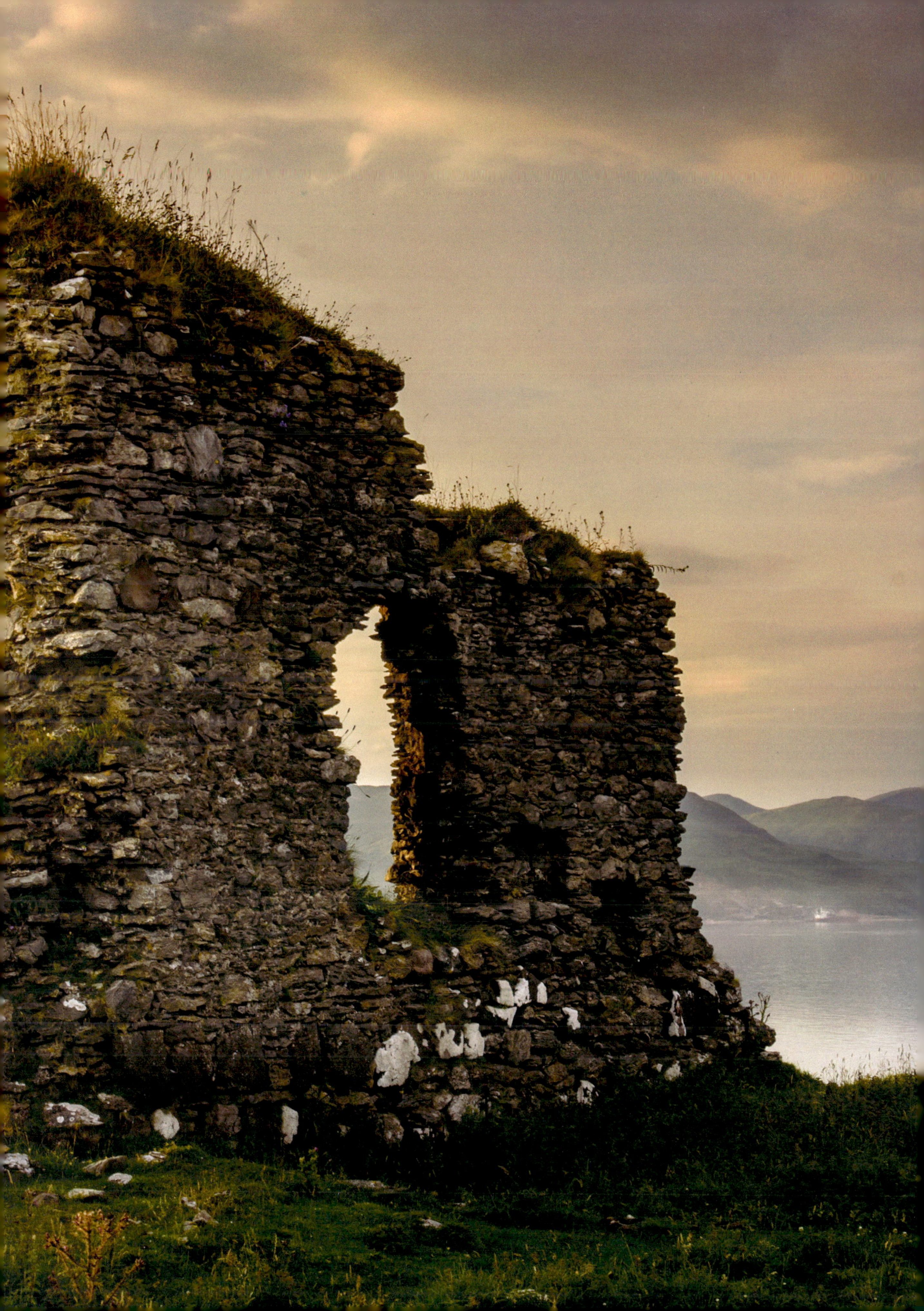

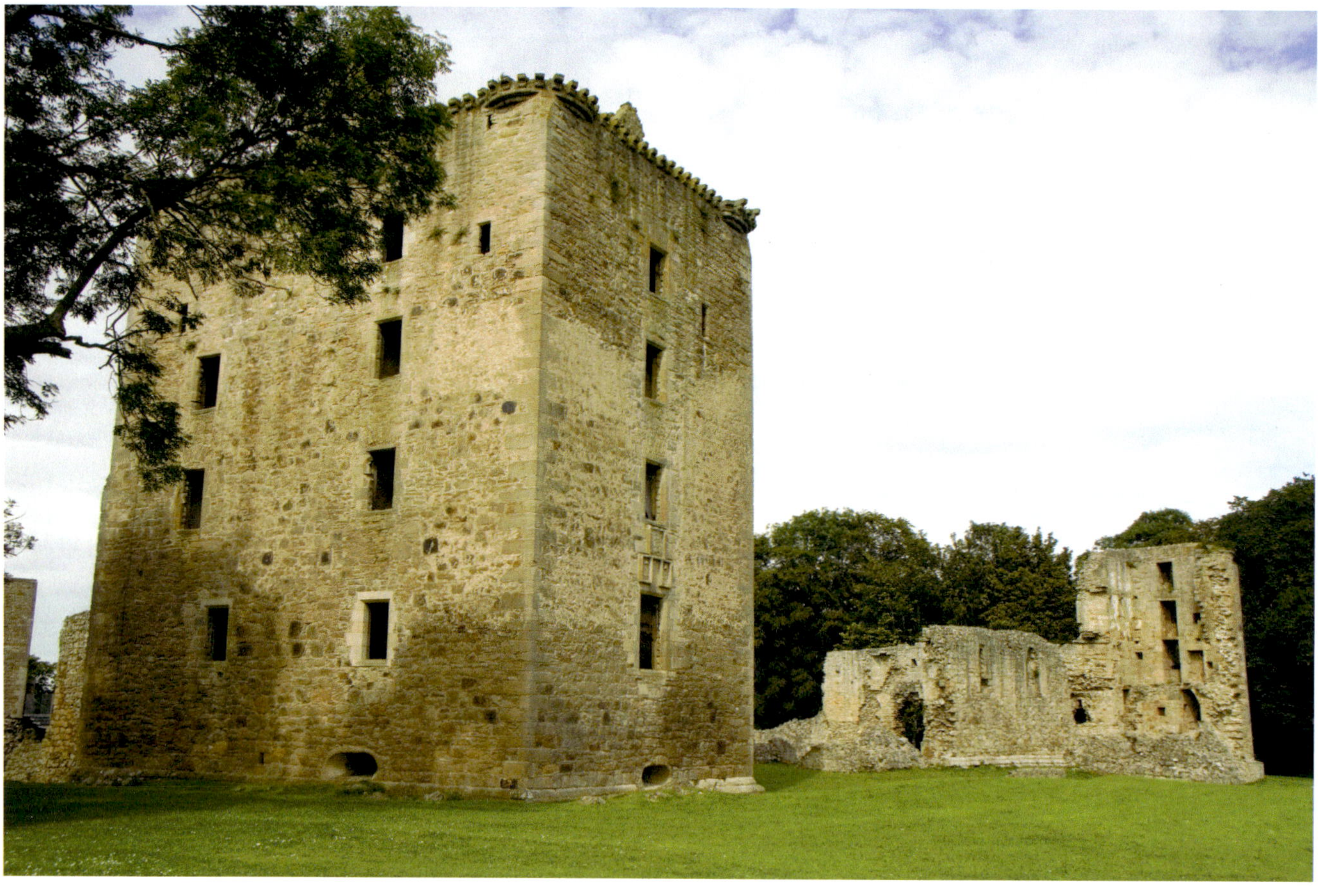

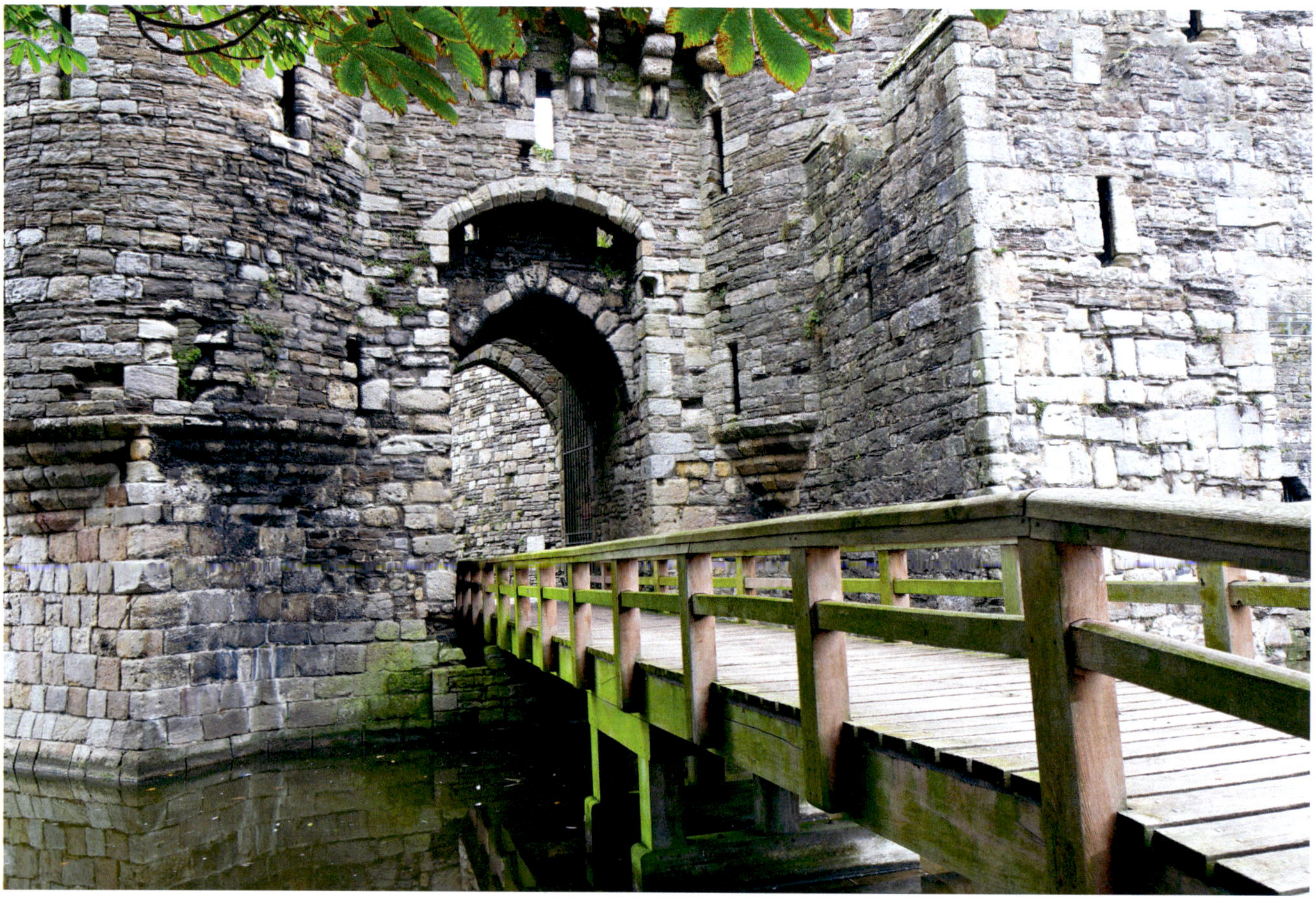

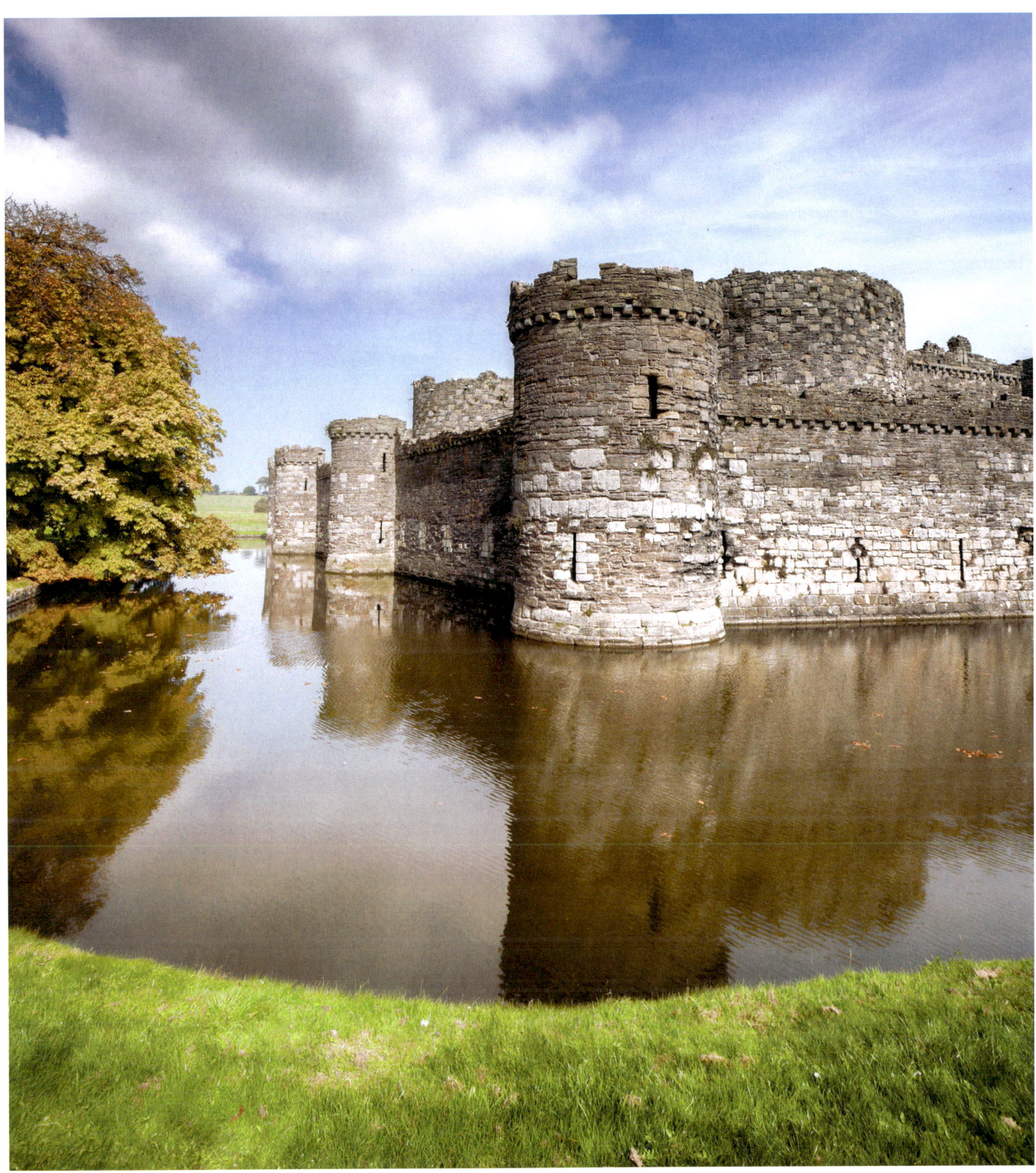

TOP LEFT:

Spynie Castle, Moray, Scotland

Spynie Castle was originally constructed as a ringwork in the 12th century, with the original wooden buildings replaced later with stone. The central stone keep was added in the 14th century, with other buildings constructed during the 15th and 16th centuries. It was a seat of the Bishop of Moray for most of its history.

BOTTOM LEFT AND ABOVE:

Beaumaris Castle, Isle of Anglesey, Wales

Beaumaris Castle was the last of Edward I's Welsh castles, and the largest. Work began in 1295 on a concentric design, with an outer curtain wall protected by a moat and sixteen towers. The inner defences stood higher, with six towers and two gatehouses defending the inner ward.

Beaumaris was envisaged as a royal residence, capable of supporting the households of the king and the Prince of Wales. At the peak of the construction work over 2500 men were employed, but the construction was never completely finished. Funds that were already in short supply had to be diverted elsewhere, and the castle was in disrepair by the early 1500s.

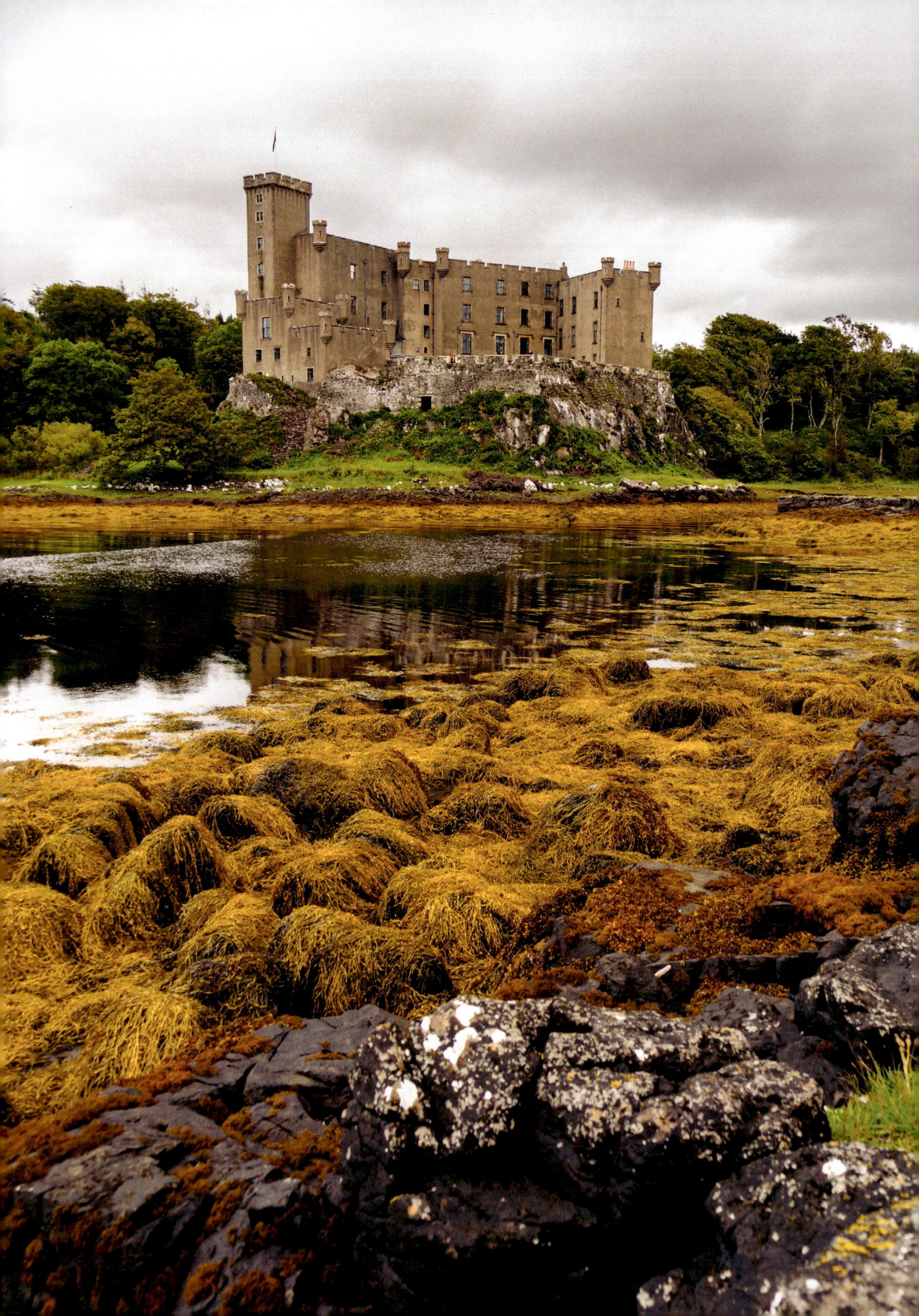

Late Middle Ages

By the Late Middle Ages, castle building was a well-developed science. Defensive works continued to evolve to meet new threats, such as increasingly sophisticated siege engines and early gunpowder weapons. Building techniques also advanced, allowing the construction of higher, stronger and more graceful structures.

Castles were, obviously, strong places that offered a refuge from attack, but they served a wider purpose. A castle was a secure base to store supplies, from which armed parties could control the surrounding countryside. They were also symbols of power and prestige, reminding everyone of the power of the king or lord who built or held the fortress. It is not possible to say how many revolts were deterred by the impossibility of defeating an overlord safe in his castle keep.

The Celtic people of this era had developed far beyond the tribal societies of the post-Roman world, but they retained their traditions, languages and warrior heritage. The post-Celtic people of Scotland, Ireland, Wales and Cornwall were at times a source of fighting men in English service, and at times the enemies they fought against. In the meantime, the clans of Scotland and Ireland often needed fortifications to guard against one another.

LEFT:
Dunvegan Castle, Isle of Skye, Scotland
Dunvegan Castle took advantage of a good defensive position on a rocky promontory; a site that had likely been fortified in the past. The castle was constructed in stages, beginning in the 13th century, with additional buildings added over the next 400 years. The appearance of the castle also evolved, until it was completely remodelled in the early 19th century.

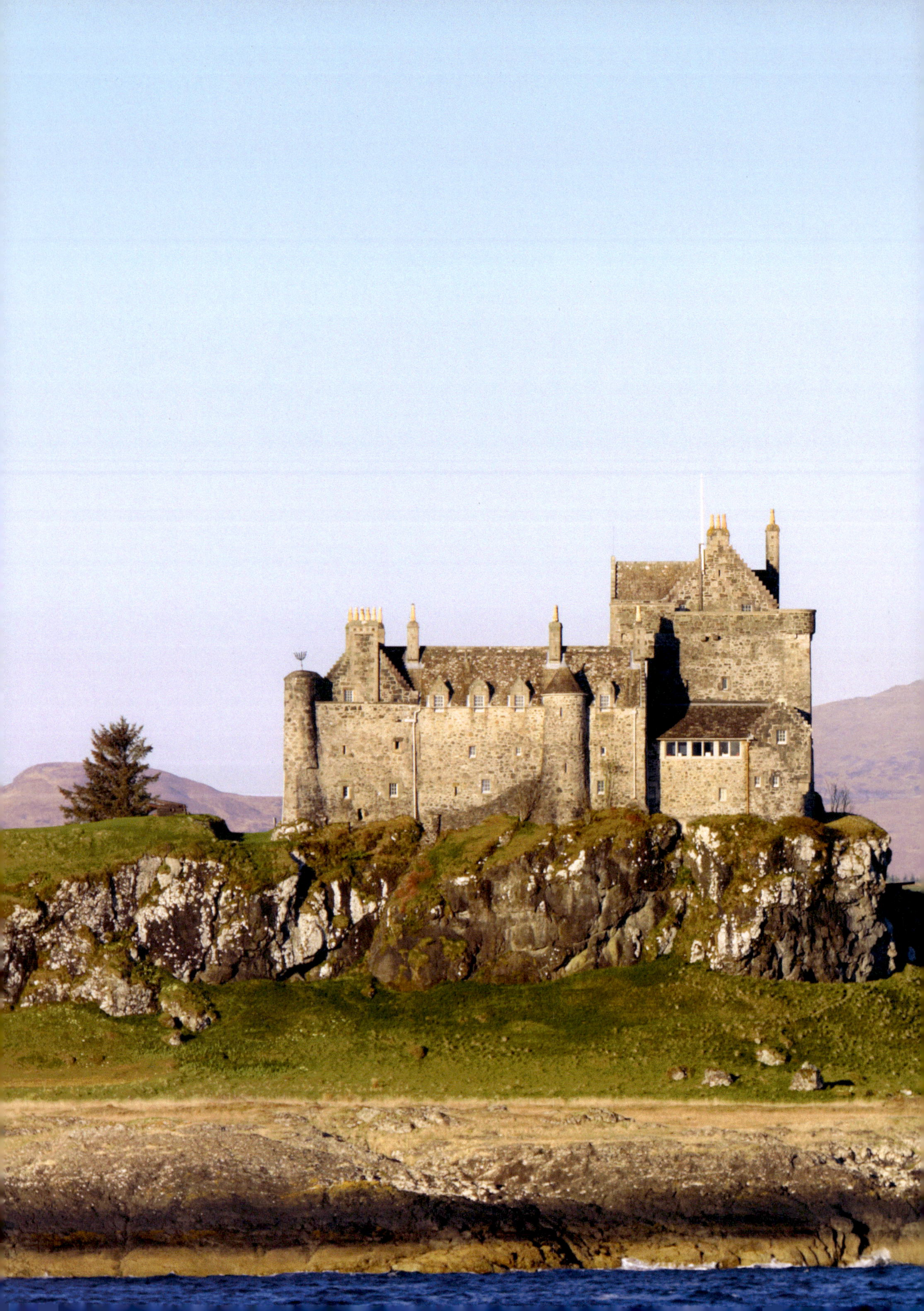

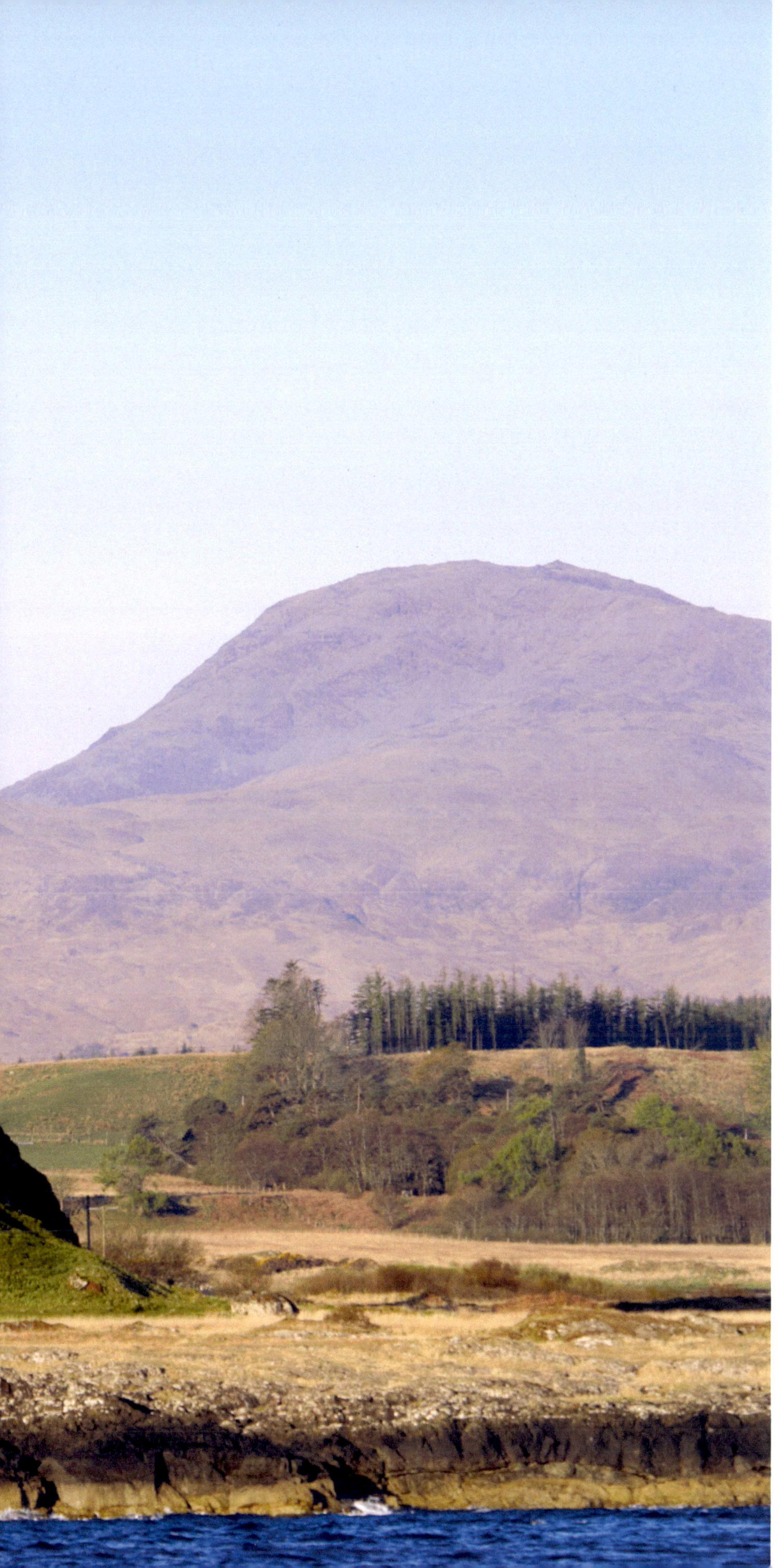

Duart Castle, Isle of Mull, Scotland

Duart Castle was constructed in the 13th century and was inhabited until the 1690s, for most of this time as a seat of clan MacLean. The castle withstood siege in 1647 but was destroyed after being surrendered to Clan Campbell in 1691. It was eventually rebuilt in its present style.

RIGHT:

MacDuff Castle, Fife, Scotland

The oldest surviving parts of MacDuff Castle date from the 14th century, though an earlier fortification may have existed on the site. The castle was destroyed on the orders of Edward I of England as punishment for the owners' choice of sides in the Scottish Wars of Independence, with new structures built there in the 16th and 17th centuries.

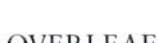

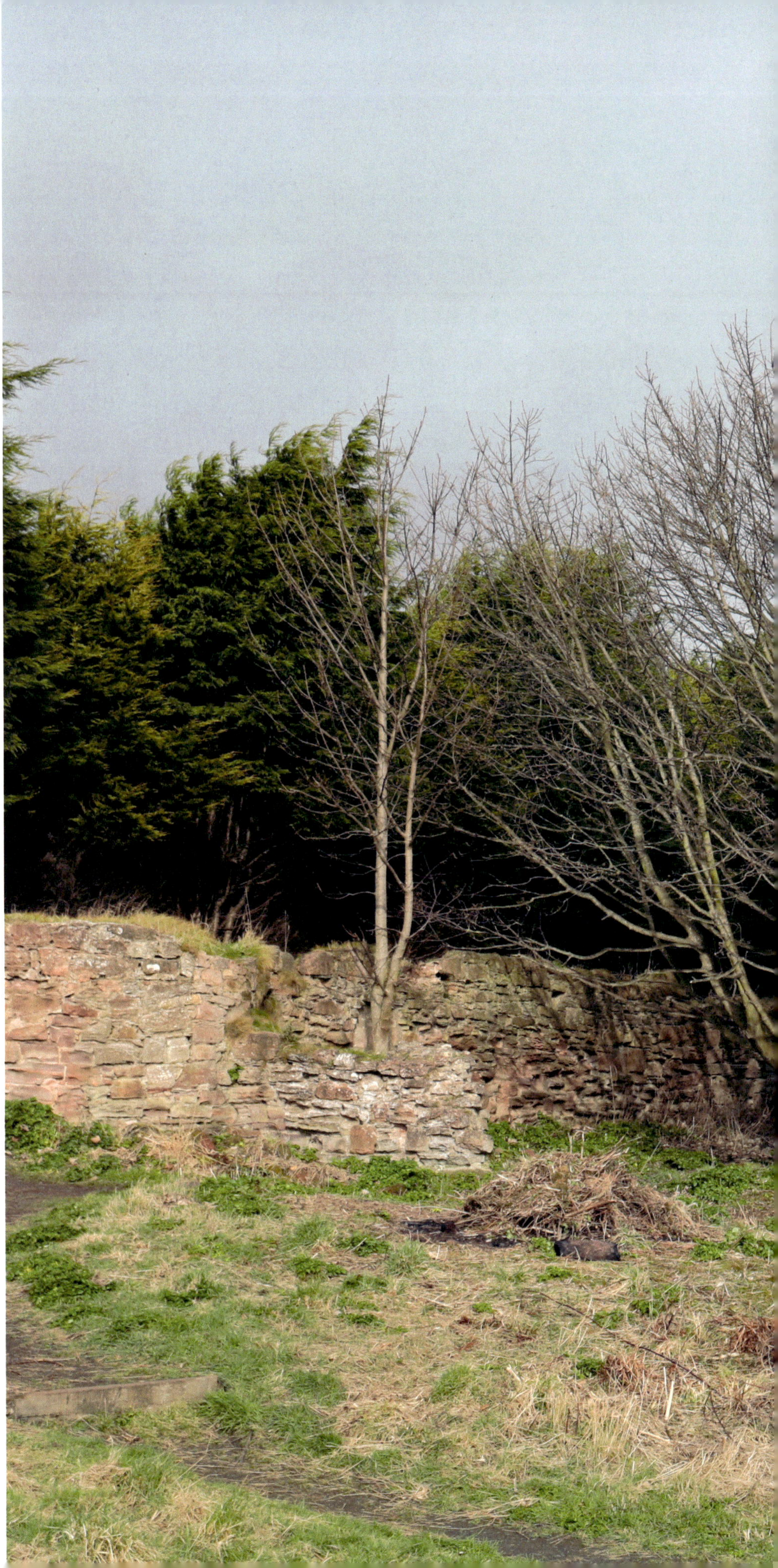

OVERLEAF:

Mugdock Castle, Stirlingshire, Scotland

Mugdock Castle near Glasgow was built in the 14th century, though little of the castle from this period survives. The castle was extended in the 15th century, but suffered badly in the English Civil War. The remains were built over to create a mansion house, which was later demolished and a new house built on the site.

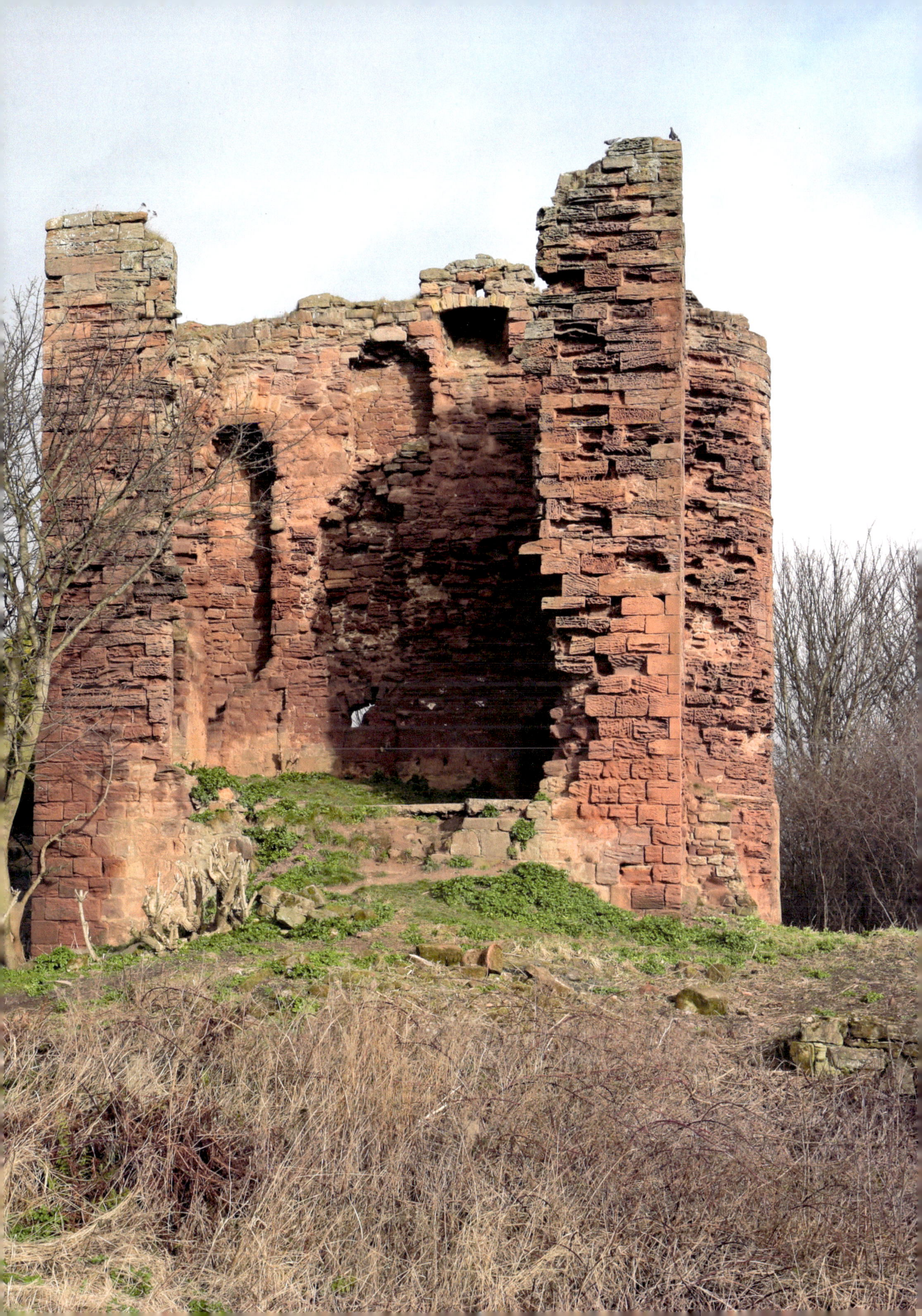

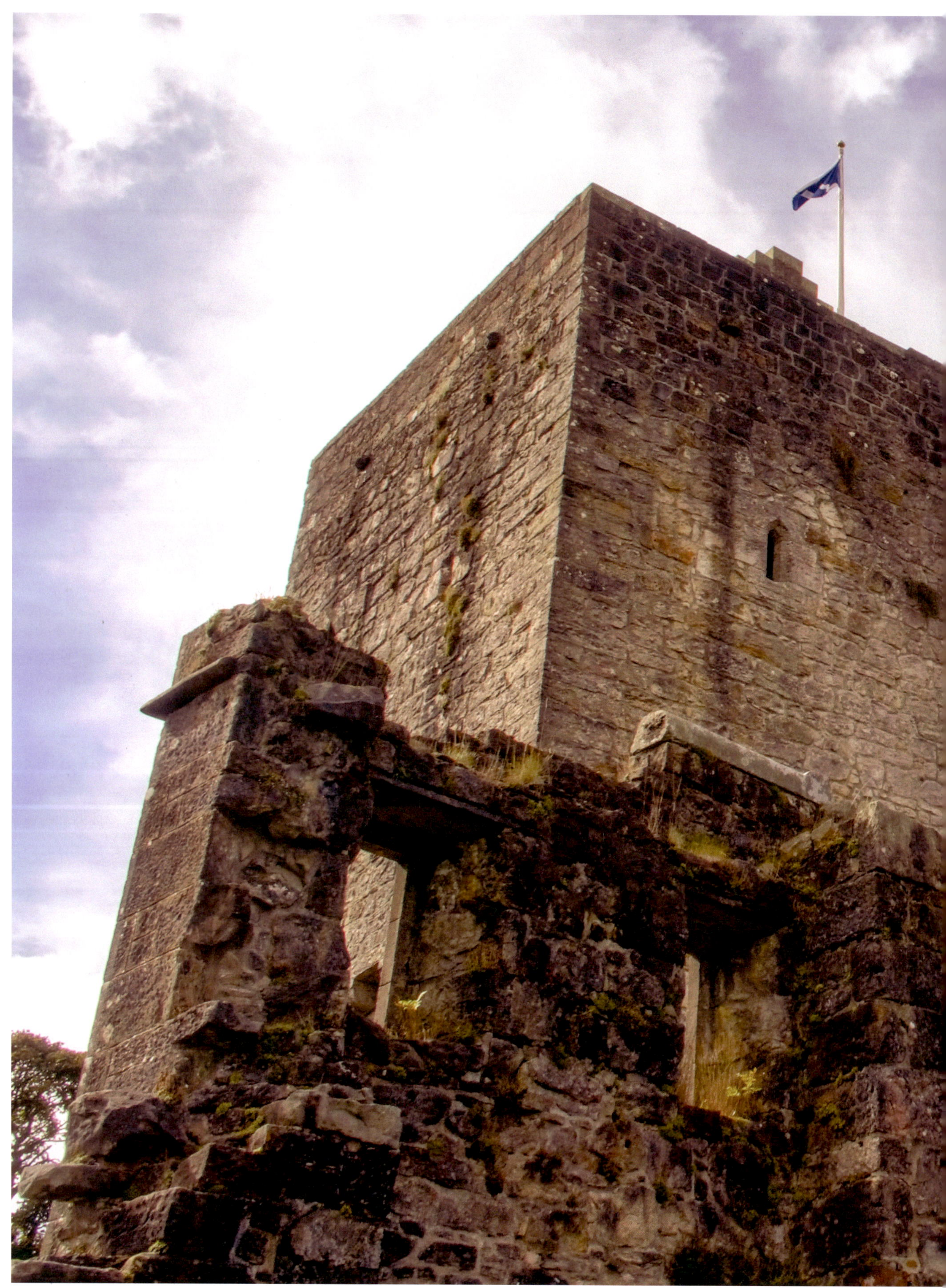

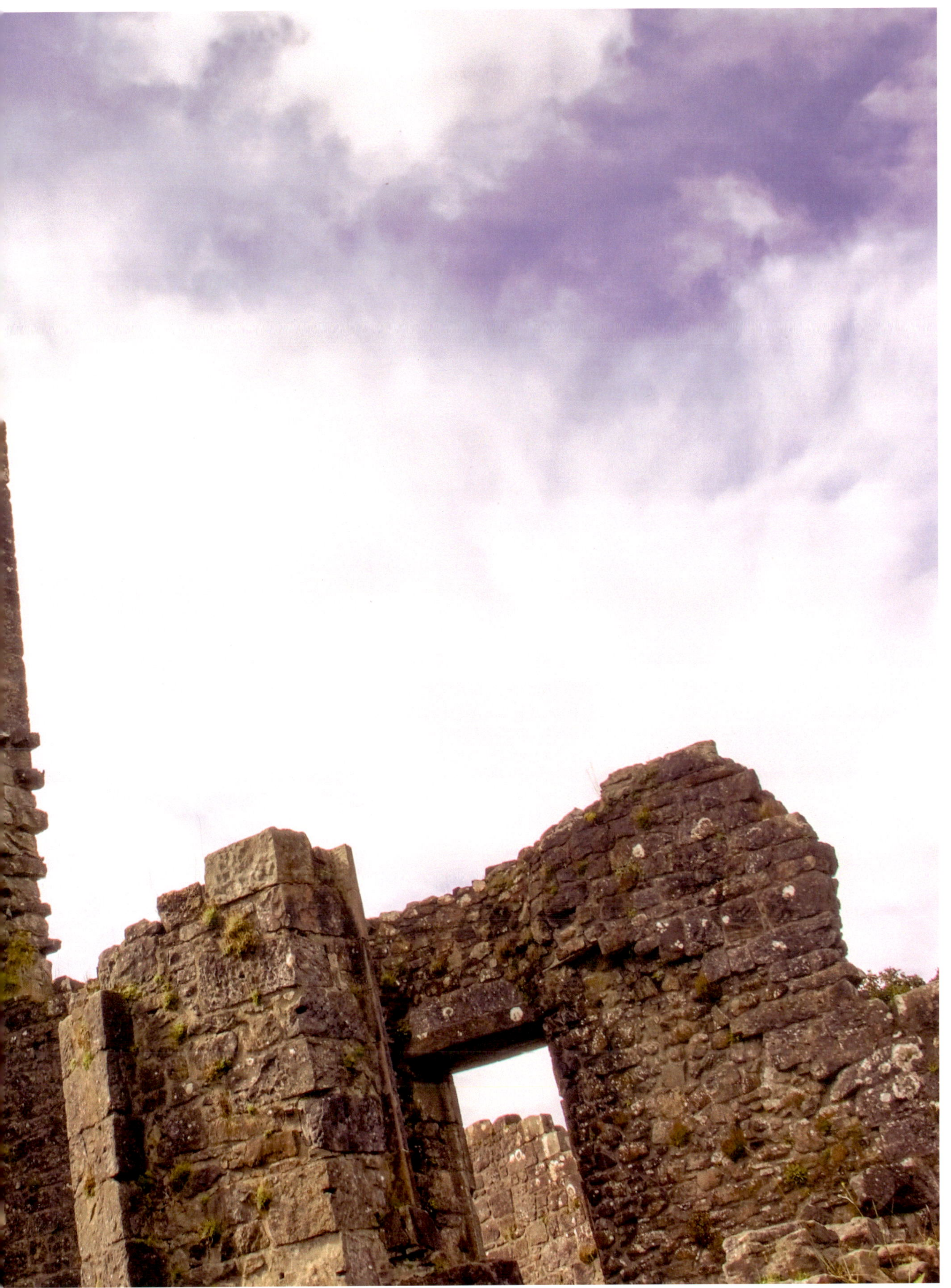

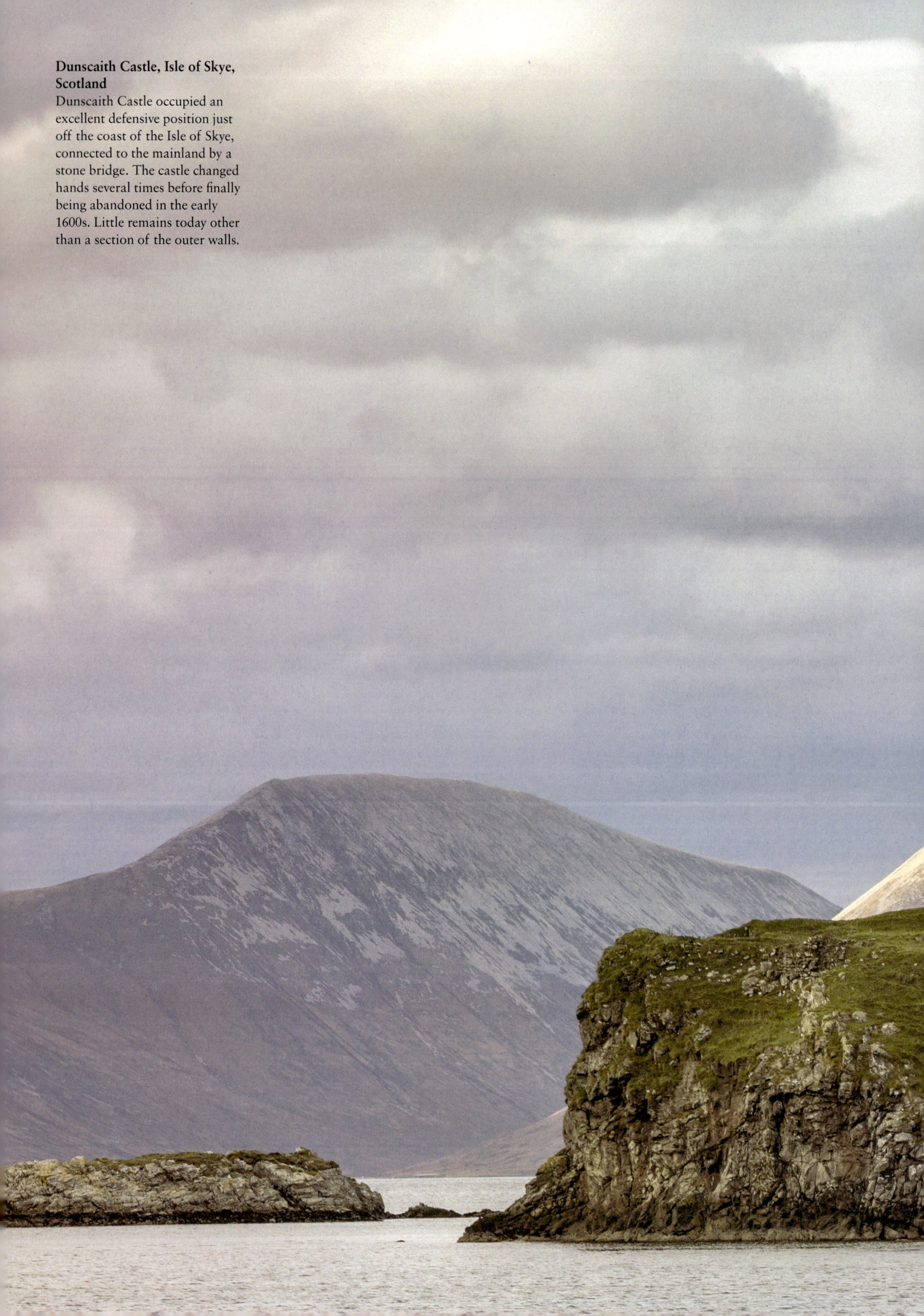

Dunscaith Castle, Isle of Skye, Scotland
Dunscaith Castle occupied an excellent defensive position just off the coast of the Isle of Skye, connected to the mainland by a stone bridge. The castle changed hands several times before finally being abandoned in the early 1600s. Little remains today other than a section of the outer walls.

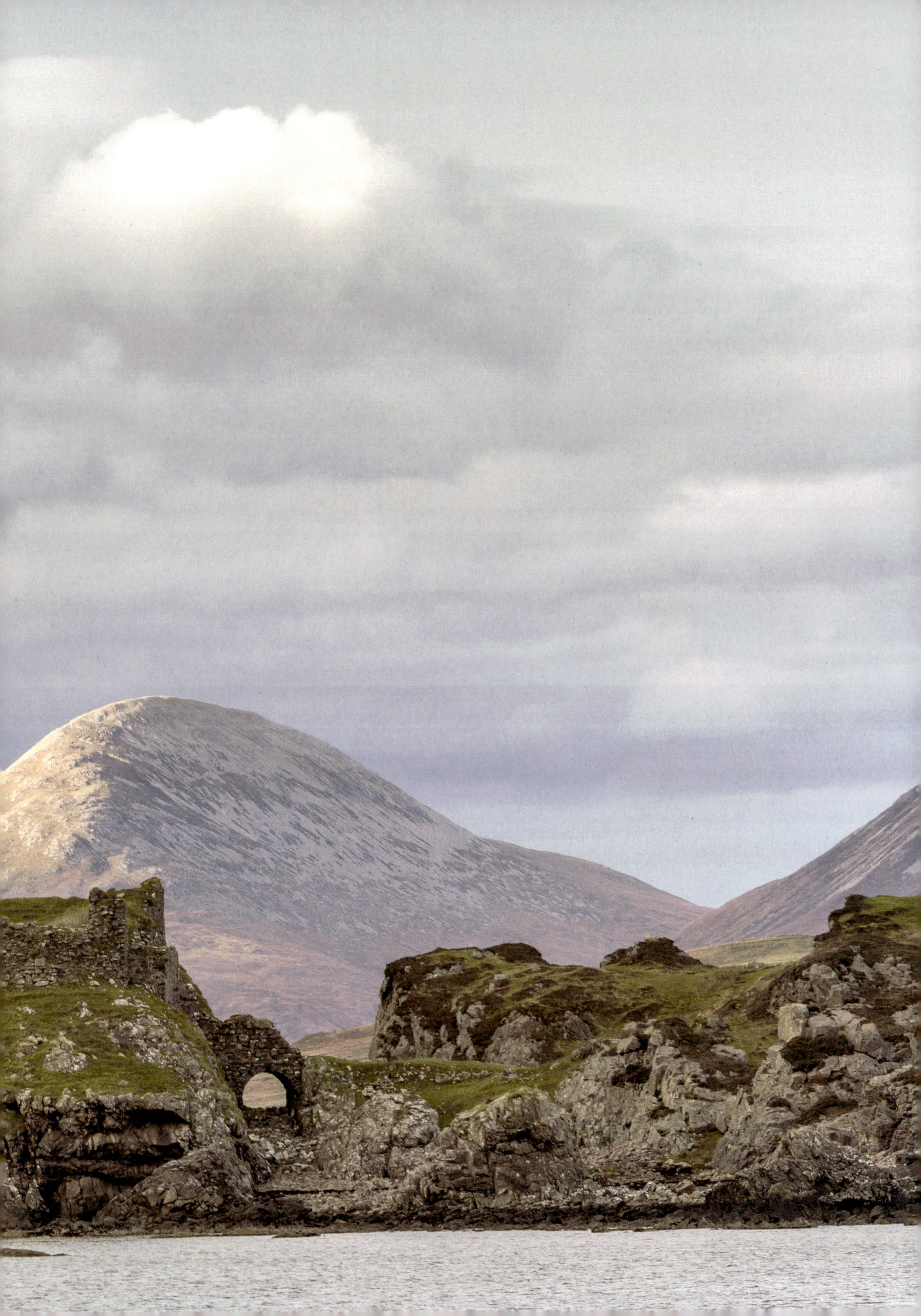

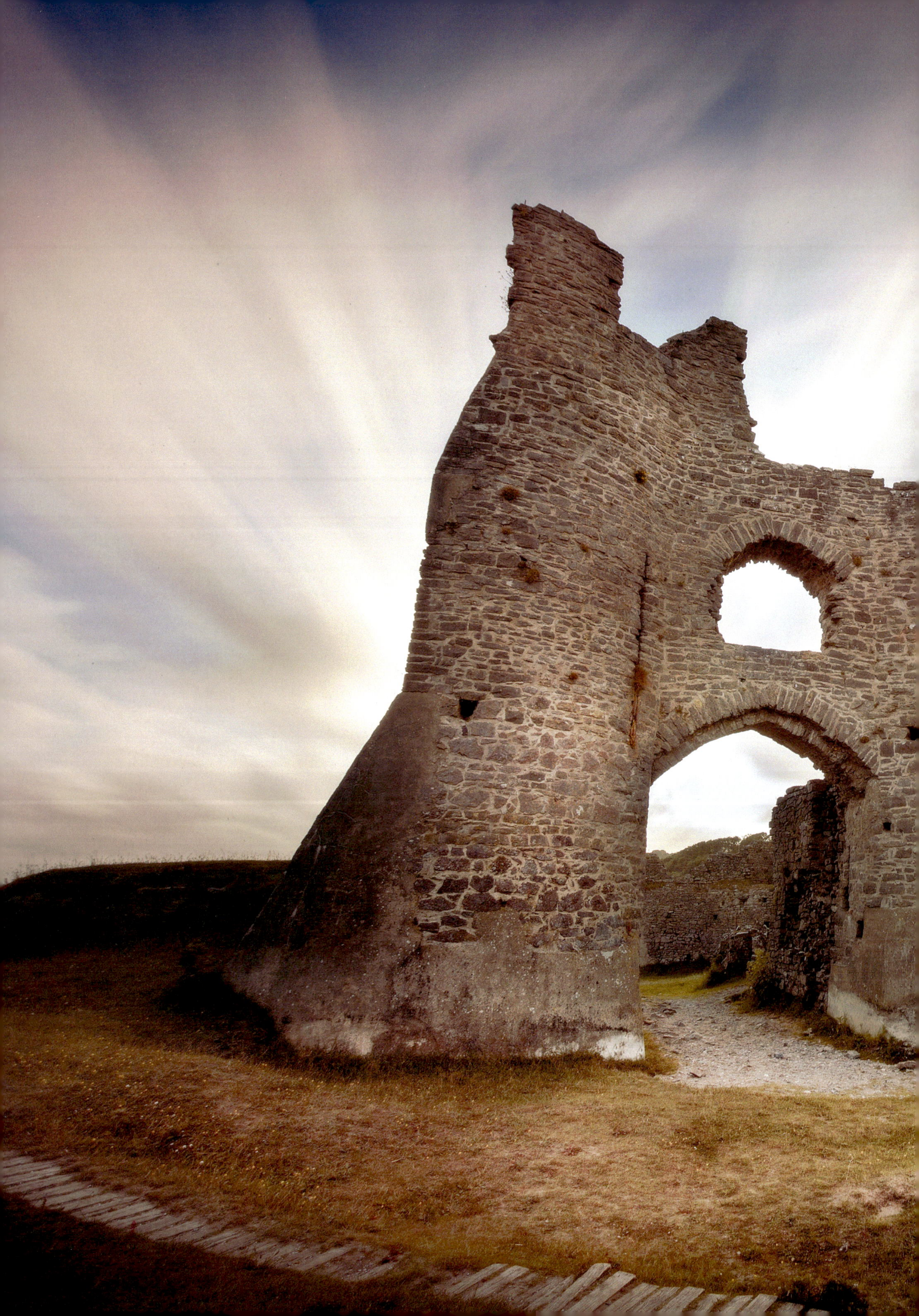

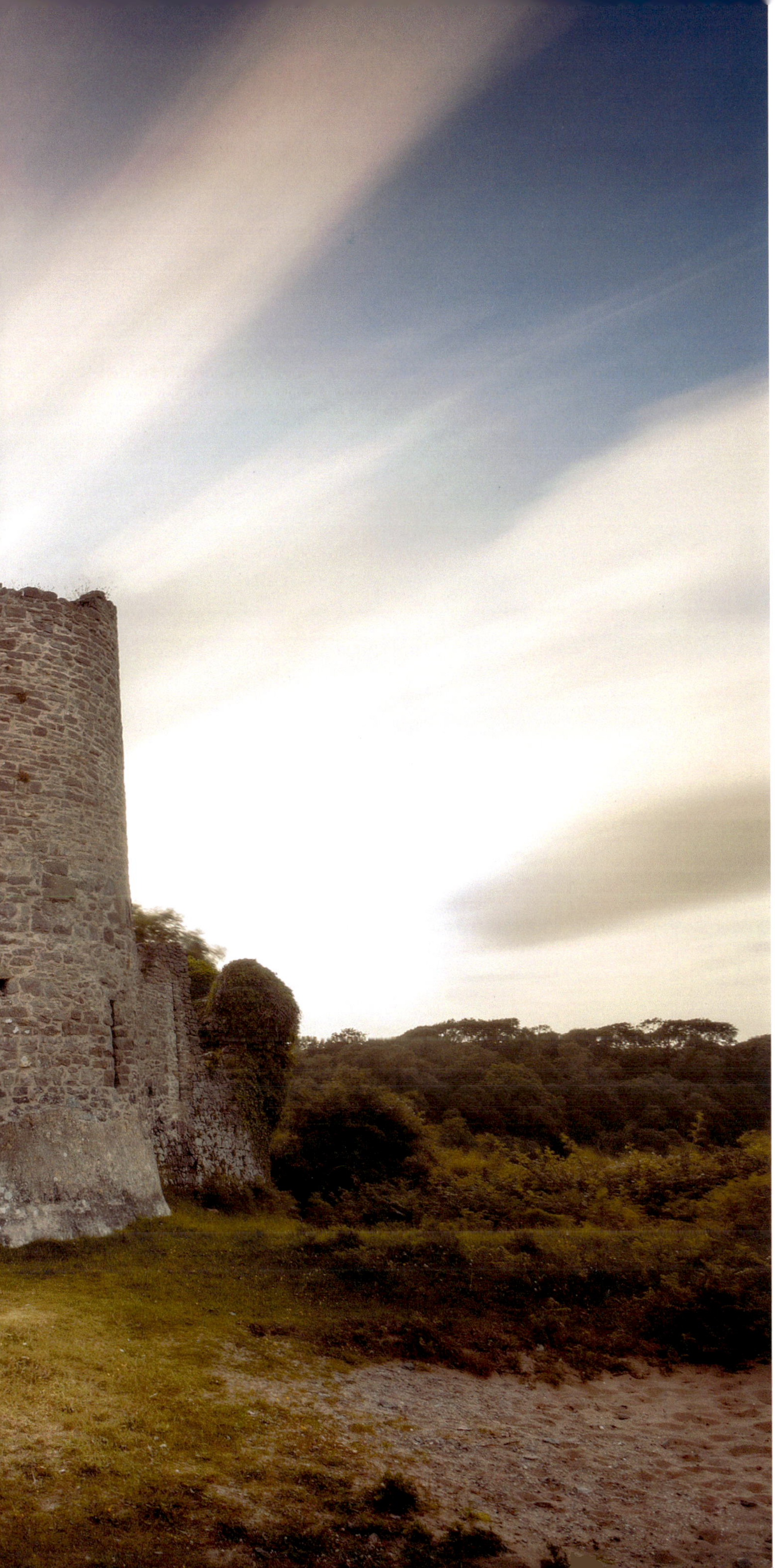

Pennard Castle, Gower Peninsula, Wales
Pennard Castle in South Wales was originally constructed as a ringwork in the 12th century. The castle was rebuilt in stone in the late 13th or perhaps early 14th century. The builders attempted to incorporate advanced features for the time, such as a strong gatehouse with two towers, but lacked the skill to implement them properly. The castle was abandoned due to the encroachment of sand blowing in from Three Cliffs Bay.

Urquhart Castle, Highlands of Scotland
Urquhart Castle occupies a good defensive site on the shore of Loch Ness. The castle was built in the mid-13th century, though there is evidence of an earlier fortification on the site. The defences were strengthened over time, but in 1690 the gatehouse was destroyed to make the castle useless to the Jacobites.

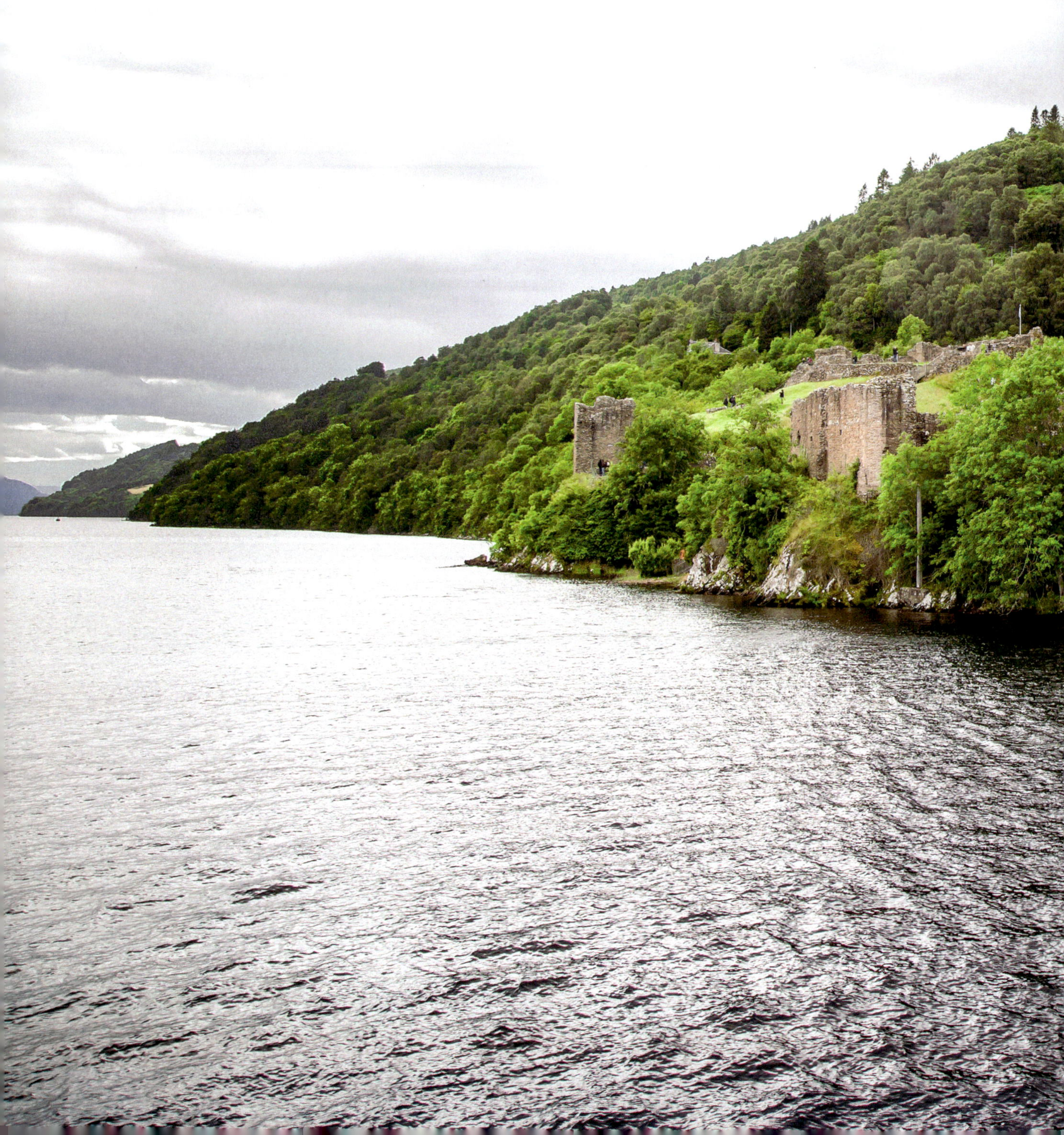

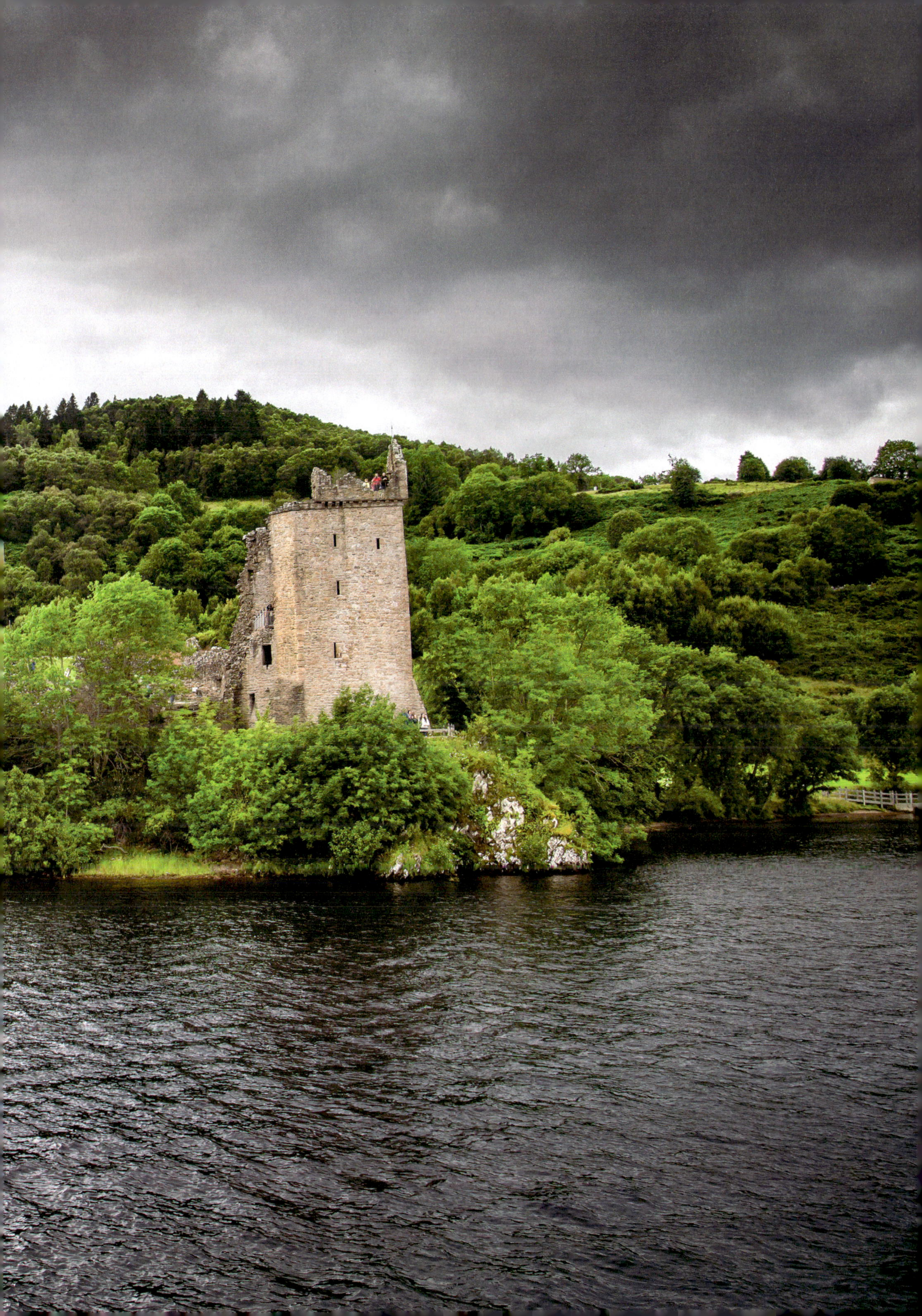

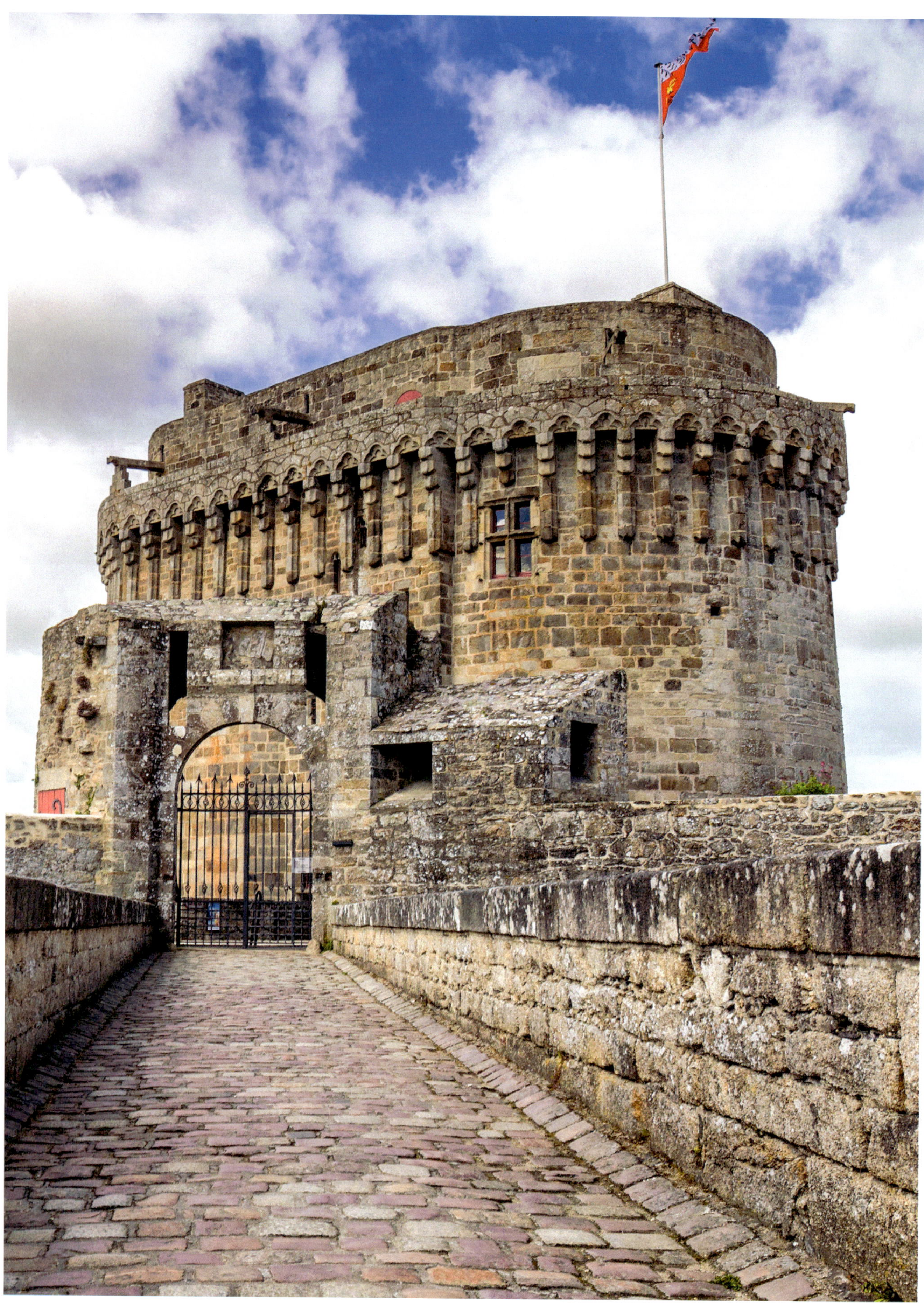

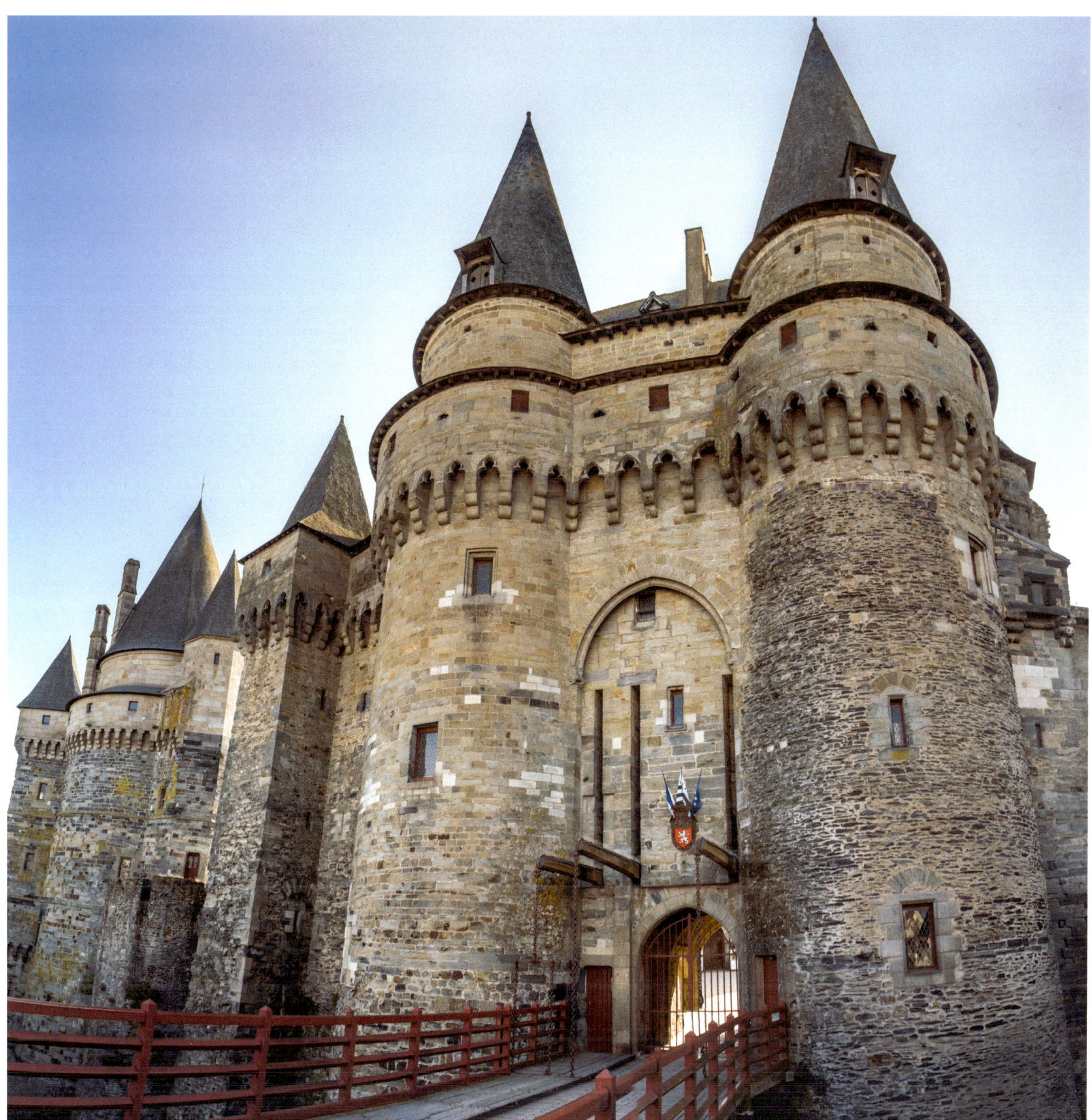

LEFT:
Château de Dinan, Côtes-d'Armor, Brittany, France
Work began on Chateau de Dinan in 1382. It formed part of the city defences but did not depend on them, ensuring security from both external attack and local revolt. The design drew on previous experience of building a pair of round towers and joining them with a forebuilding. The result was a well defended yet comfortable living space for the Dukes of Brittany. The castle was later extended by incorporating parts of the city defences.

ABOVE:
Château de Vitré, Ille-et-Vilaine, Brittany, France
Chateau de Vitre was built on the site of earlier fortifications. The original wooden fort was destroyed and replaced with a stone structure in the 1100s, and this was rebuilt as the present castle in the early 1200s. Later additions included a gatehouse and towers plus modifications to accommodate gunpowder artillery, after which most modifications were designed to improve habitability rather than defence.

OVERLEAF:
Tantallon Castle, East Lothian, Scotland
Tantallon Castle was built on a promontory, with cliffs on three sides and a curtain wall on the fourth. Construction began in the 1350s, creating a fortress sufficient to withstand siege and naval bombardment in 1491, and again in 1528. The more advanced artillery of 1651 did serious damage, with the castle finally falling to an army under Oliver Cromwell.

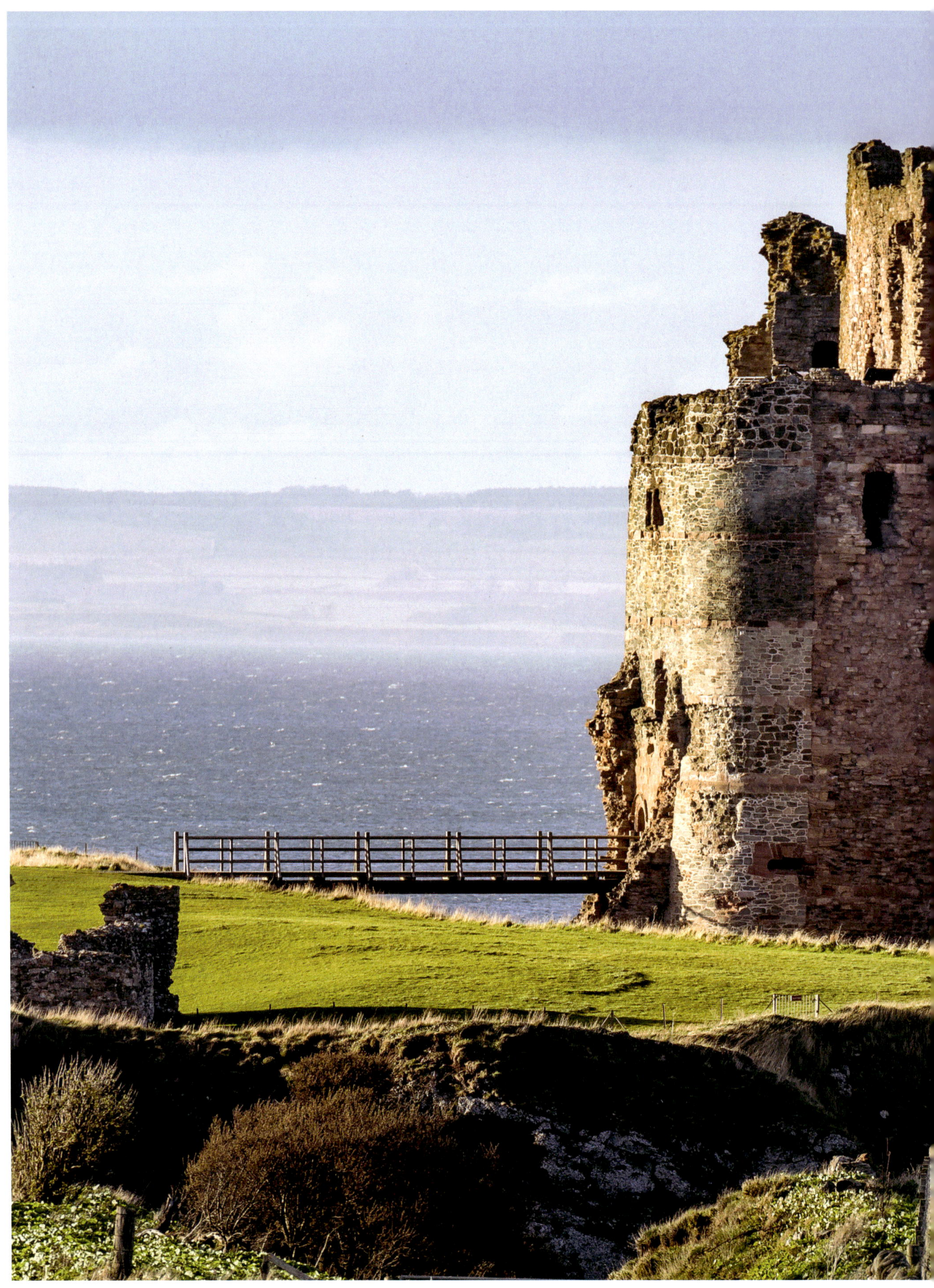

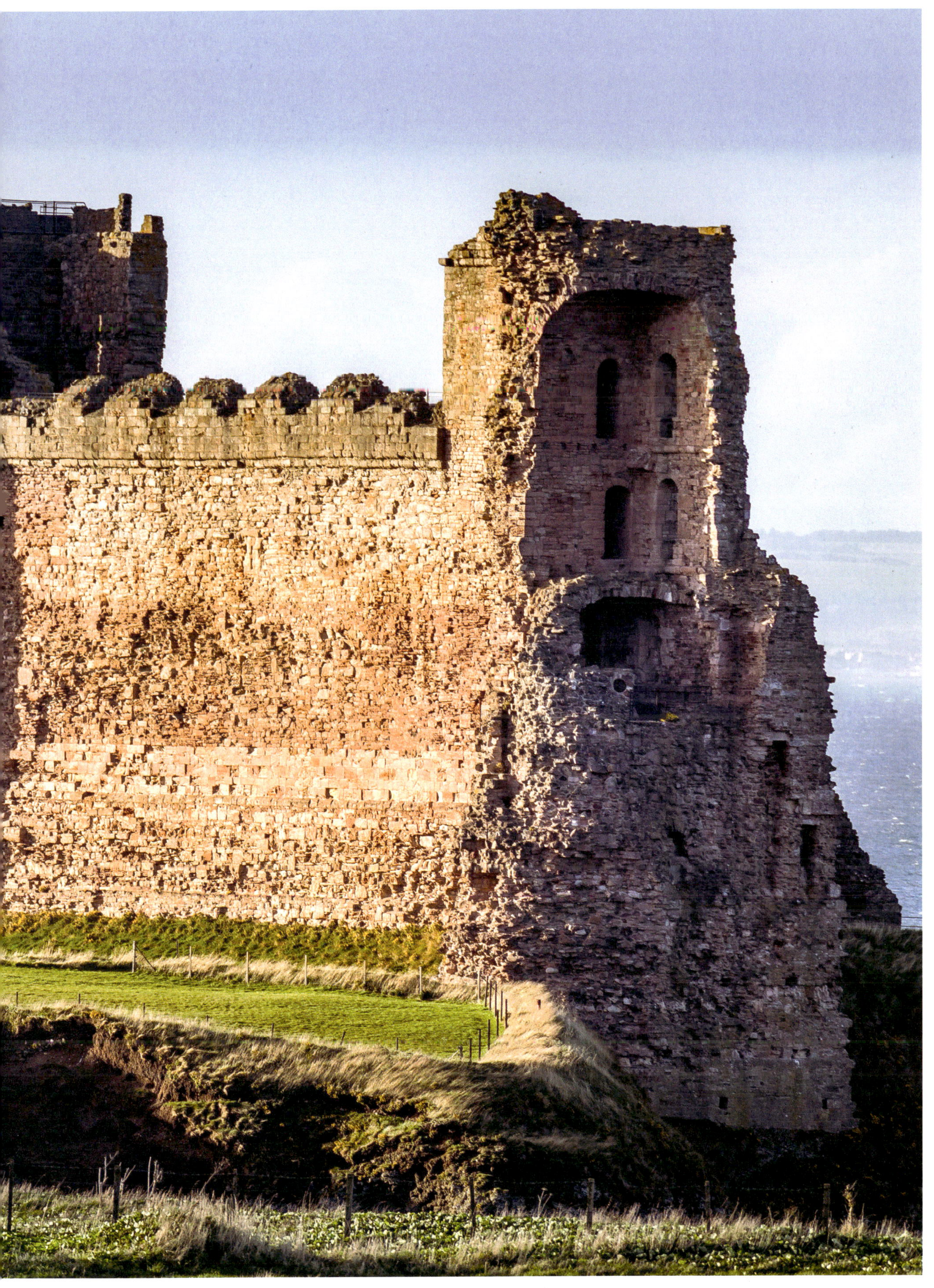

RIGHT:

Castle Tioram, Eilean Tioram Island, Scotland

Castle Tioram stands on the island of Eilean Tioram, on the west coast of Scotland. The original structure was begun in the 13th century, and was extensively updated in the 14th. Wooden buildings were rebuilt in stone, and the outer wall strengthened. The castle was already in poor repair in 1715, when it was badly damaged by fire. This was probably deliberate, to prevent occupation by the enemy.

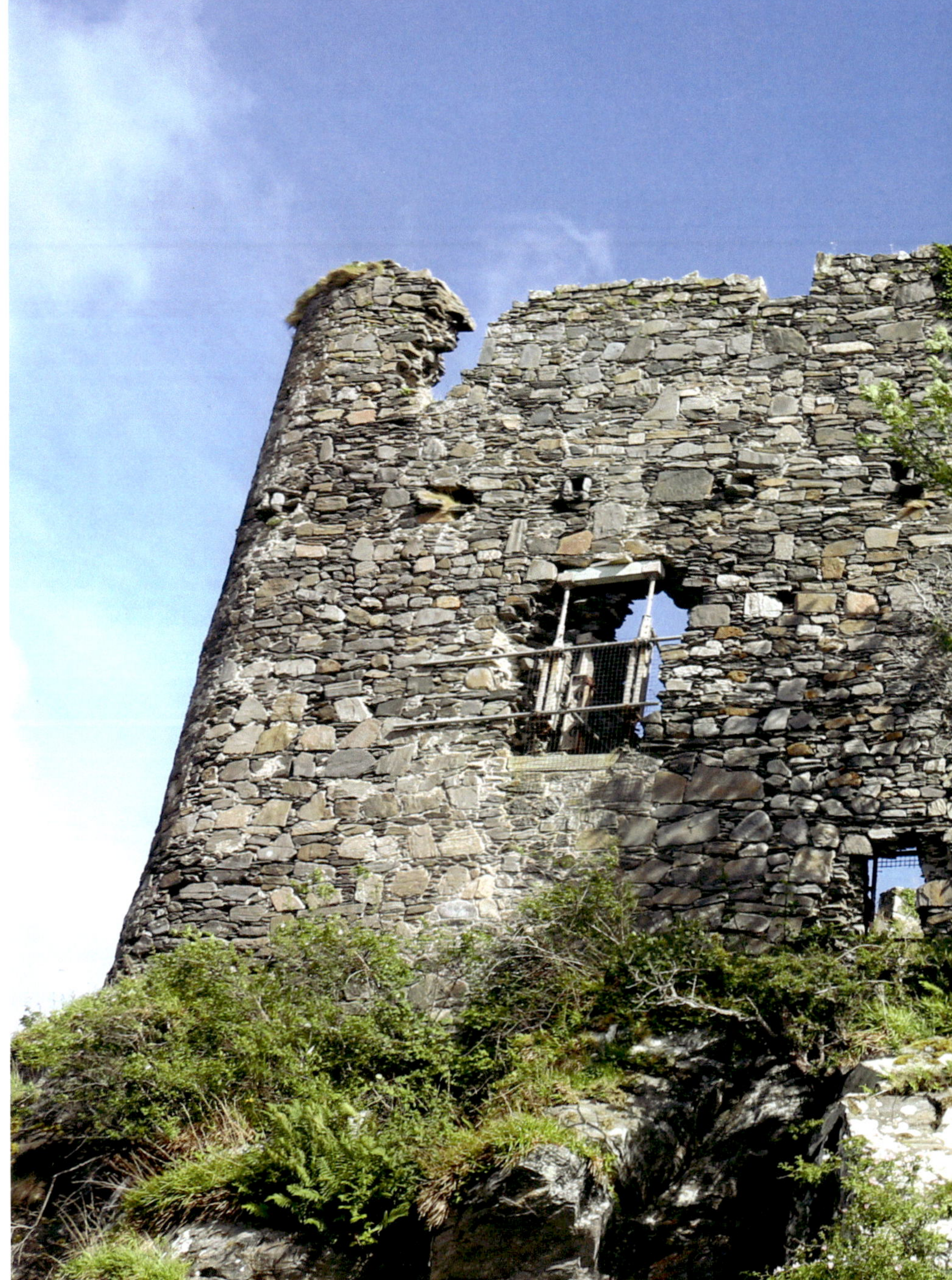

OVERLEAF:

Llawhaden Castle, Pembrokeshire, Wales

Llawhaden Castle was built by the bishops of St David's. The first fortification was of earth and timber, constructed during the 12th century. Rebuilt in stone, the castle evolved into its present form during the 13th and 14th centuries, finally being abandoned after the dissolution of the monasteries in the 16th century.

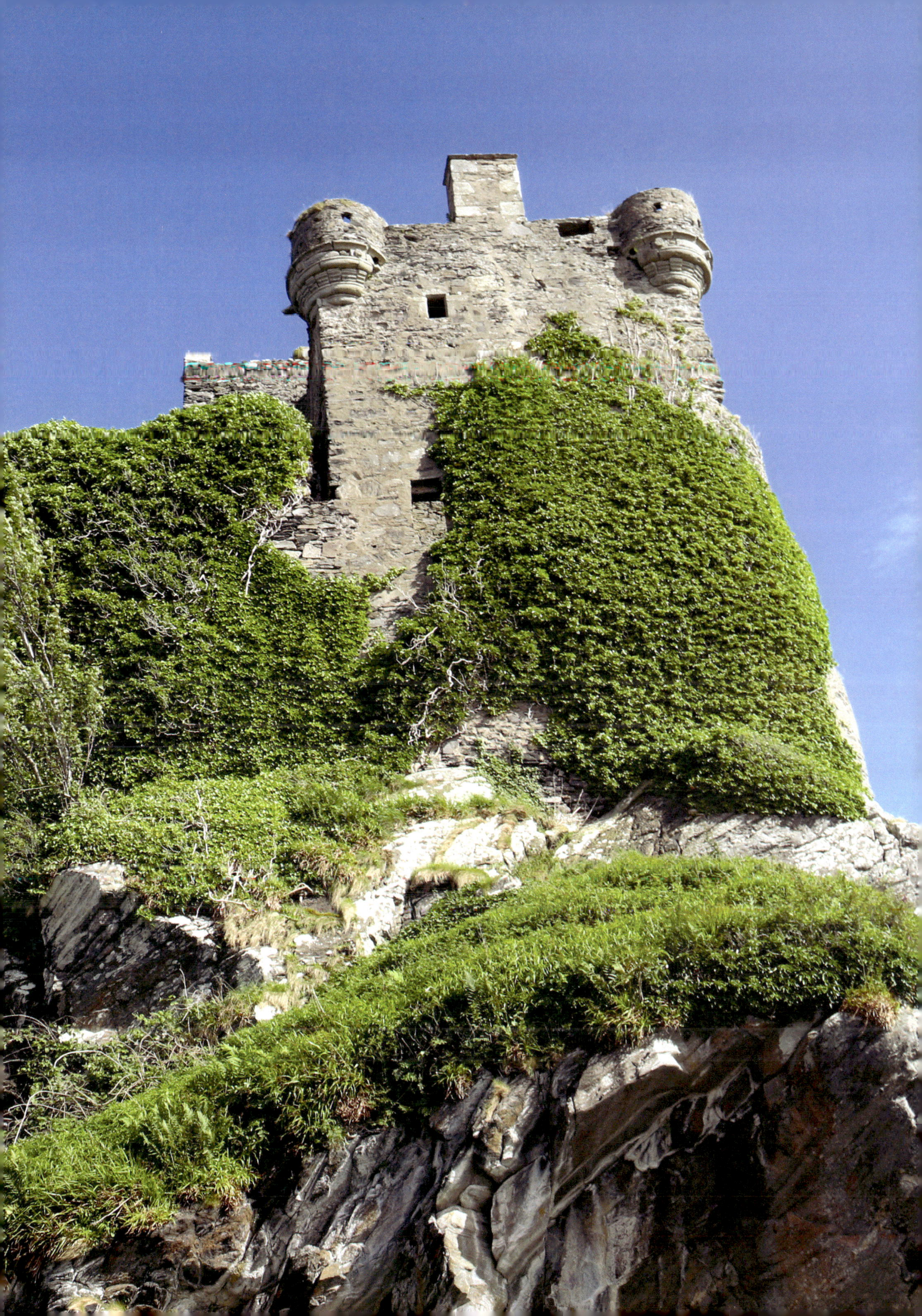

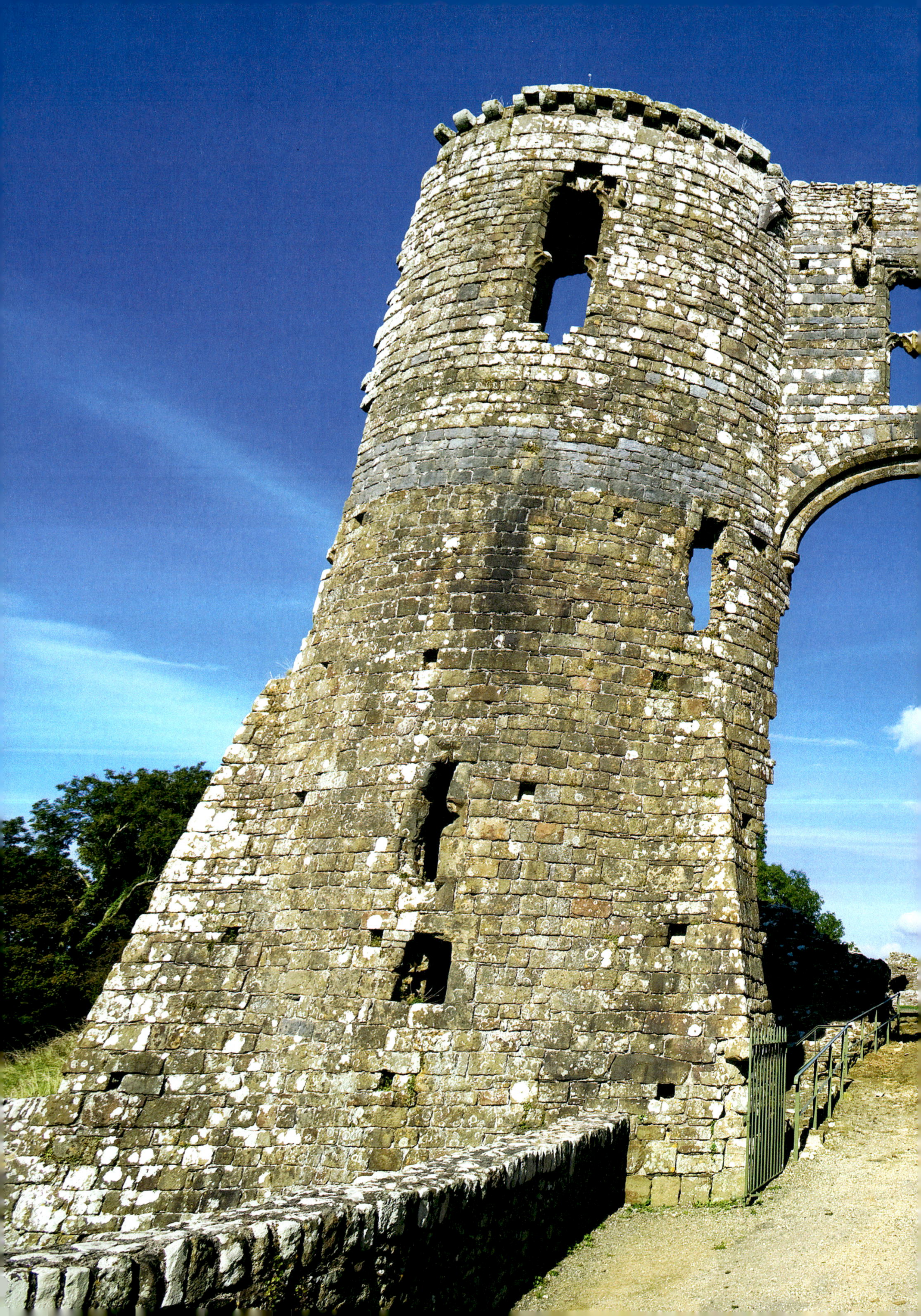

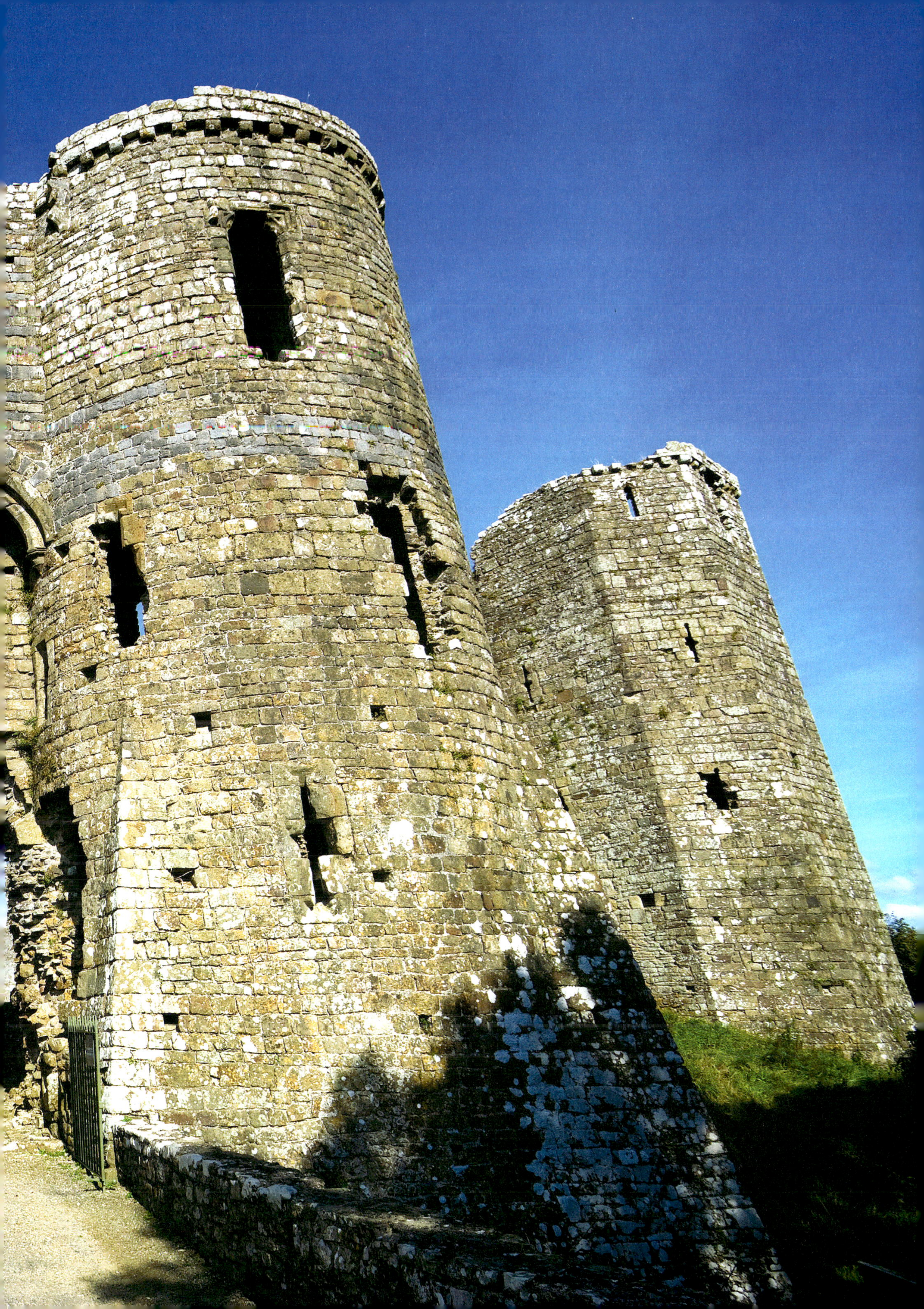

Threave Castle, Dumfries and Galloway, Scotland

Threave Castle, near Castle Douglas, is a tower house built in the late 14th century. It later received upgraded defences, including an artillery house, which did not prevent its fall during the siege of 1455. The castle was again besieged in 1640, this time by Covenanters. The castle was eventually surrendered and its defences partially dismantled.

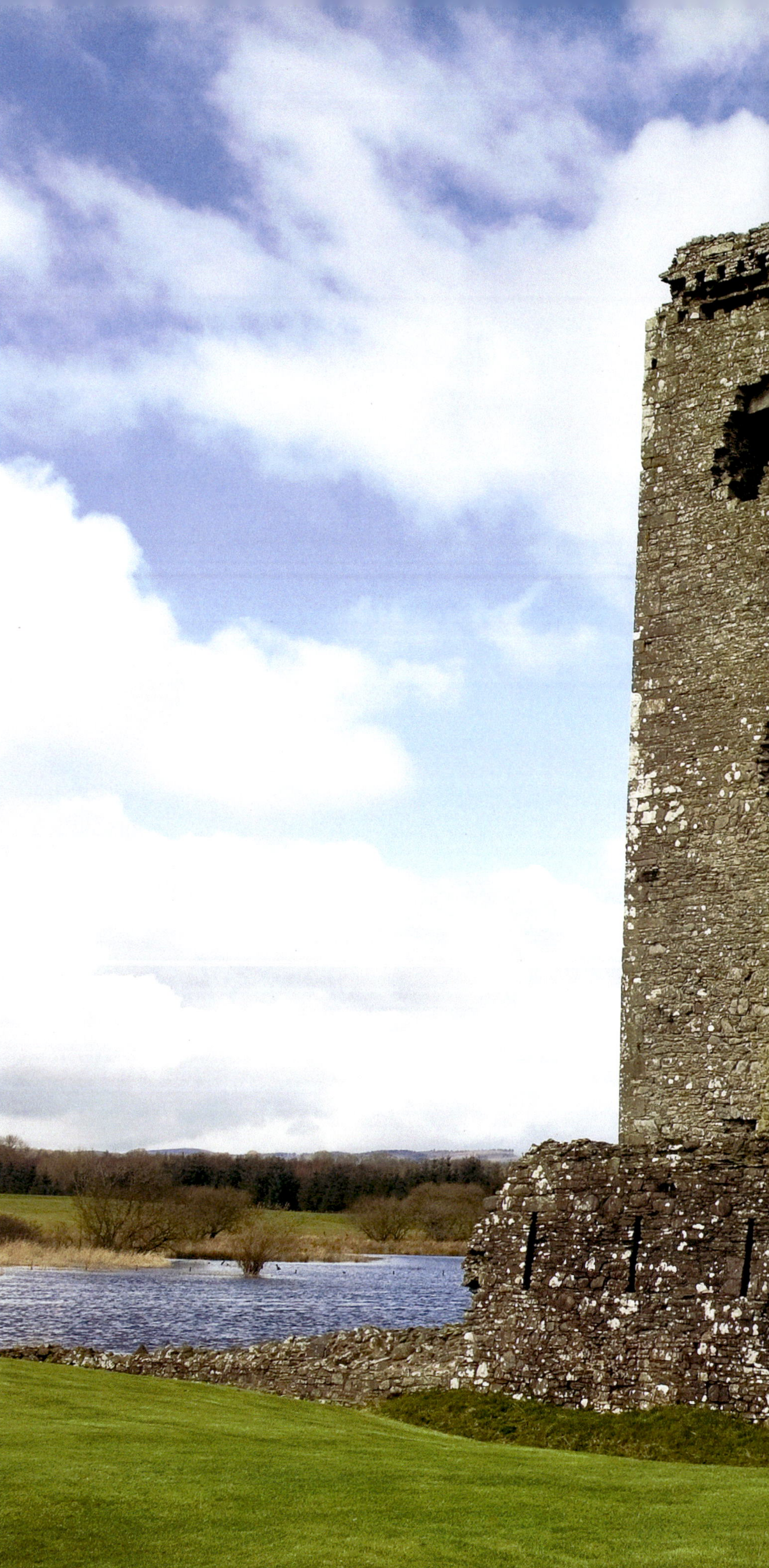

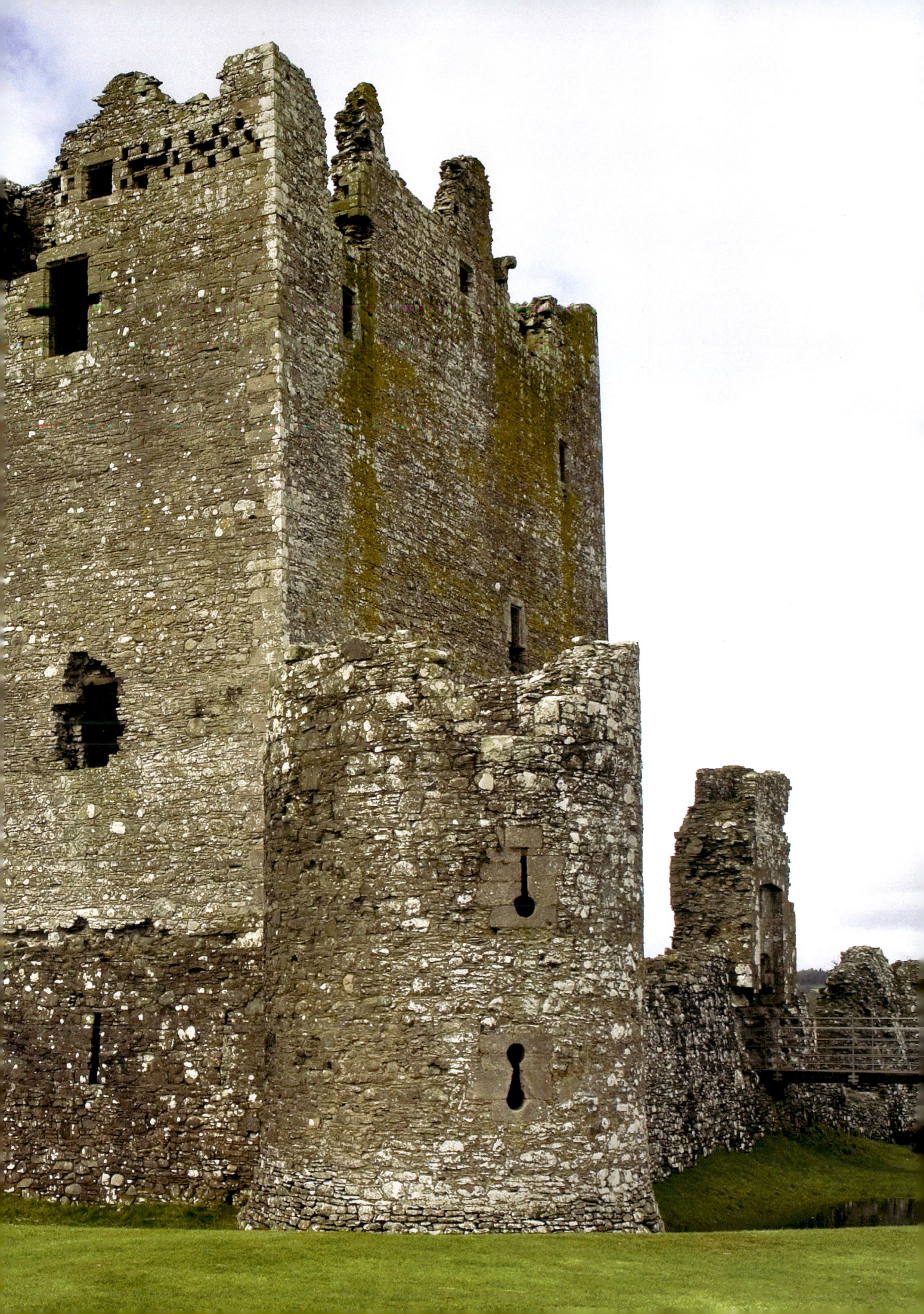

Strome Castle, Highlands of Scotland
Strome Castle, on the shores of Loch Carron in western Scotland, was built as a tower house in the mid-1400s, and had several owners over the next decades. The castle was in MacDonald hands in 1602 when it was besieged by the Mackenzies. The siege was on the point of failure when an unfortunate incident occurred involving well water being poured on the gunpowder supply and an escaped prisoner who knew about it. The garrison surrendered and the Mackenzies blew up the defences – presumably with their own, dry gunpowder.

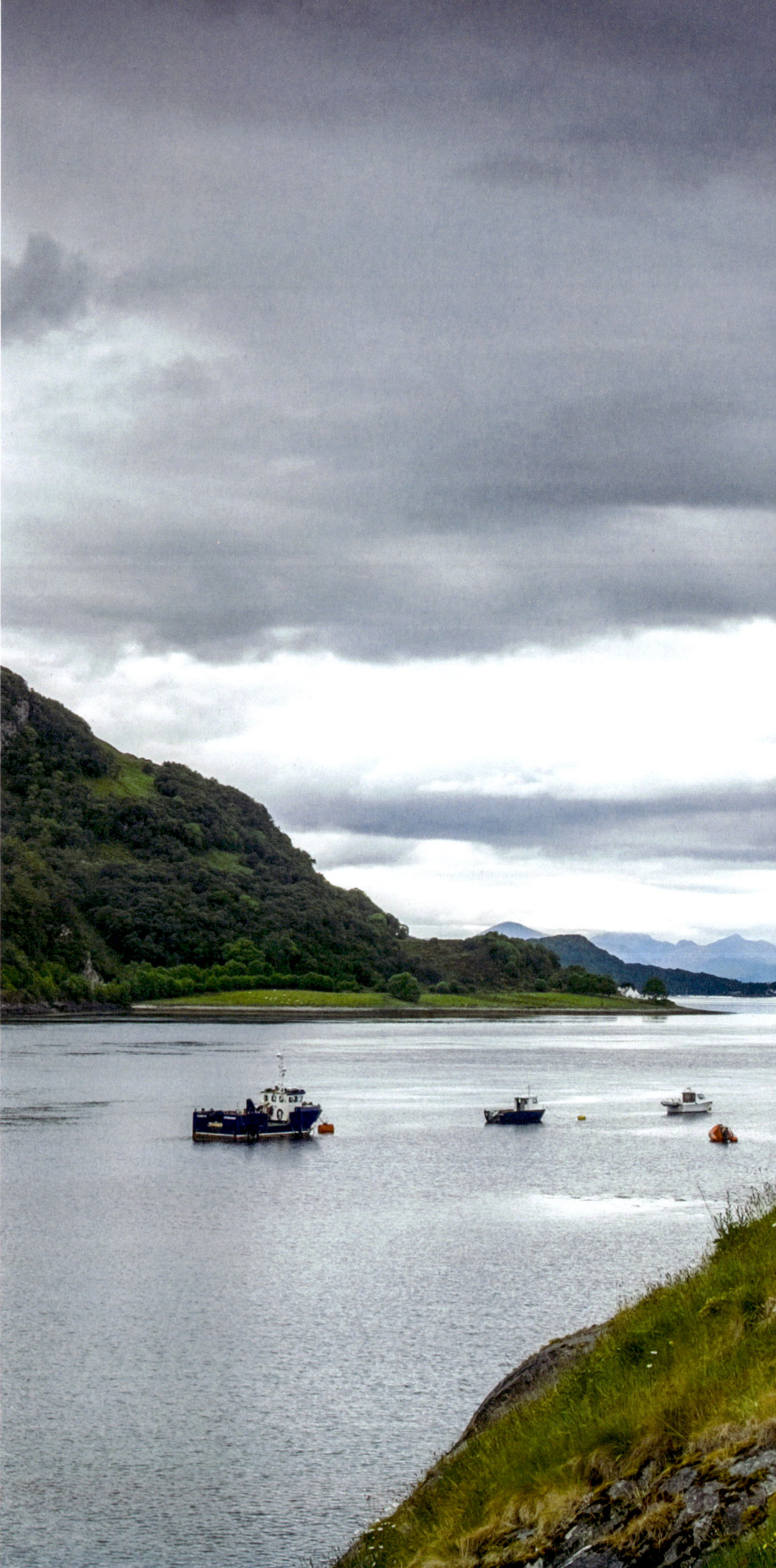

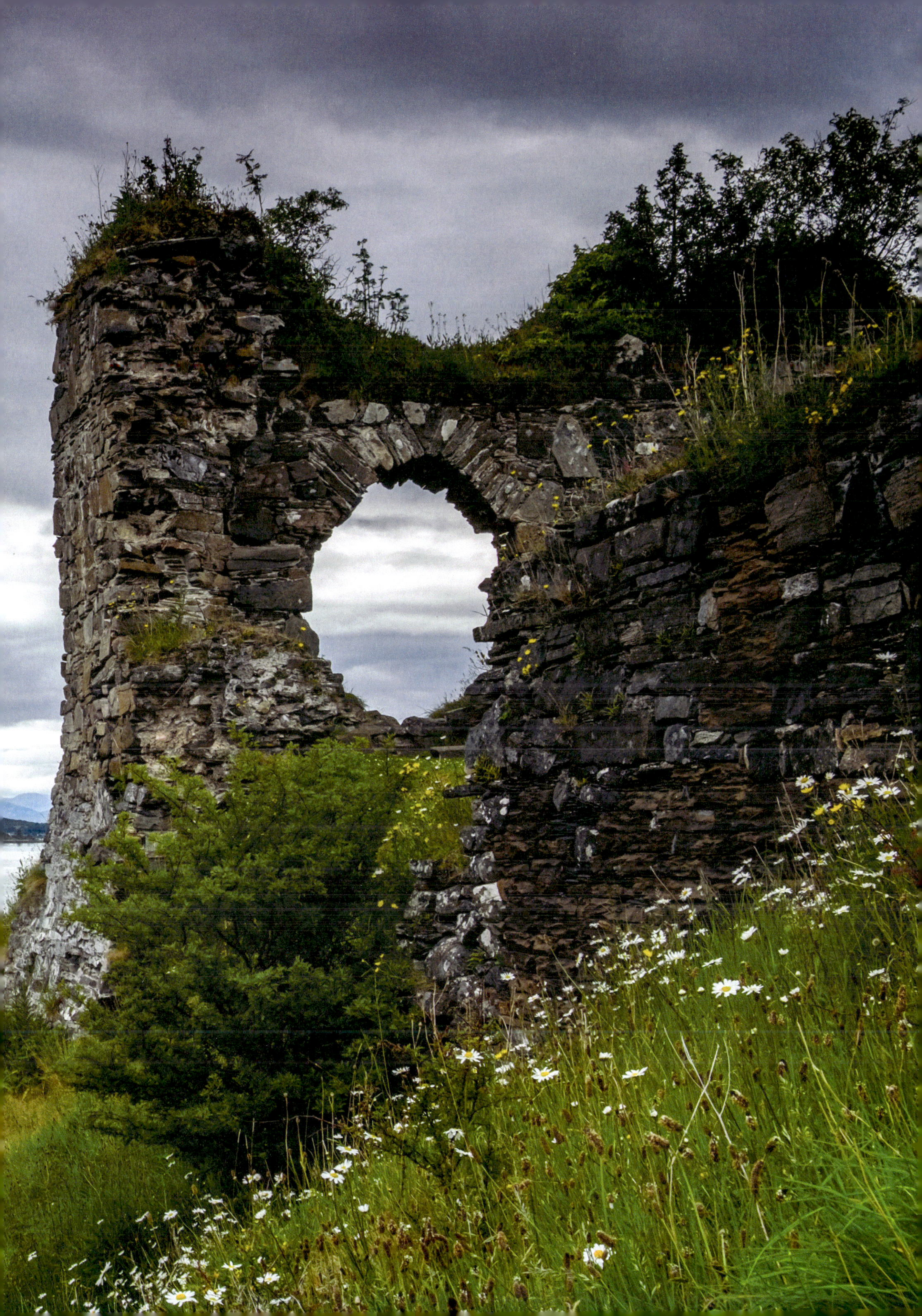

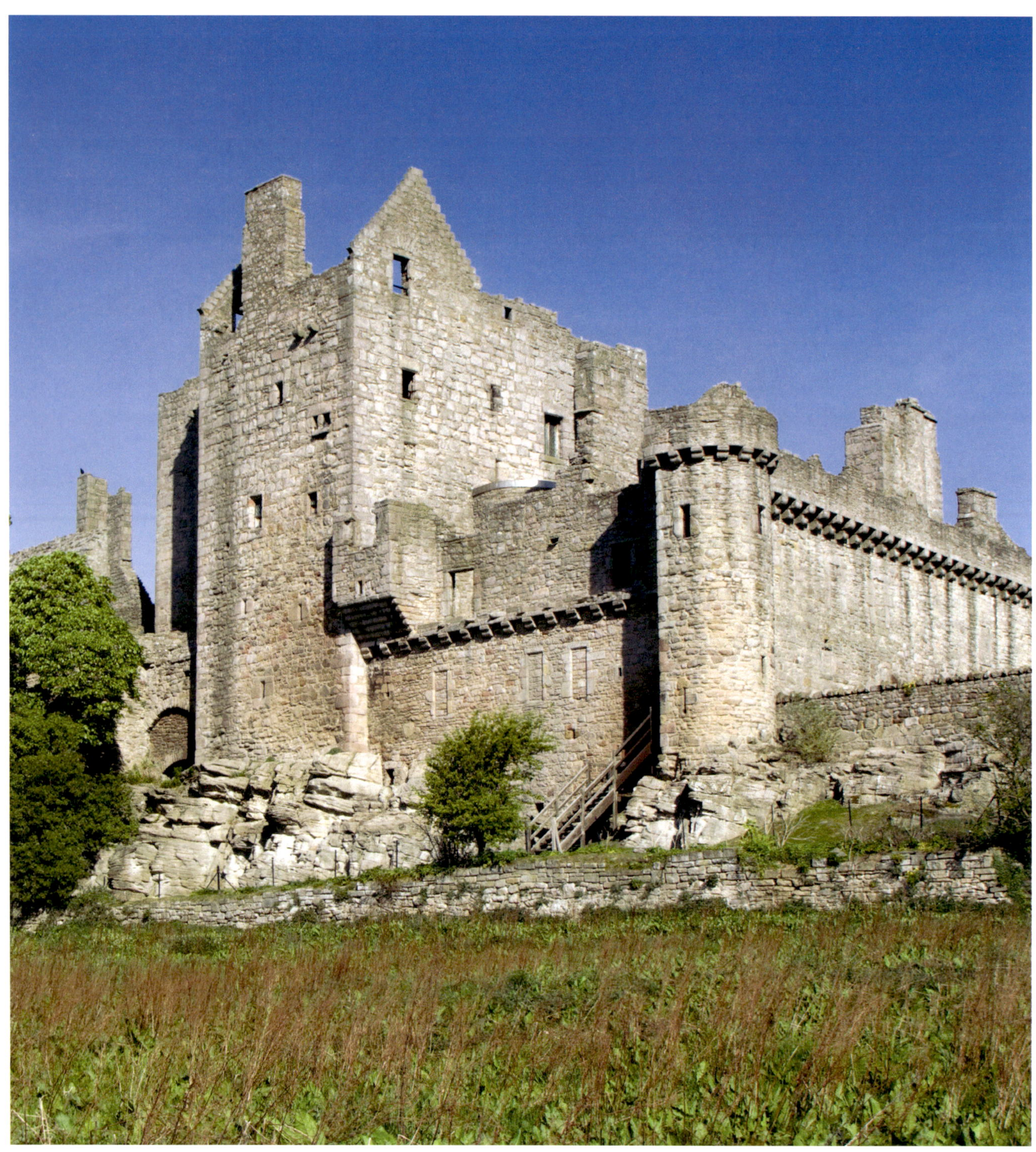

ABOVE AND RIGHT:

Craigmillar Castle, Edinburgh, Scotland

Craigmillar Castle was begun in the late 1300s, with work continuing for the next two centuries. It is best known for its association with Mary, Queen of Scots, who stayed there in 1563 and 1566. It was here that the plot to eliminate Mary's husband, Lord Darnley, was agreed.

Craigmillar Castle was burned by the English in 1544 and later restored. In 1572 it was used as a base for the siege of Edinburgh Castle, which was at the time in the hands of supporters of Mary, Queen of Scots. The castle was kept in good repair and is well preserved today.

OVERLEAF:

Craigmillar Castle, Edinburgh, Scotland

Craigmillar Castle was built as a four-storey tower house with access granted by this spiral staircase. The tower house dates from the late 14th century and is the oldest part of the castle. Some buildings were added as late as the 17th century.

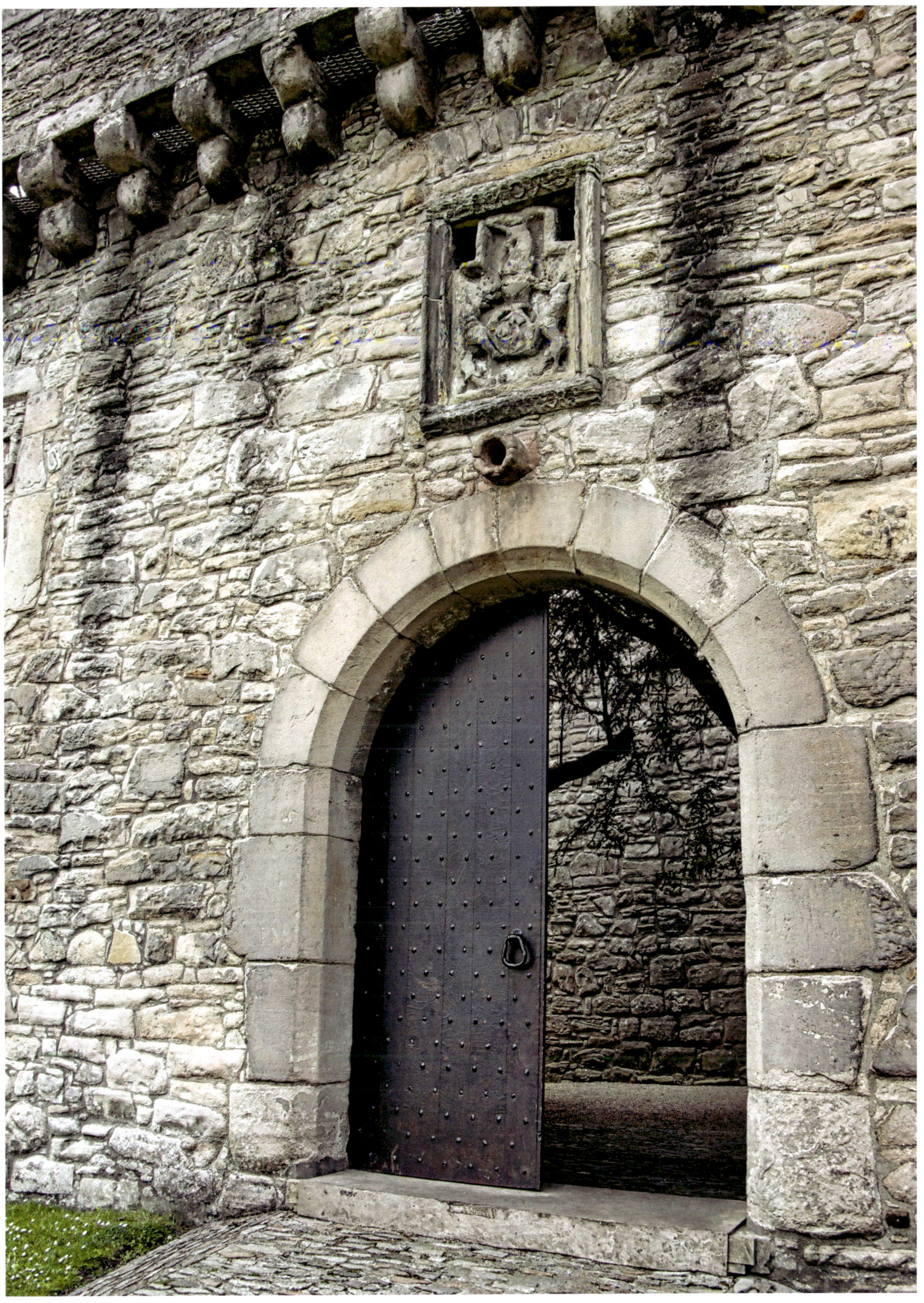

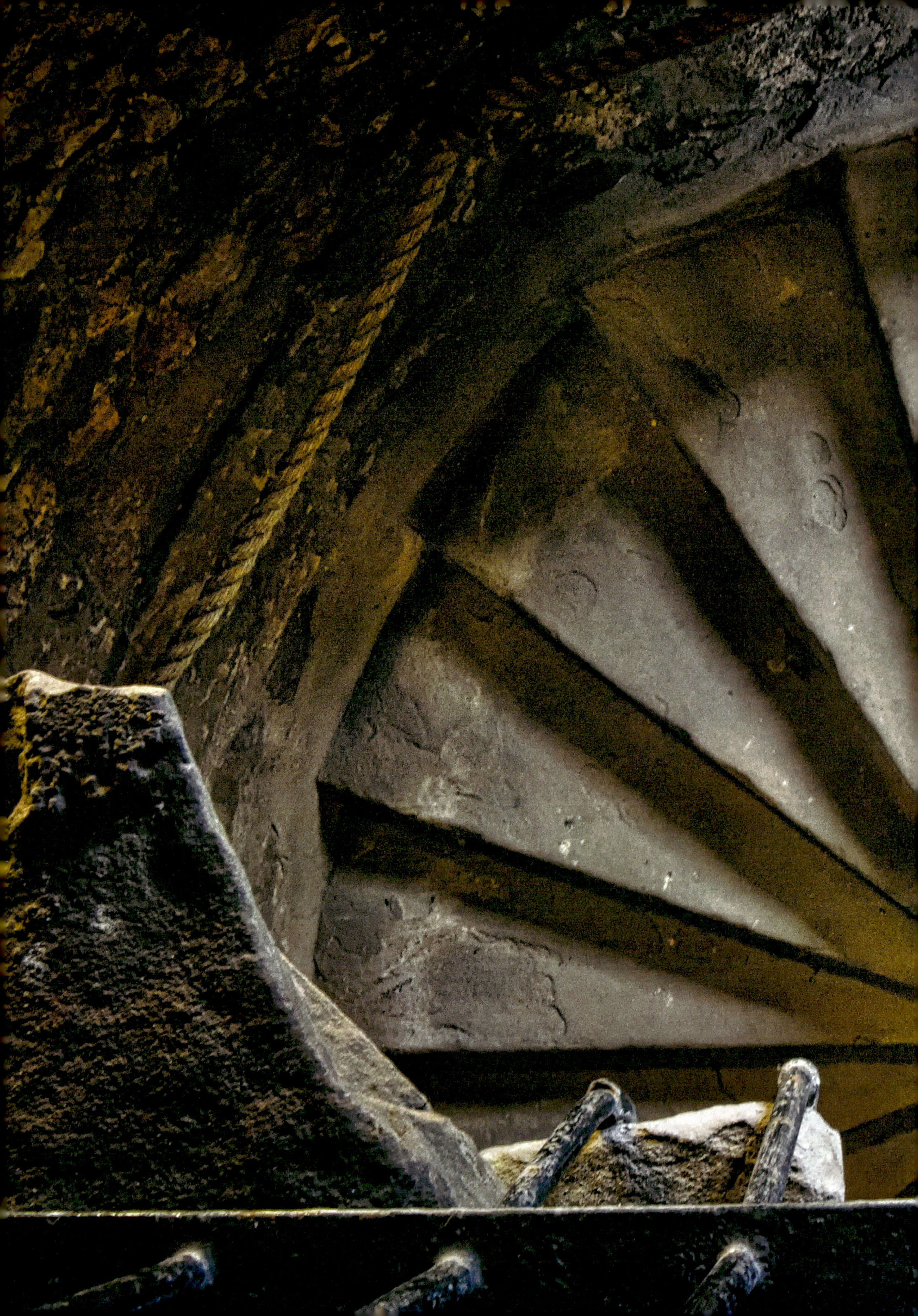

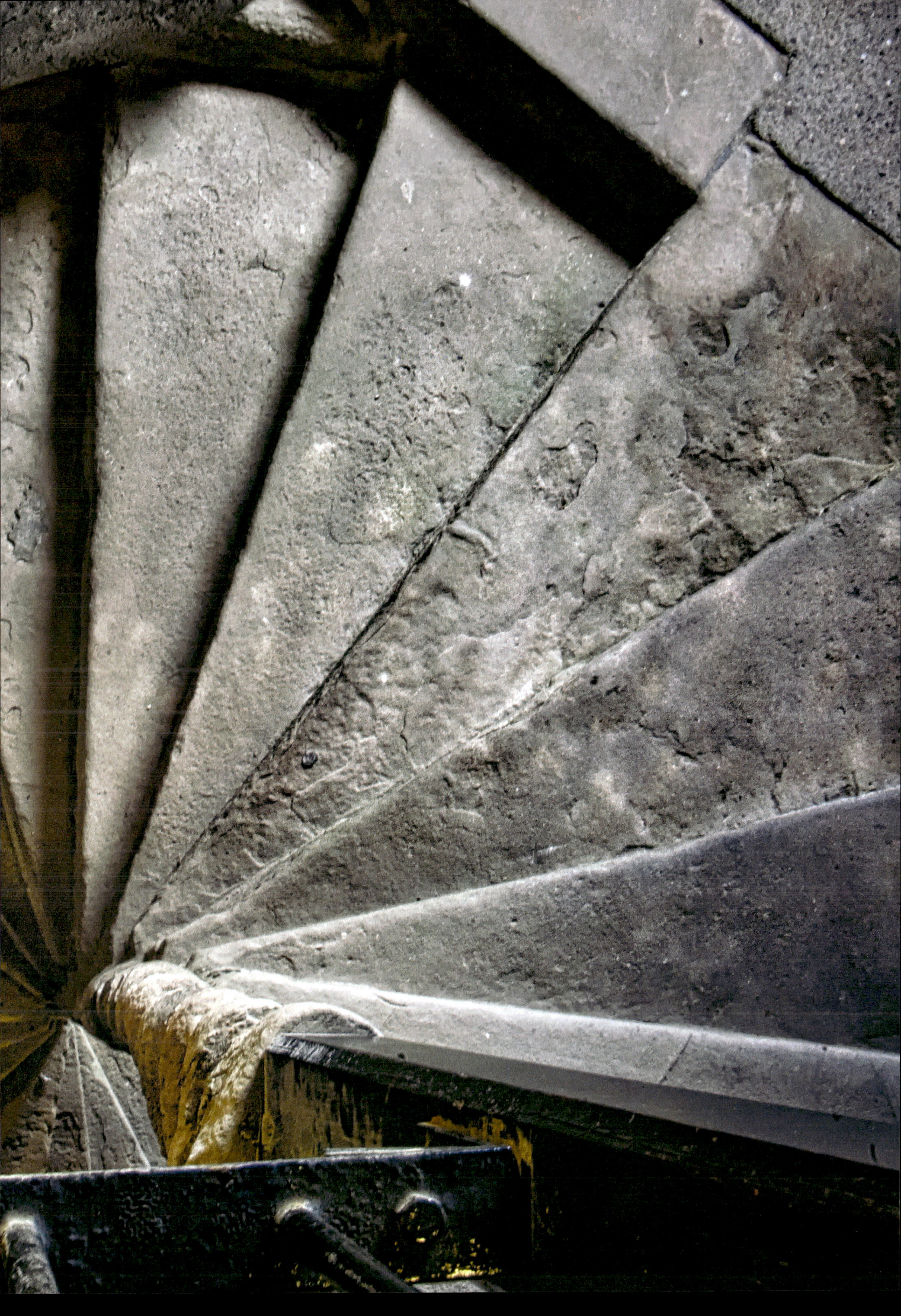

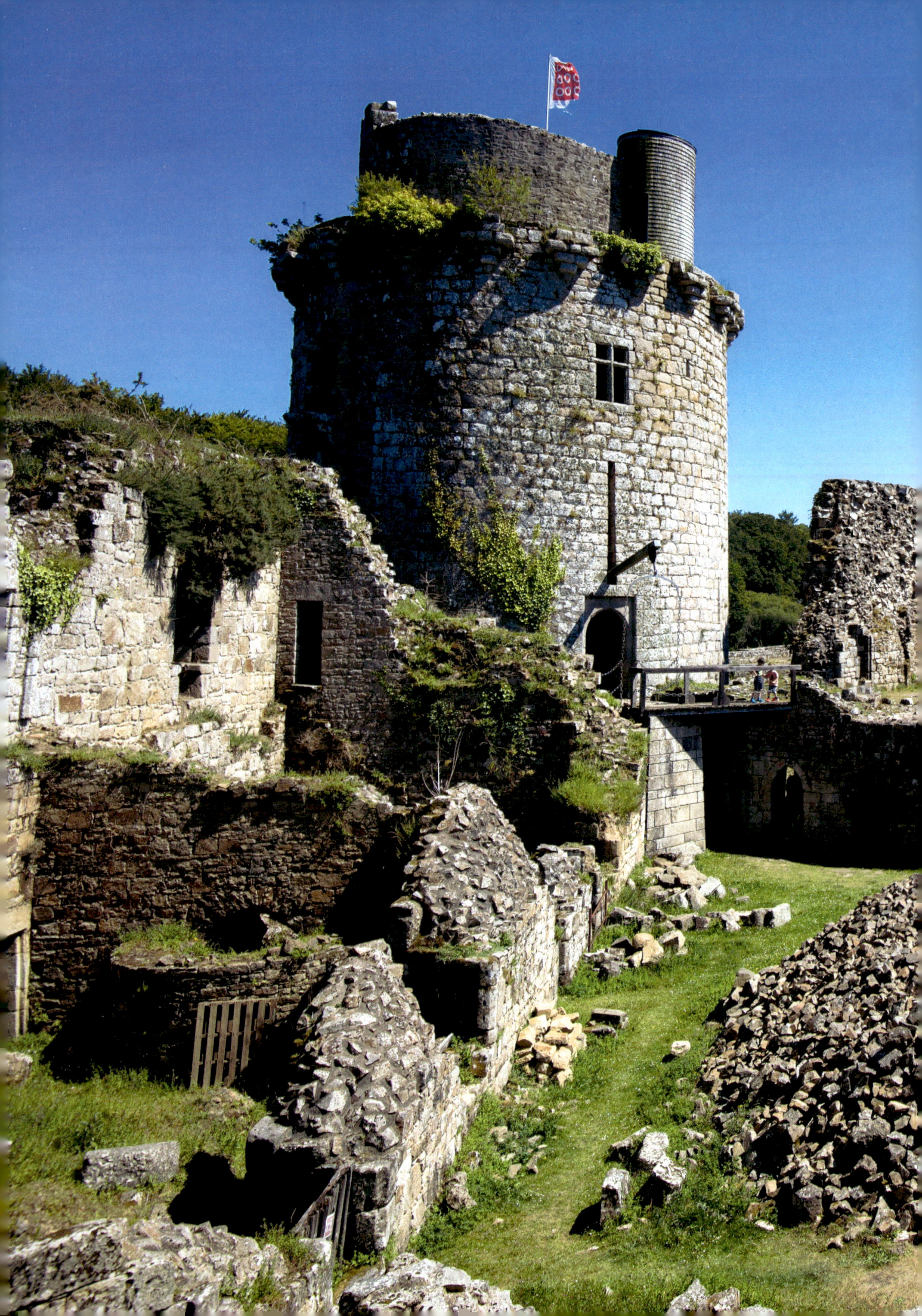

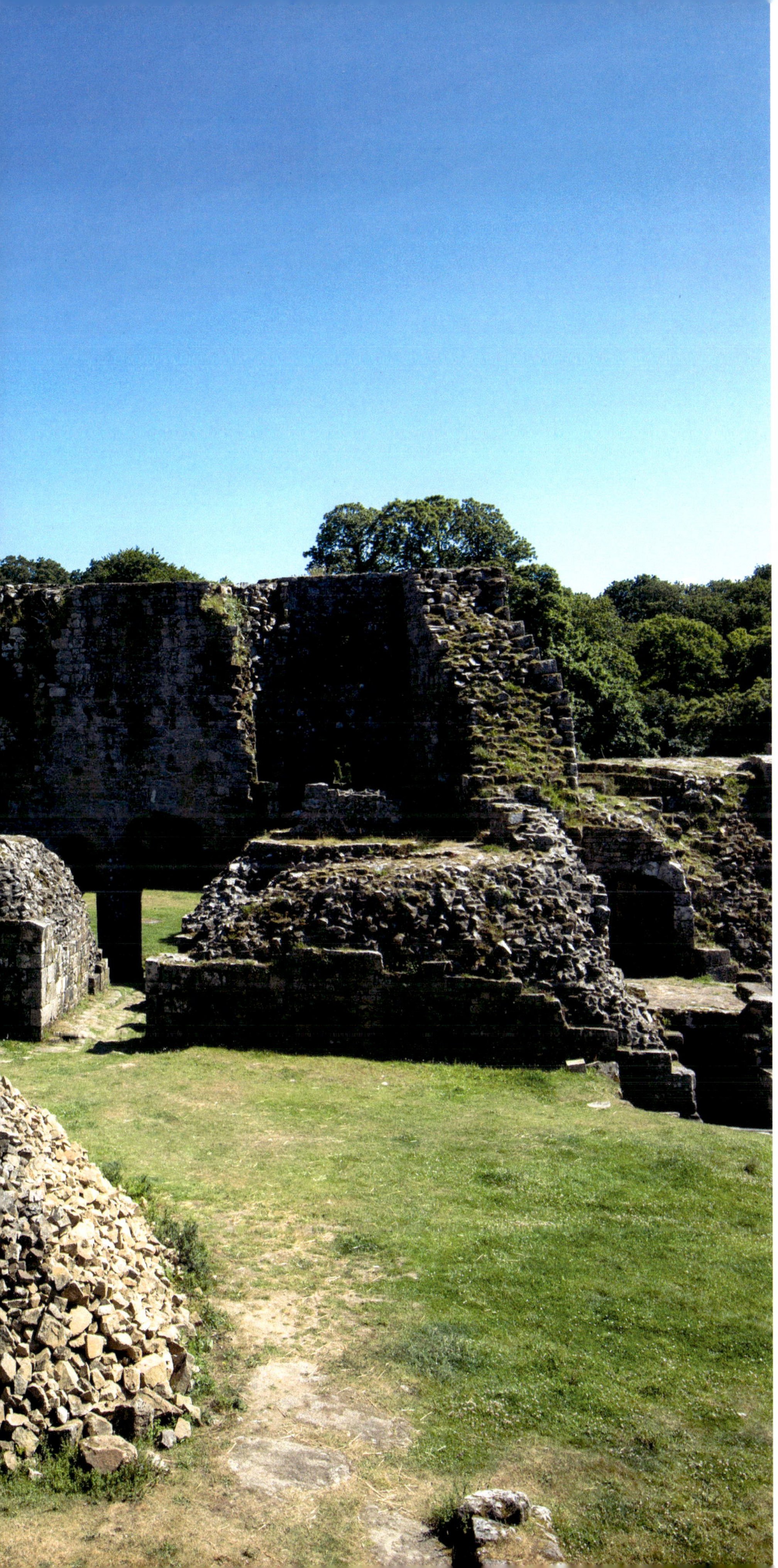

Château de Tonquédec, Brittany, France

Château de Tonquédec was built in the 15th century. An earlier castle stood on the site, dating from the 12th century, but was abandoned for political reasons. After reconstruction beginning in 1406, the castle was updated over the next two centuries before once again being dismantled in the early 1600s.

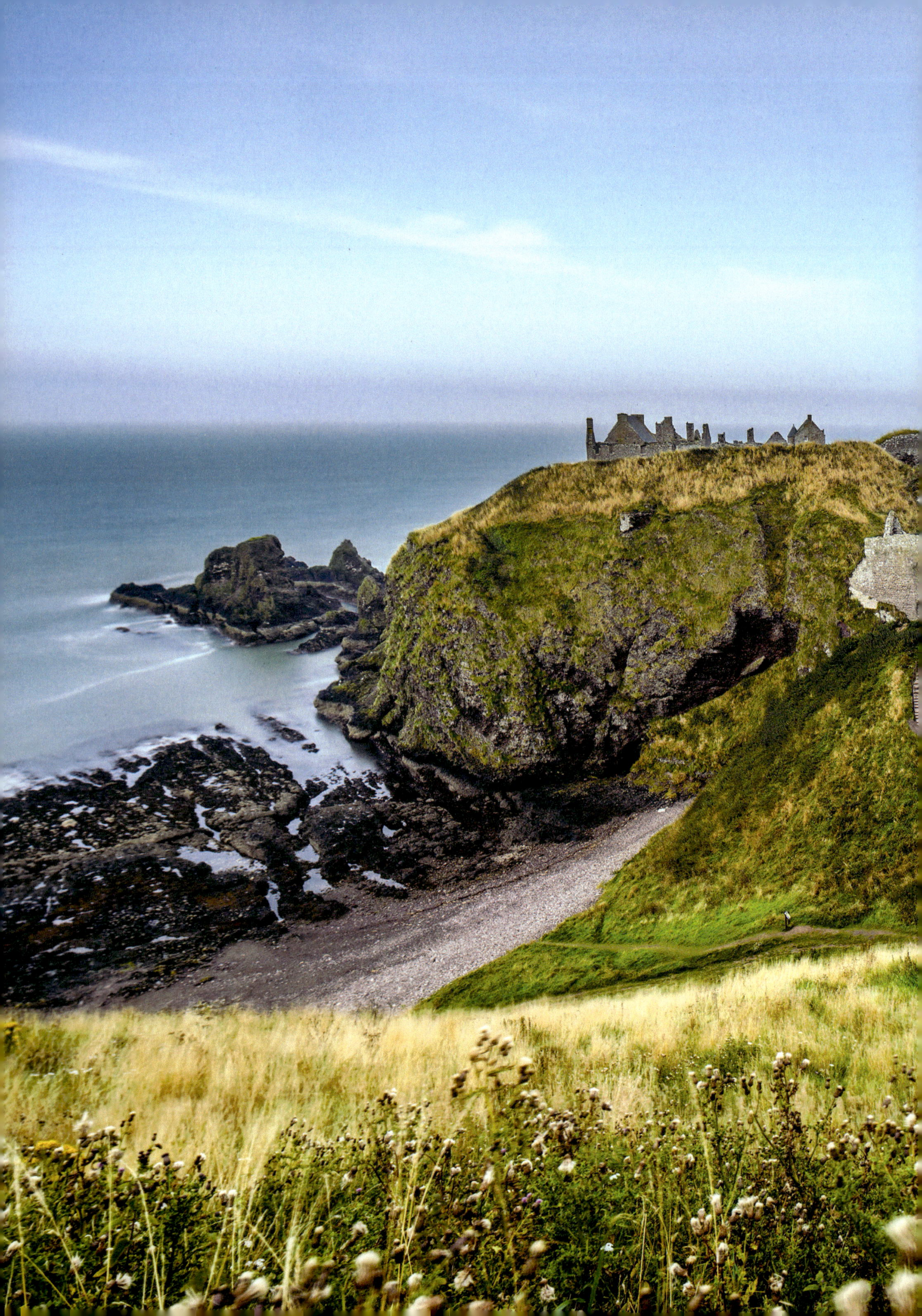

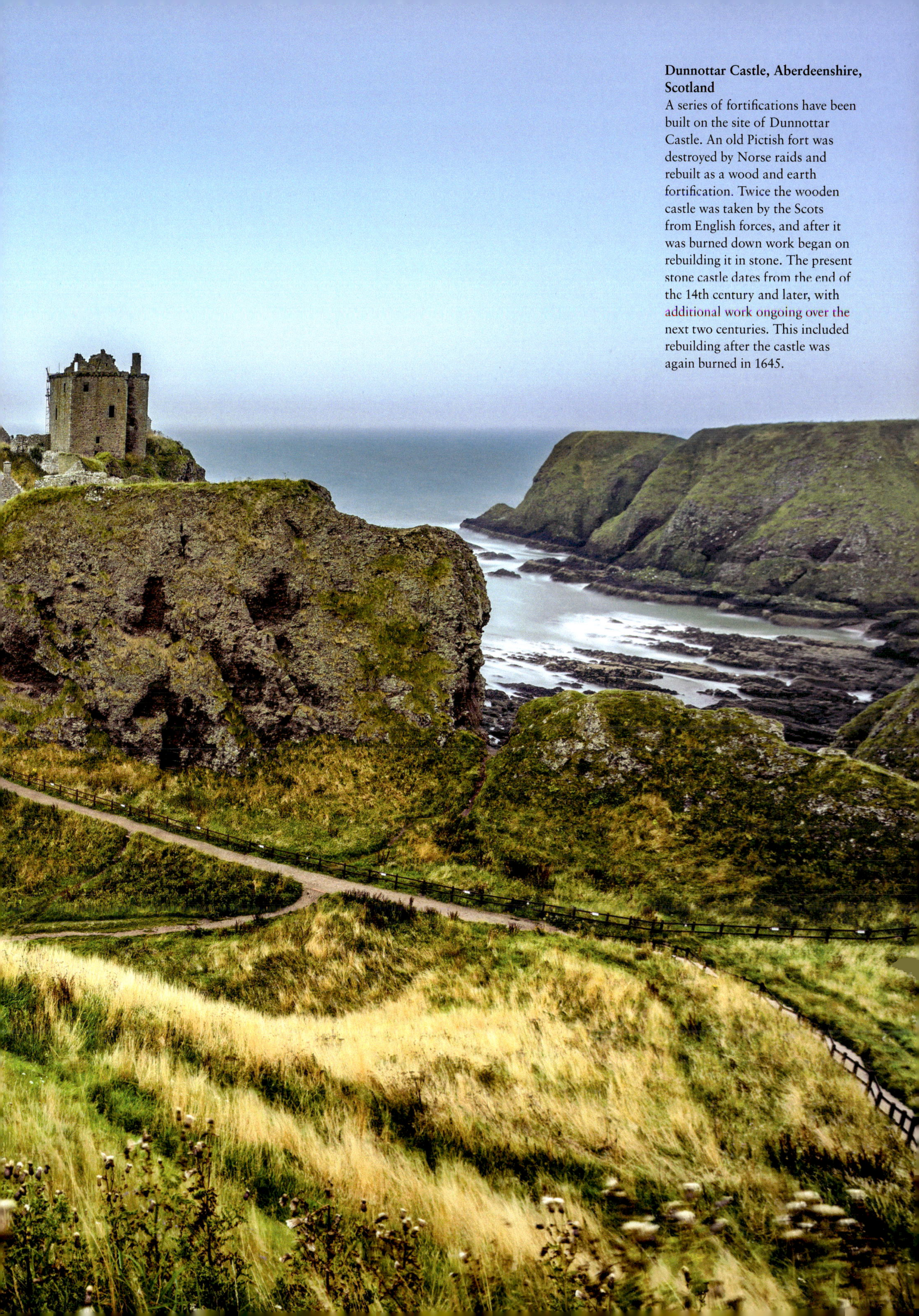

Dunnottar Castle, Aberdeenshire, Scotland
A series of fortifications have been built on the site of Dunnottar Castle. An old Pictish fort was destroyed by Norse raids and rebuilt as a wood and earth fortification. Twice the wooden castle was taken by the Scots from English forces, and after it was burned down work began on rebuilding it in stone. The present stone castle dates from the end of the 14th century and later, with additional work ongoing over the next two centuries. This included rebuilding after the castle was again burned in 1645.

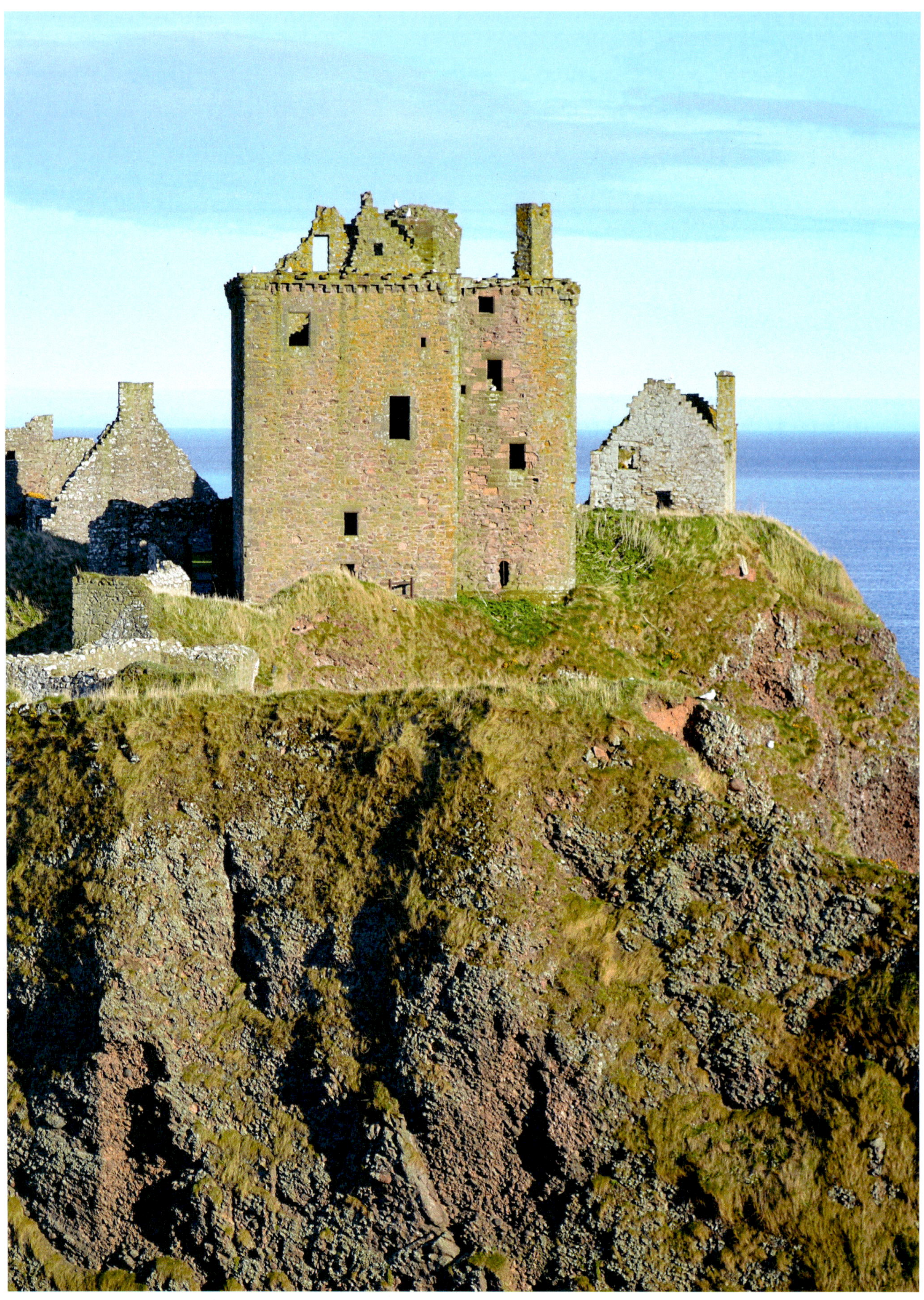

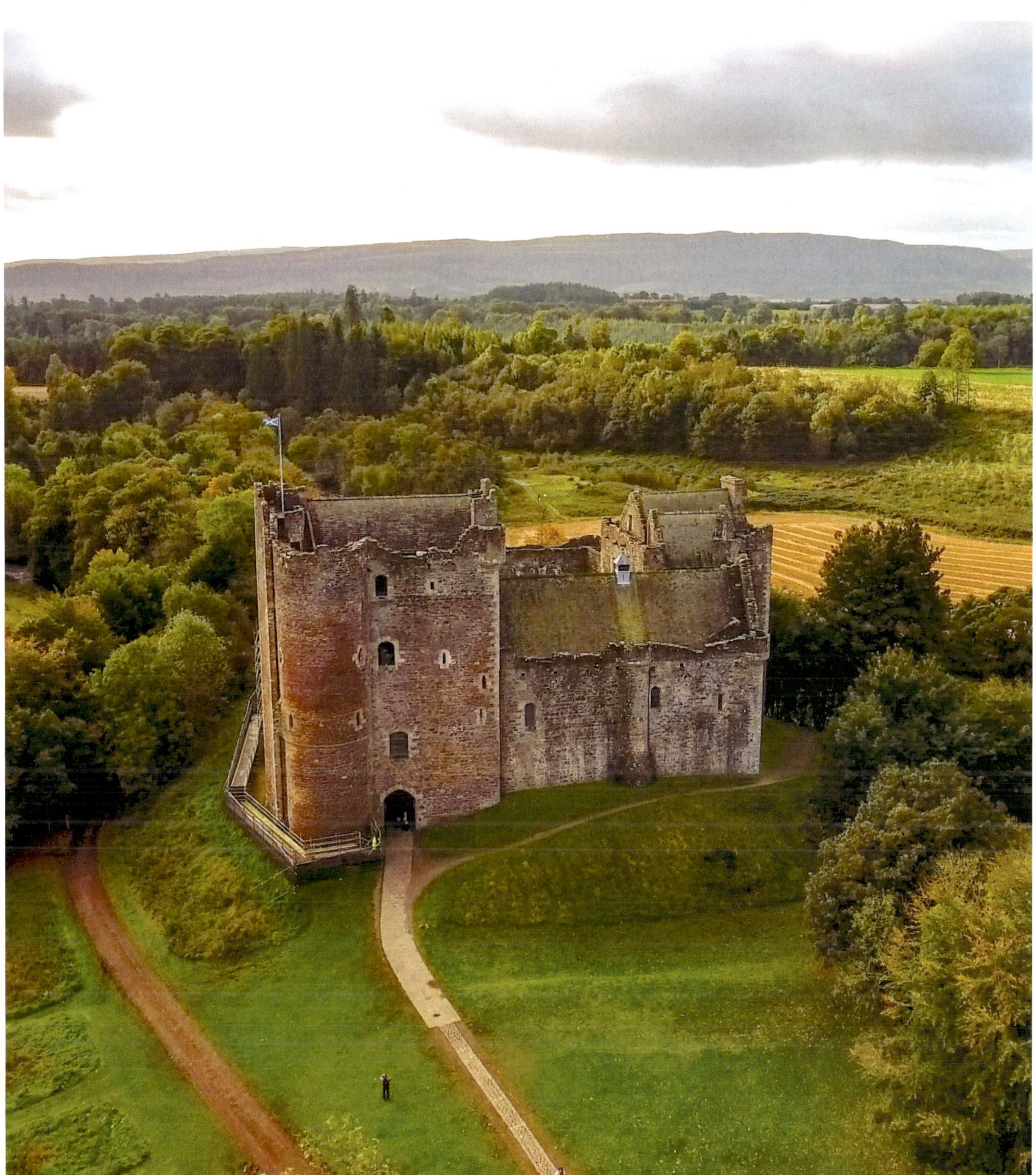

LEFT:
Dunnottar Castle, Aberdeenshire, Scotland
Dunnottar Castle is famous for hosting the Honours of Scotland while Edinburgh was in the hands of Oliver Cromwell. The castle was besieged in 1651–52, finally surrendering after many months. During the siege, the Honours were sneaked out to avoid capture by Cromwell's forces.

ABOVE:
Doune Castle, Stirlingshire, Scotland
Doune Castle near Stirling was originally built in the 13th century. The present structure resulted from rebuilding work in the late 14th century and has seen relatively little alteration since, although repair work was undertaken in the late 1500s and again in the 1800s.

OVERLEAF:
Duntulm Castle, Isle of Skye, Scotland
Duntulm Castle was built on the site of an earlier fortification built by the Picts and later taken over by invading Norsemen. Work began on the stone castle in the 14th century, with additional works over the next 200 years including an extra defensive tower. Duntulm Castle was abandoned in the early 1700s.

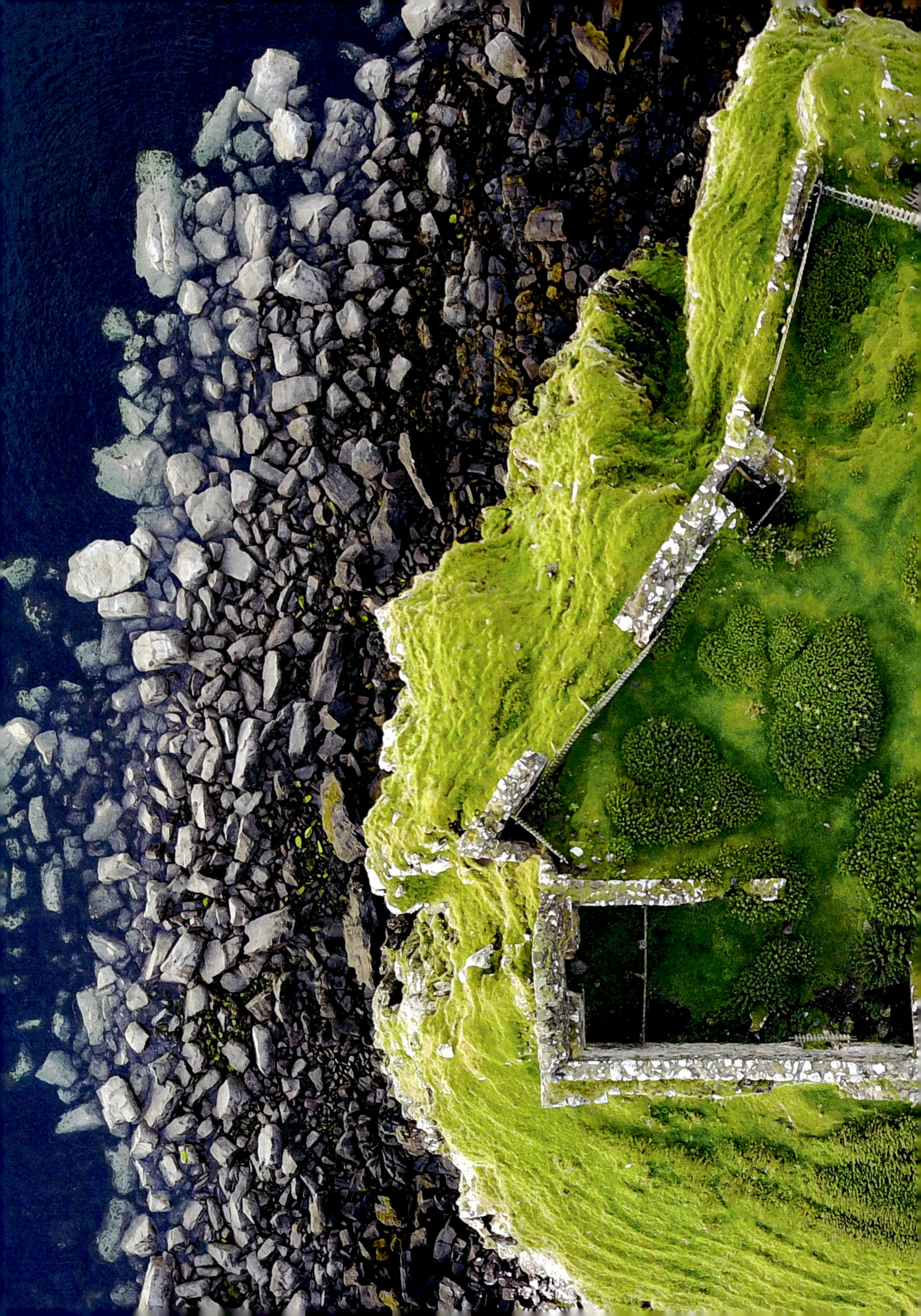

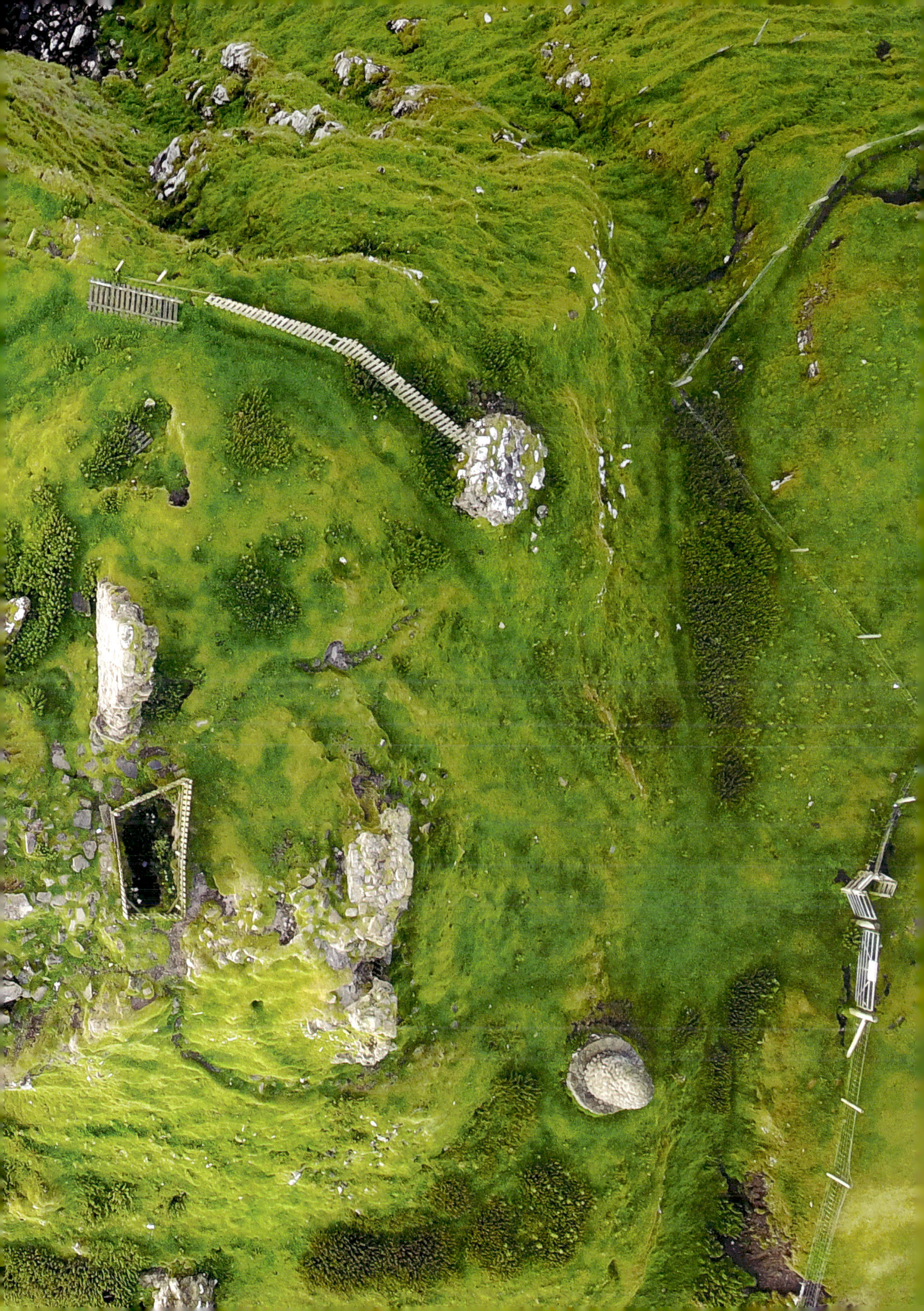

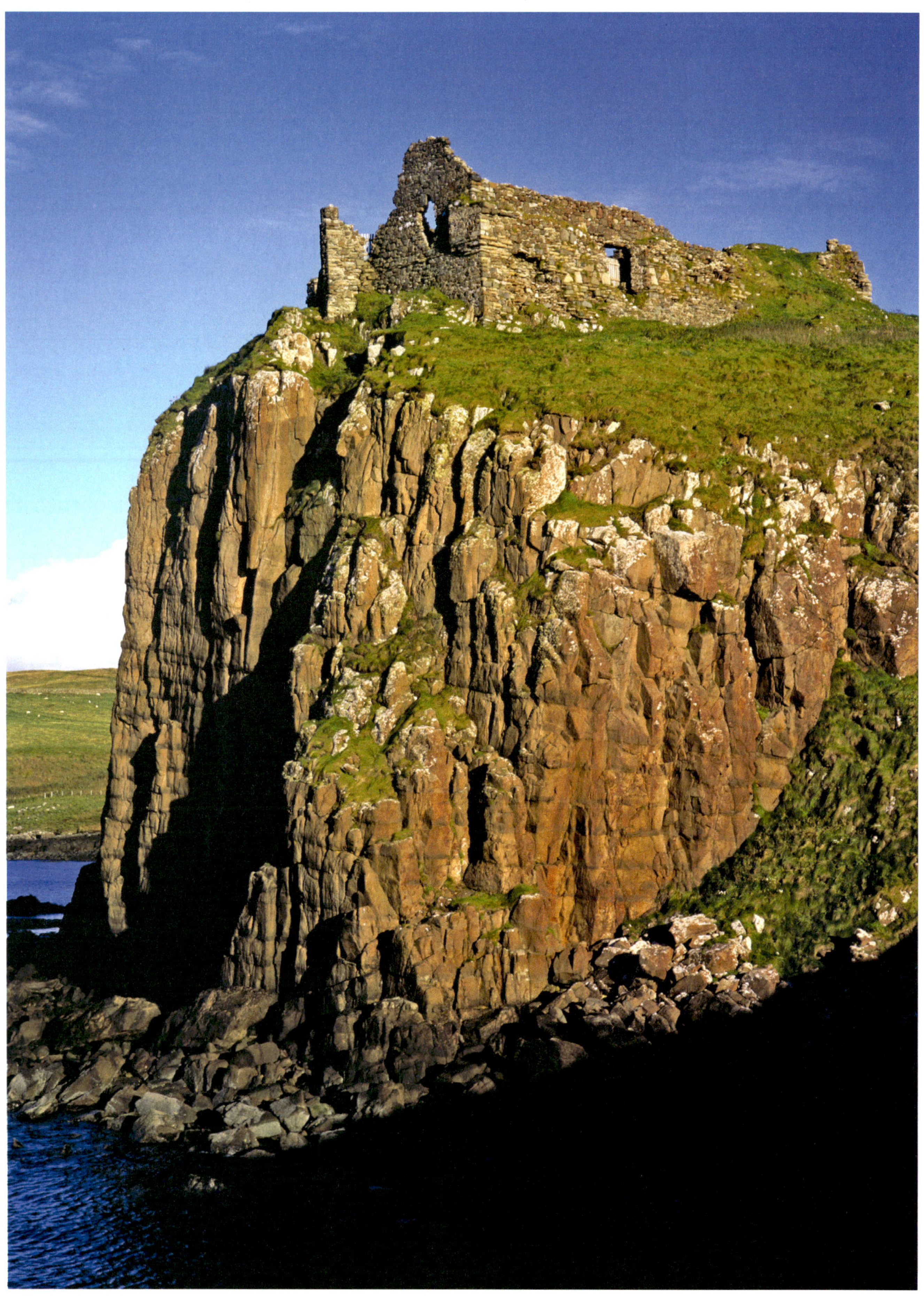

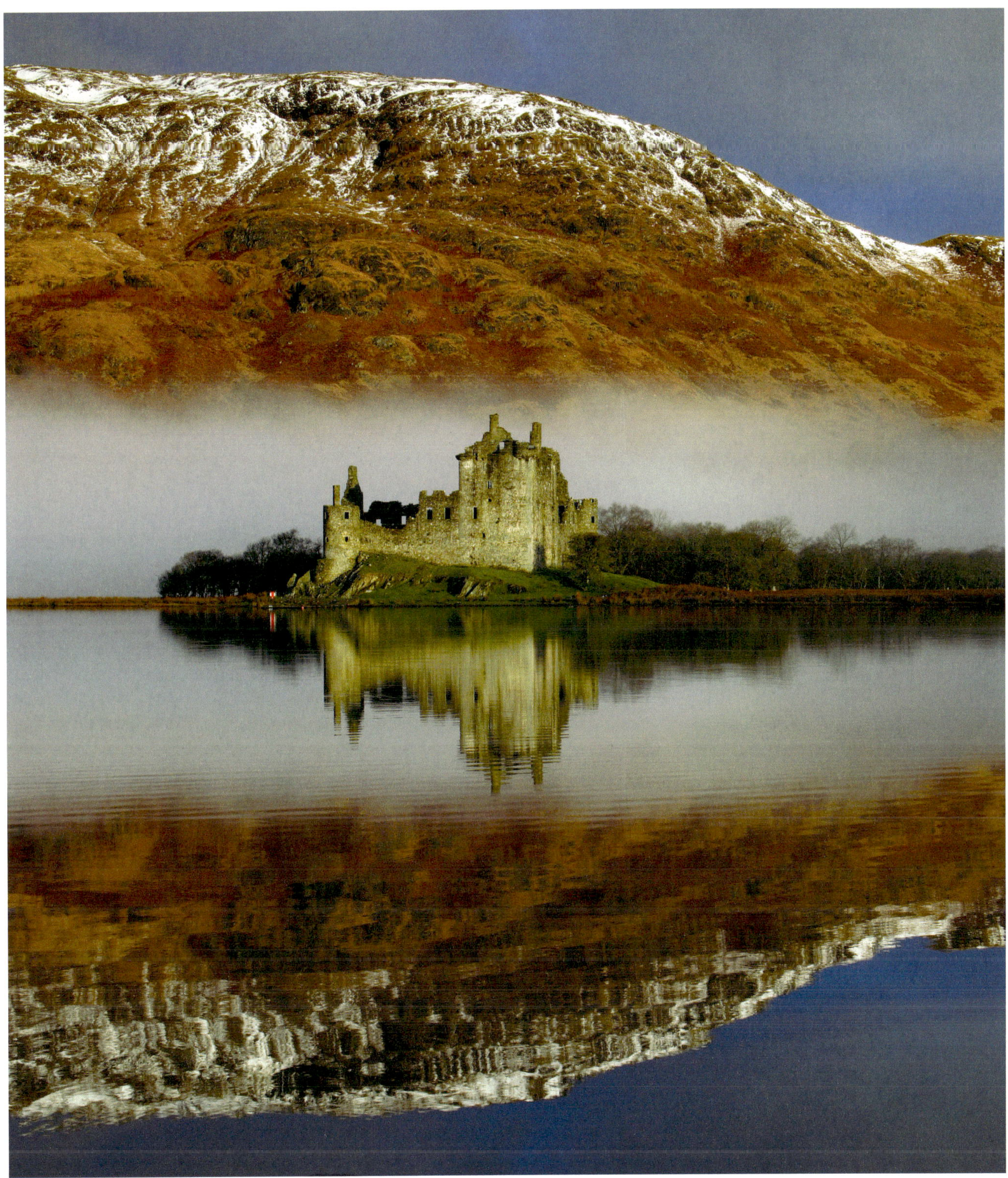

LEFT:
Duntulm Castle, Isle of Skye, Scotland
Duntulum Castle occupies an excellent defensive location, protected by sea cliffs on most sides and a ditch on the only landward approach. The four-storey tower, now collapsed, and the walls were constructed of local basalt.

ABOVE AND OVERLEAF:
Kilchurn Castle, Argyll and Bute, Scotland
Kilchurn Castle was constructed on an island in Loch Awe, though today the site is connected to the mainland. Work began around 1440 on the five-storey keep, with some later remodelling and additional buildings added over the next two centuries. In the late 1600s, additional structures were added to Kilchurn Castle, creating a barracks for 200 troops. Kilchurn was garrisoned by loyalist forces during the uprisings of 1715 and 1745, but had been eclipsed by other, more recent, fortifications in the area. The castle was abandoned in 1760 after suffering severe storm damage.

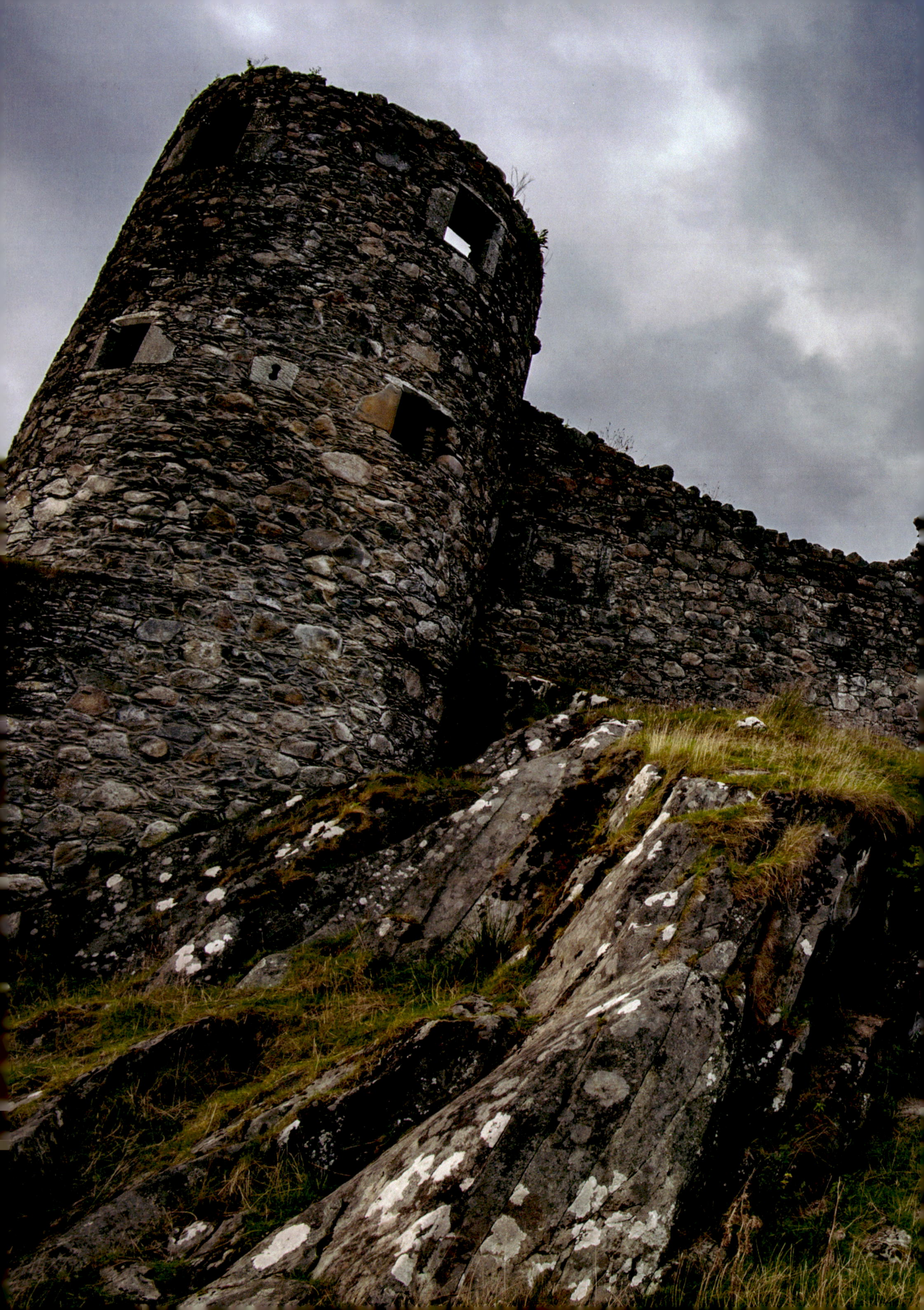

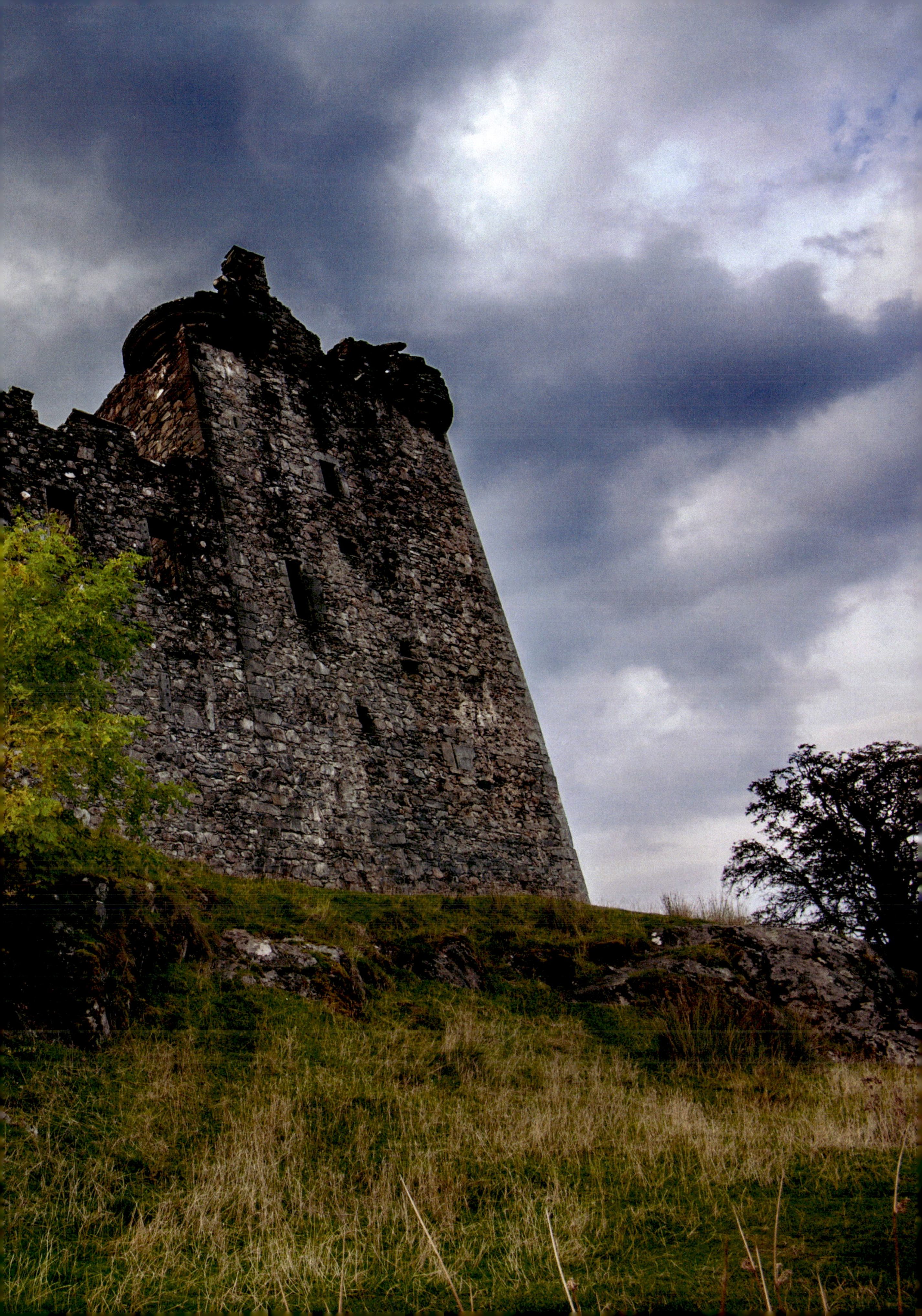

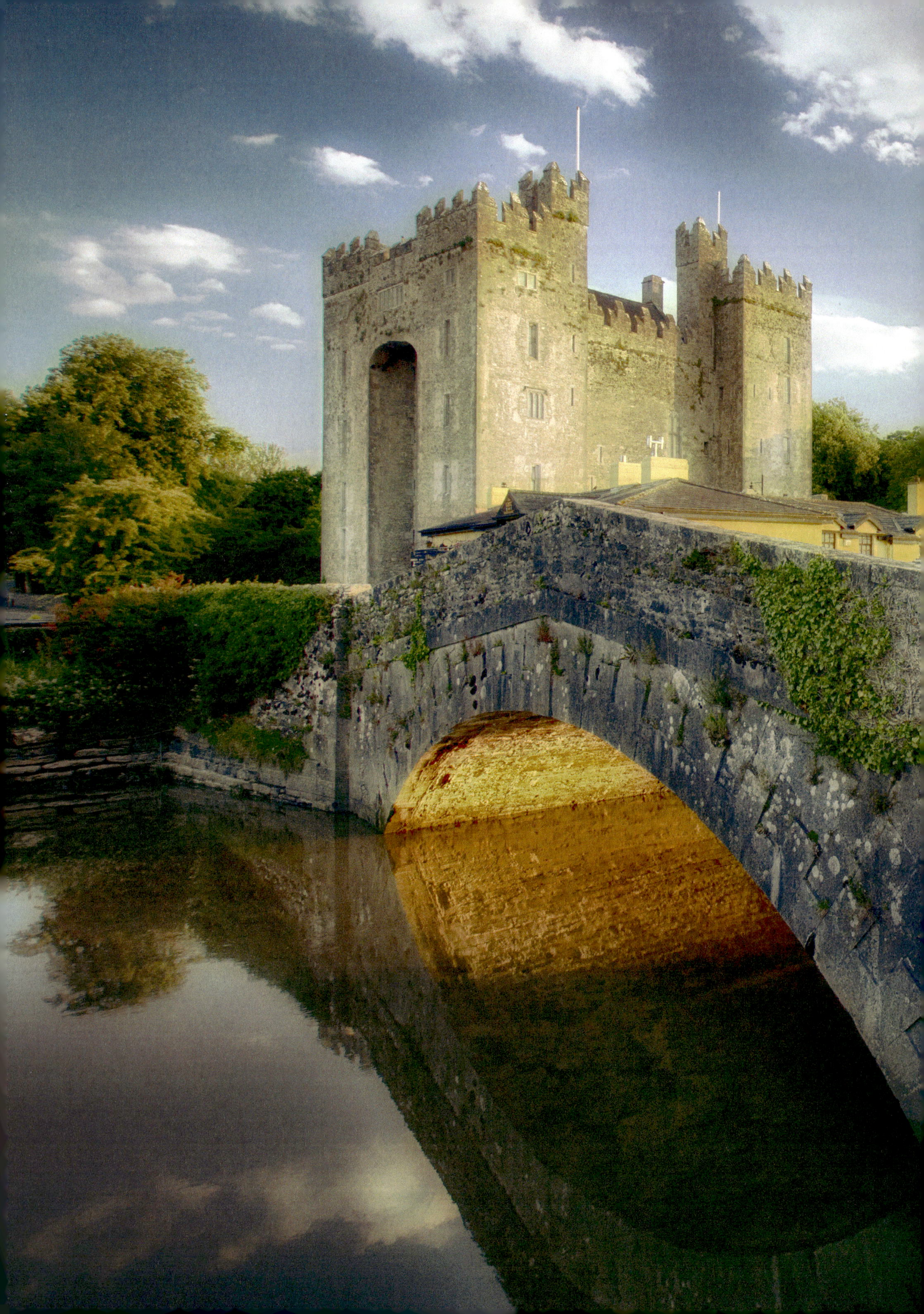

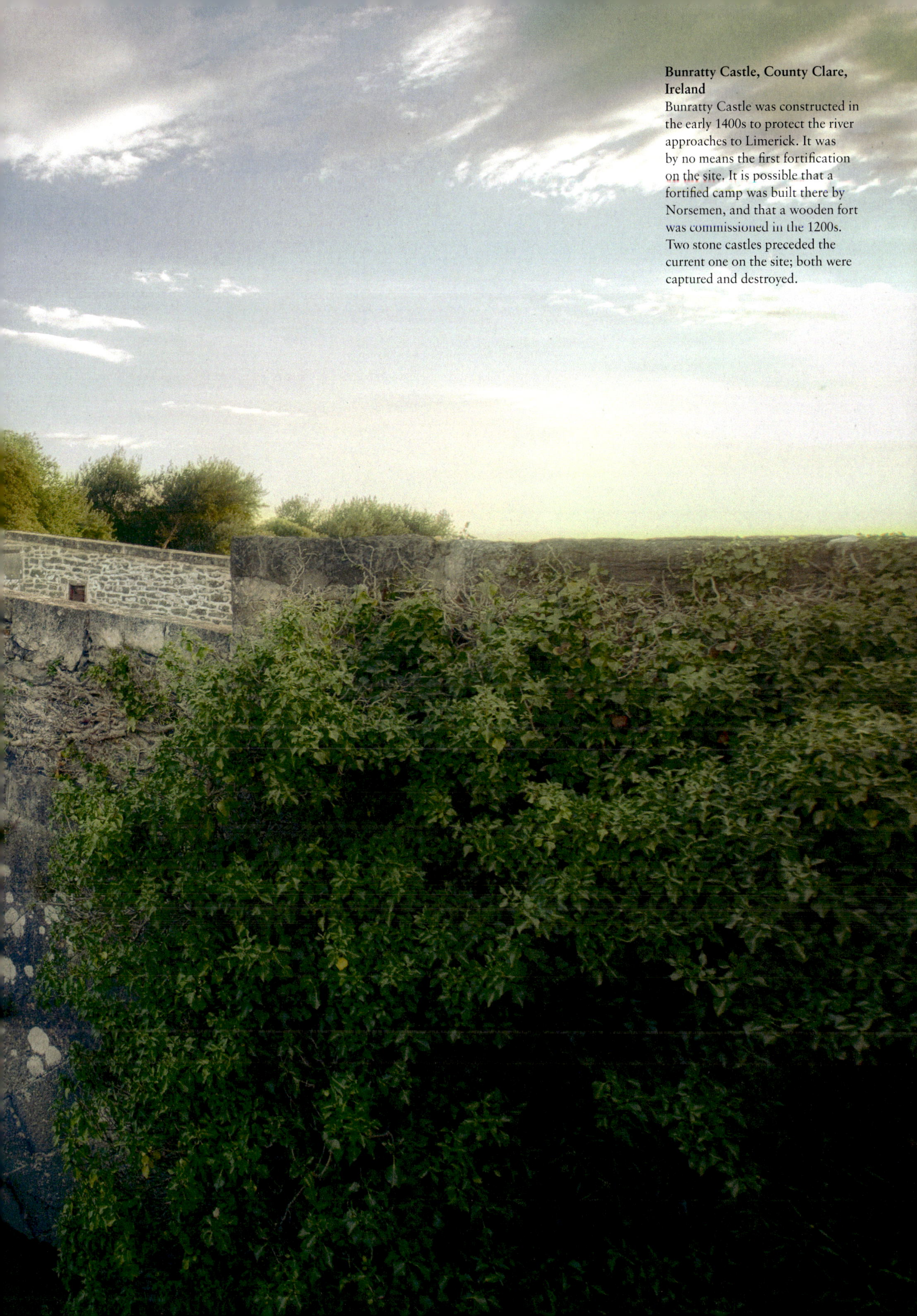

Bunratty Castle, County Clare, Ireland
Bunratty Castle was constructed in the early 1400s to protect the river approaches to Limerick. It was by no means the first fortification on the site. It is possible that a fortified camp was built there by Norsemen, and that a wooden fort was commissioned in the 1200s. Two stone castles preceded the current one on the site; both were captured and destroyed.

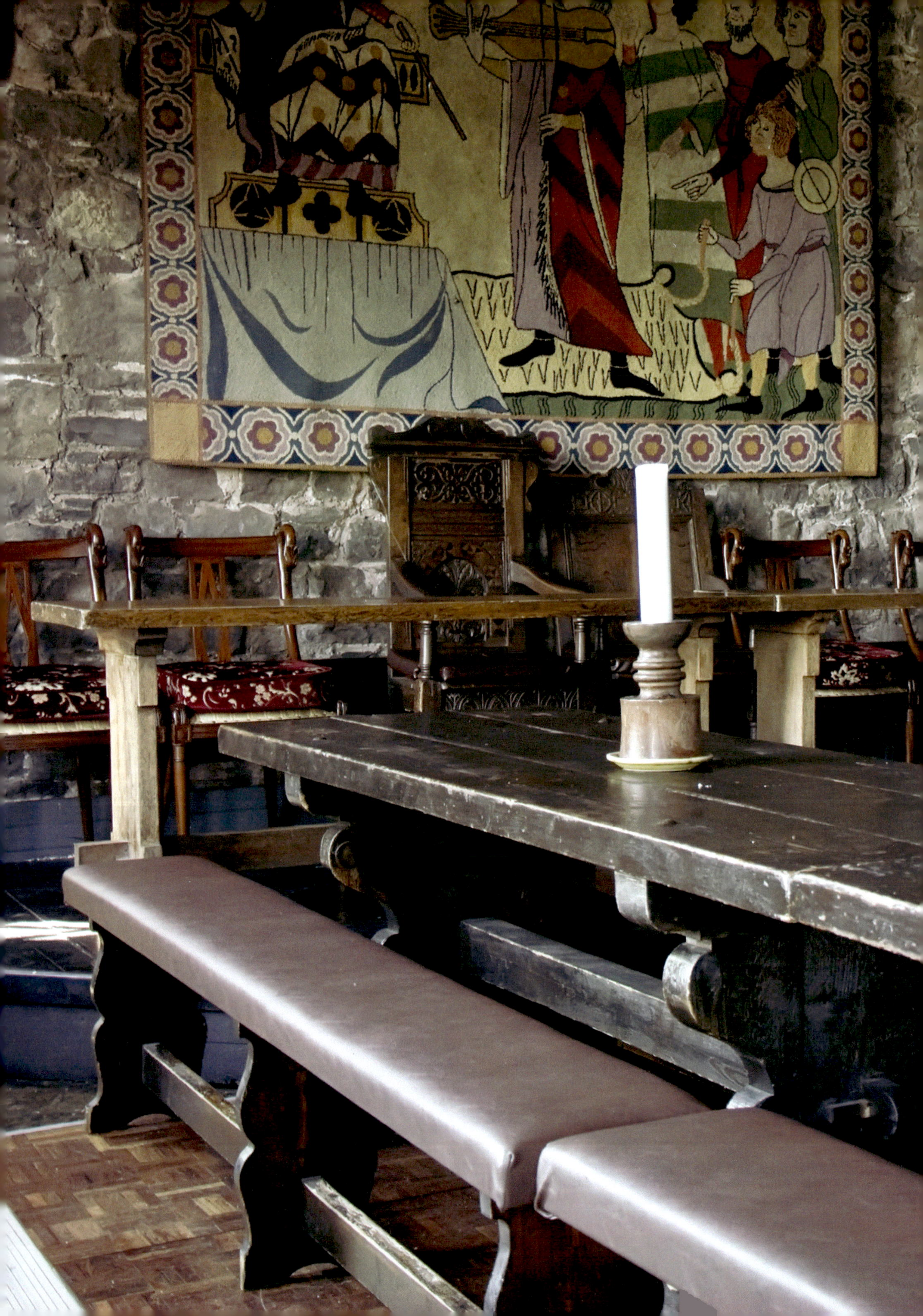

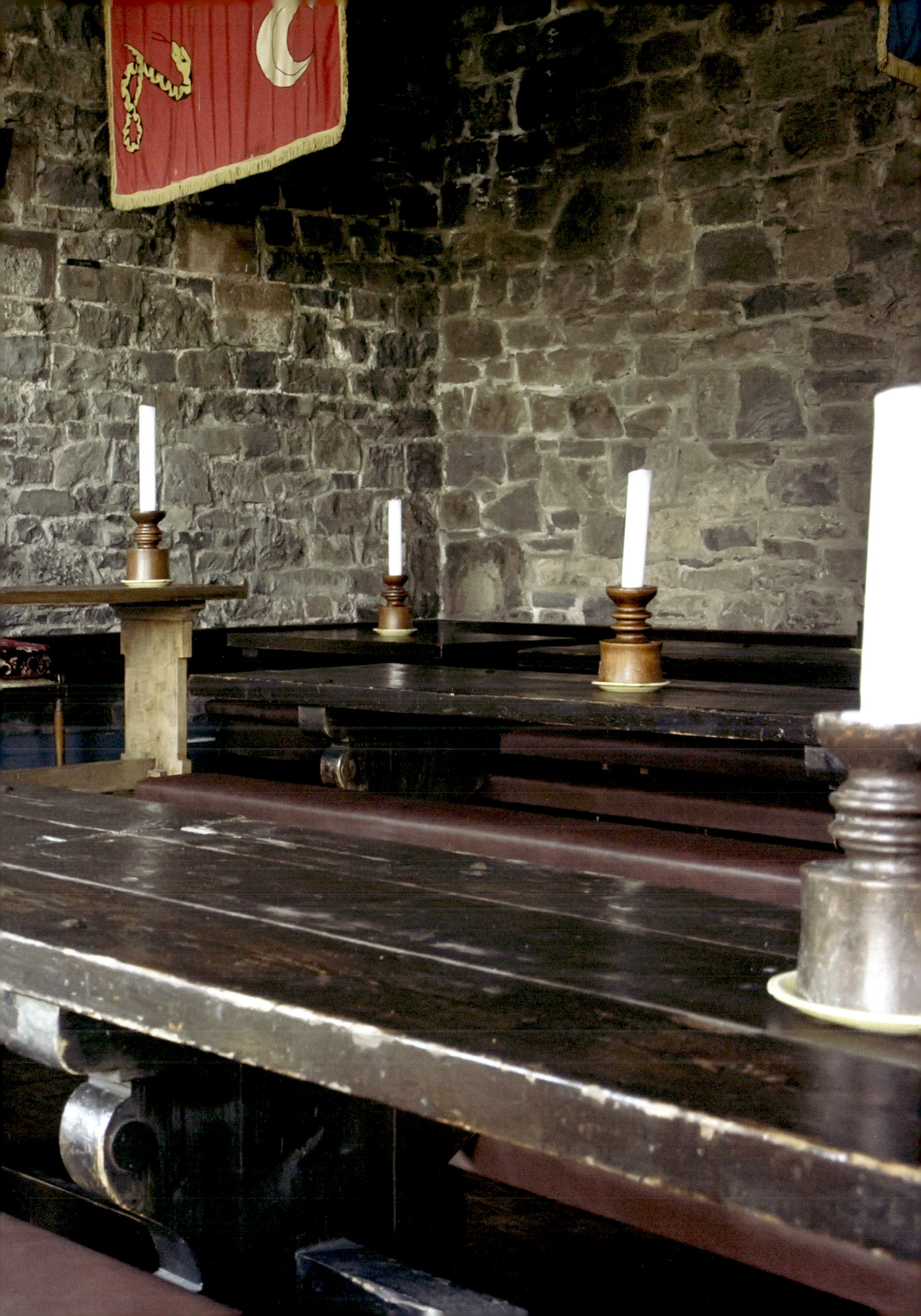

PREVIOUS PAGES:

Bunratty Castle, County Clare, Ireland

The banqueting hall at Bunratty Castle is set up as it might have been in the 1600s. The castle changed hands at the end of that century and was occupied until the early 1800s, after which it decayed until restored during the 1950s.

RIGHT:

Castle Stalker, Argyll, Scotland

Castle Stalker stands on an island at the mouth of Loch Laich. It was constructed on the site of an earlier castle, built in the early 1300s, and was inhabited until the mid-1800s. After decades in disrepair, the castle was restored in the 1960s.

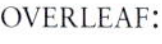

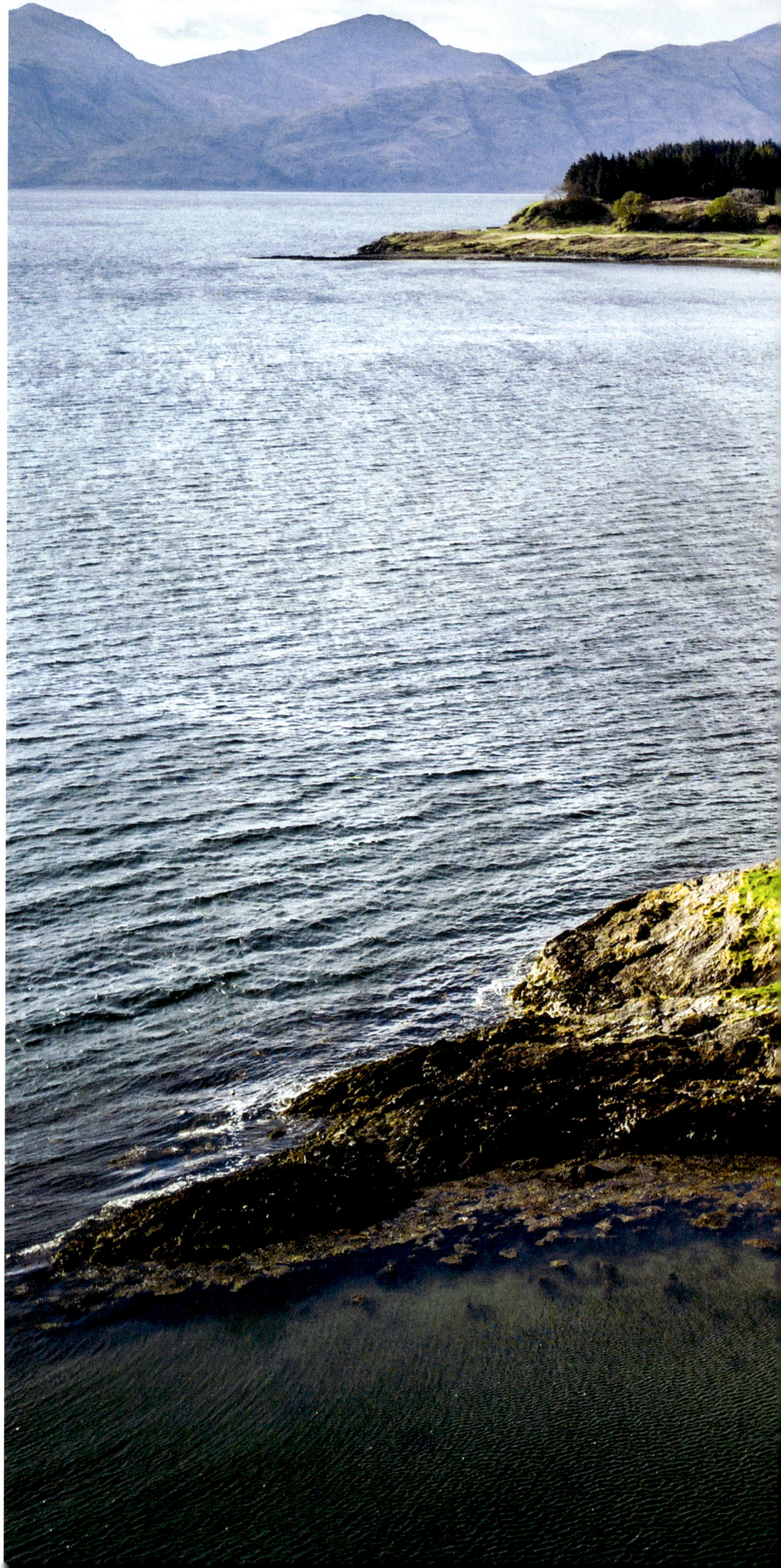

OVERLEAF:

Blackness Castle, Falkirk, Scotland

Blackness Castle on the Firth of Forth was constructed in the 1440s to protect the port at Blackness, which served the royal palace at Linlithgow. A previous fortification existed on the site before this. The castle was later modified to incorporate extensive artillery defences, but was captured in 1650 by Oliver Cromwell.

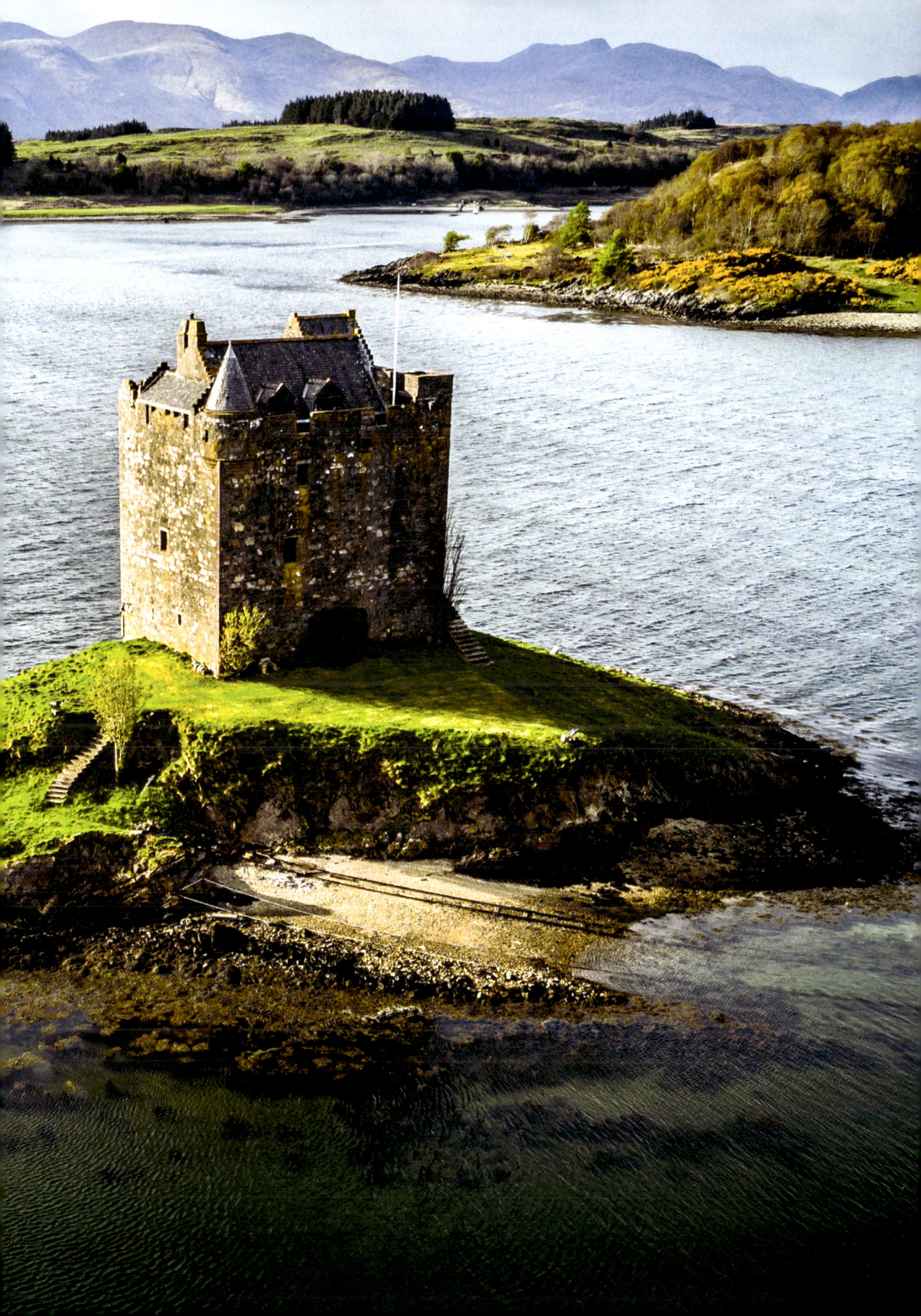

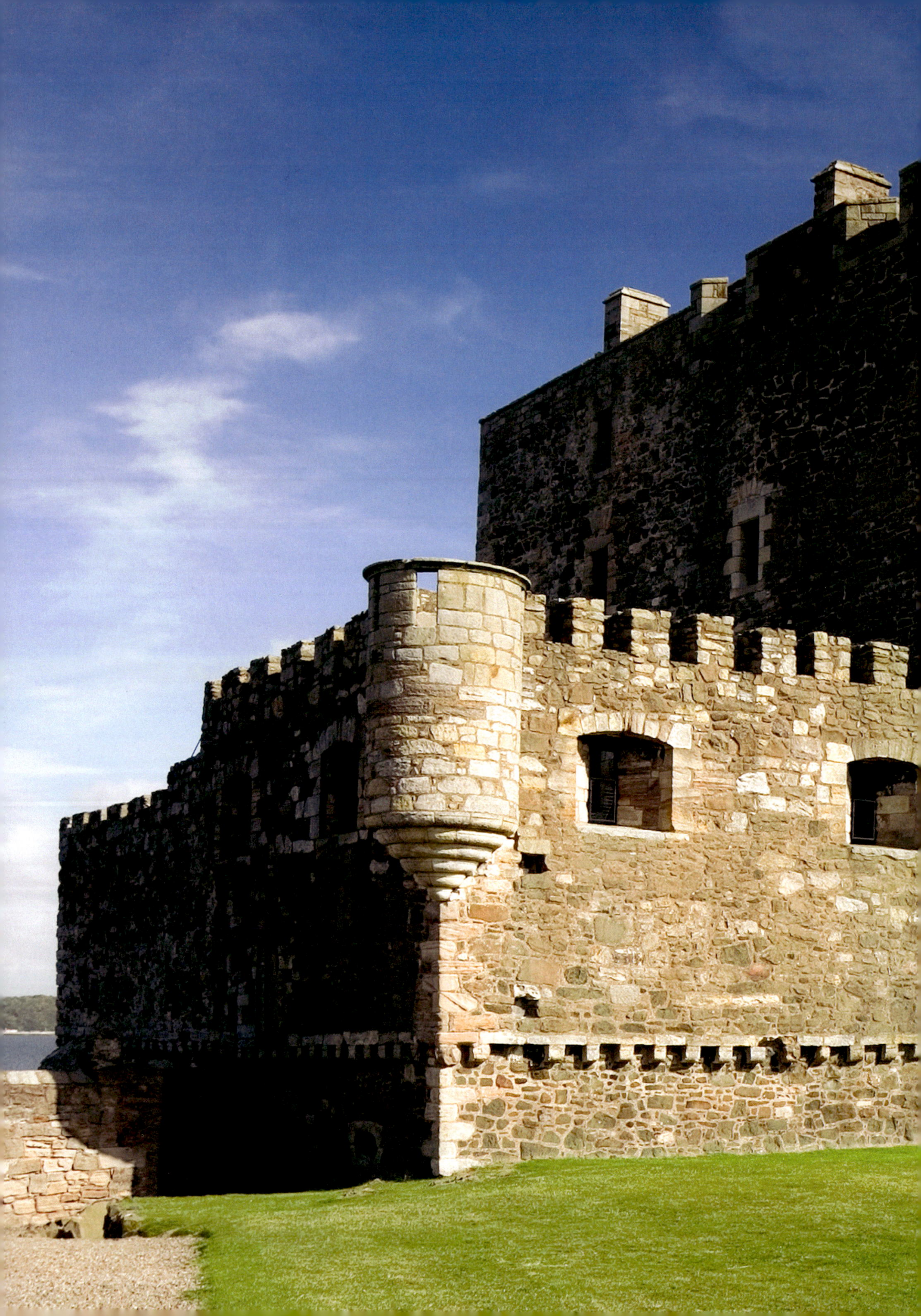

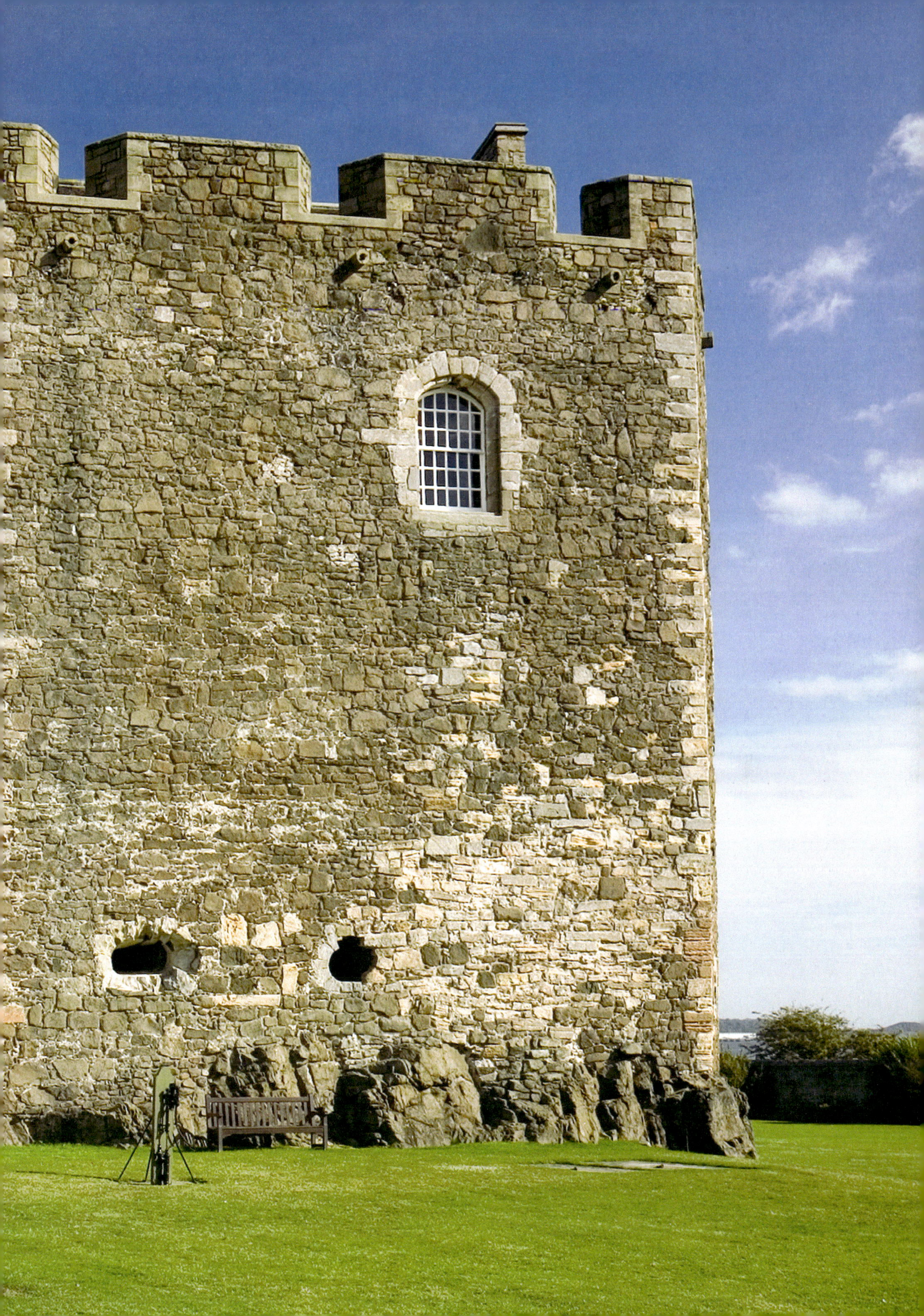

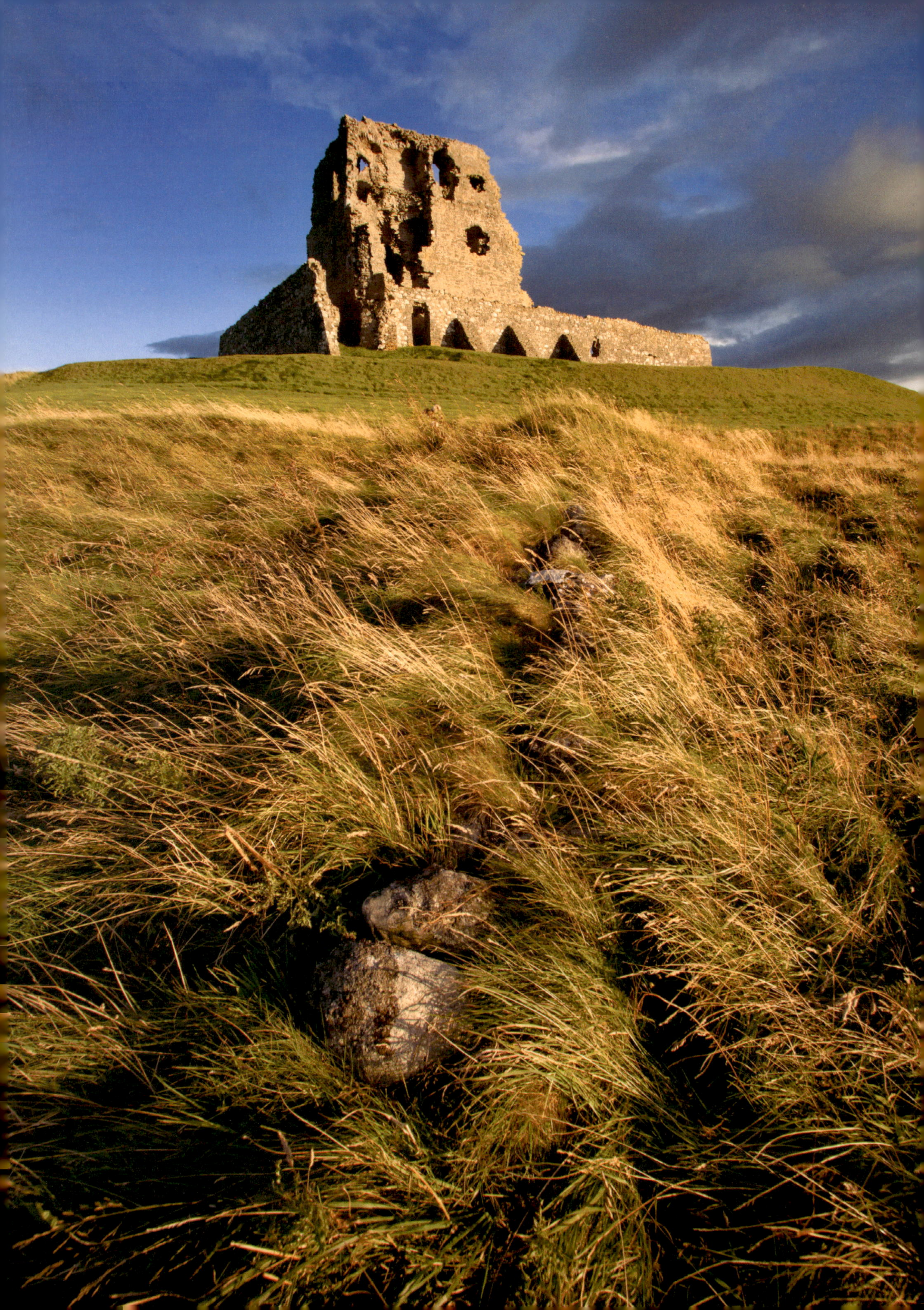

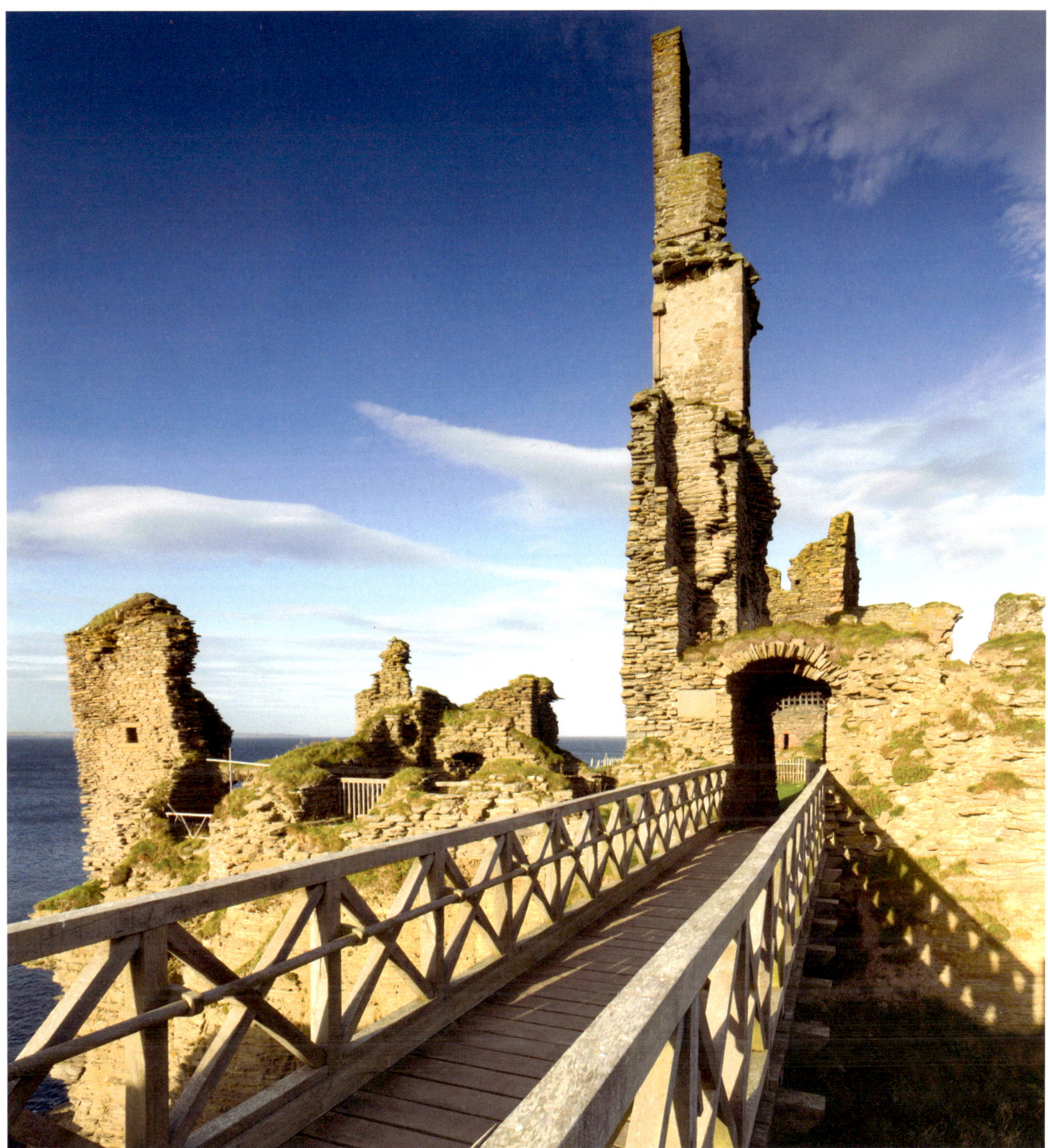

LEFT:

Auchindoun Castle, Moray, Scotland

Auchindoun Castle was built in the mid-1400s, taking advantage of ancient earthworks dating from the Iron Age. Despite its defensive location, the castle was burned in 1592, with new buildings added during the reconstruction works. It was used as a base by Jacobite forces in 1689 but was later abandoned. The castle was ruined by 1725.

ABOVE:

Castle Sinclair Girnigoe, Caithness, Scotland

Sinclair Girnigoe Castle, near Wick, was built on a site now known to have been inhabited since the Mesolithic era. The castle was built in the late 1400s, possibly by adapting an existing fortification, and was later expanded by encircling additional land with a new moat and building there.

Upon completion of the expansion in the early 1600s, an attempt was made to change the castle's name to Sinclair, but an administrative error resulted in the modern double name.

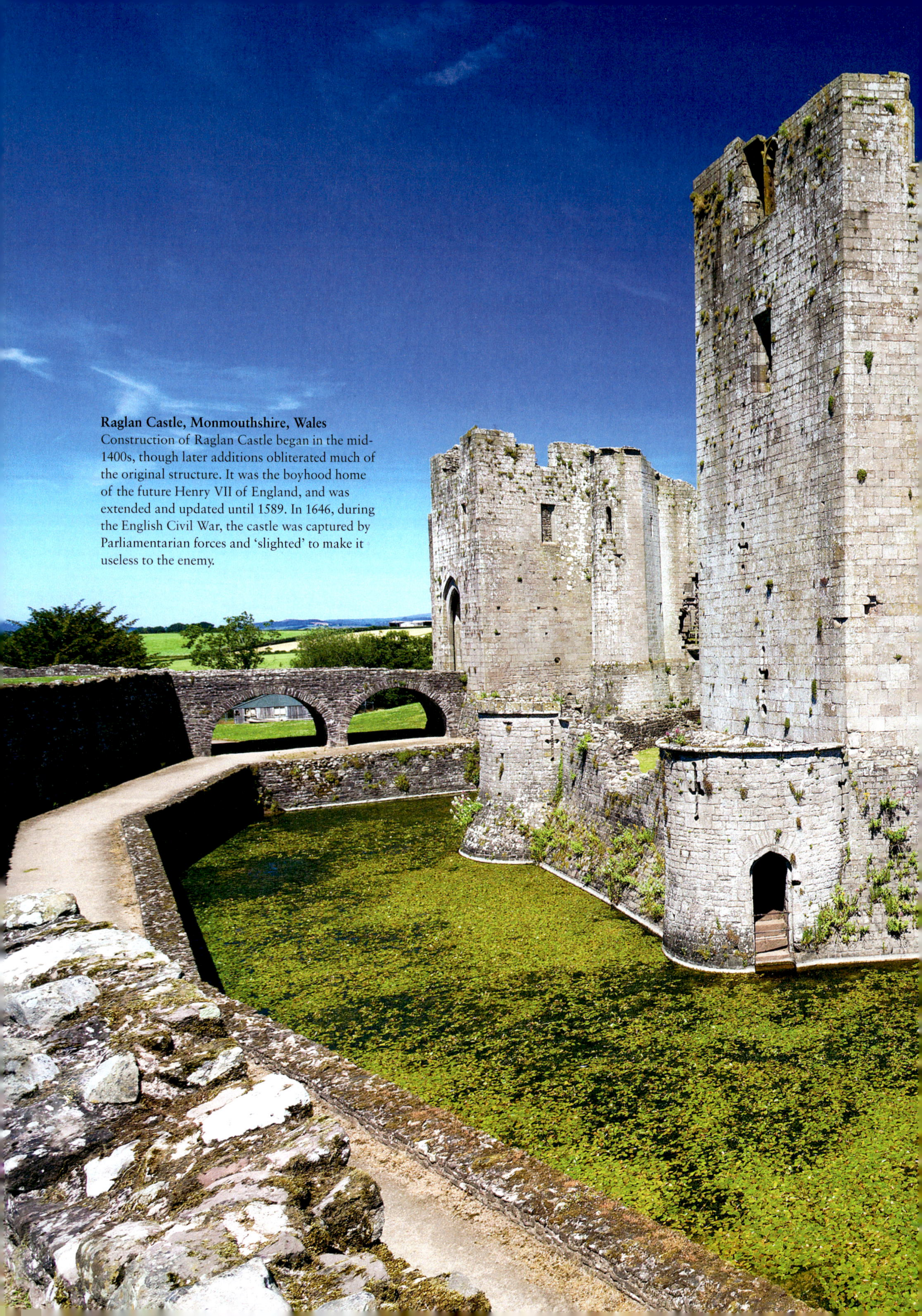

Raglan Castle, Monmouthshire, Wales
Construction of Raglan Castle began in the mid-1400s, though later additions obliterated much of the original structure. It was the boyhood home of the future Henry VII of England, and was extended and updated until 1589. In 1646, during the English Civil War, the castle was captured by Parliamentarian forces and 'slighted' to make it useless to the enemy.

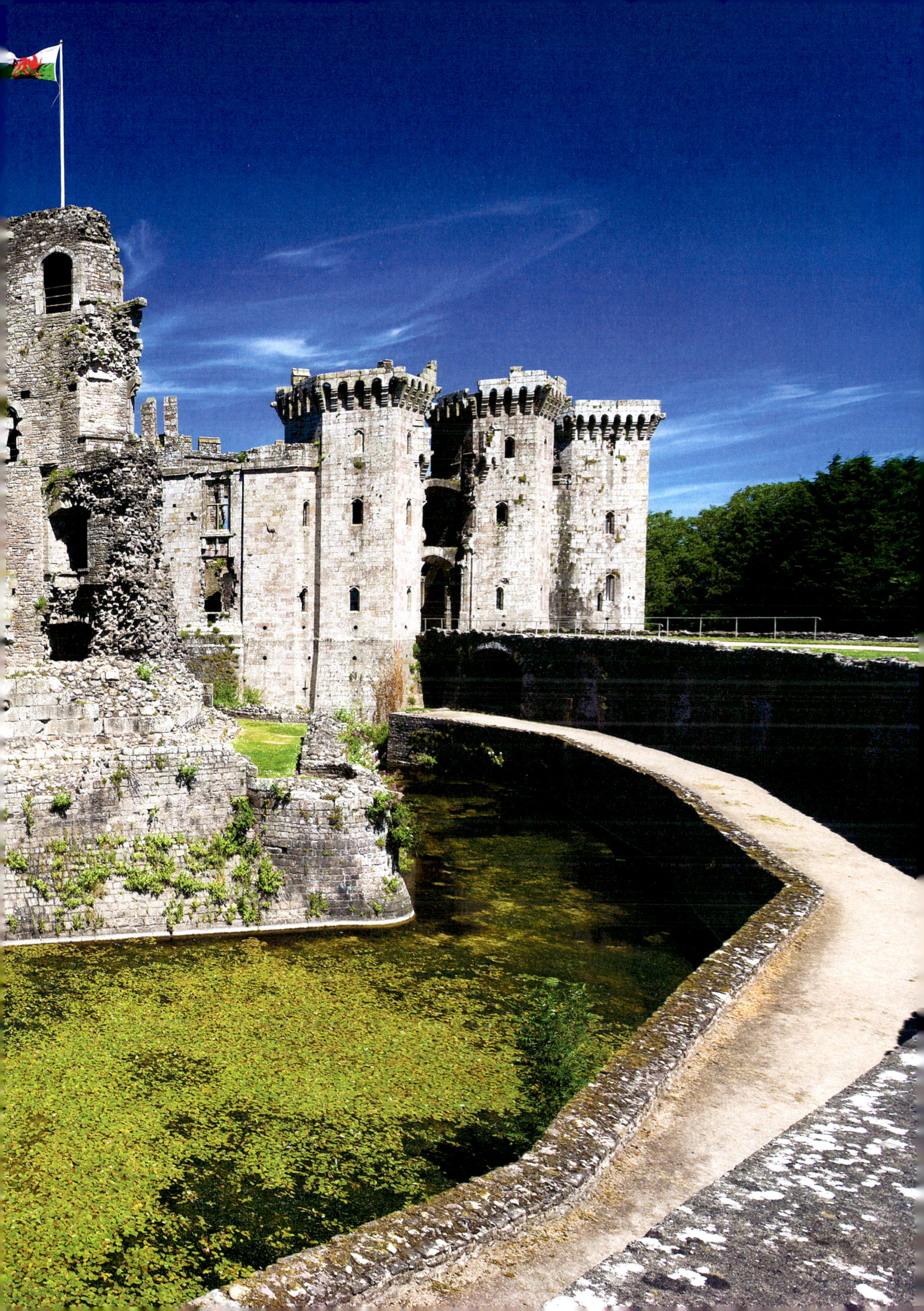

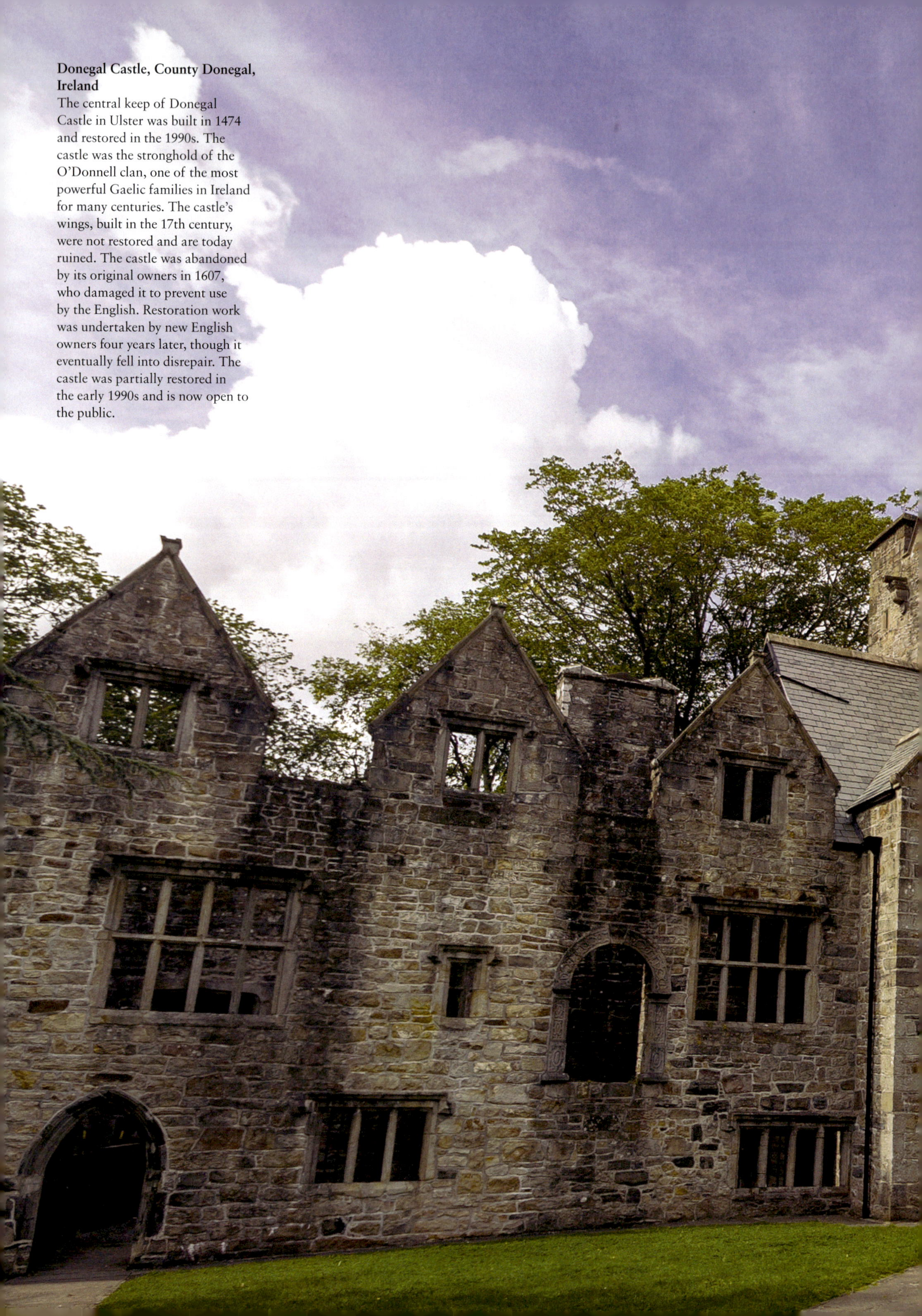

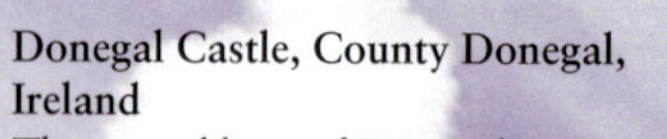

Donegal Castle, County Donegal, Ireland

The central keep of Donegal Castle in Ulster was built in 1474 and restored in the 1990s. The castle was the stronghold of the O'Donnell clan, one of the most powerful Gaelic families in Ireland for many centuries. The castle's wings, built in the 17th century, were not restored and are today ruined. The castle was abandoned by its original owners in 1607, who damaged it to prevent use by the English. Restoration work was undertaken by new English owners four years later, though it eventually fell into disrepair. The castle was partially restored in the early 1990s and is now open to the public.

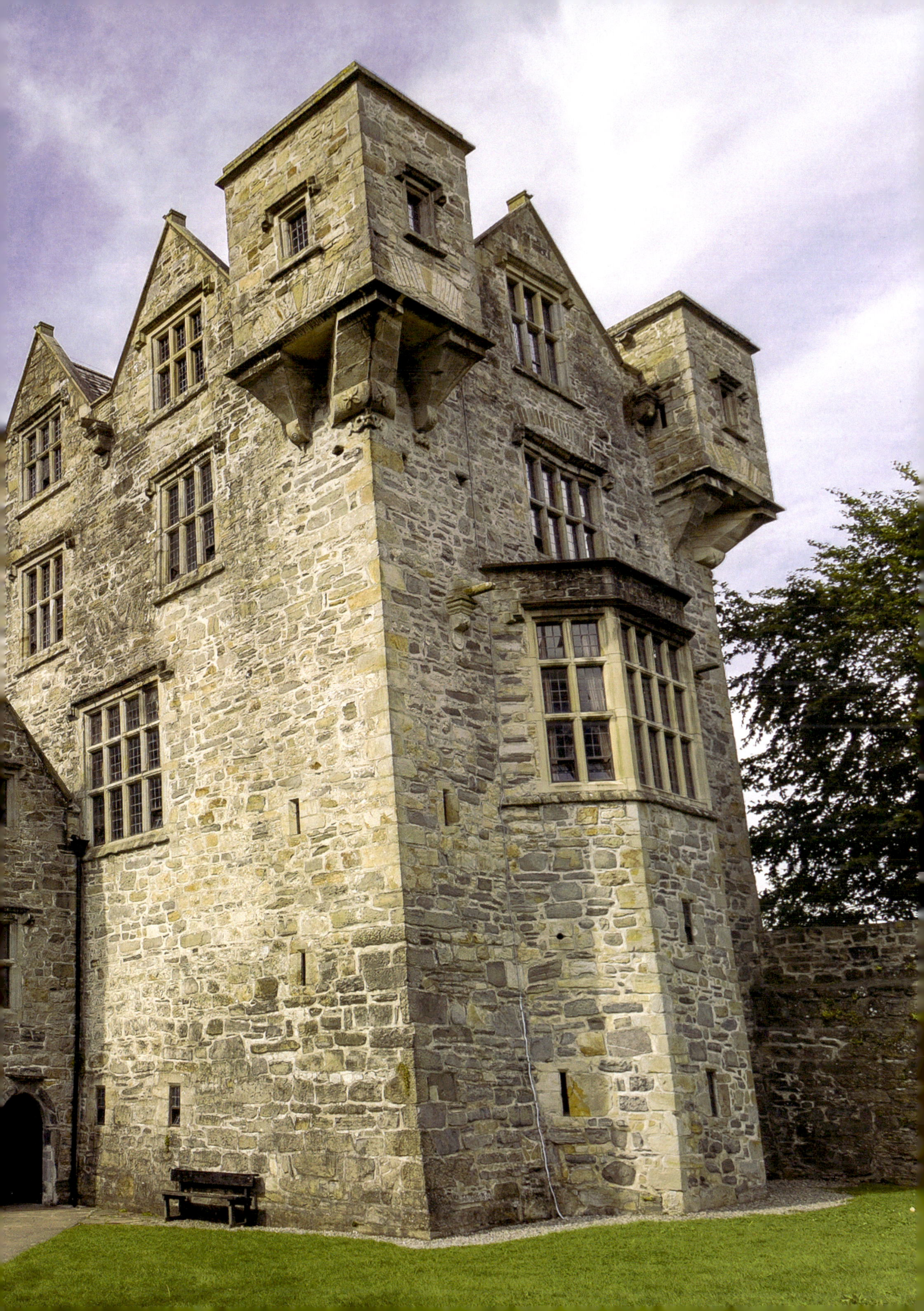

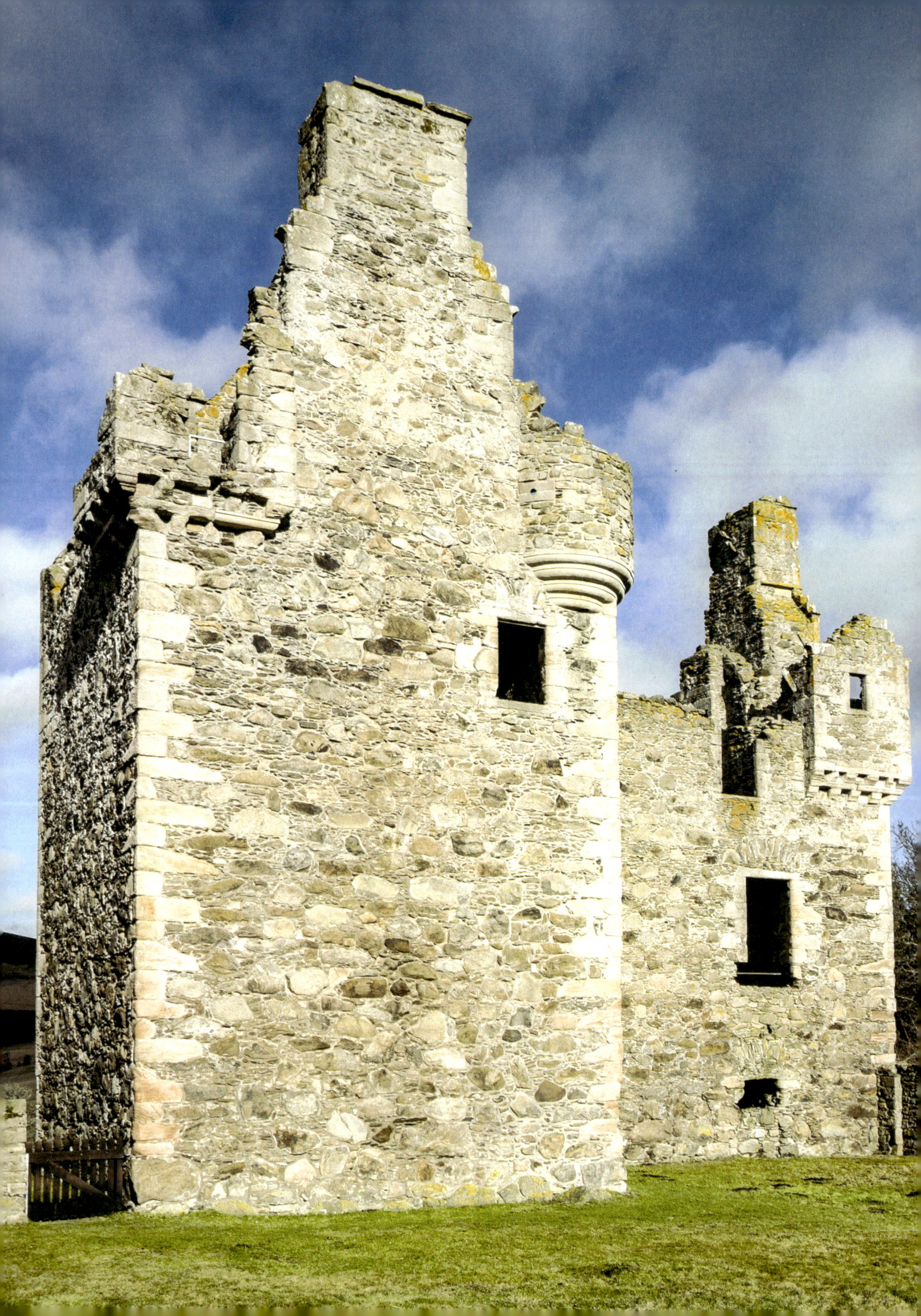

Early Modern Era

The Early Modern Era was characterized by religious reformation, wars of religion and civil war in England. Older castles, though now very vulnerable to attack with gunpowder artillery, were still useful as bases and defensive sites. Fortifications were deliberately 'slighted' when captured to prevent reuse. This typically took the form of blowing up towers or collapsing a section of the walls to leave the castle open on one side.

Castles increasingly became manor houses, with comfort and convenience more important than defensive capabilities. Many castles from earlier eras were altered during this time, with the addition of windows and ornamental features, while new construction was typically designed to impress visitors rather than intimidate them.

Architectural styles also evolved. Converted castles were sometimes extensively remodelled to give a uniform appearance, but some retained older styling on their original buildings. This can create a confusing image for the modern viewer, who may be seeing the end result of several alterations rather than what any particular builder or owner had in mind at the time.

LEFT:
Glenbuchat Castle, Aberdeenshire, Scotland
Glenbuchat Castle was built in 1590, as a tower house with two smaller blocks on opposite corners. Constructed at a time when gunpowder weapons were readily available, the castle has gun-loops rather than arrow slits. The entryway was designed so that anyone attacking the door could be fired upon from two directions.

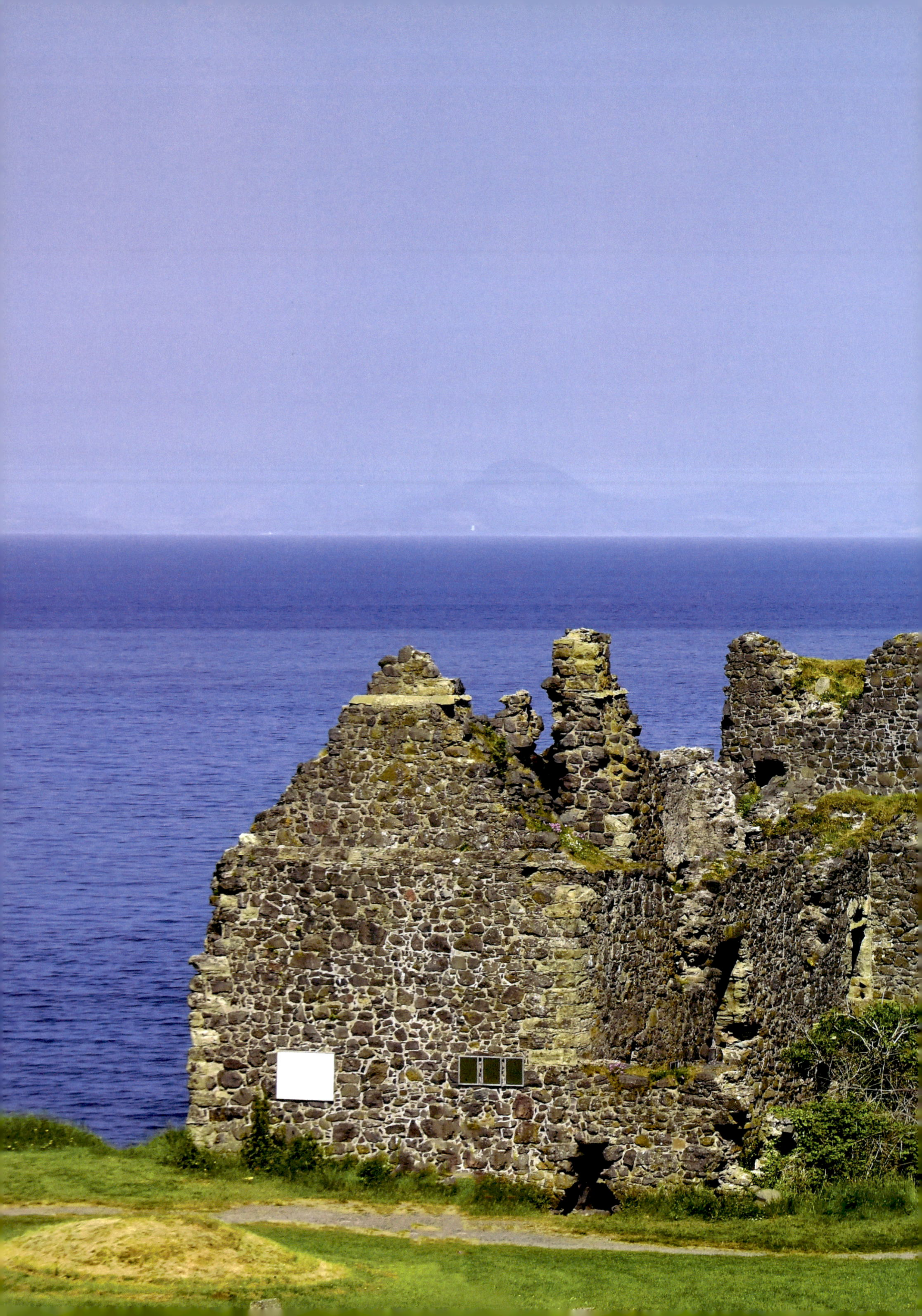

Dunure Castle, South Ayrshire, Scotland

Dunure Castle on the west coast of Scotland dates from the 15th century, though there is evidence of a castle on the site from a much earlier time. Dunure Castle was visited by Mary, Queen of Scots, in 1563 and in 1569 was the site of a complex three-way fight resulting from a dispute over the lands attached to nearby Crossraguel Abbey. The castle was heavily damaged and abandoned soon afterward.

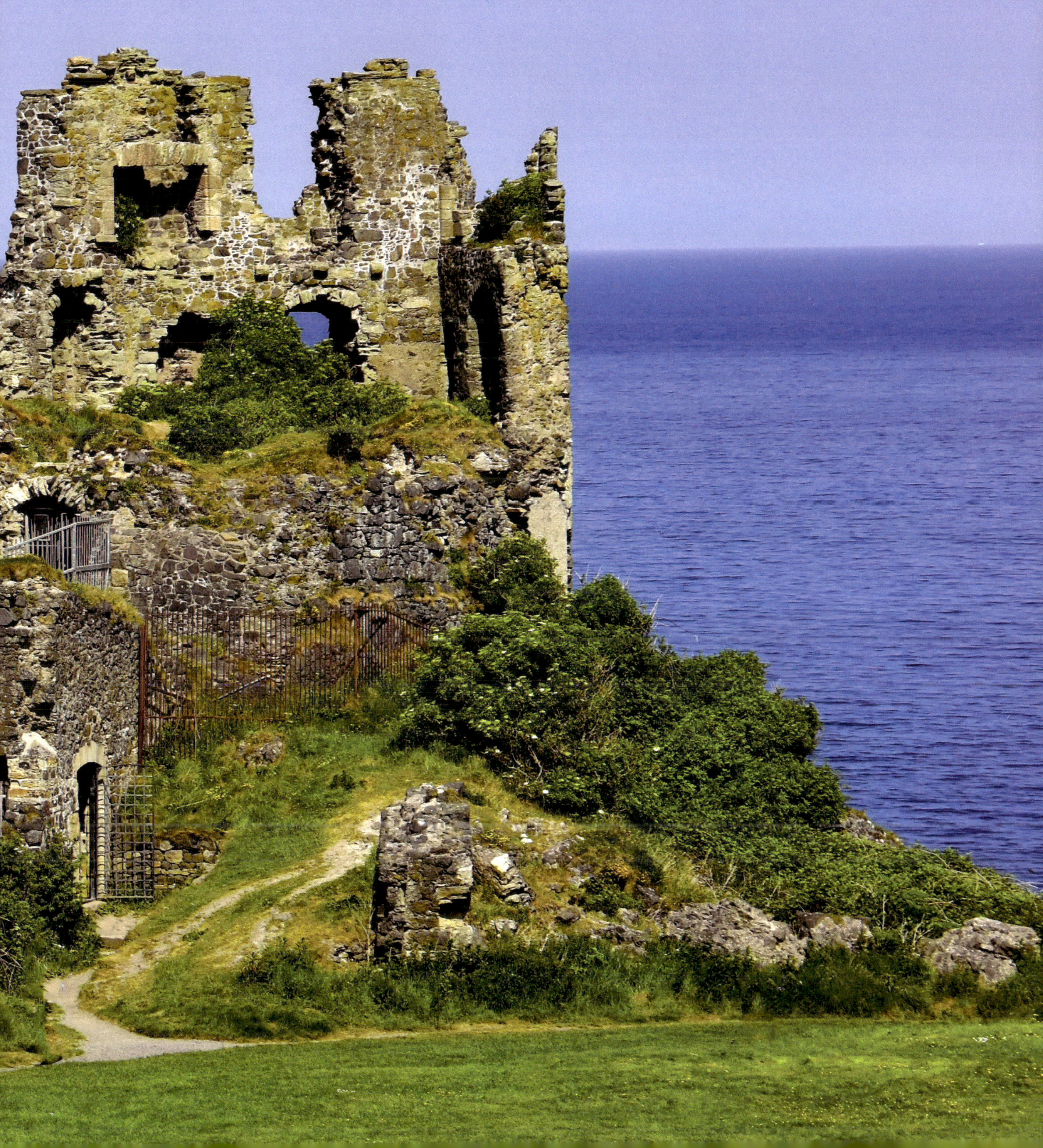

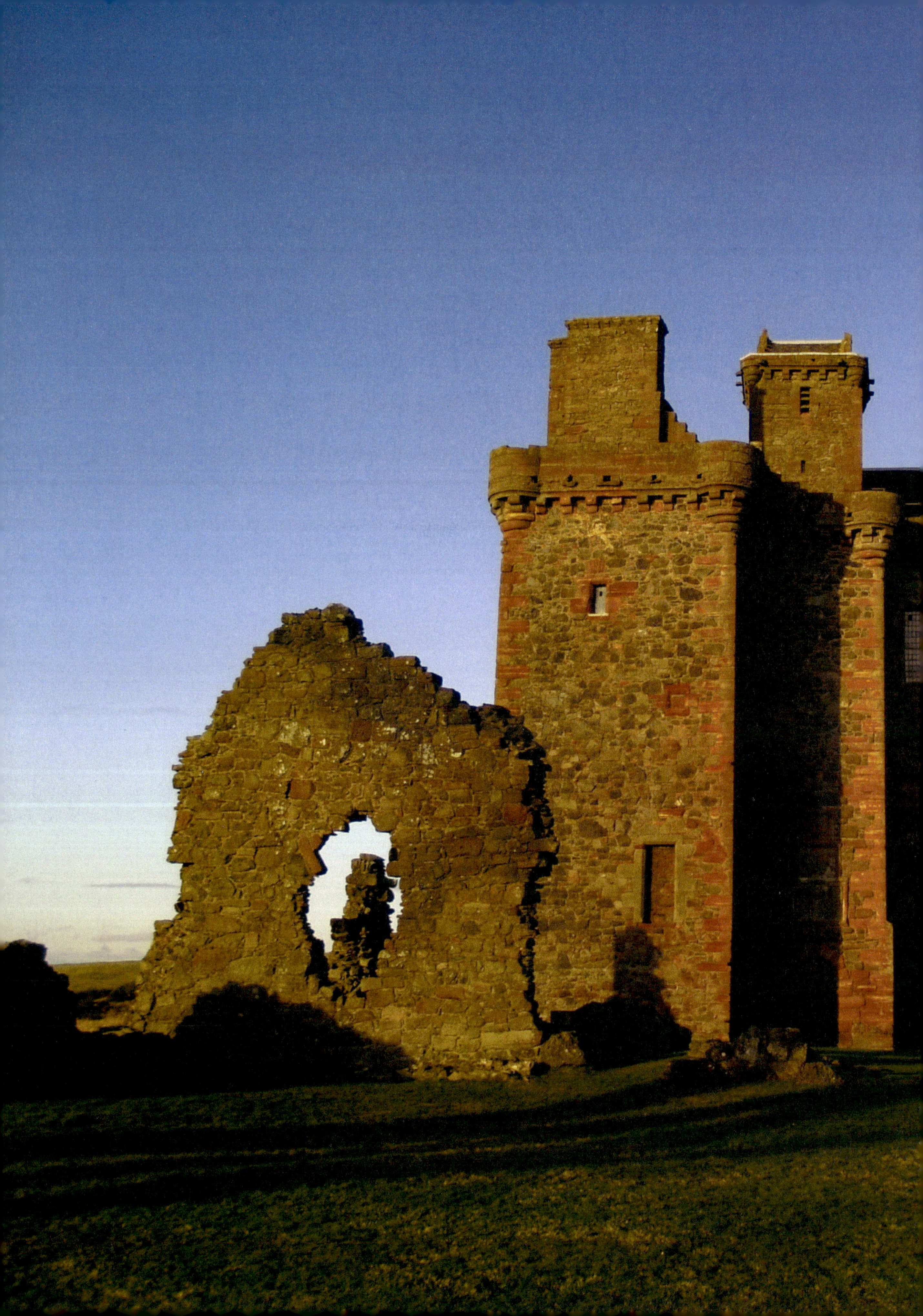

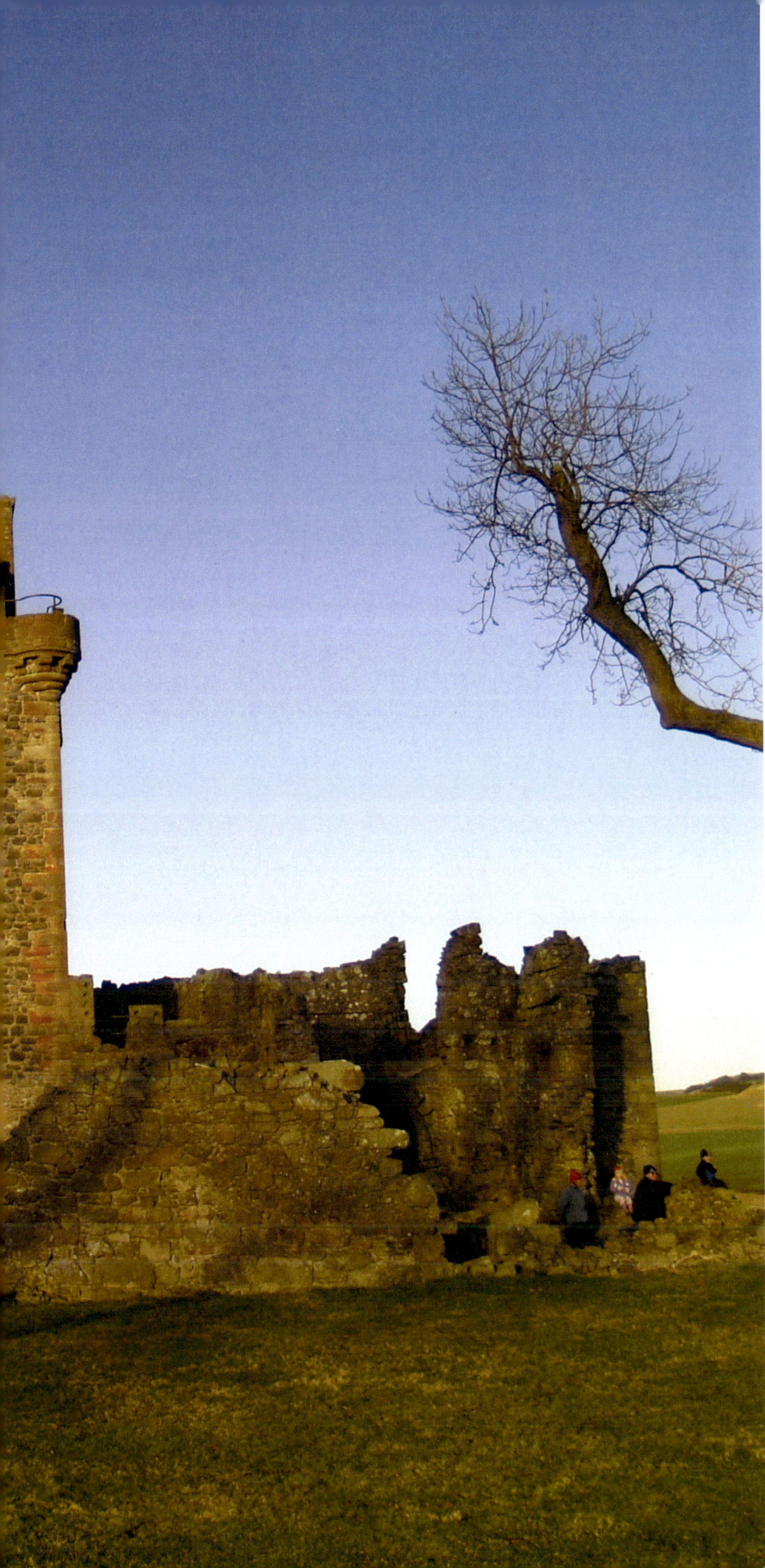

Balvaird Castle, Perthshire, Scotland

Balvaird Castle (also spelled as Balverd Castle or Balverde Castle) was built around 1500, probably on the site of an earlier fortification. The original tower house was augmented with an outer wall and gatehouse in 1567. The first floor of the tower house was later extended over the gatehouse.

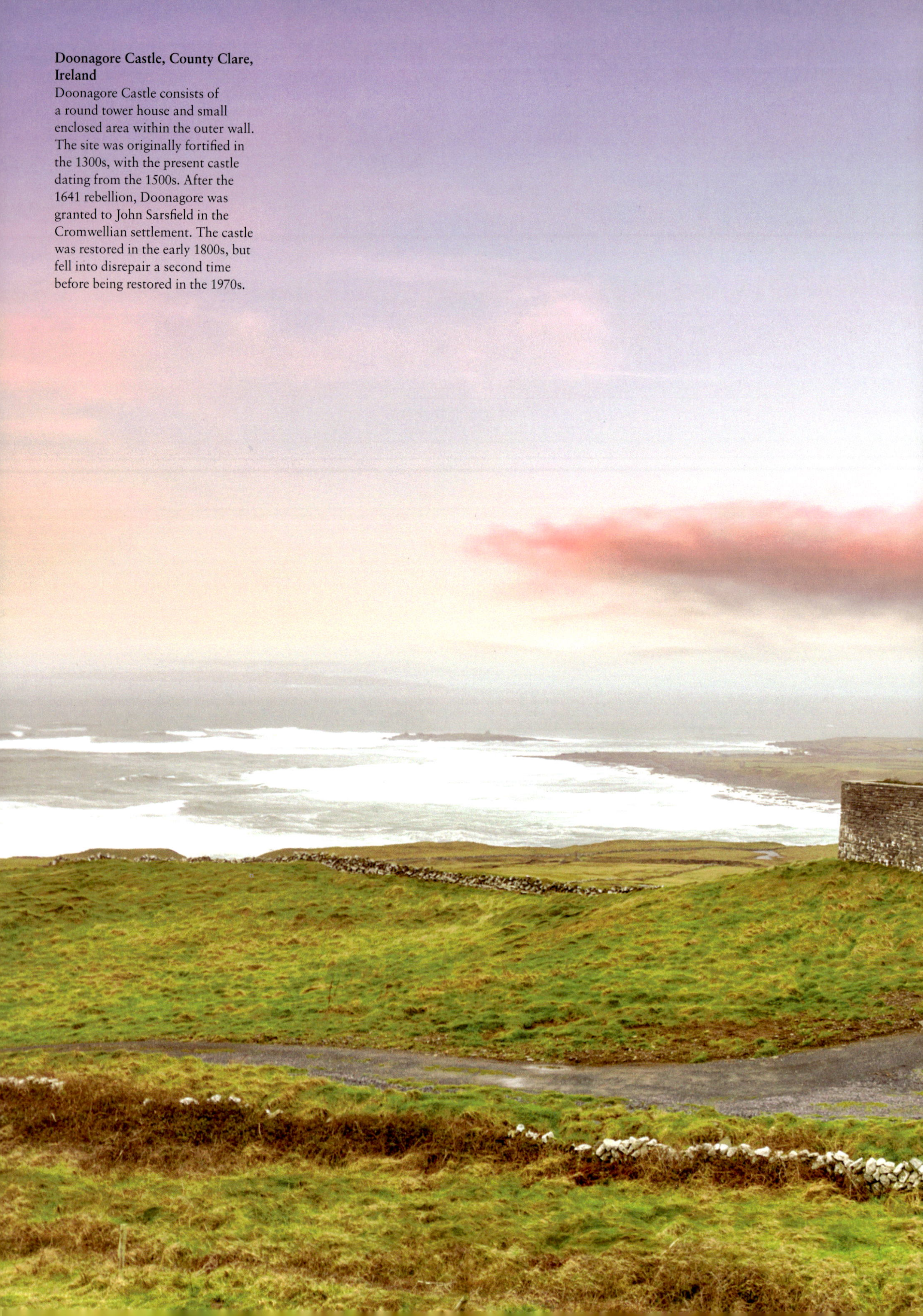

Doonagore Castle, County Clare, Ireland

Doonagore Castle consists of a round tower house and small enclosed area within the outer wall. The site was originally fortified in the 1300s, with the present castle dating from the 1500s. After the 1641 rebellion, Doonagore was granted to John Sarsfield in the Cromwellian settlement. The castle was restored in the early 1800s, but fell into disrepair a second time before being restored in the 1970s.

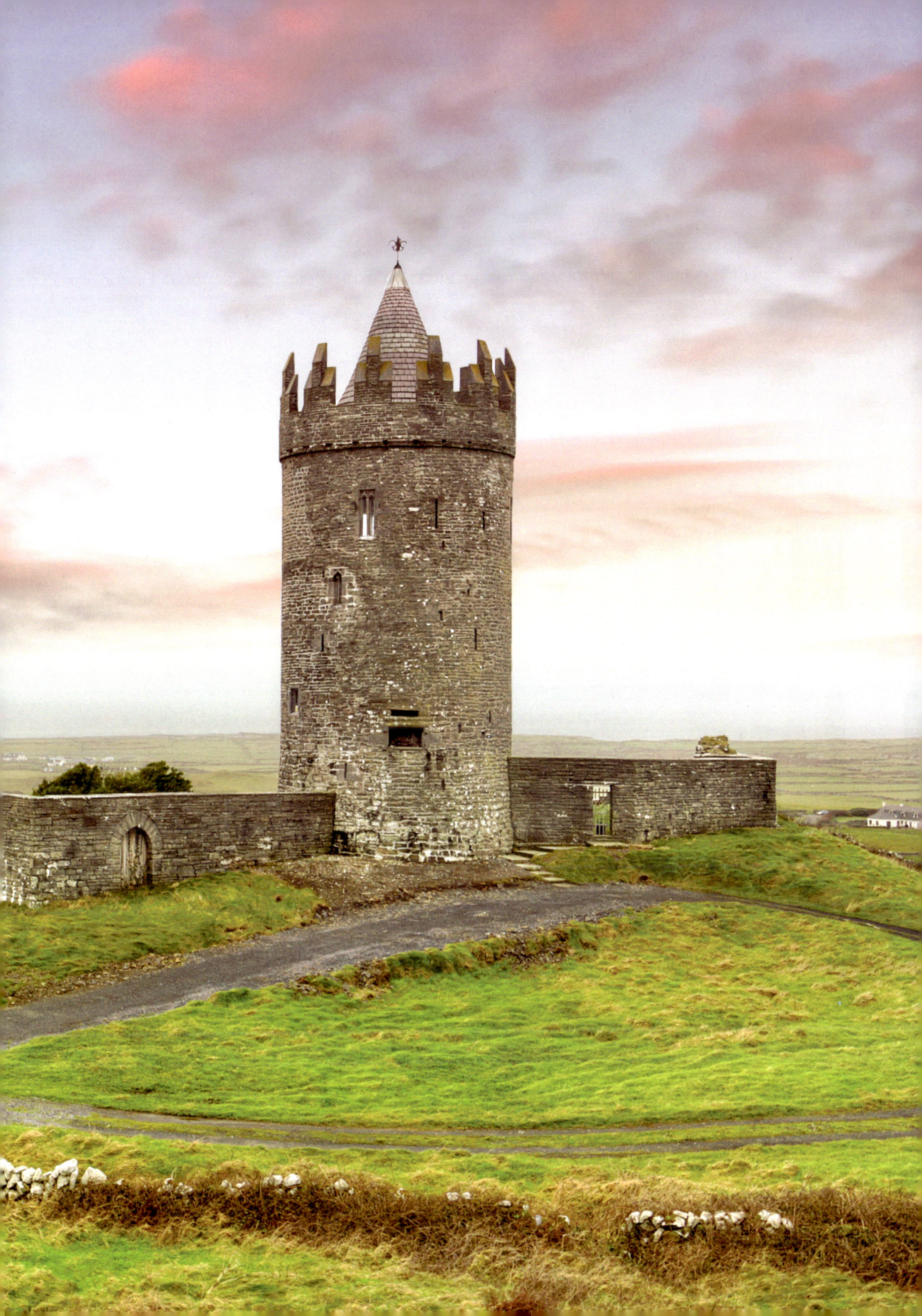

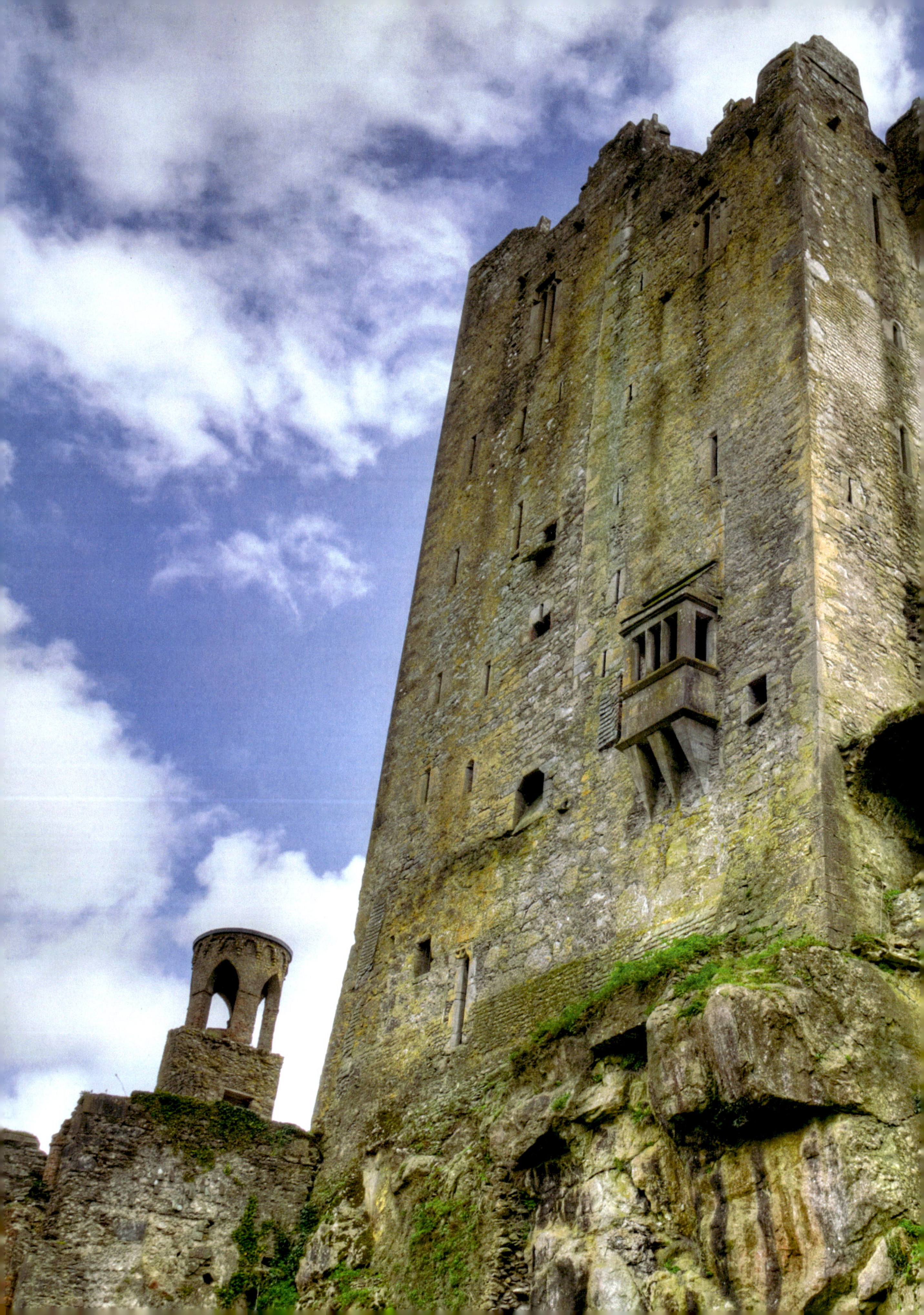

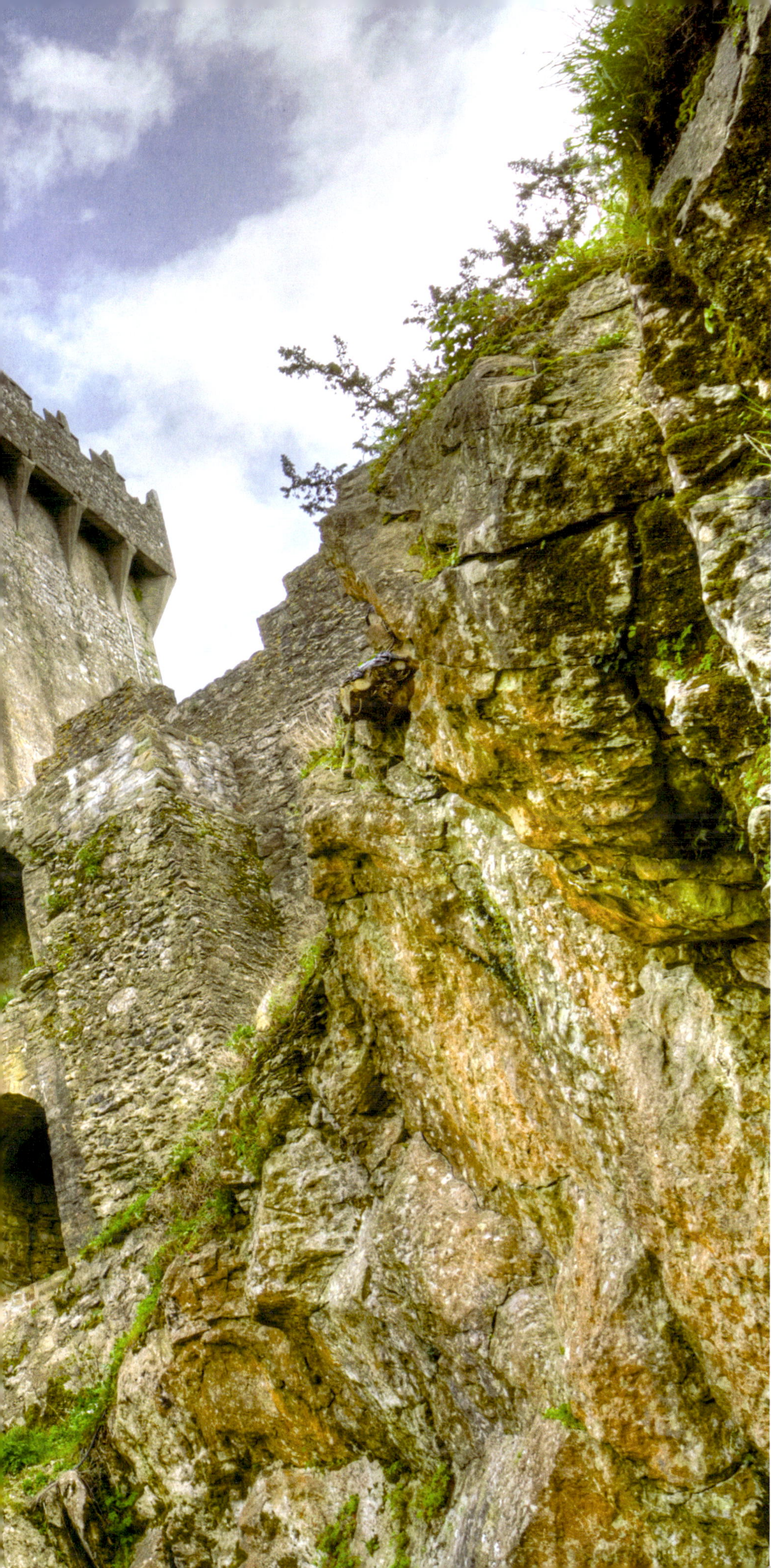

Blarney Castle, County Cork, Ireland
Blarney Castle near Cork was built on the site of an earlier stone fortification dating from around 1200. This was destroyed in the mid-1400s and rebuilt in its present form, at which time the Blarney Stone was built into the castle wall. (The Blarney Stone is today famous for inspiring great eloquence among those who kiss it.) Blarney Castle was successfully besieged by Parliamentarian forces in 1646, but survived to pass through several owners before falling into partial ruin.

Dunluce Castle, County Antrim, Northern Ireland

Dunluce Castle occupies a very strong defensive position atop a volcanic rock outcrop. The site was fortified previously, but the present castle was not built until the 1300s. It was significantly updated and improved in the late 1500s. Following the defeat of the Spanish Armada in 1588, the castle benefited from a Spanish ship being wrecked nearby, from which artillery was added to the castle defences.

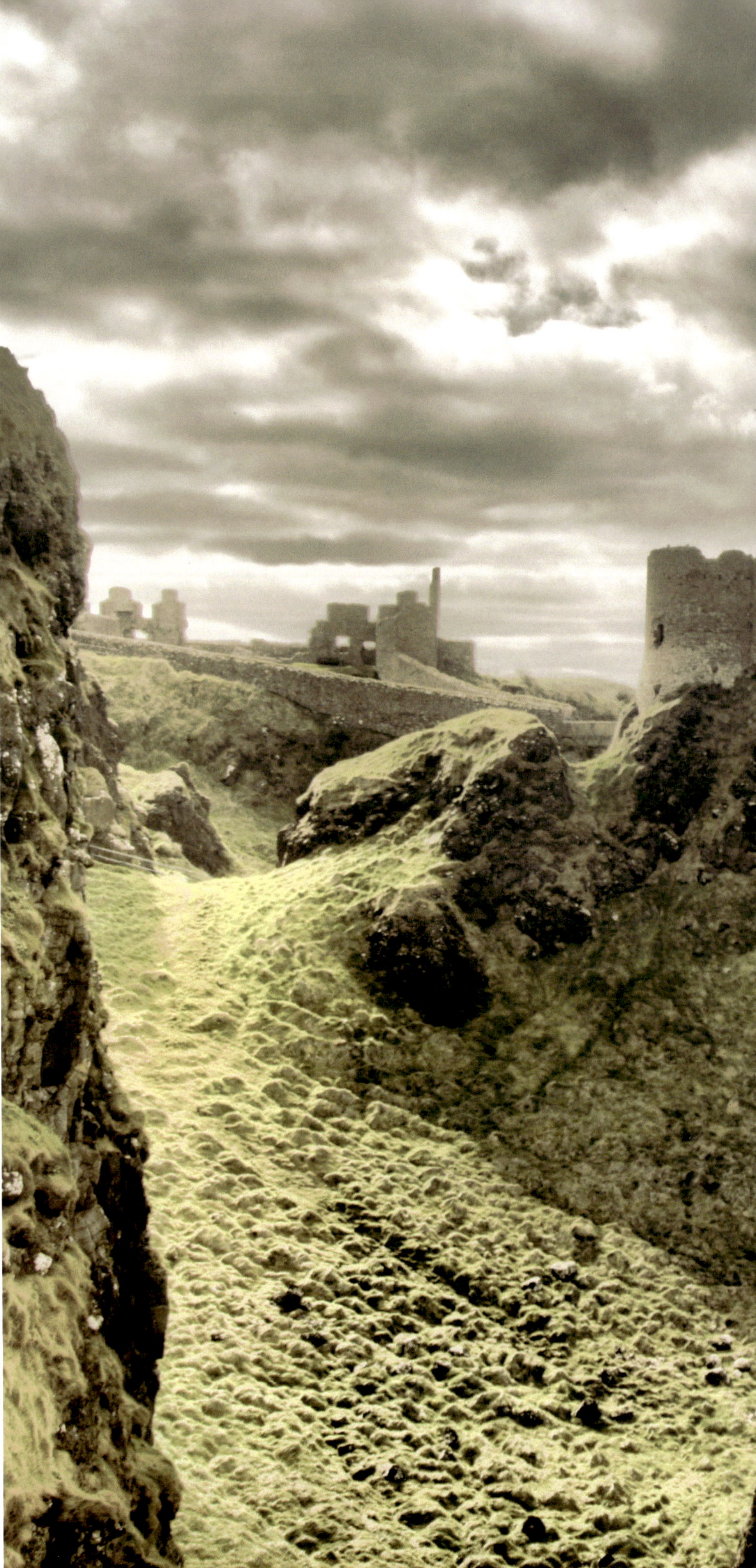

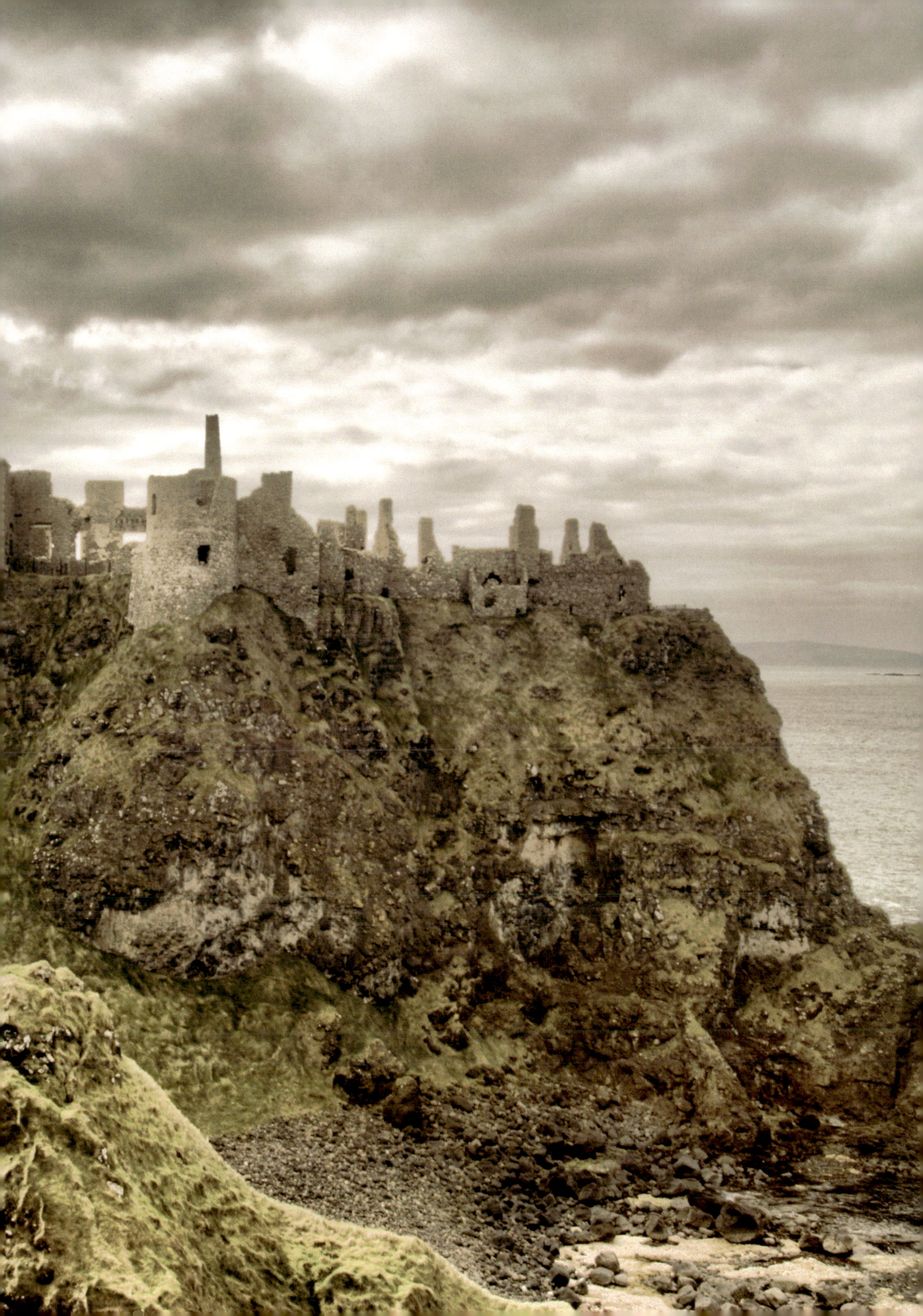

Huntly Castle, Aberdeenshire, Scotland

Huntly Castle was built on the site of a motte-and-bailey castle dating from the 1180s. Construction on the central buildings began around 1410, but these were burned in 1452 by the Earl of Moray. The castle was rebuilt in a more ambitious manner, which was then converted in 1550 into a palace. Despite damage inflicted by the forces of King James VI, the castle survived to be further remodelled in the early 1600s.

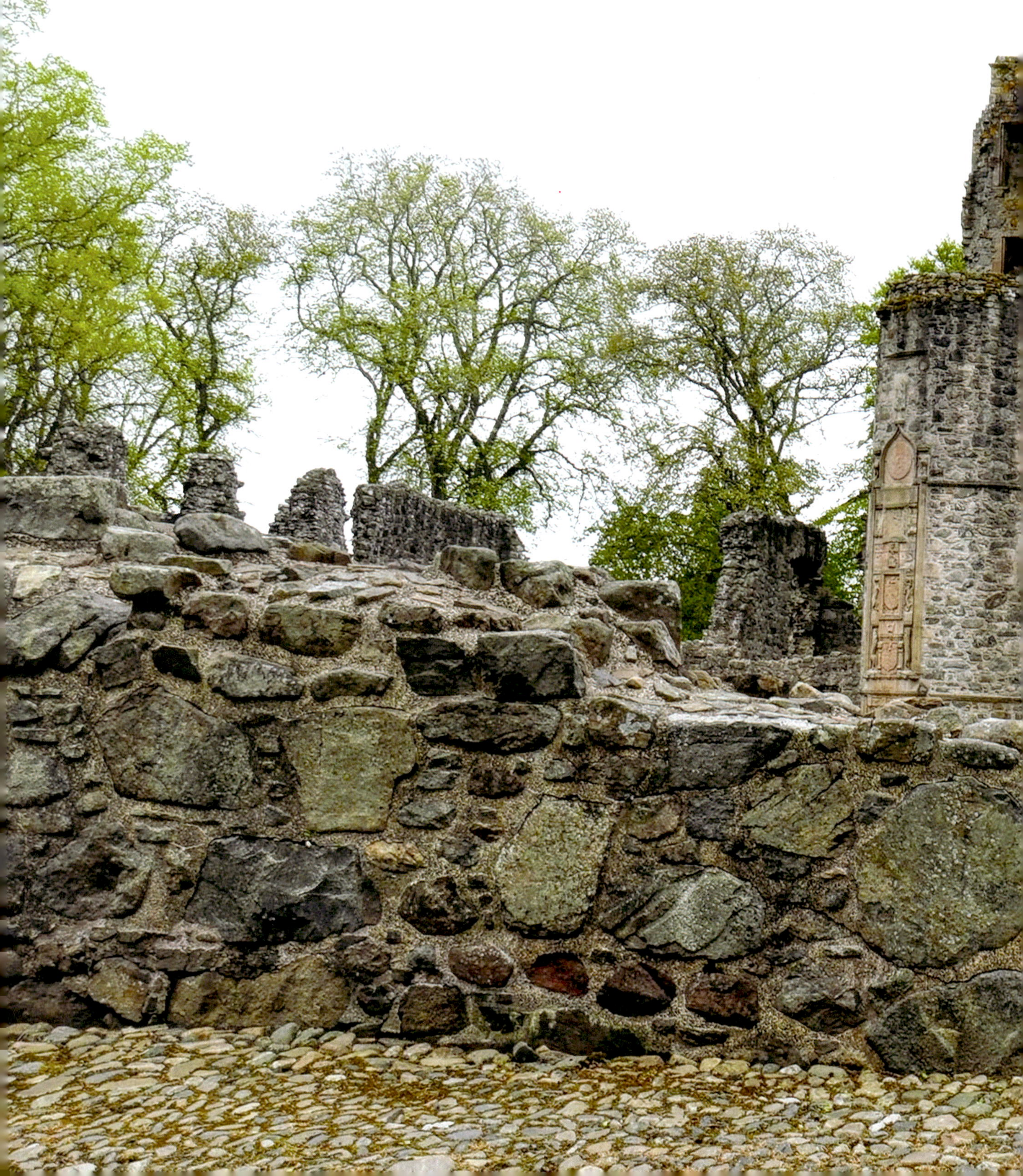

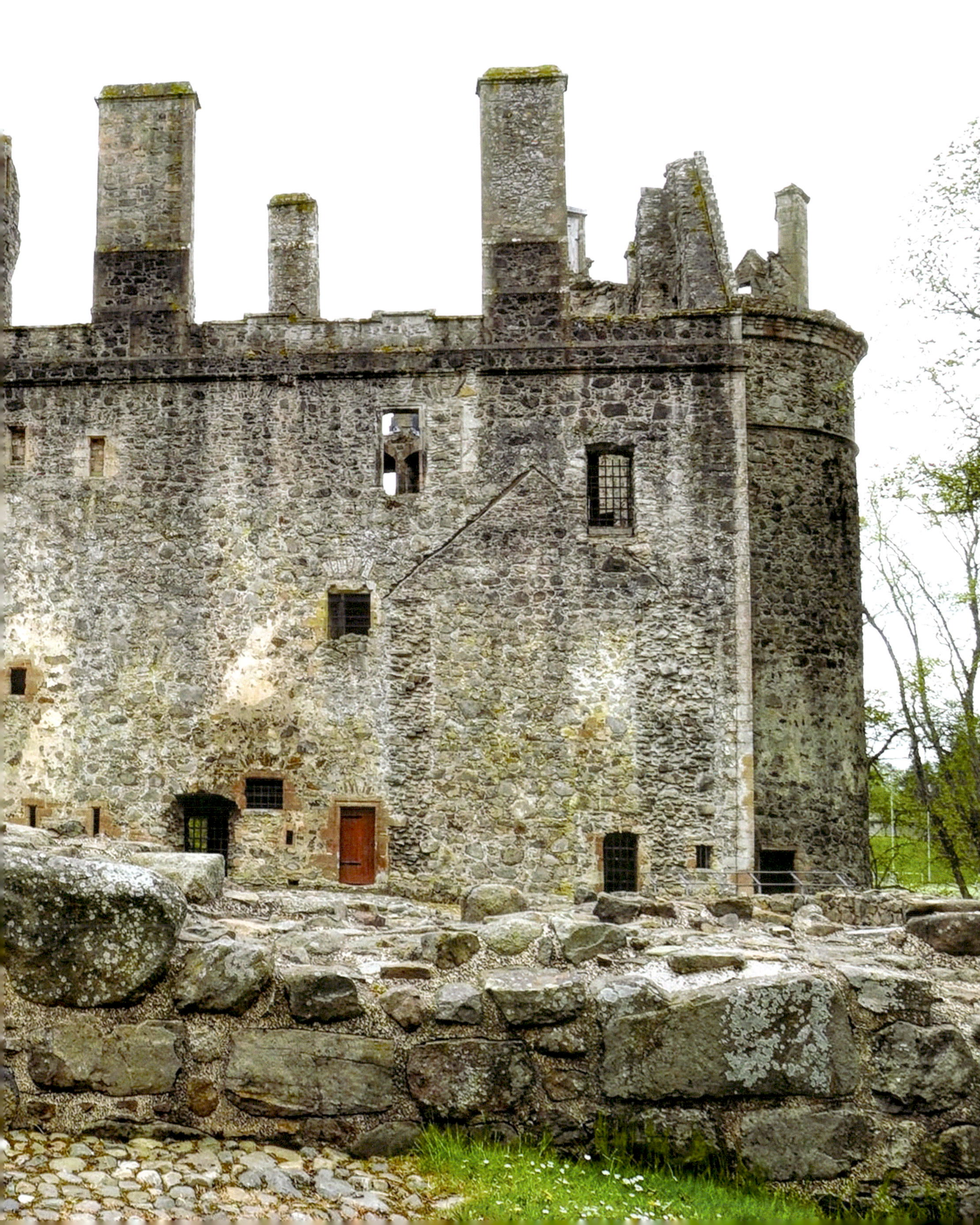

Kisimul Castle, Outer Hebrides, Scotland

Kisimul Castle stands on a small island near Barra in the Outer Hebrides. The site may have been fortified from the 11th century, though the surviving castle was started in the 15th century. Additions were made later, including improvements to the defences that enabled it to withstand attack on several occasions. The castle was abandoned in the 1800s and declined, but was restored in the 20th century.

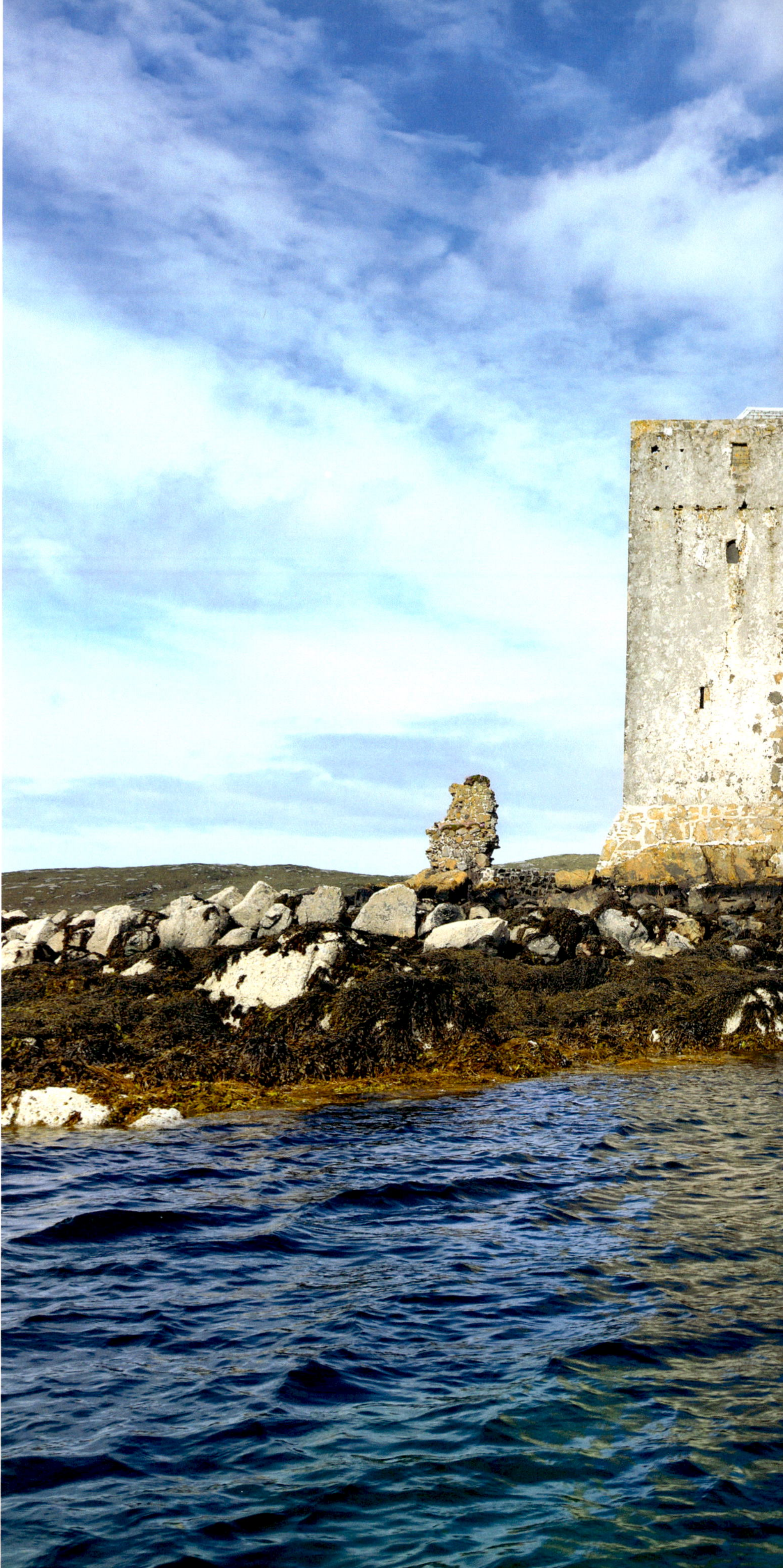

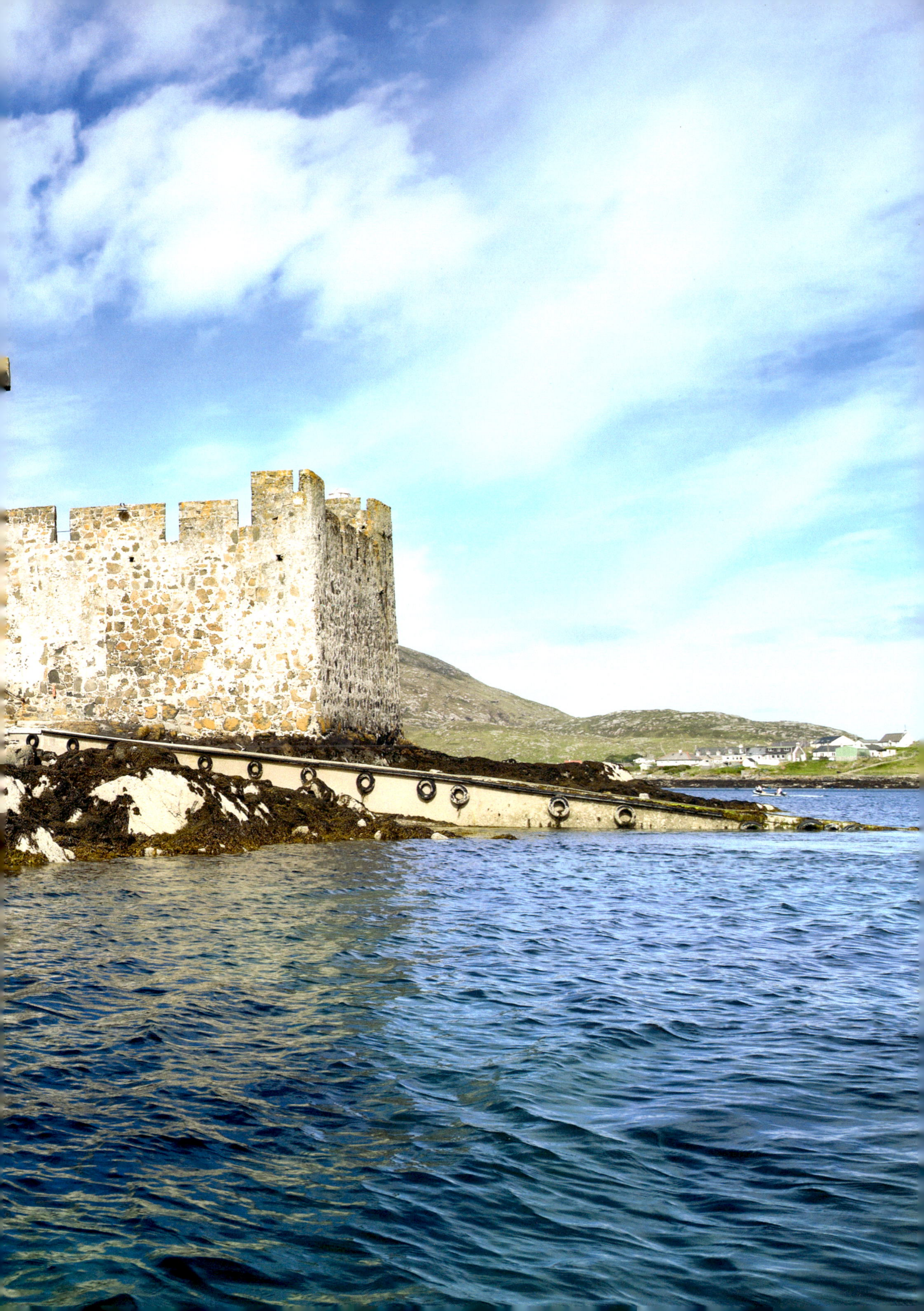

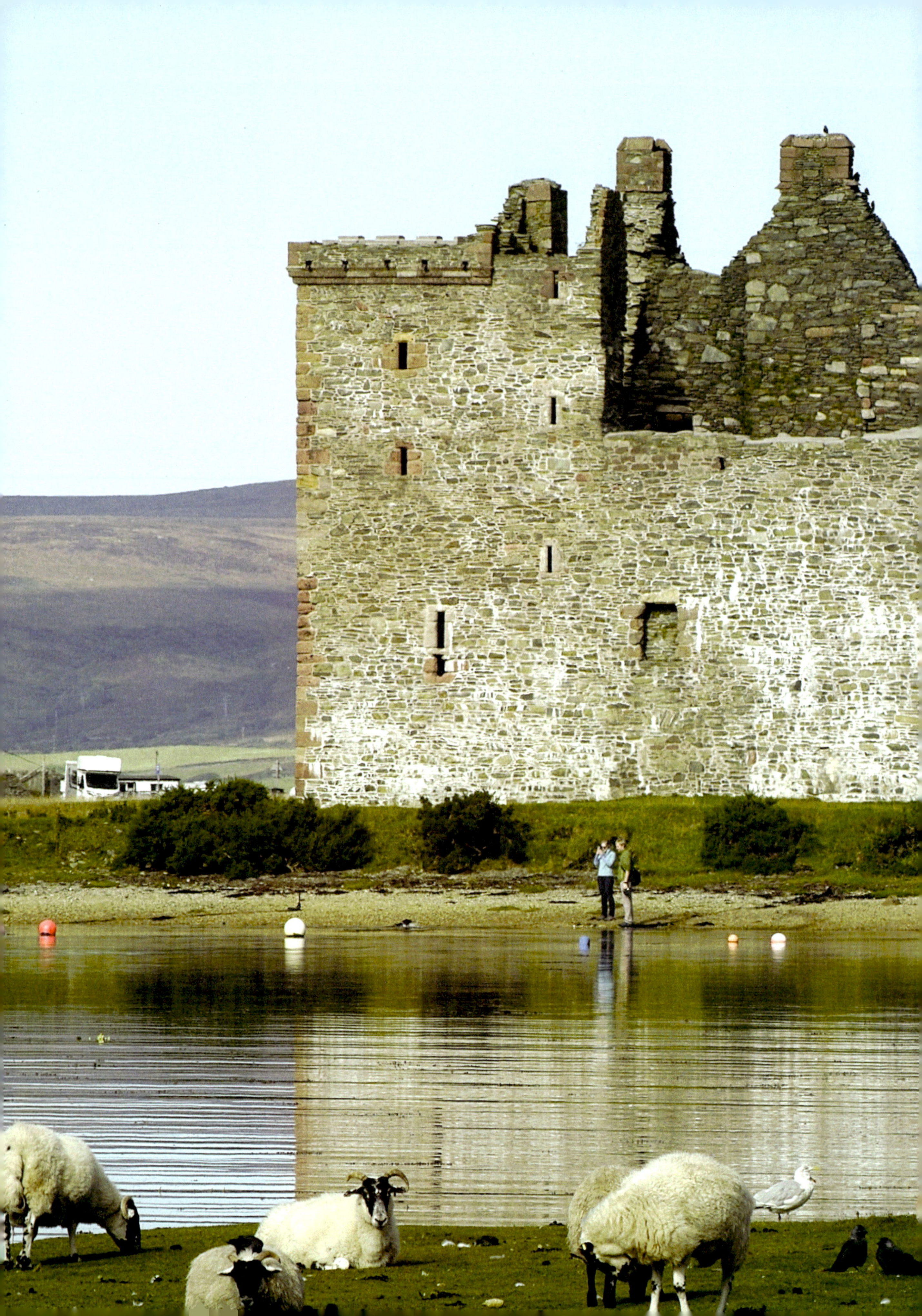

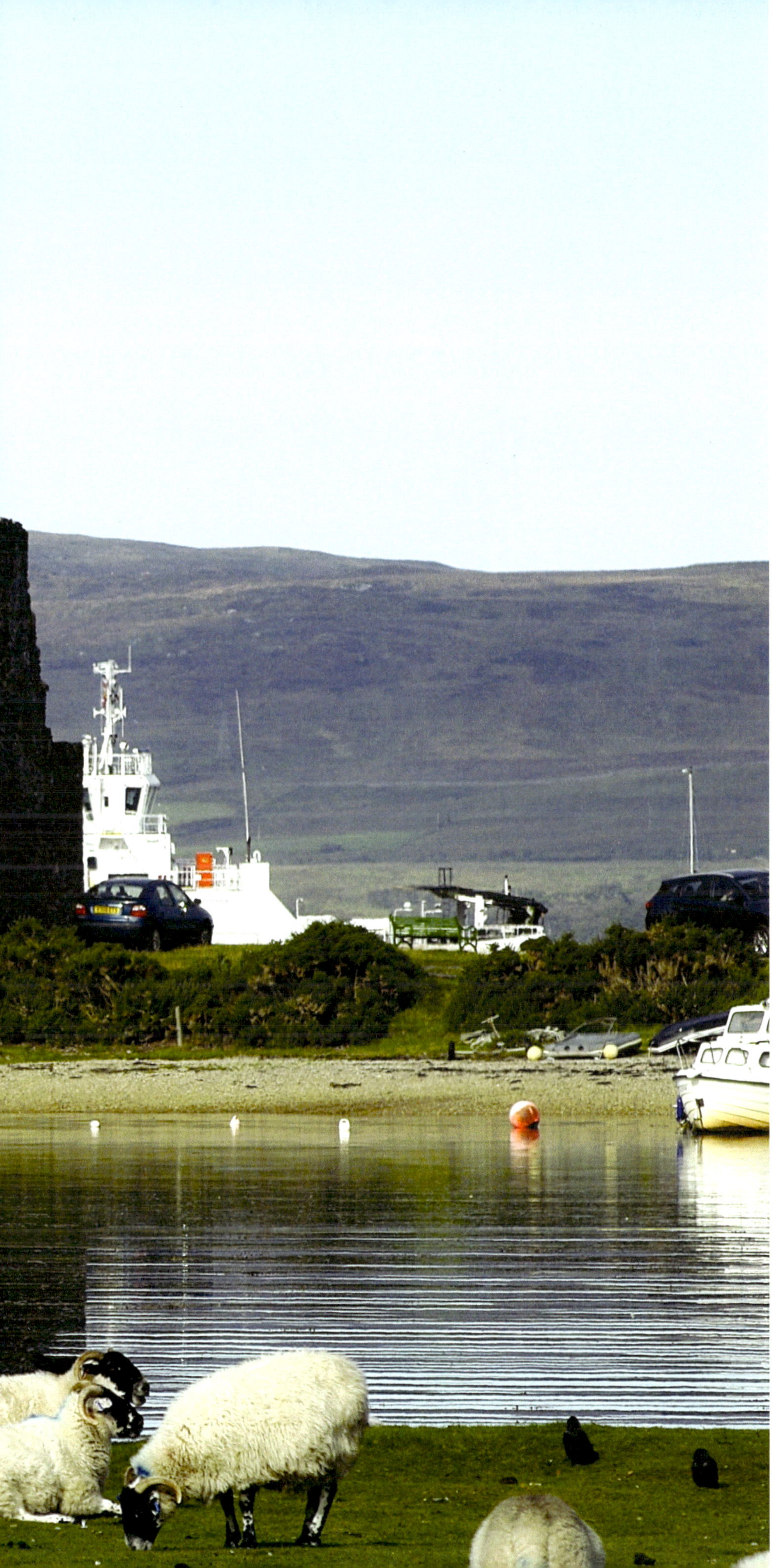

Lochranza Castle, Isle of Arran, Scotland

Lochranza Castle on the Isle of Arran was originally built in the 13th century but was gradually remodelled into its present form, which is an L-shaped tower house and quite different to the original structure. Lochranza Castle is said to be where Robert the Bruce made landfall in Scotland on his return from Ireland in 1306. It was abandoned in the late 18th century.

Ross Castle, County Kerry, Ireland

Ross Castle was probably built in the late 15th century. The central tower house was surrounded by a fortified enclosure known as a bawn, which was defended by a wall and towers. Part of this was removed in the 18th century to install barracks buildings, which were in use for much of the next century.

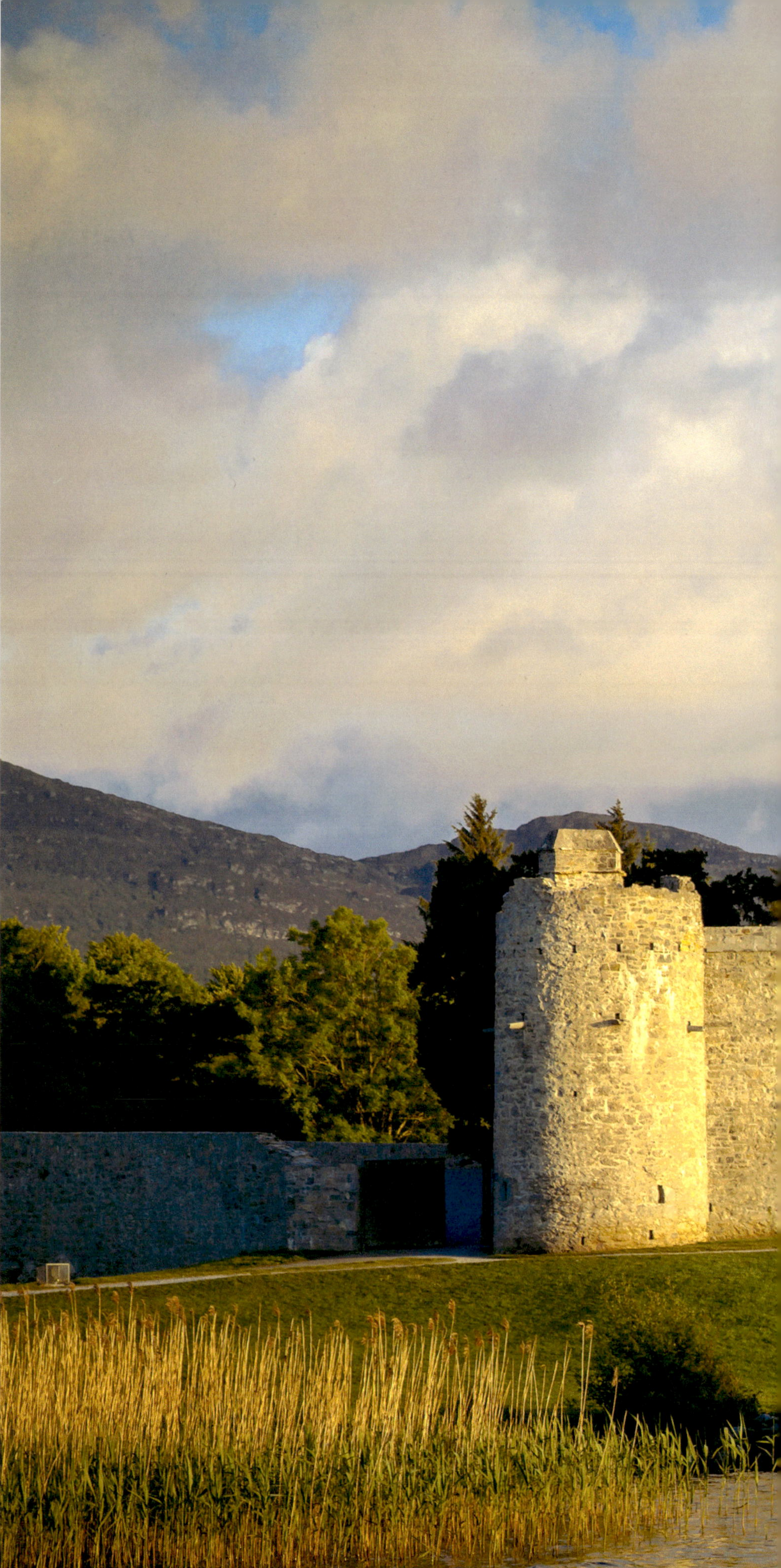

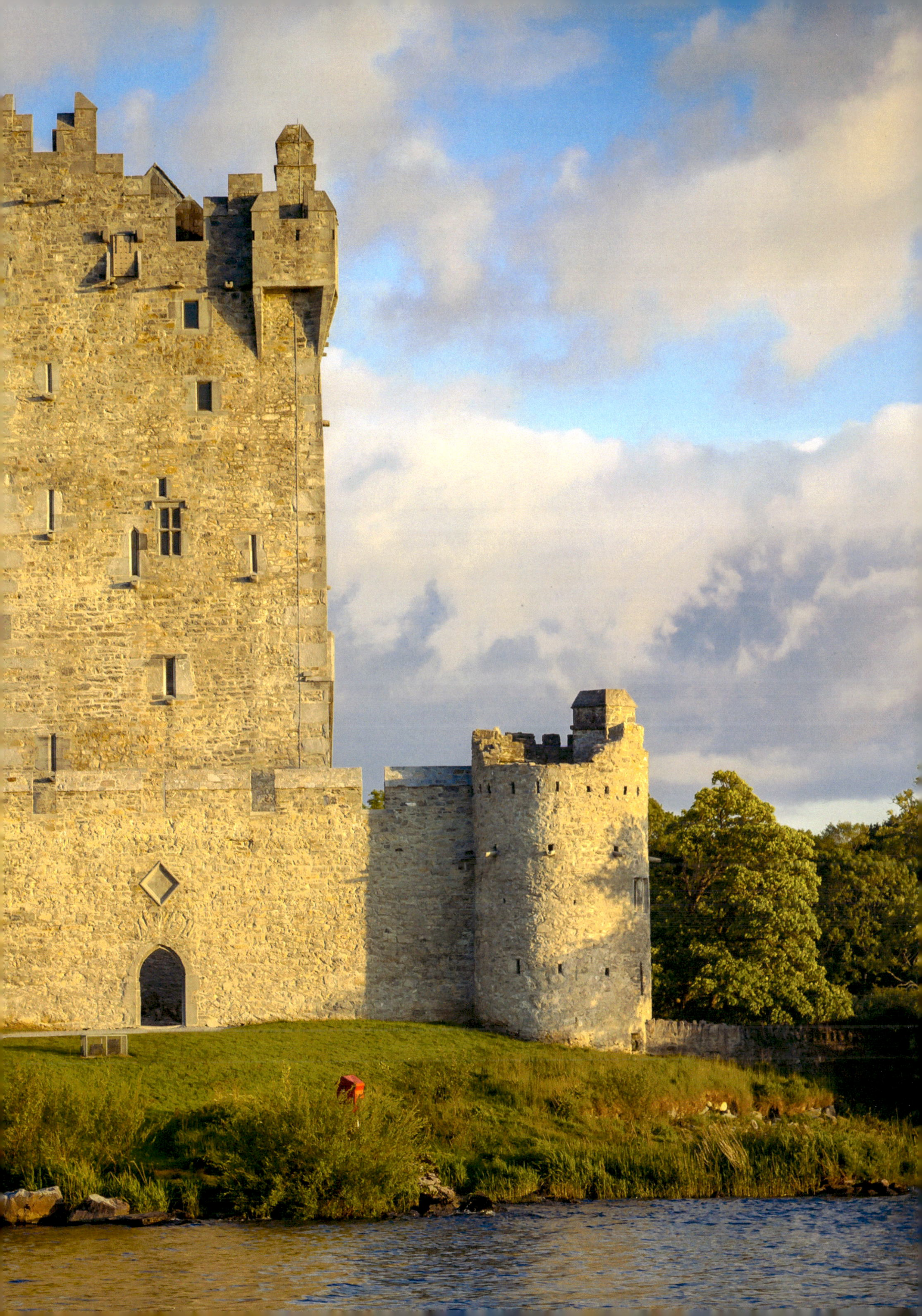

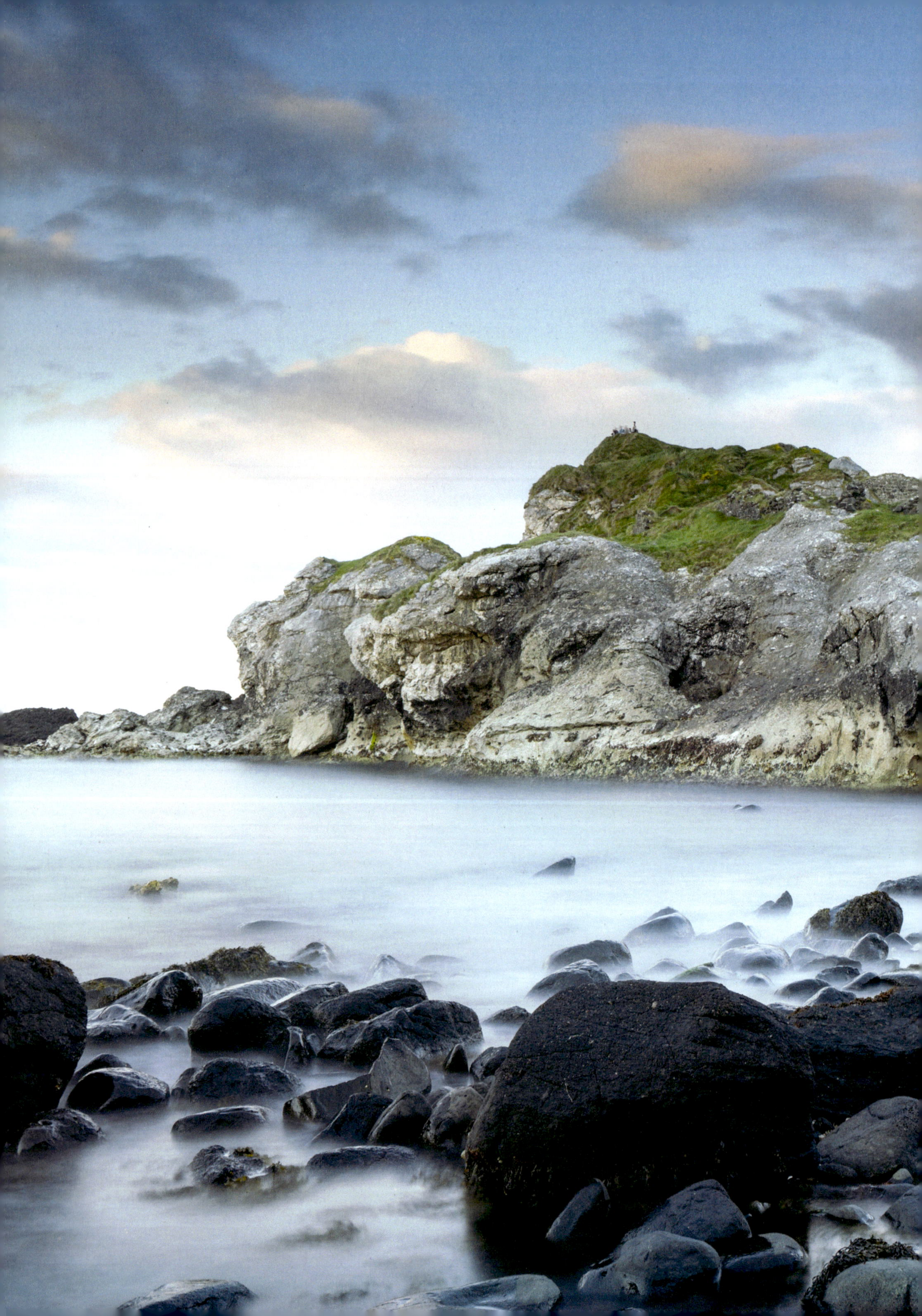

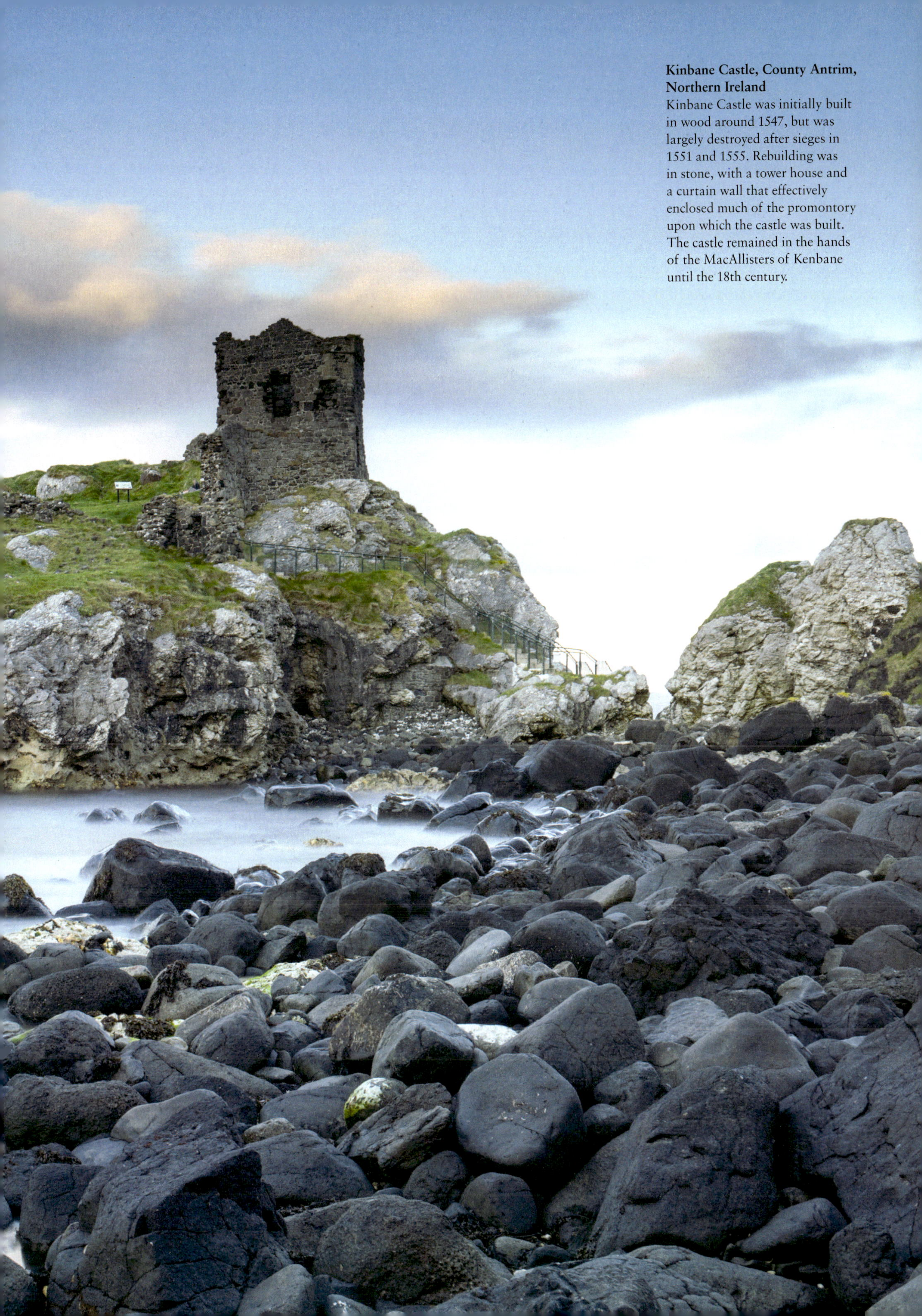

Kinbane Castle, County Antrim, Northern Ireland
Kinbane Castle was initially built in wood around 1547, but was largely destroyed after sieges in 1551 and 1555. Rebuilding was in stone, with a tower house and a curtain wall that effectively enclosed much of the promontory upon which the castle was built. The castle remained in the hands of the MacAllisters of Kenbane until the 18th century.

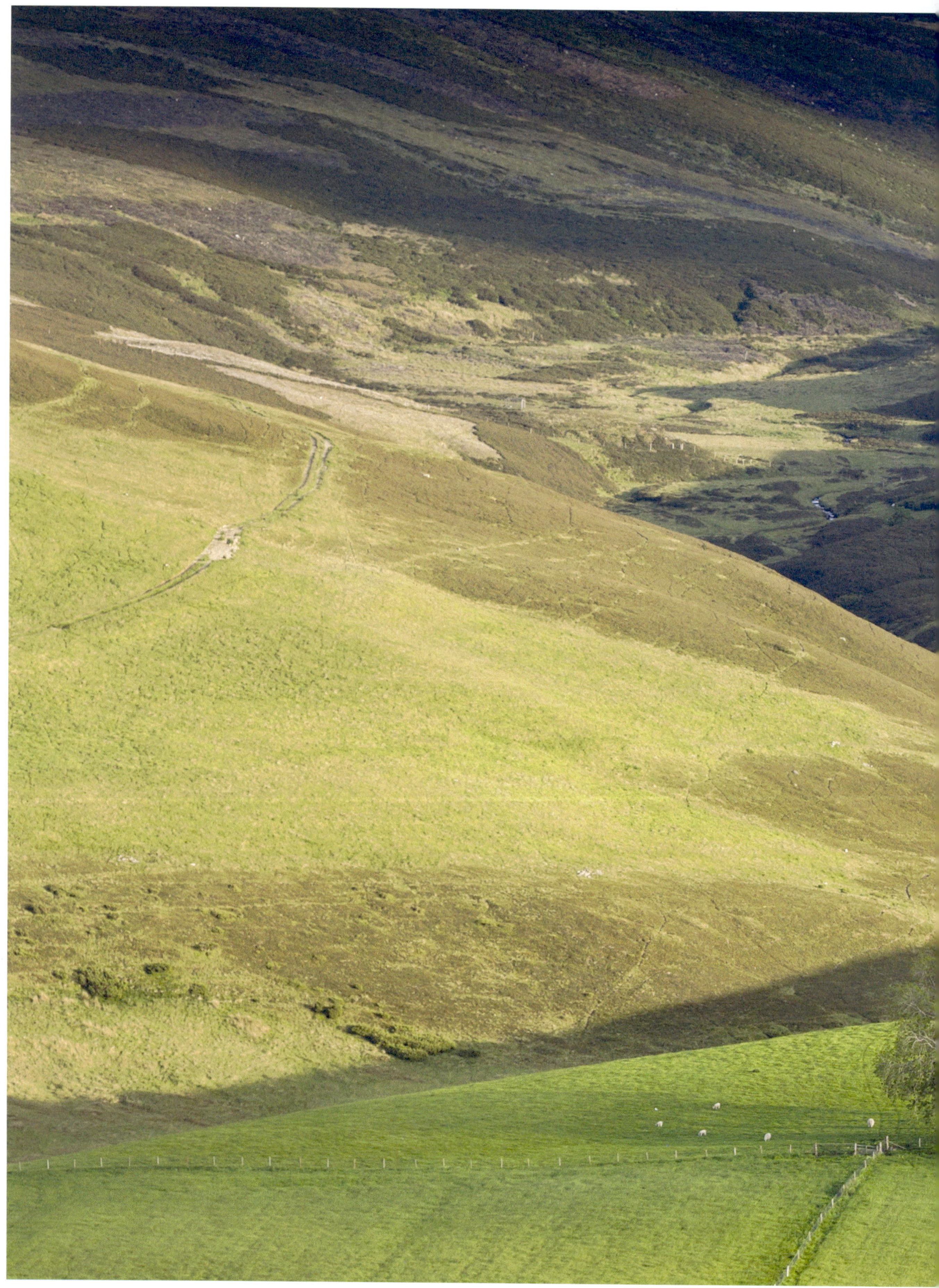

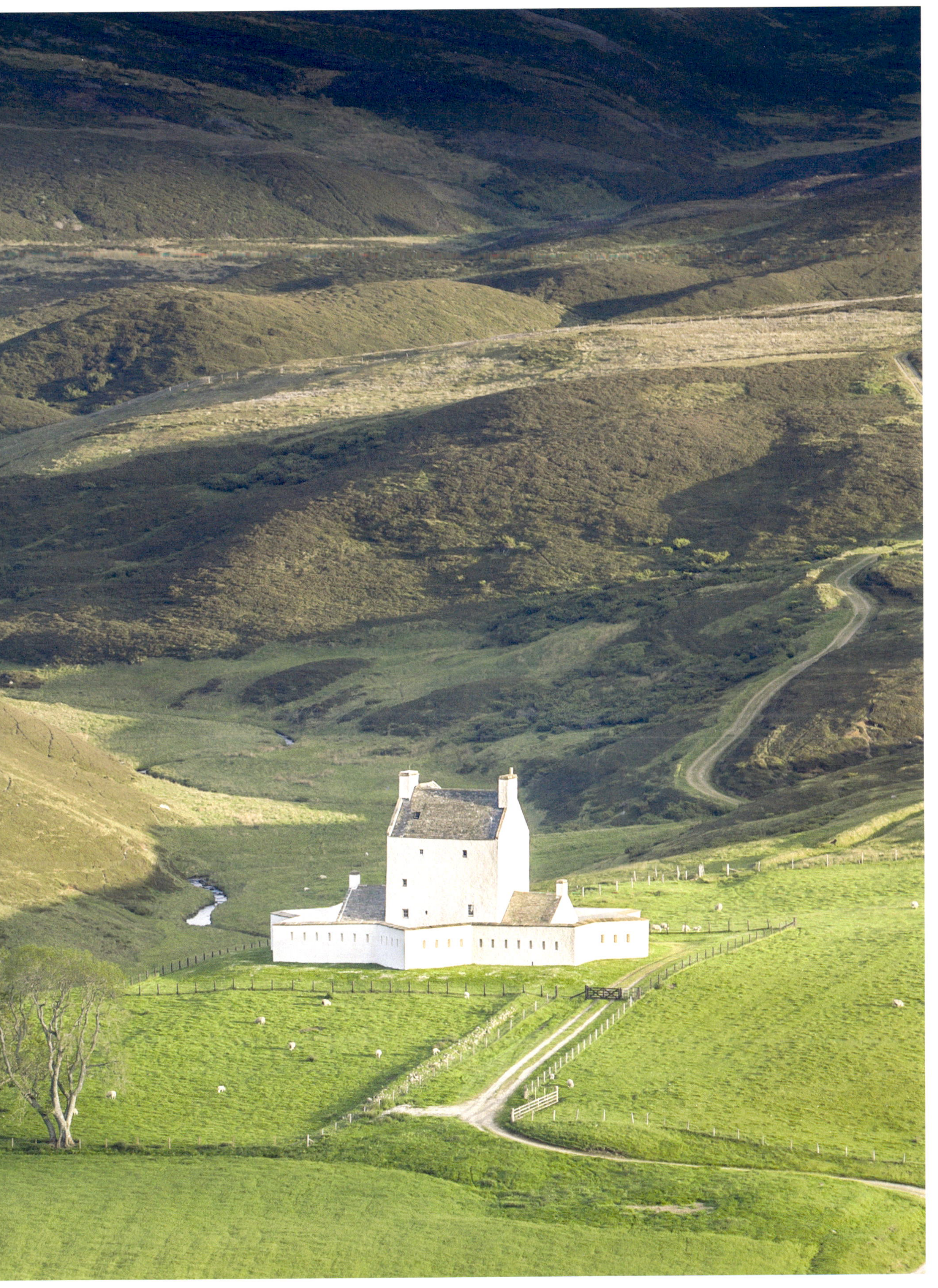

PREVIOUS PAGES:

Corgarff Castle, Aberdeenshire, Scotland

Corgarff Castle was built around 1550 as a tower house surrounded by a walled enclosure. It was badly damaged by fire after the women of the owning Forbes family refused to surrender to the Gordon clan, even though their men were away at war. The castle was burned again in 1689 and 1715, and was later reconstructed for use as a barracks and military post.

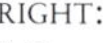

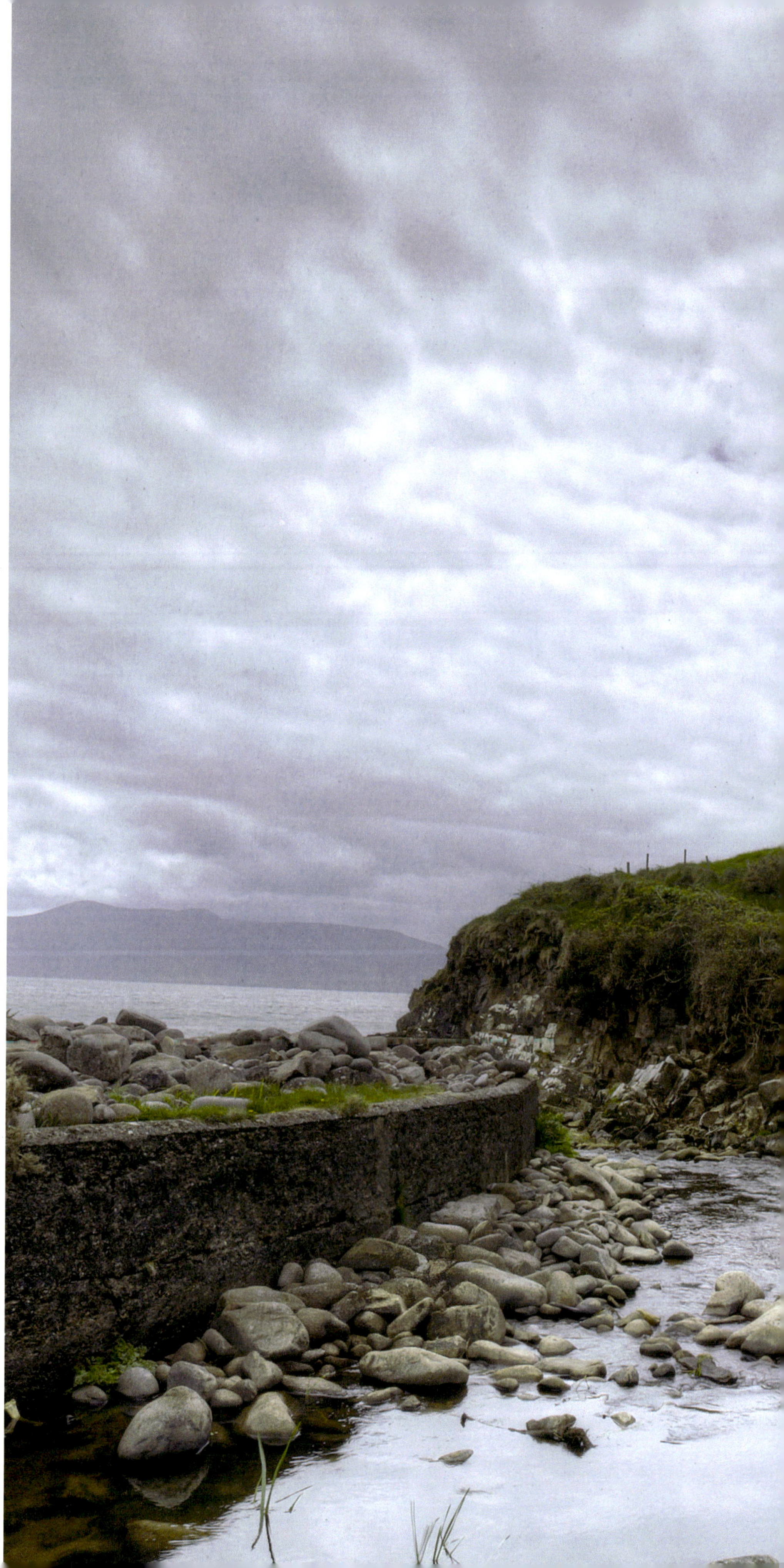

RIGHT:

Minard Castle, County Kerry, Ireland

Minard Castle on the Dingle Peninsula was one of three tower houses built there in the mid-16th century, and is the only one to remain largely intact. The castle was built close to an Iron Age earthwork, which was used by besieging English forces to site their artillery in 1640. The castle was heavily damaged by cannon and then blown up with powder charges, forcing the surviving defenders to surrender.

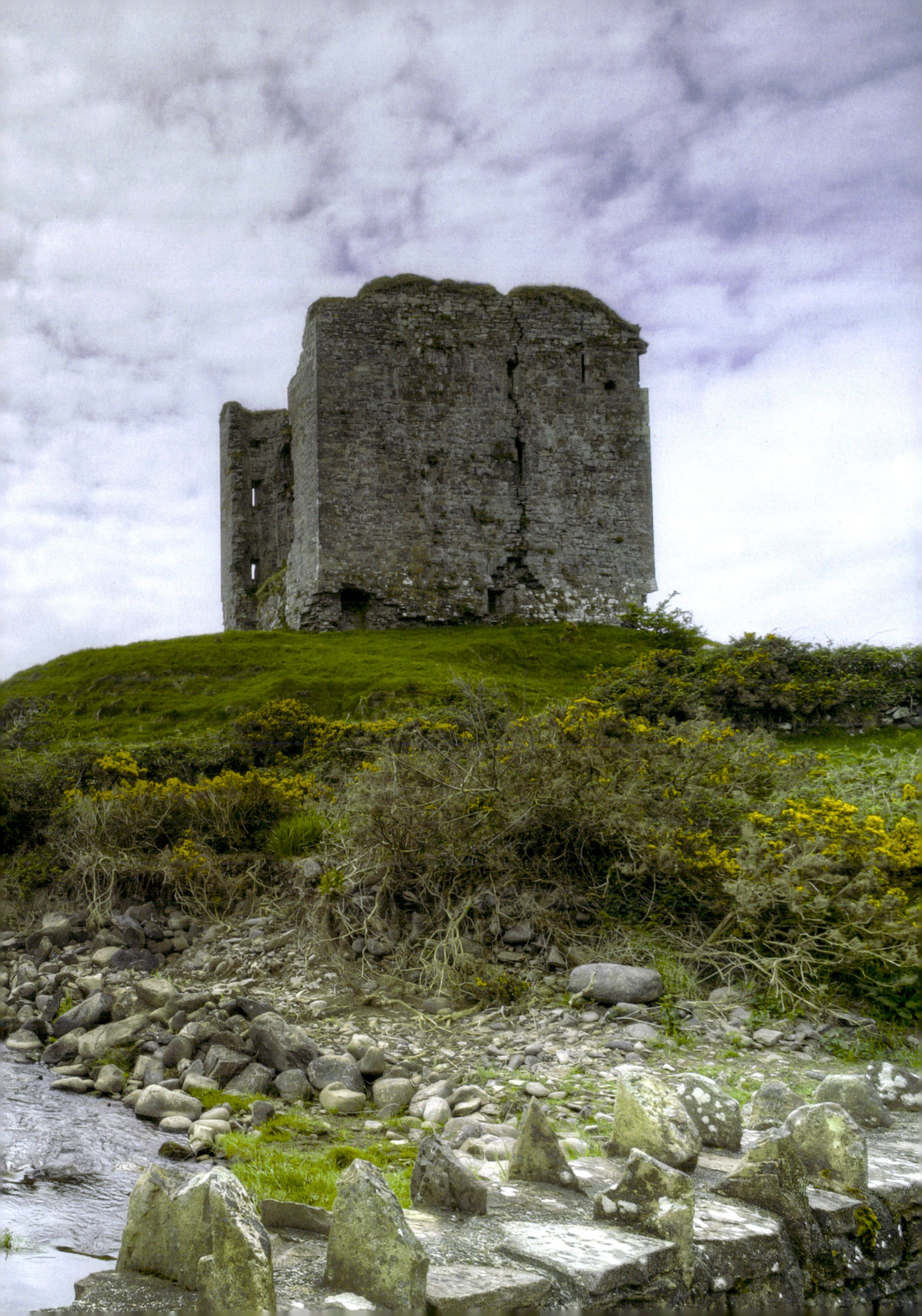

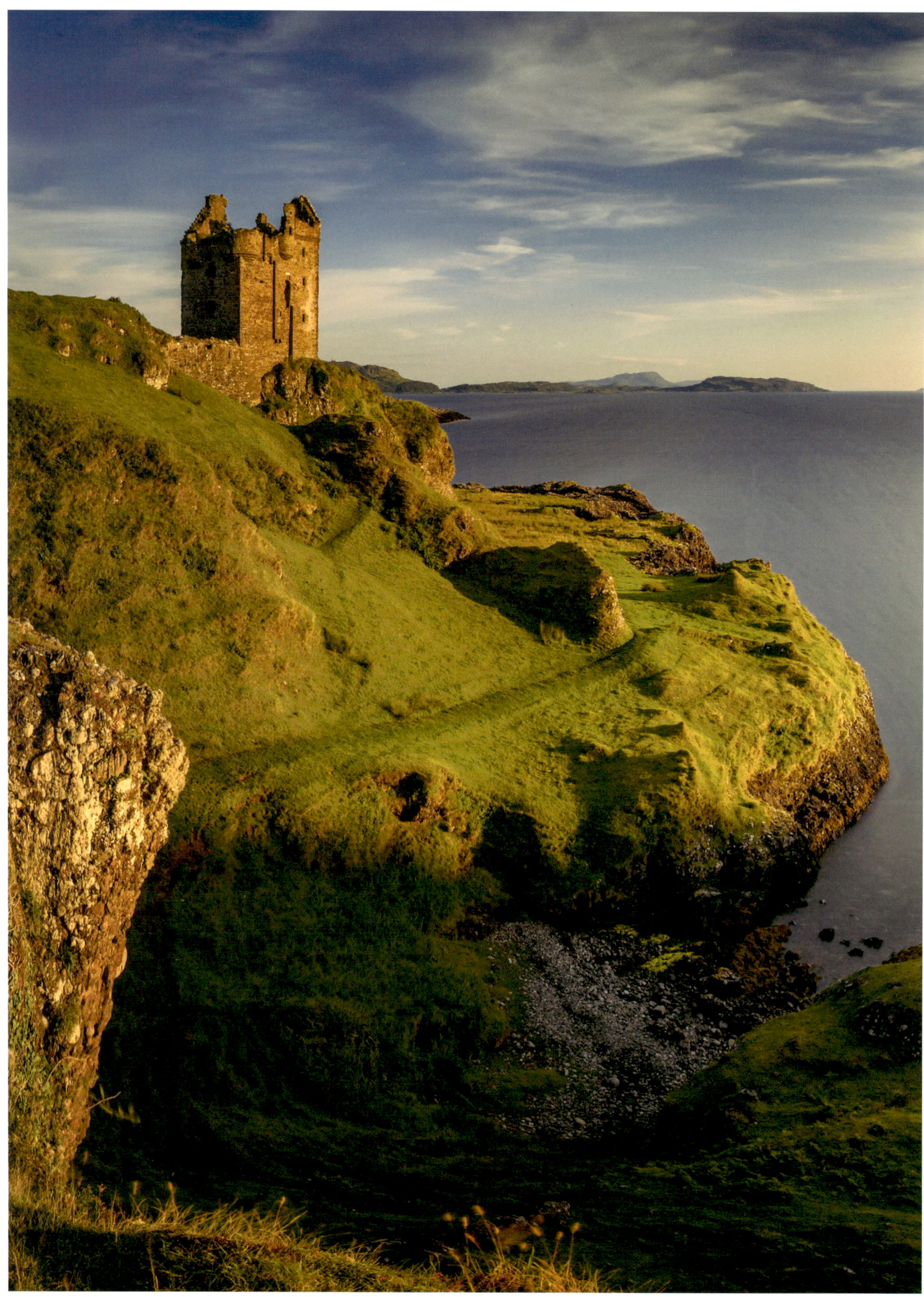

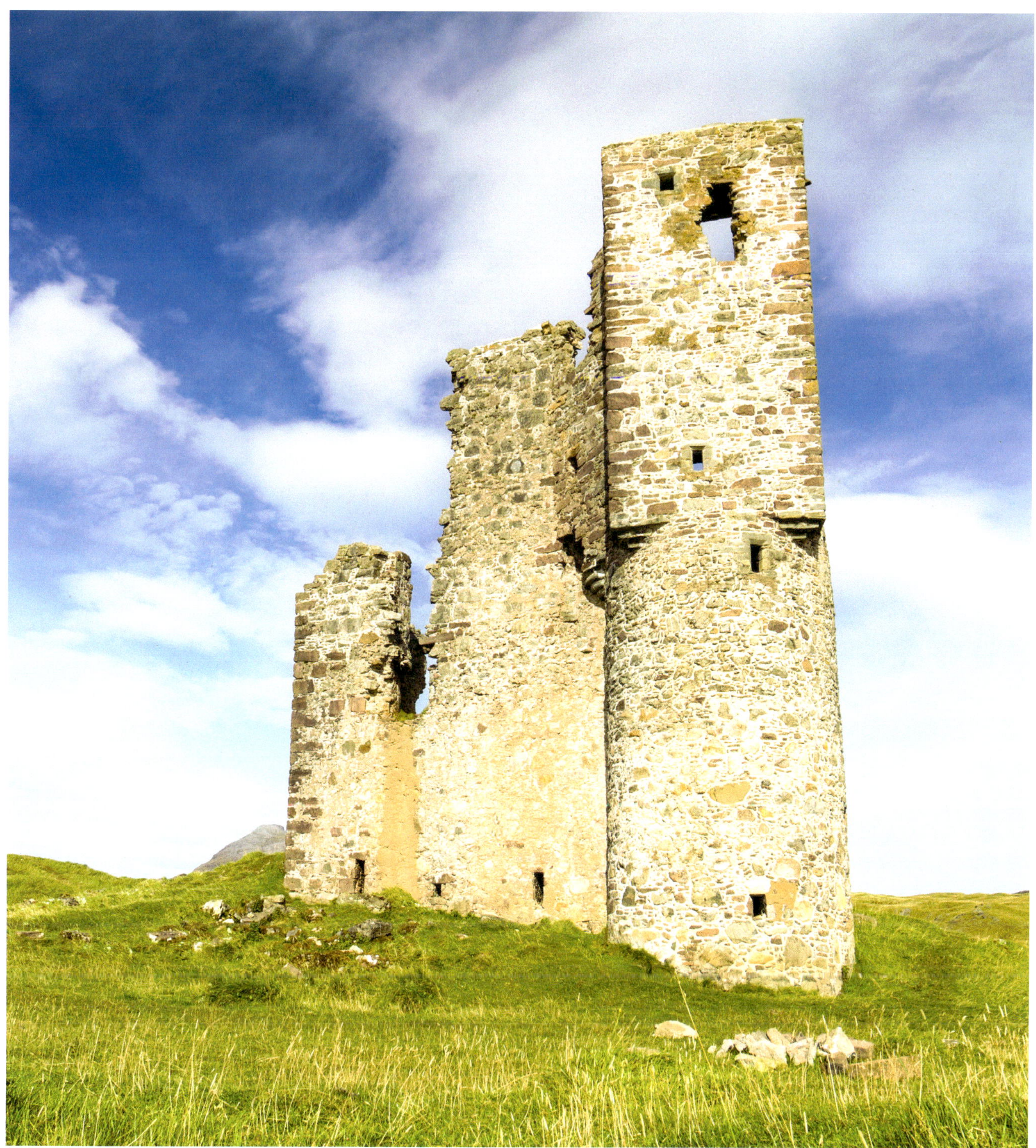

LEFT:

Gylen Castle, Argyll and Bute, Scotland

Gylen Castle in the Inner Hebrides occupies a defensive location on the south coast of the island of Kerrera. The castle was built in 1582 by Clan MacDougall, possibly over an earlier fortification on the site. It was burned after falling to the Covenanters in 1647 during the Wars of the Three Kingdoms, and never reoccupied.

ABOVE:

Ardvreck Castle, Sutherland, Scotland

Ardvreck Castle stands on the shore of Loch Assynt in Sutherland, Scotland, on a promontory that almost becomes an island when the water is high. It was probably built at the end of the 15th century. In 1650 it was a prison for the Marquis of Montrose, who was subsequently executed in Edinburgh.

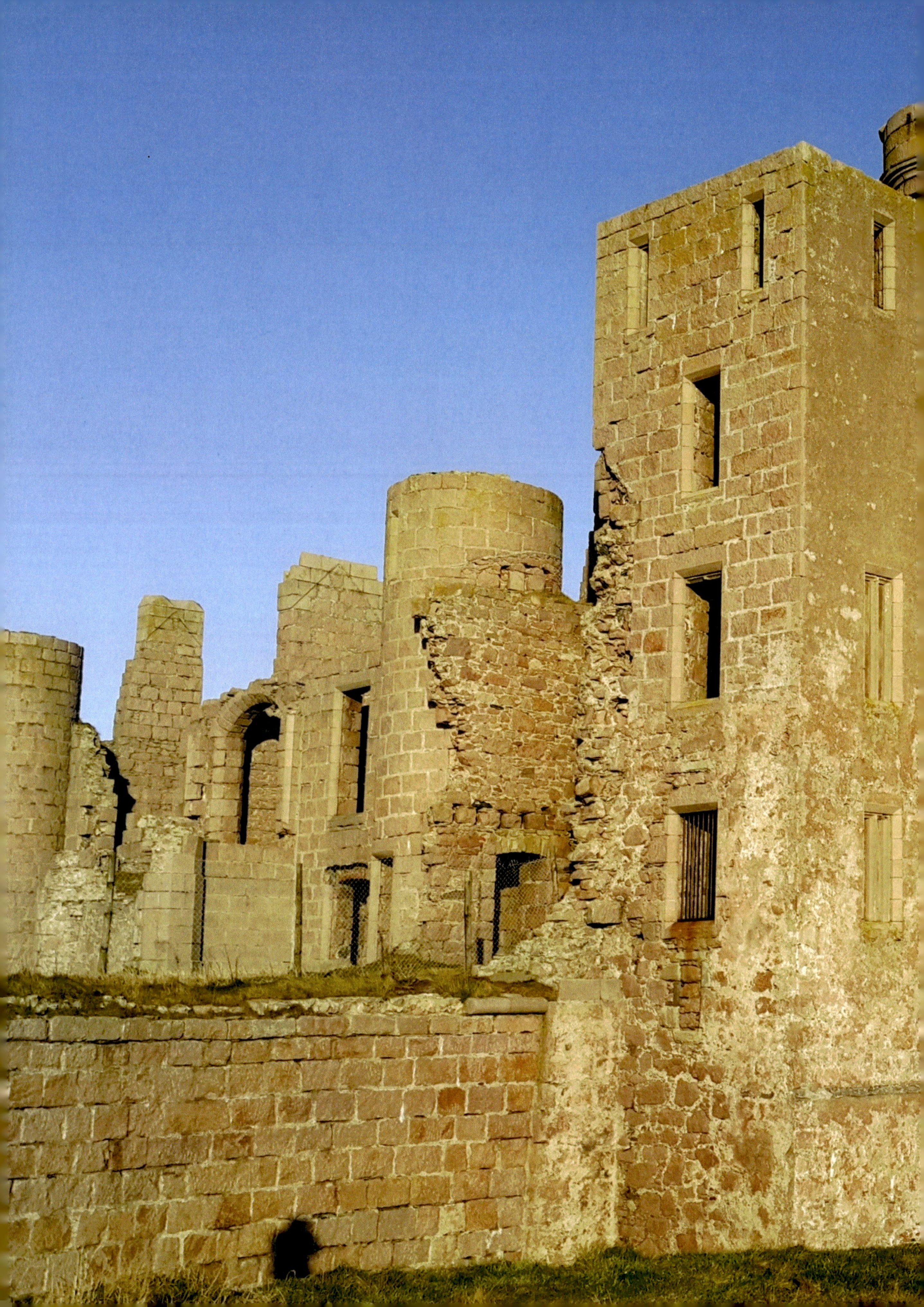

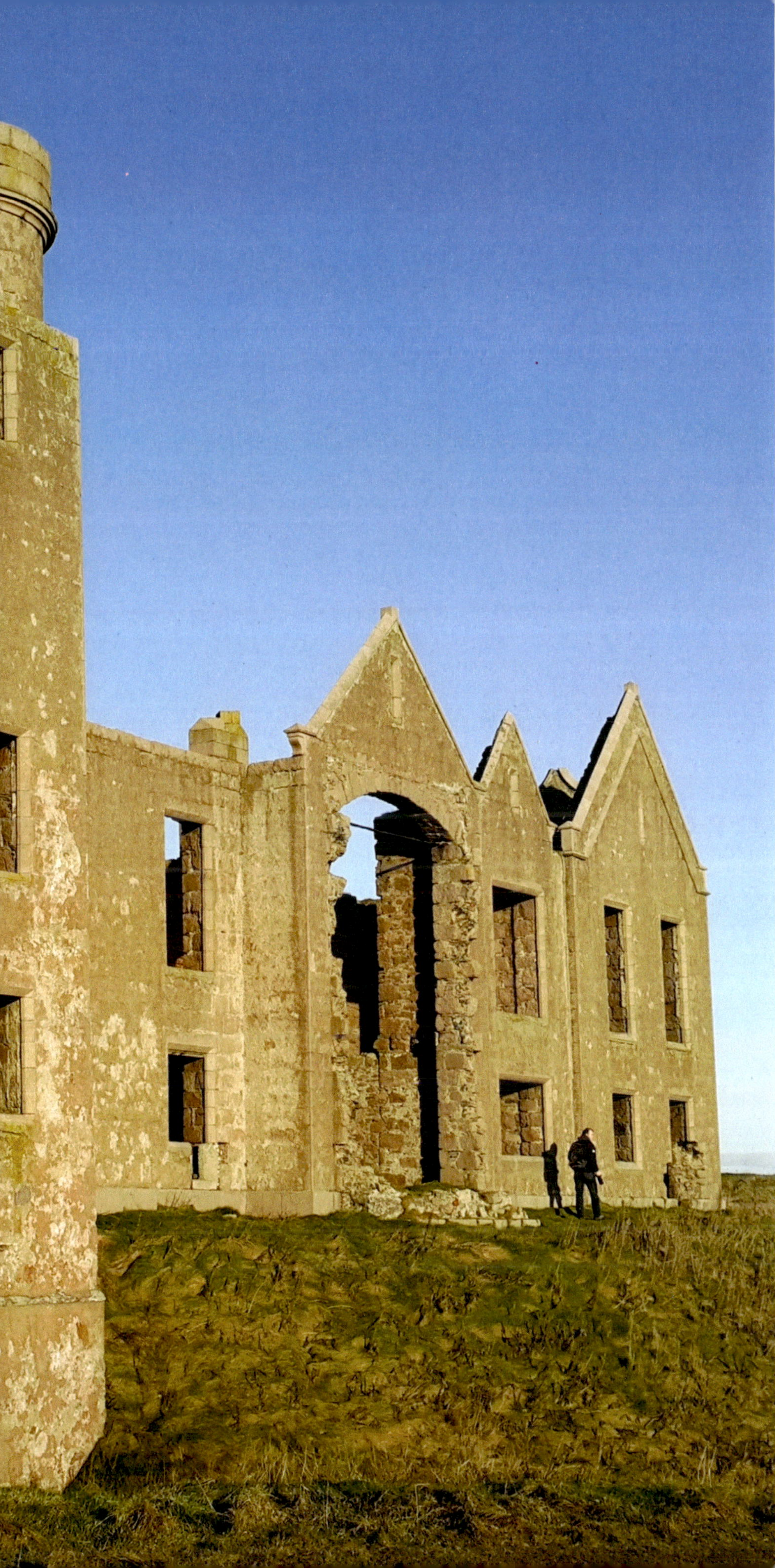

New Slains Castle, Aberdeenshire, Scotland
New Slains Castle stands close to the site of Old Slains Castle, which was built in the 1200s and destroyed in 1594 after the owners rebelled against the crown. The new castle was begun some time after 1597 and extended in 1664. In 1836 a final remodelling took place, with the castle falling into ruin a century later.

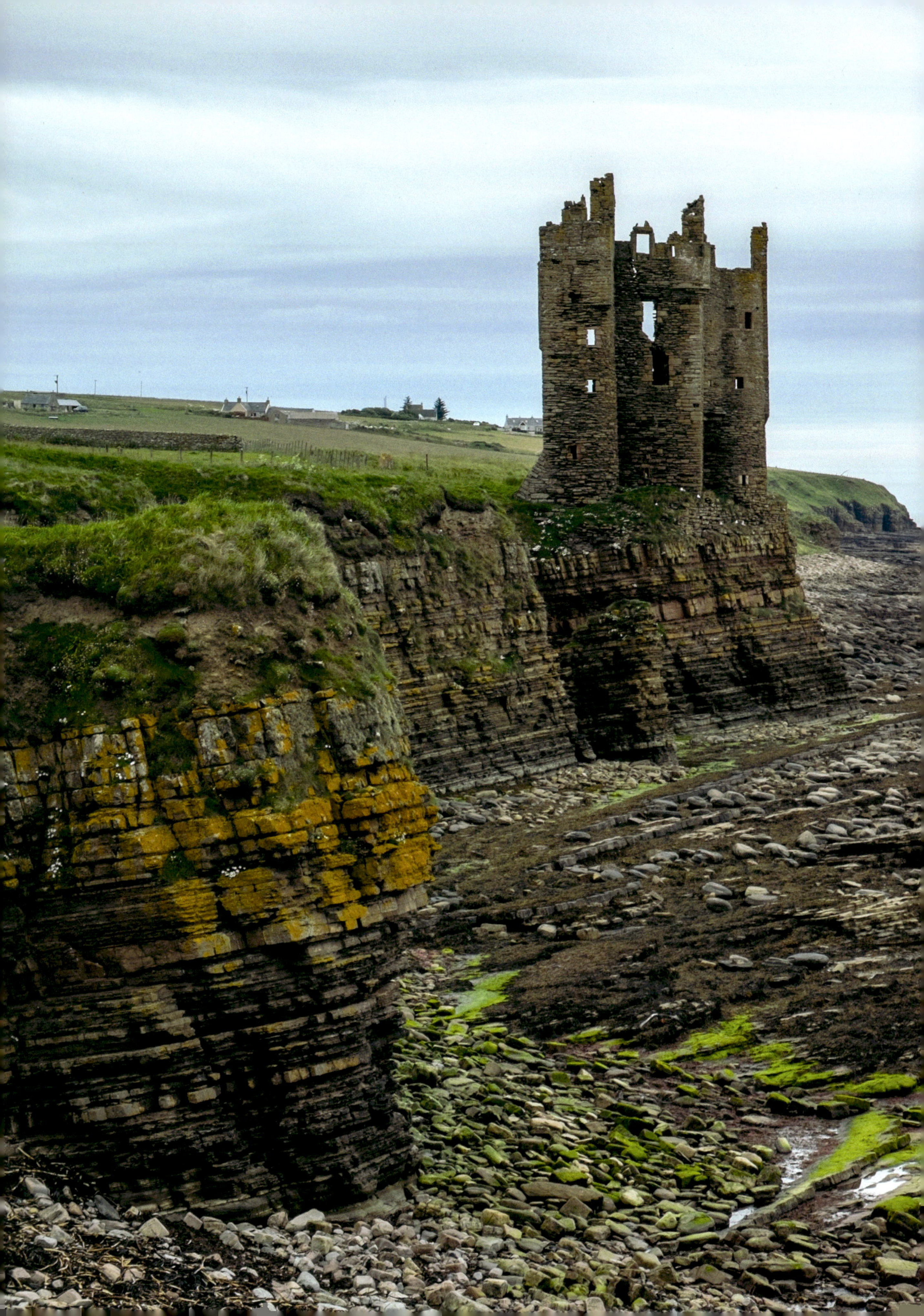

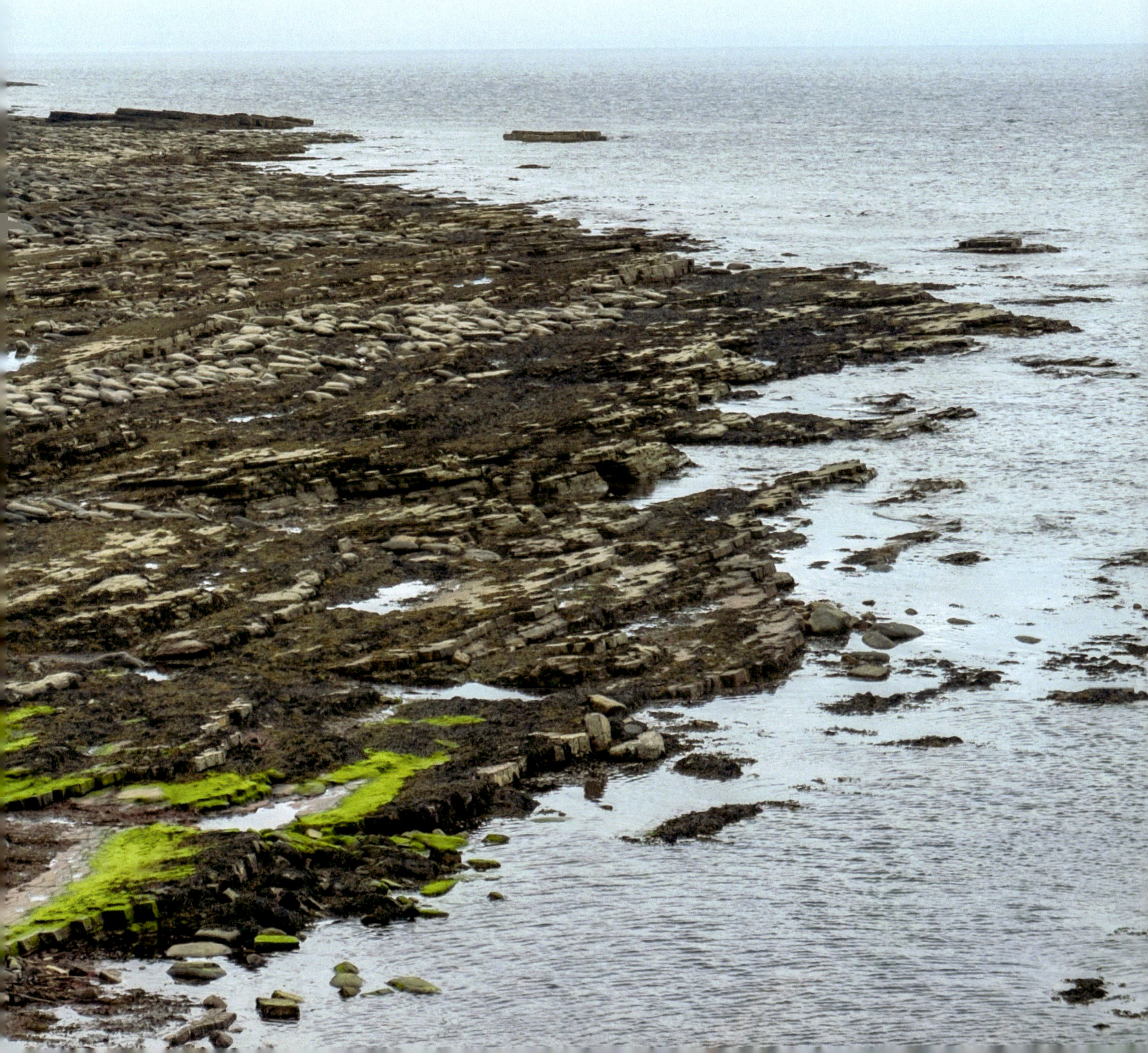

Keiss Castle, Sutherland, Scotland
Keiss Castle may have been built on the site of an earlier fortification. It took the form of a tower house with towers at opposite corners, creating a 'Z-plan' configuration that is quite common in castles of the era. Keiss Castle was in existence before 1623, but the exact date of its construction is unclear. It fell into disrepair in the later 17th century. The area was fortified during World War II, to protect the Royal Navy Fleet anchorage at Scapa Flow and merchant traffic along the coast.

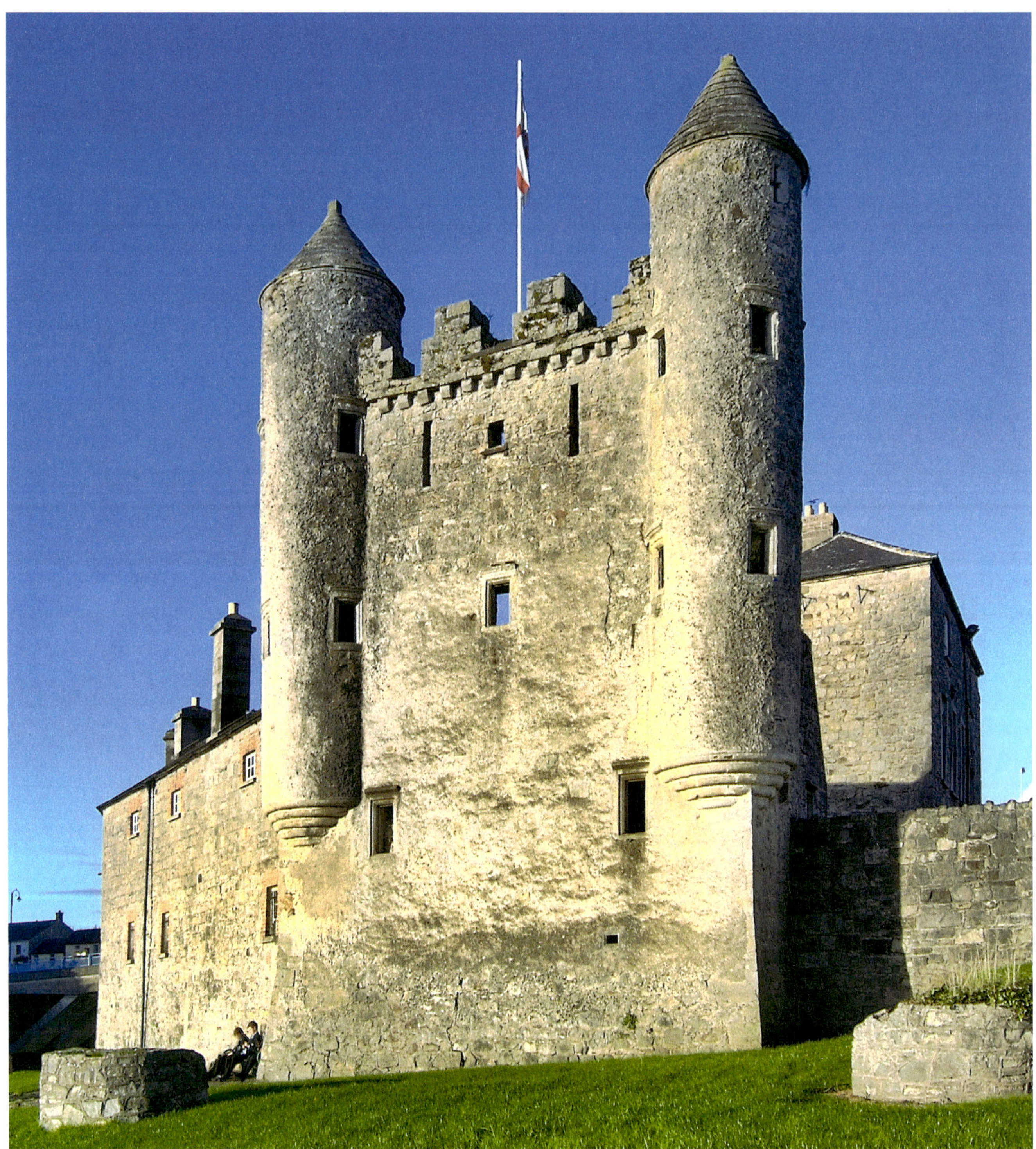

ABOVE:

Enniskillen Castle, County Fermanagh, Northern Ireland

Enniskillen Castle takes the form of a central keep and outer wall with its own towers. It was built in the 16th century and captured by the English in 1594. The castle was modified in 1607 and was later converted into a barracks.

RIGHT:

Parke's Castle, County Leitrim, Northern Ireland

Parke's Castle was built in 1610 using materials from an earlier castle on the site. The outer defences of a curtain wall with towers were retained. One side of the fortified bawn was originally defended by the lough (lake), but water levels have since dropped, allowing access to the base of the wall on that side.

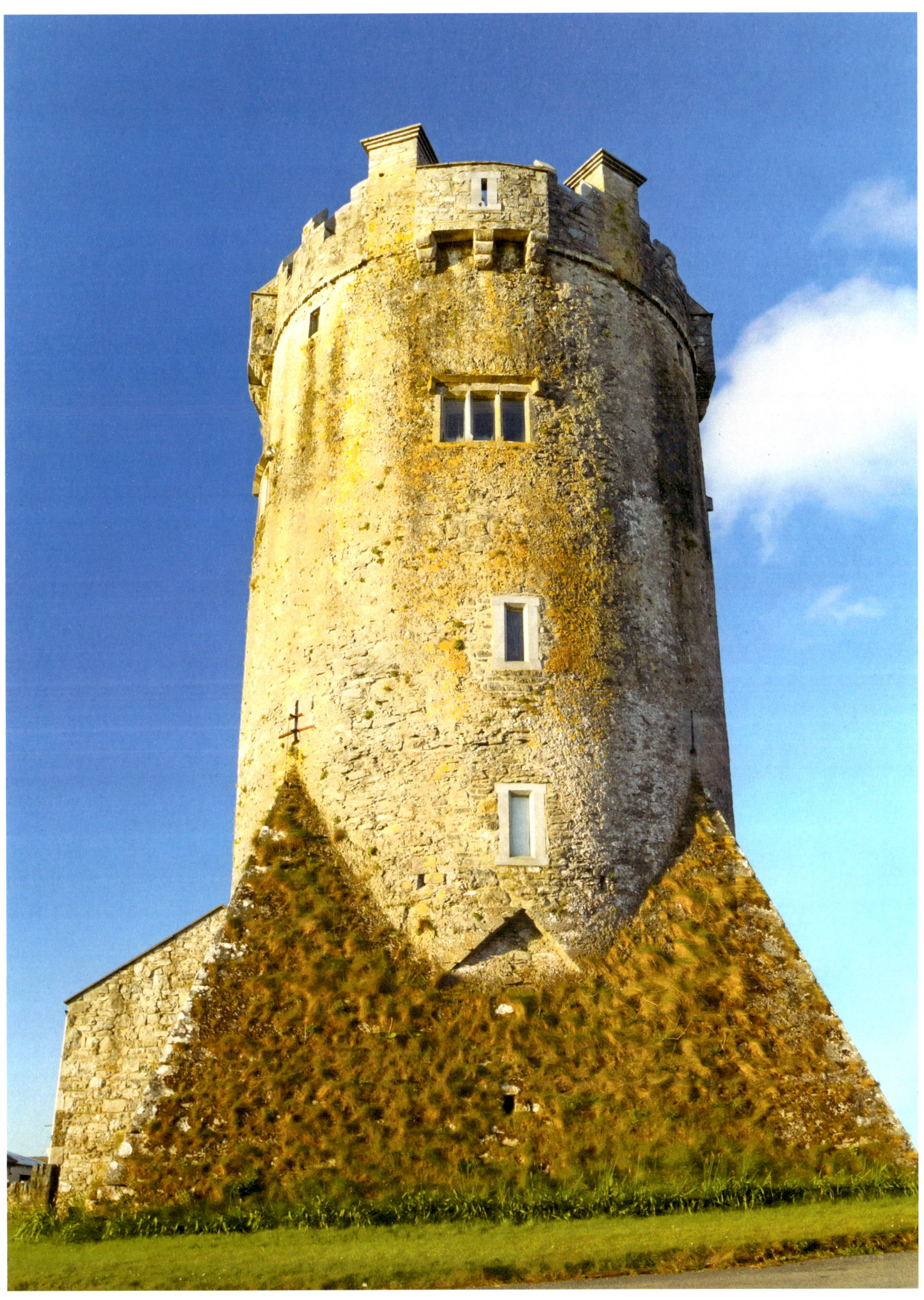

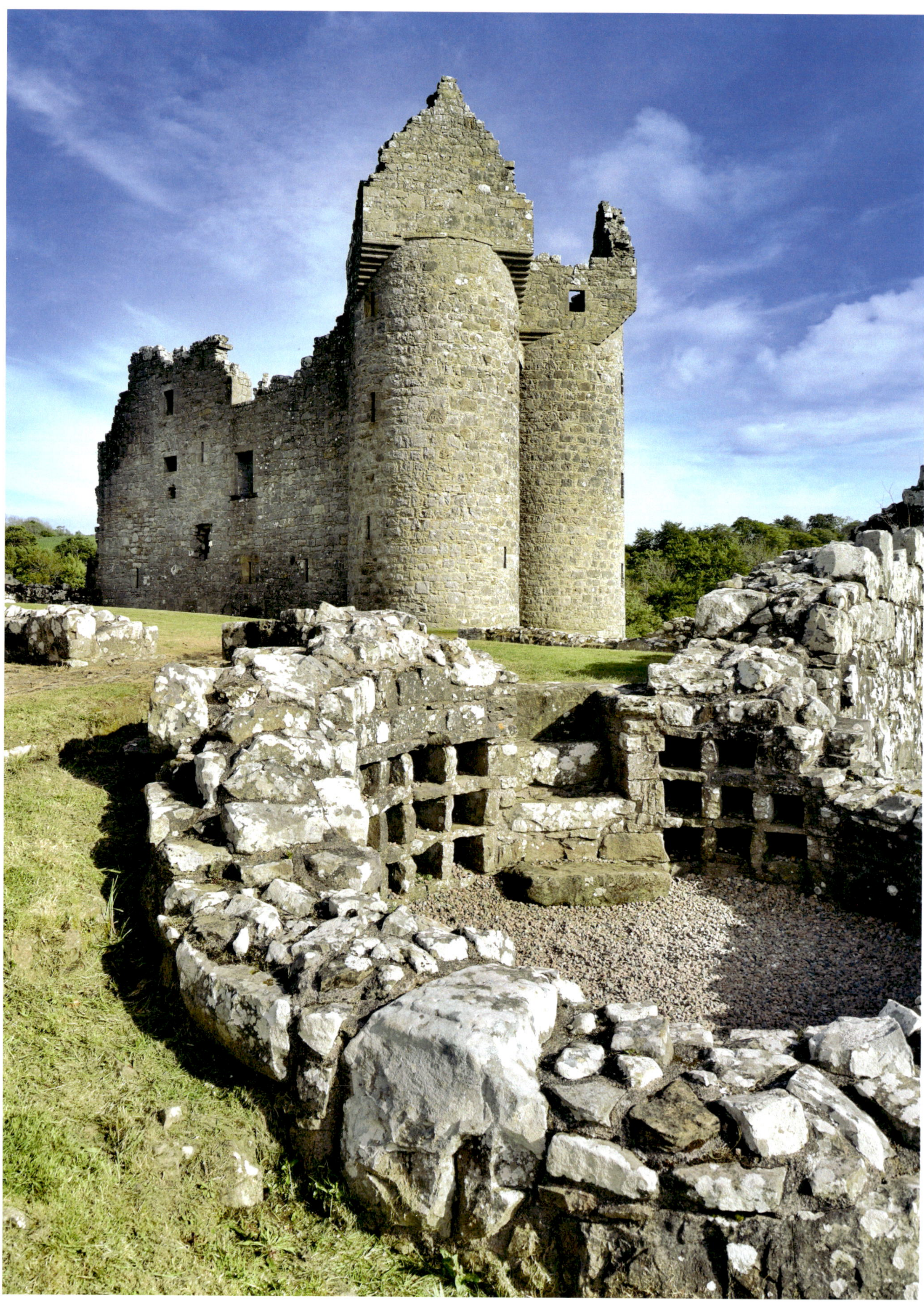

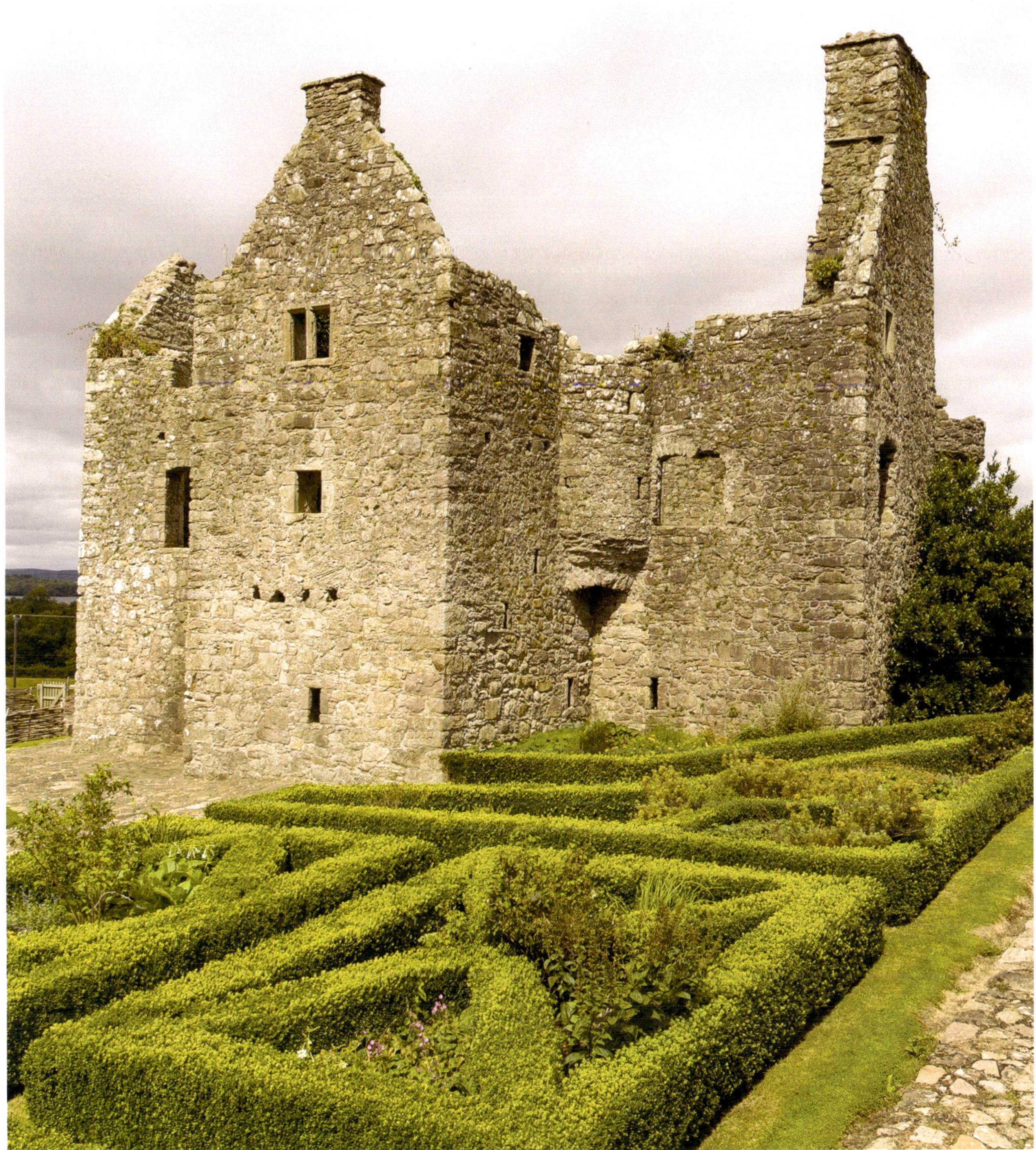

LEFT:
Monea Castle, County Fermanagh, Northern Ireland
Monea Castle takes the form of a four-storey tower house of distinctly Scottish appearance, with round towers flanking its entrance. As completed in 1618, the castle stood within a fortified bawn. The castle was heavily damaged by fire in the 18th century and fell into ruin.

ABOVE:
Tully Castle, County Fermanagh, Northern Ireland
Tully Castle was built in 1619. Standing within a bawn fortified with corner towers, the castle was a typical defensive residence used by English and Scottish landowners. It was attacked and burned in 1641 by Irish rebels, who killed all the occupants except the owning Hume family, who had been granted safe passage.

Birr Castle, County Offaly, Ireland
Birr Castle is an example of the evolution of fortified places into comfortable stately homes. It was modified in the early 19th century, with some pseudo-medieval features dating from that time. The Parsons family, who have owned the castle since the 1600s, had a great scientific heritage, working on several important advances there.

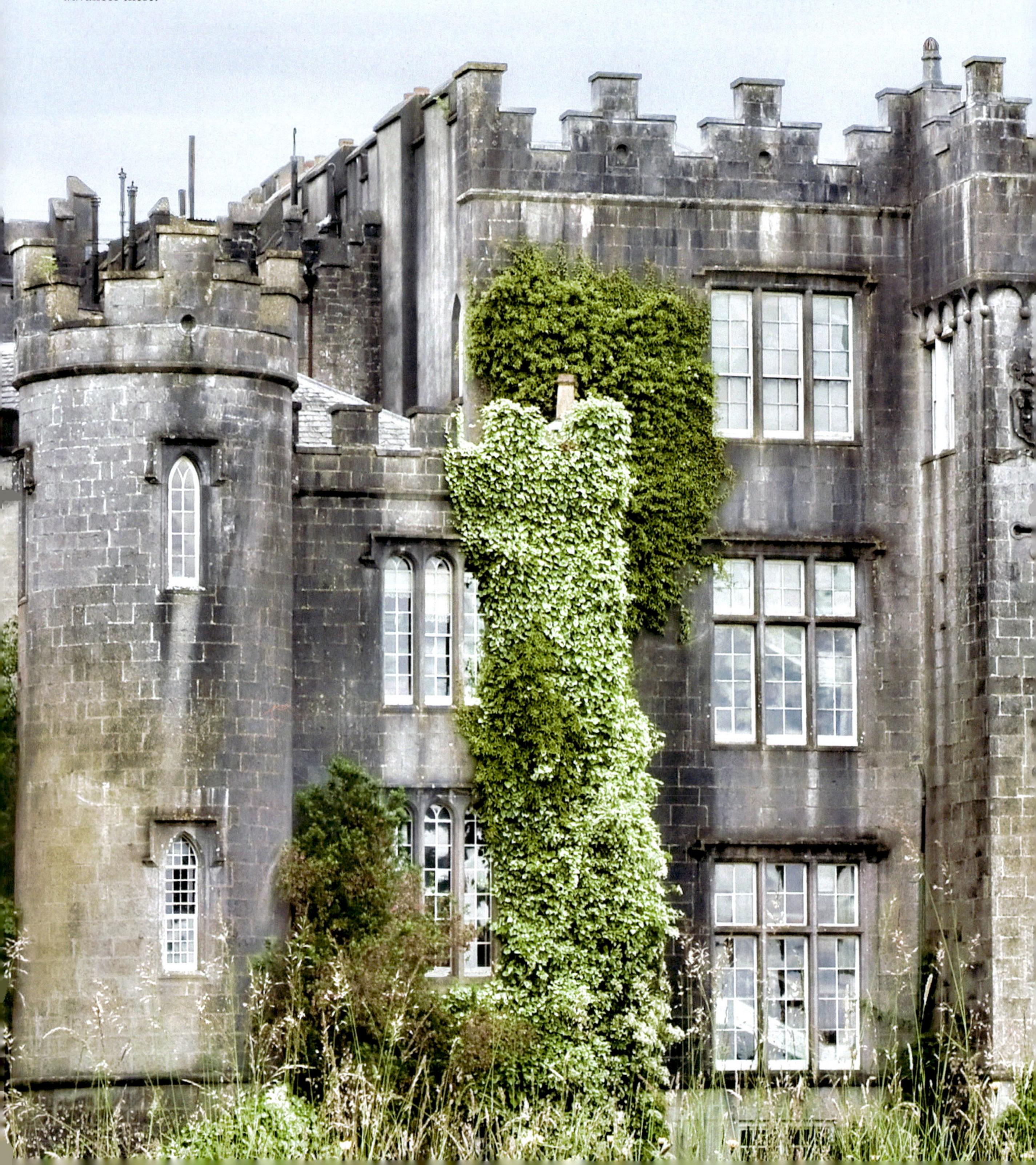

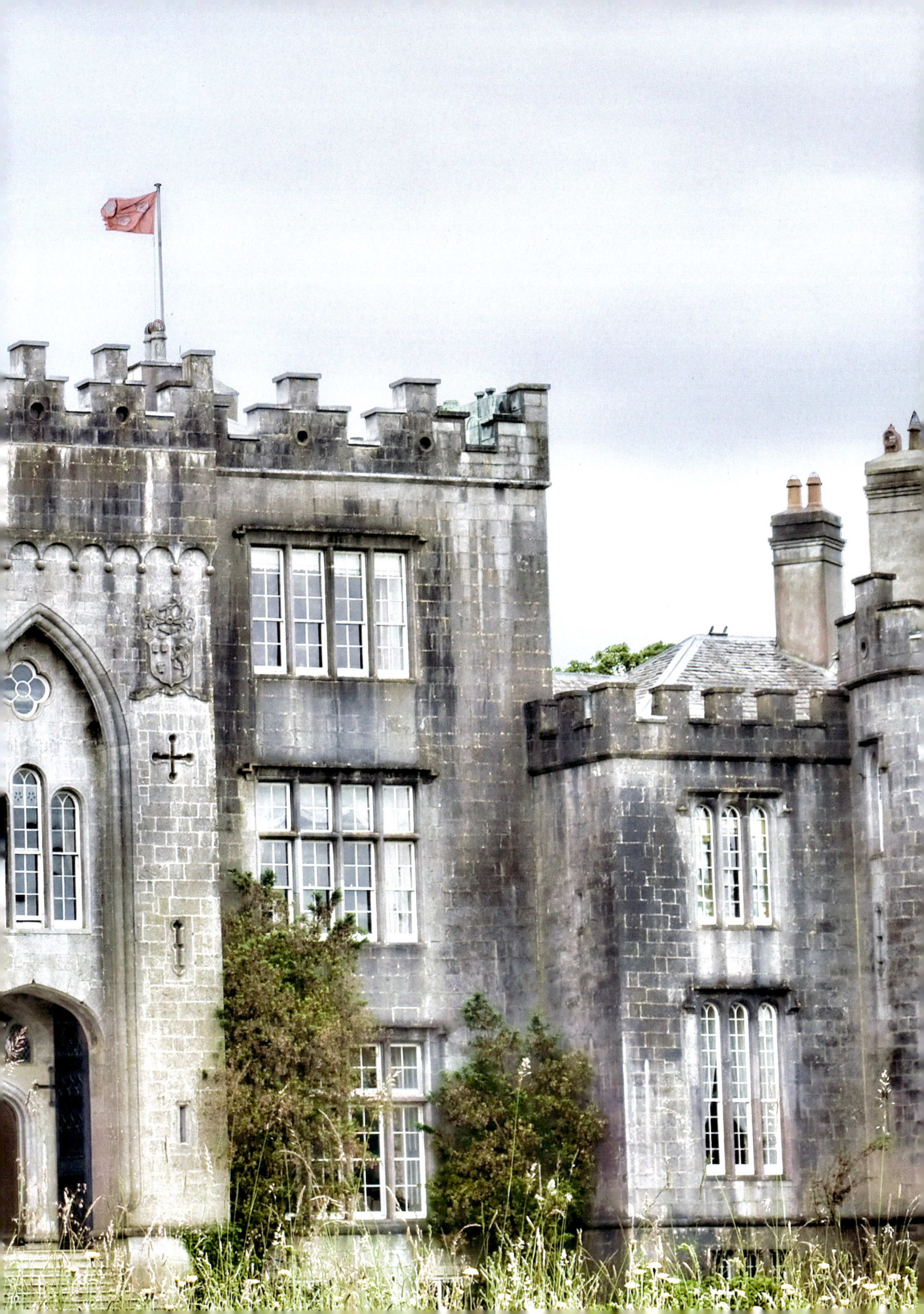

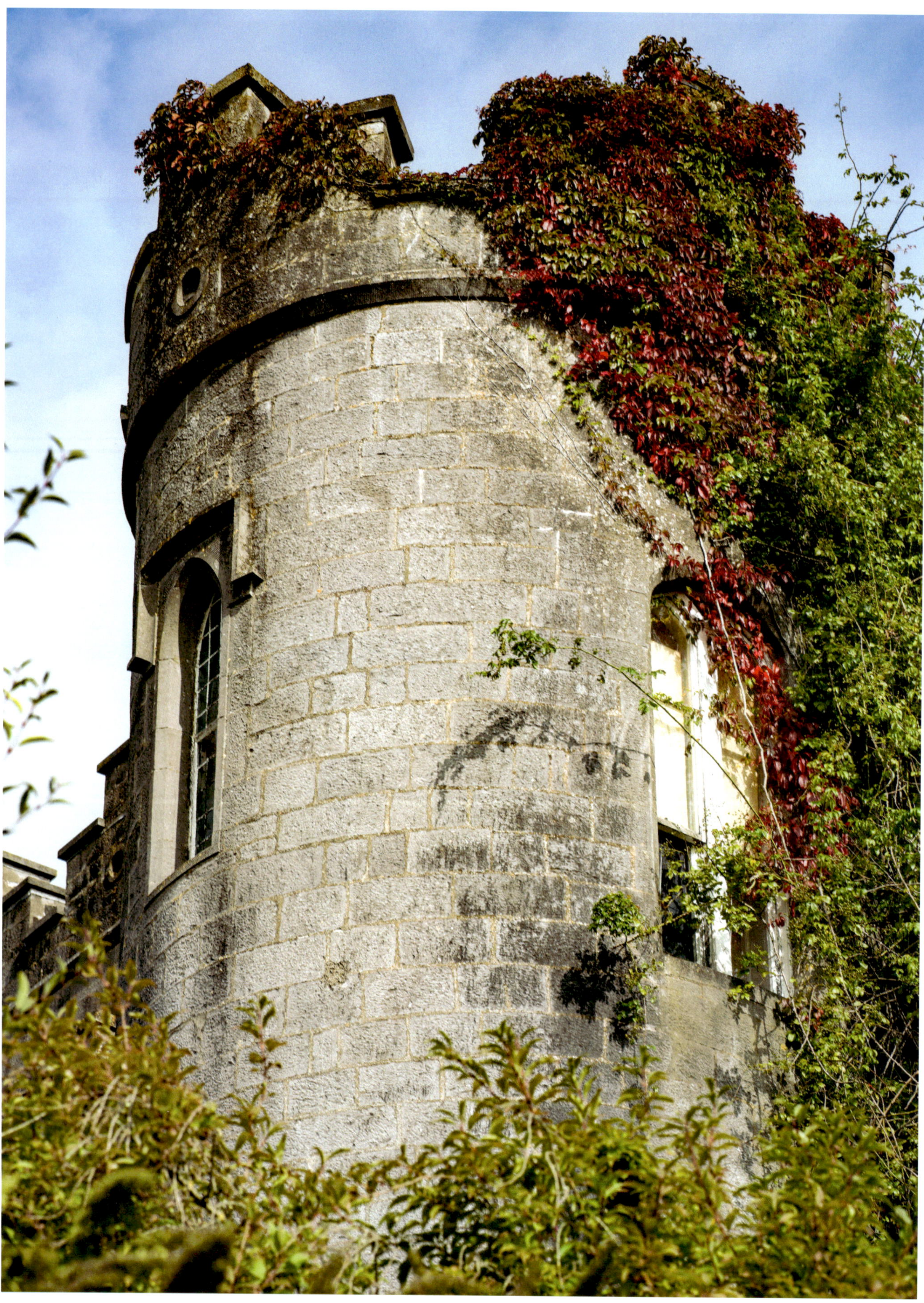

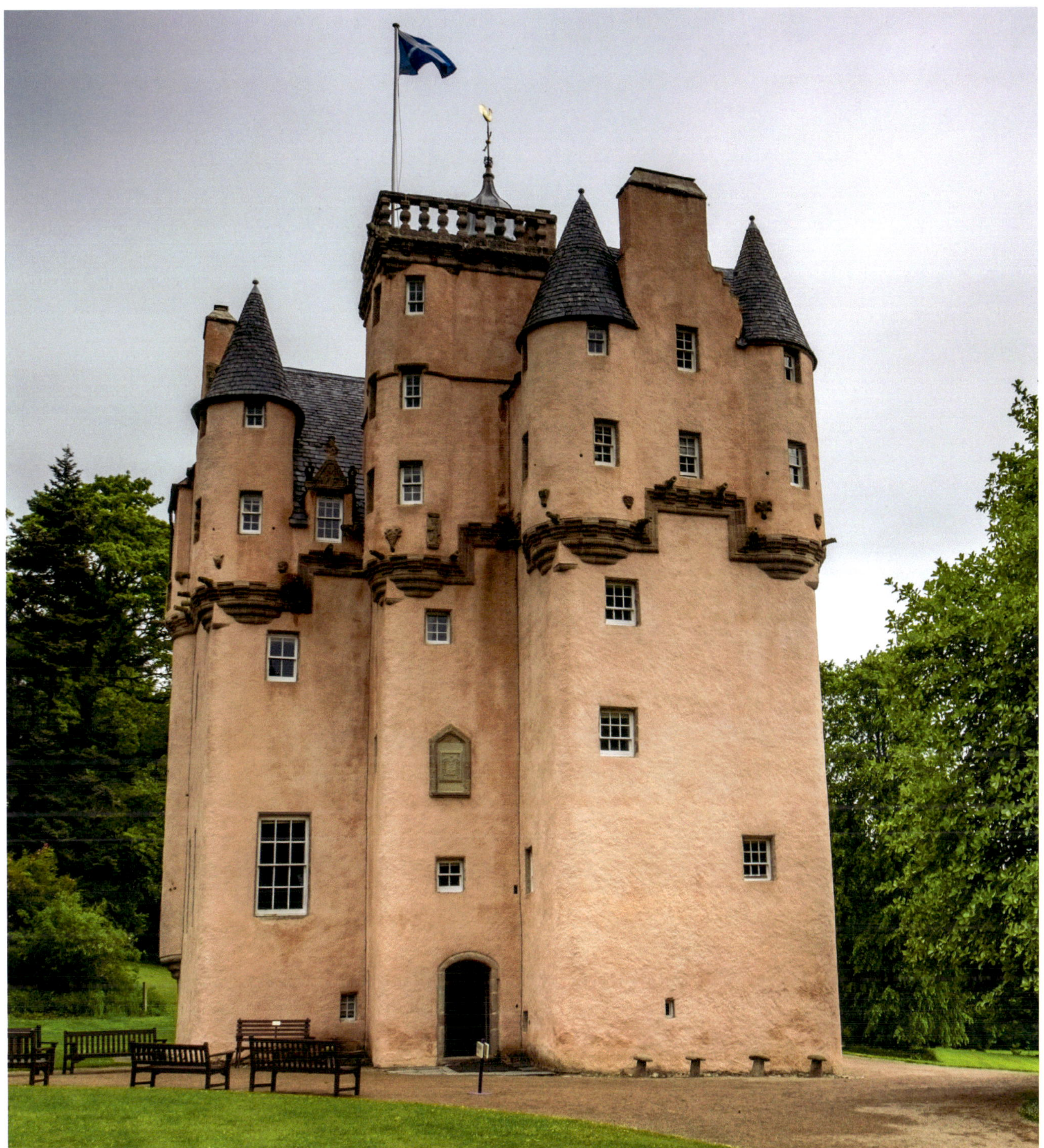

LEFT:

Birr Castle, County Offaly, Ireland

The round towers of Birr Castle were remodelled in a gothic style during the rebuilding of the early 19th century. Few features of the original design have survived, but the towers still show signs of damage caused by artillery fire during two sieges in the 1600s.

ABOVE:

Craigievar Castle, Aberdeenshire, Scotland

Craigievar Castle is a seven-storey tower house. It is built on an L-plan, allowing the entrance to be defended by sites of fire from within the structure. Construction began around 1610, and was completed in 1626. The tower house has been little modified, but additional buildings that once existed were later demolished.

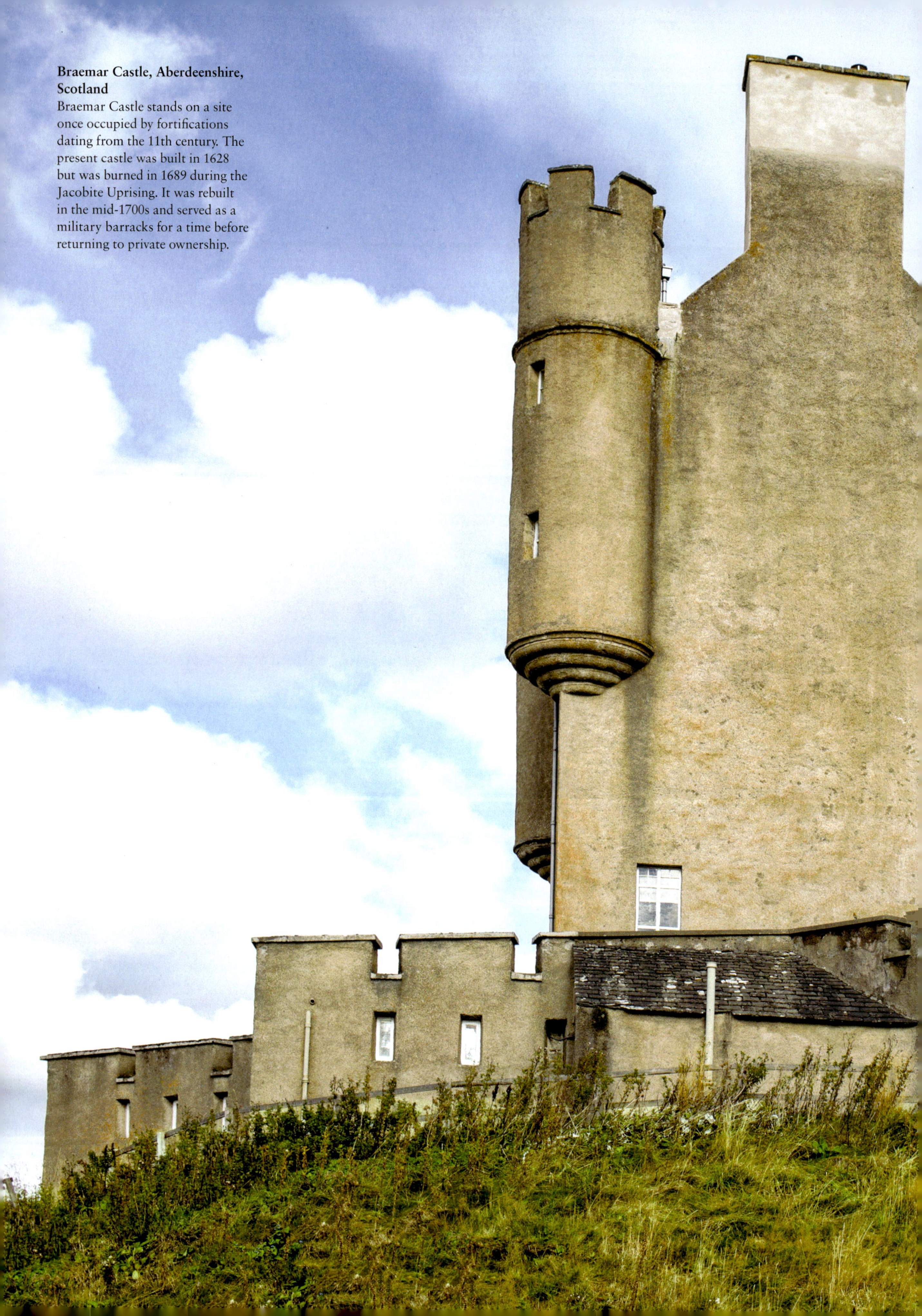

Braemar Castle, Aberdeenshire, Scotland
Braemar Castle stands on a site once occupied by fortifications dating from the 11th century. The present castle was built in 1628 but was burned in 1689 during the Jacobite Uprising. It was rebuilt in the mid-1700s and served as a military barracks for a time before returning to private ownership.

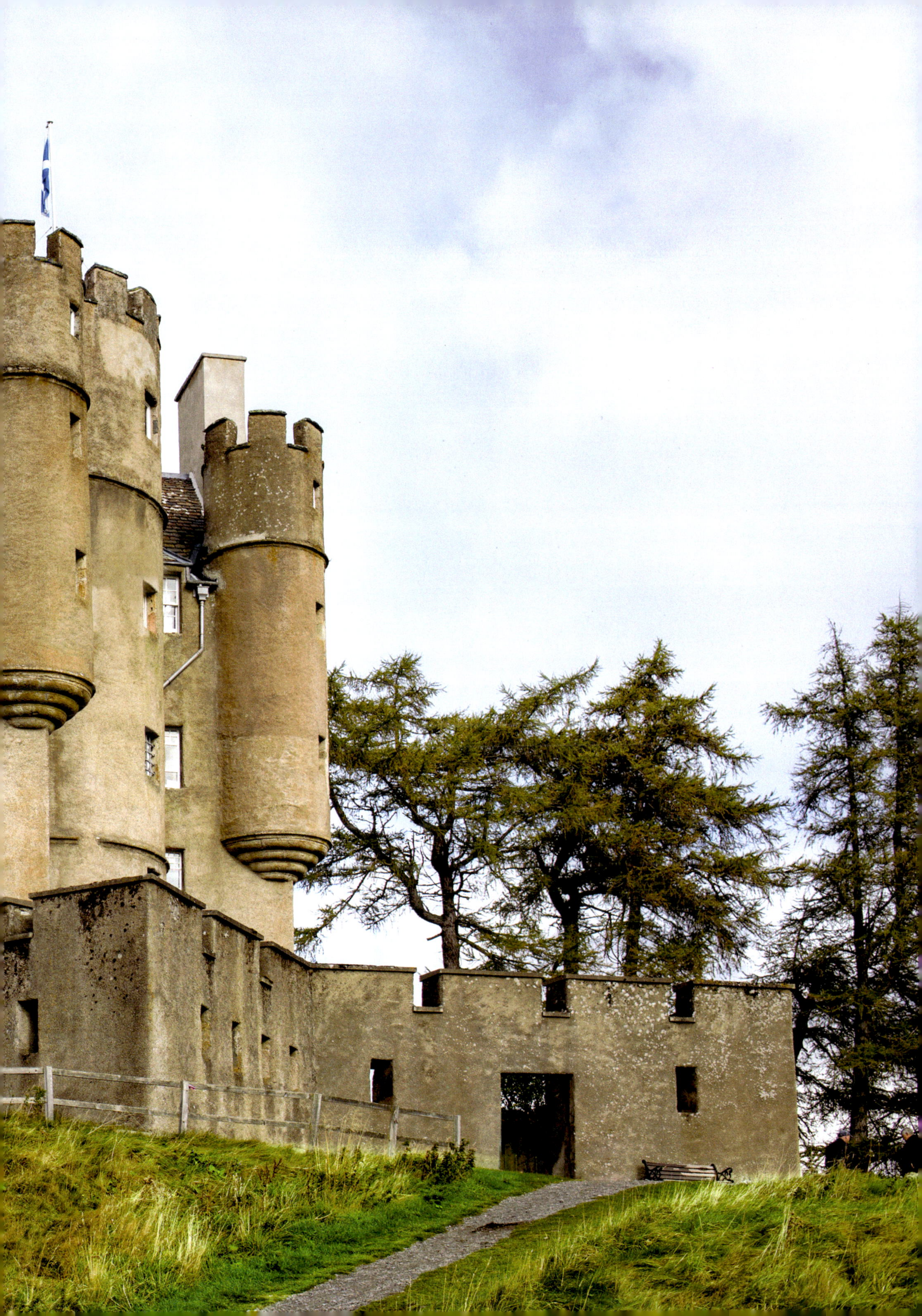

RIGHT AND OVERLEAF:

Fraser Castle, Aberdeenshire, Scotland

Fraser Castle grew over many years from the original three-storey tower house built in the mid-1400s. In 1570, work began to add the large round tower and additional towers to the existing structure, greatly expanding the available space and creating a grand residence where previously a small defensive structure had existed. Additional extensions were begun in the 1630s, and in 1797 further modernization work was undertaken. The end result was a building that was still the same castle but which had grown enormously.

Fraser Castle fell into disrepair until it was purchased in the 1920s and renovated, retaining the original style and general appearance. It is today owned by the National Trust for Scotland, which also maintains the extensive surrounding estates.

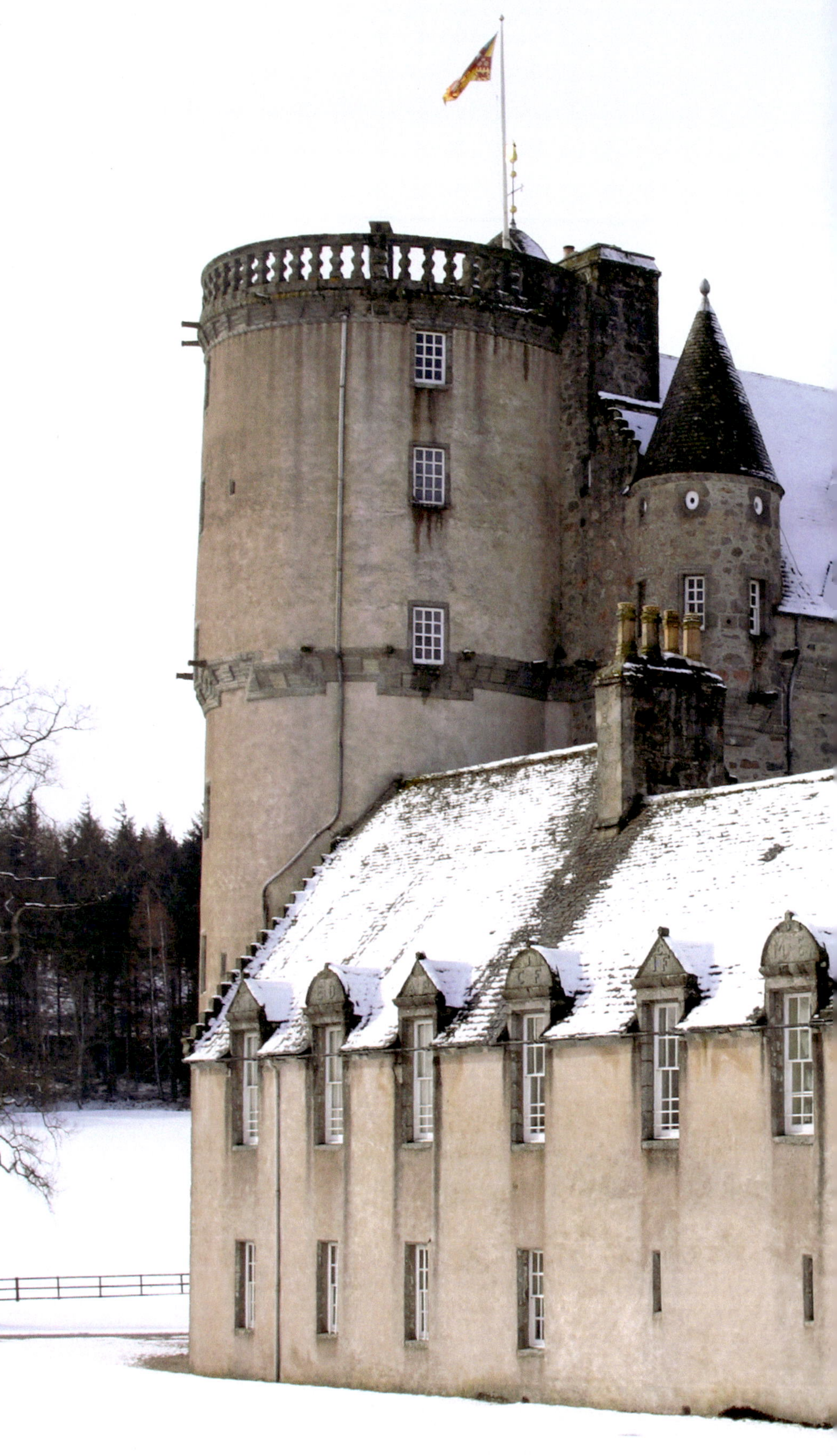

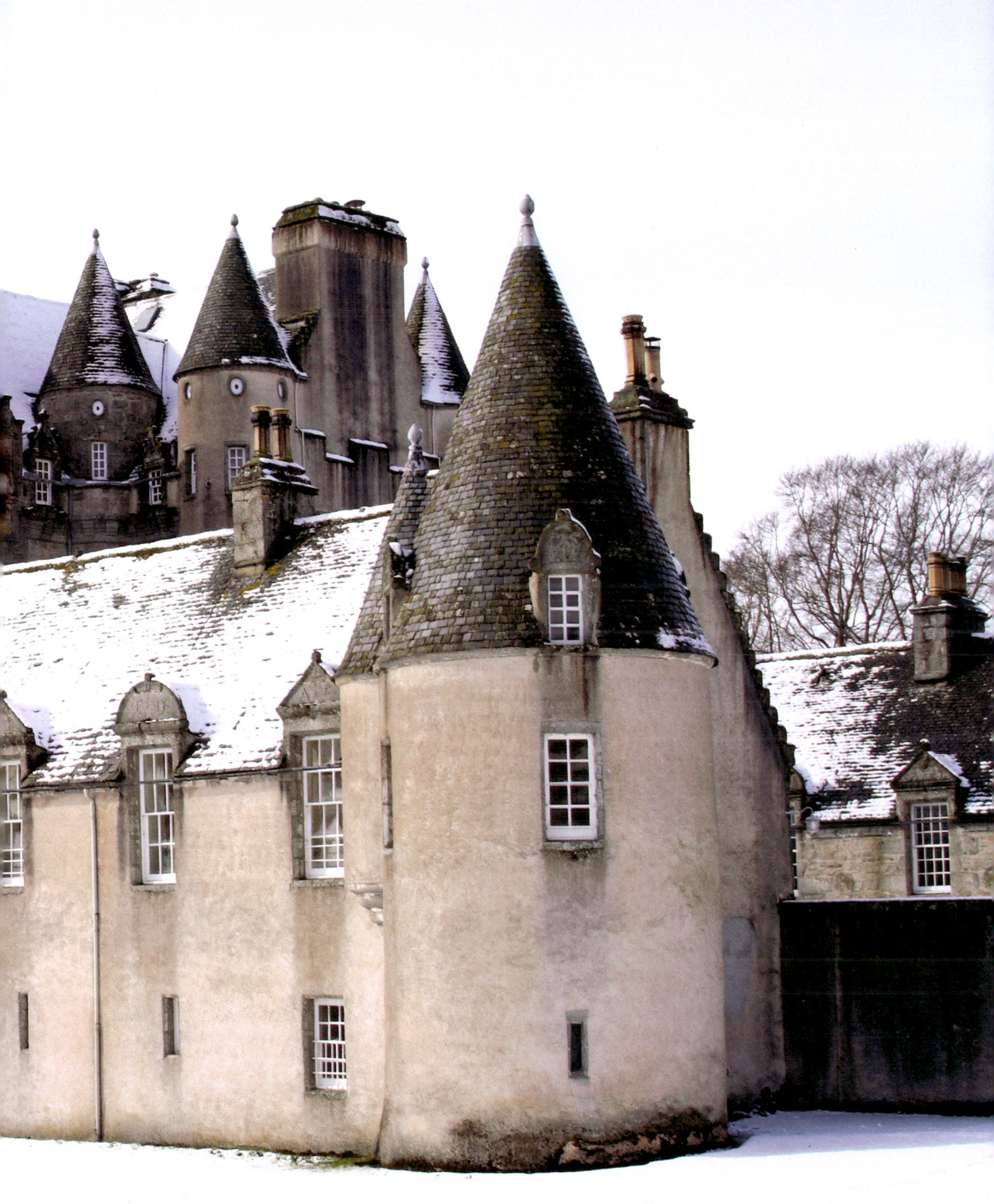

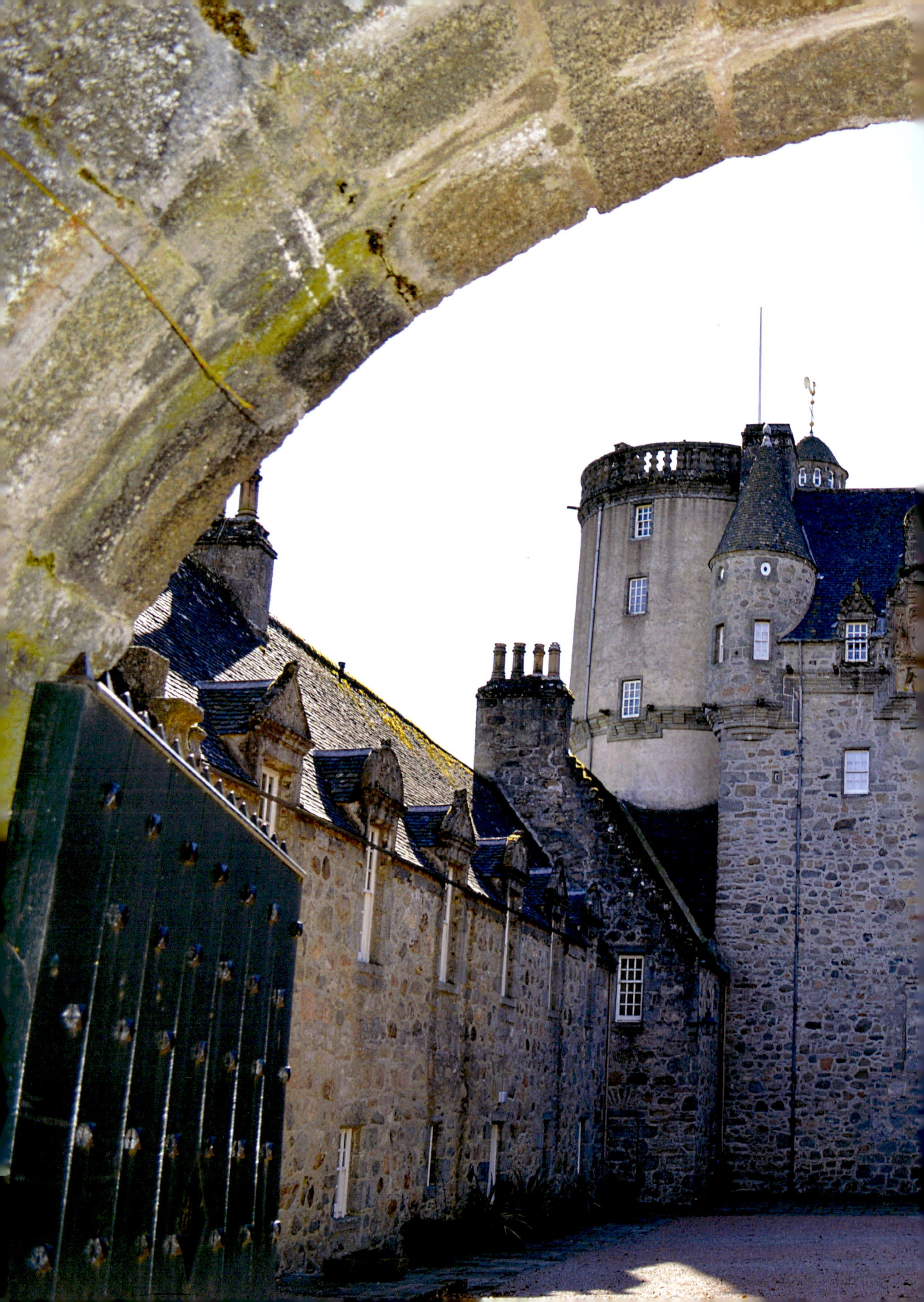

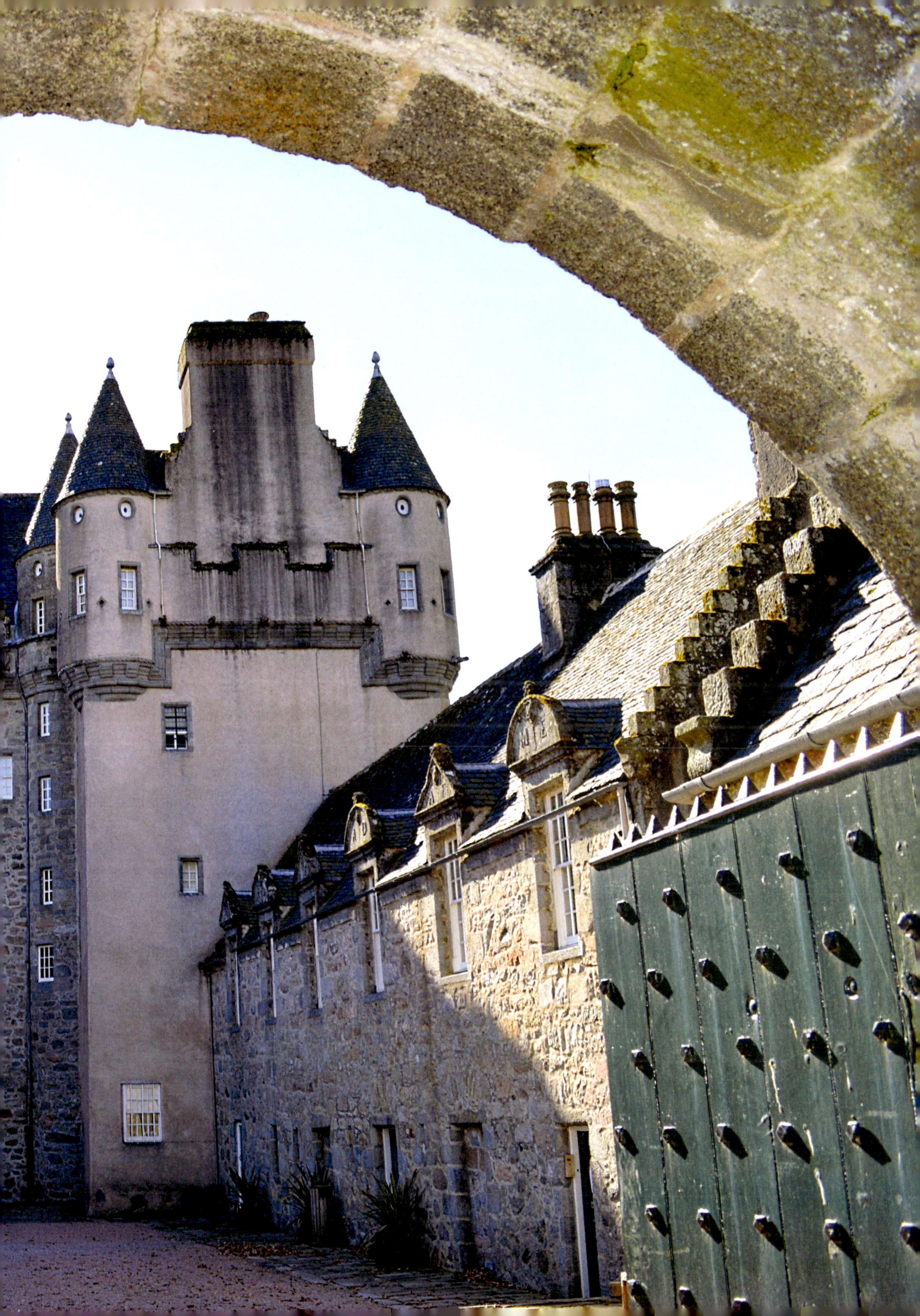

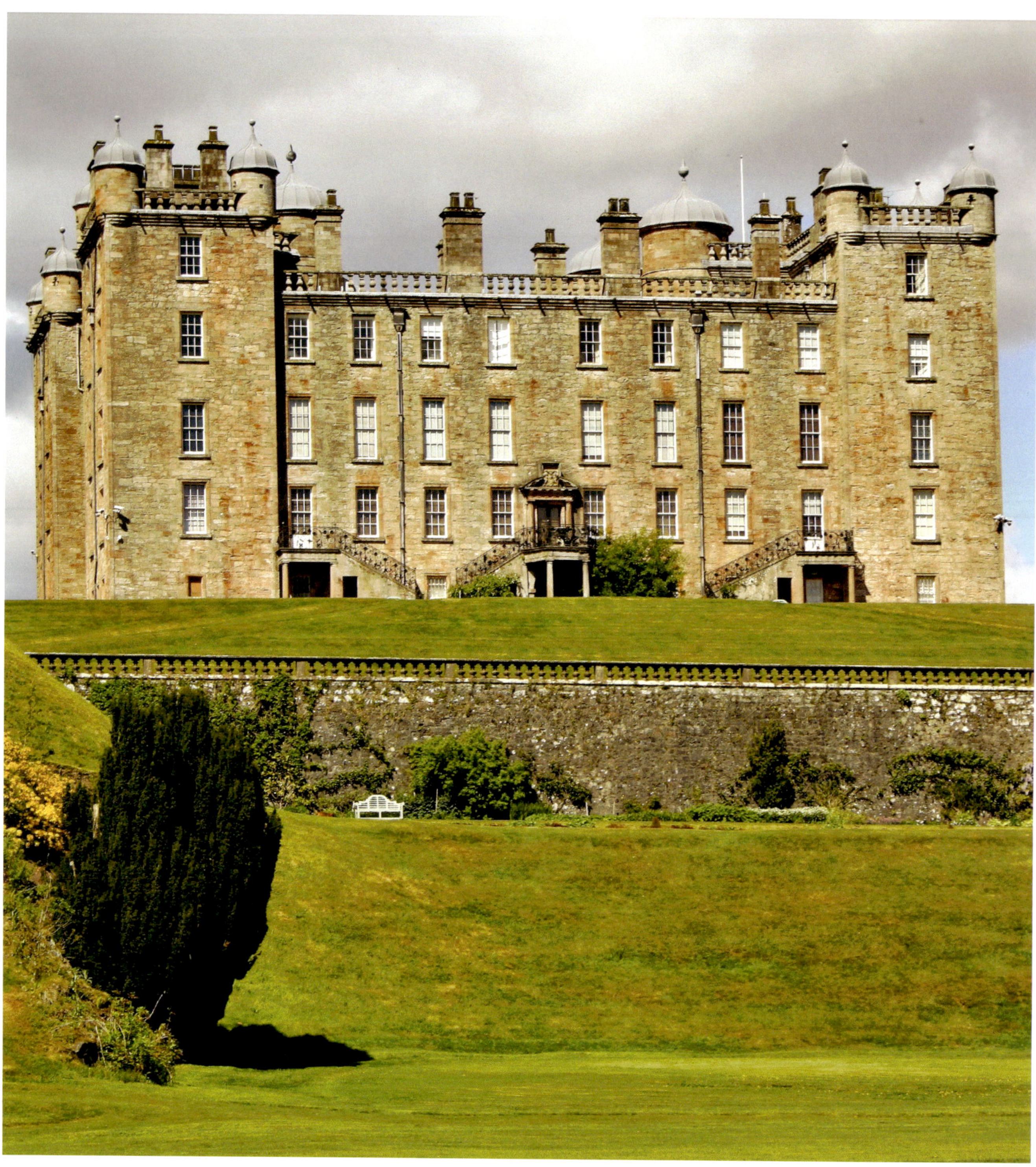

ABOVE:
Drumlanrig Castle, Dumfries and Galloway, Scotland
Drumlanrig Castle is a currently inhabited stately home. Work began on its construction in 1679 and was completed by 1689. Like many castles, Drumlanrig was constructed on a site that had been of strategic value for many centuries. Roman fortifications have been found nearby.

RIGHT, TOP:
Dunguaire Castle, County Galway, Ireland
Constructed in 1520, Dunguaire Castle stands on Galway Bay. Its design is fairly typical, consisting of a tower house and external wall. The castle has changed hands several times and was restored in the early 20th century, playing host to literary greats such as W.B. Yeats and George Bernard Shaw.

RIGHT, BOTTOM:
Ashford Castle, County Galway, Ireland
Ashford Castle dates from the early 1200s, though it has been heavily modified over the years. Some reconstruction took place in the late 1500s, and in the mid-1800s large extensions were added to create the modern structure. The castle is today a luxury hotel.

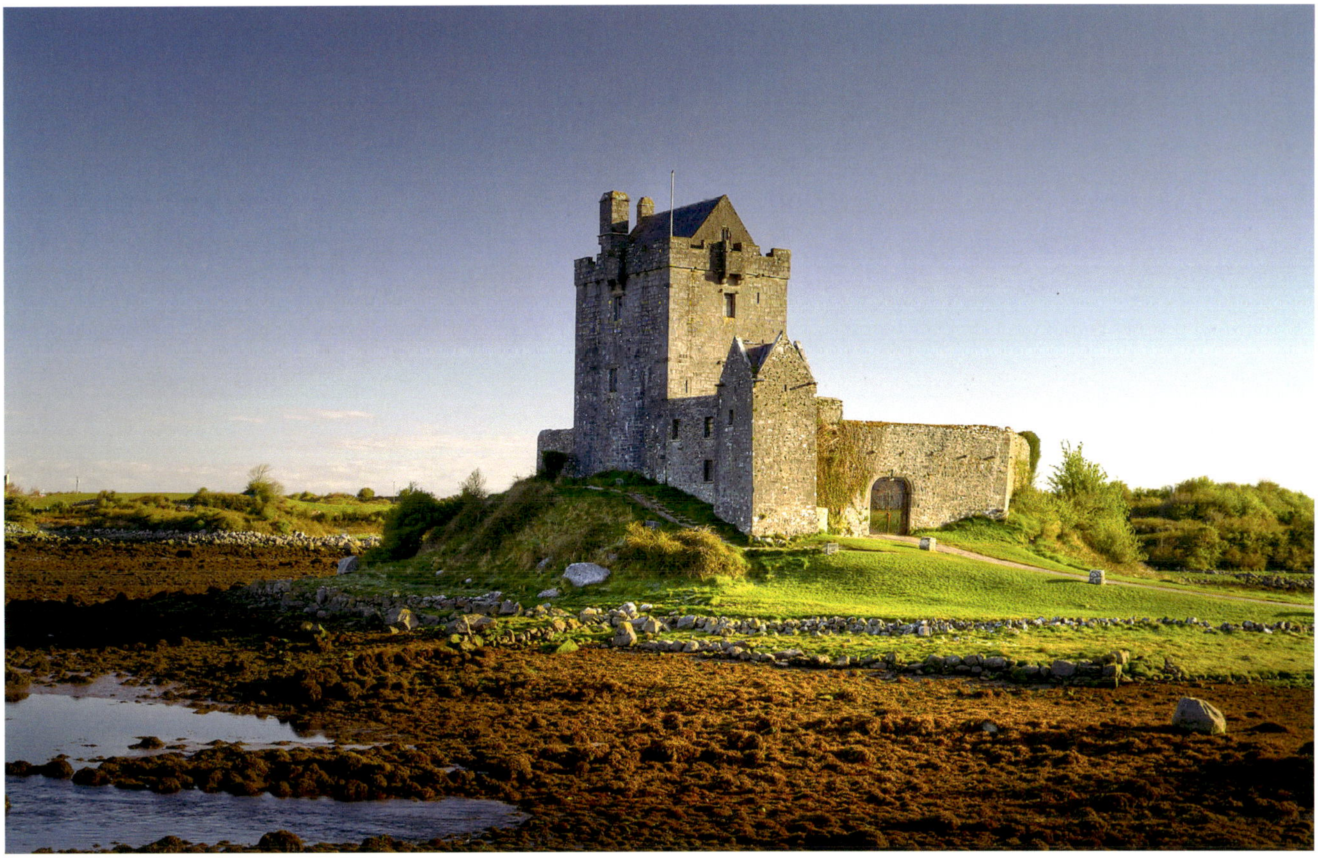

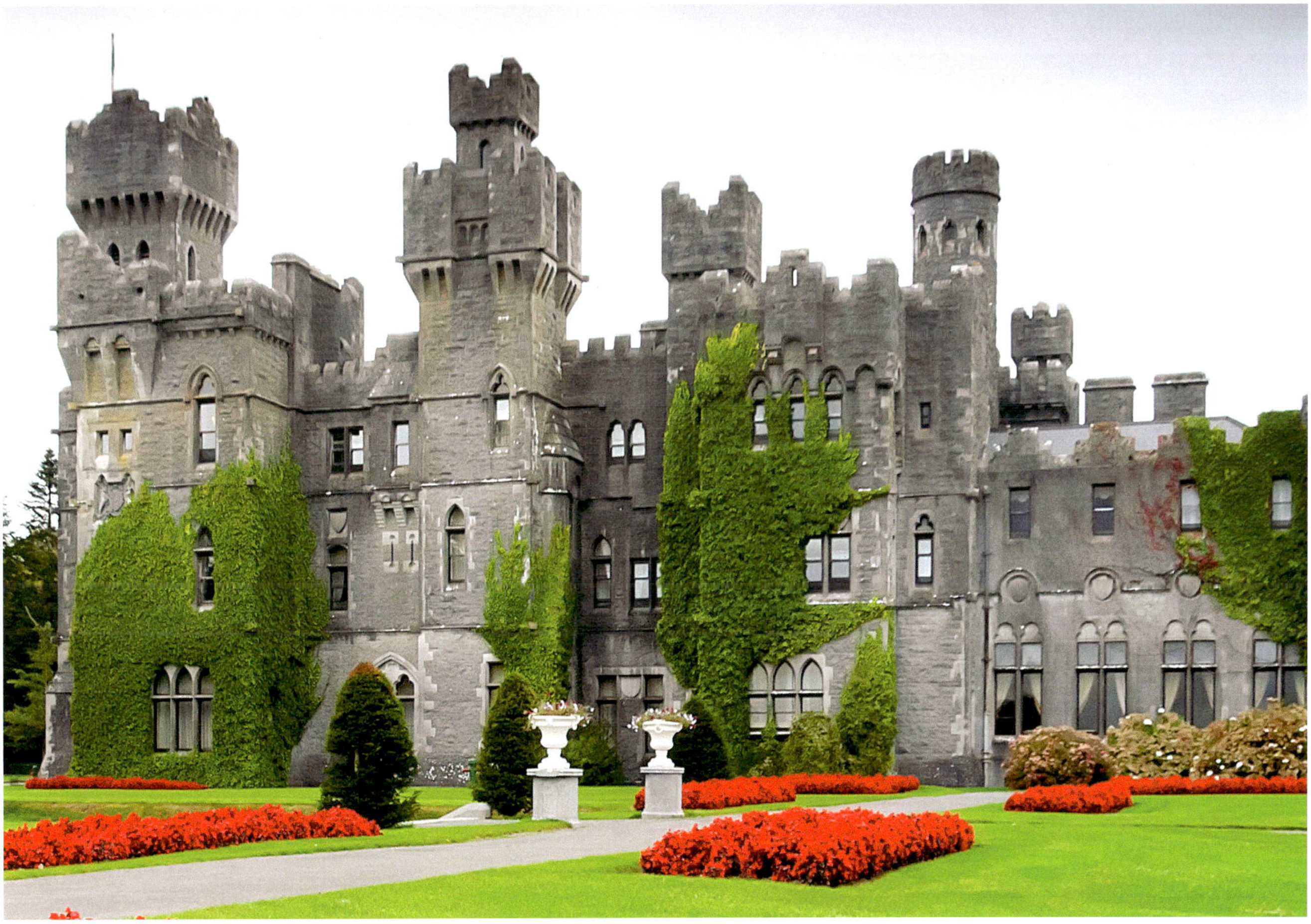

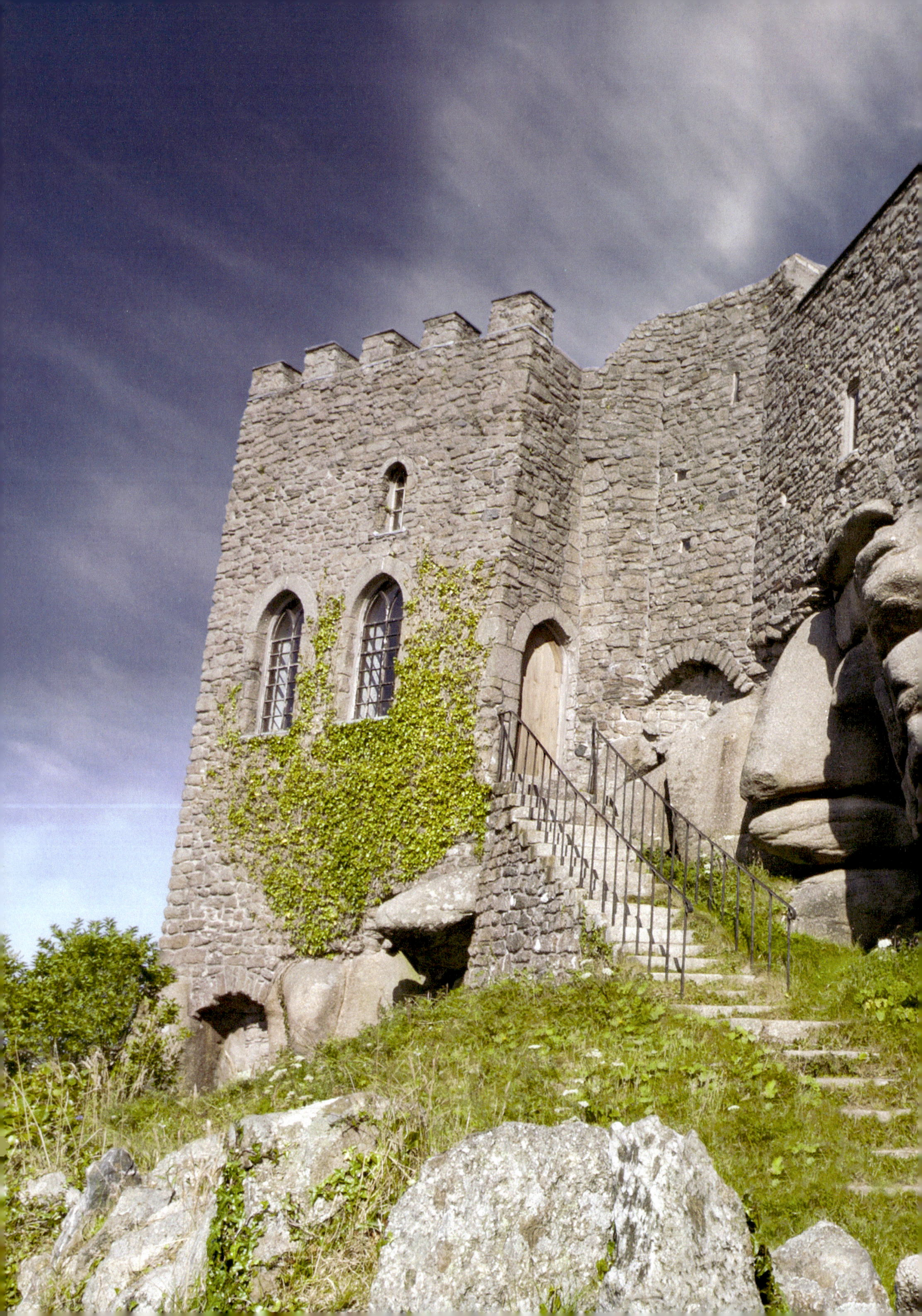

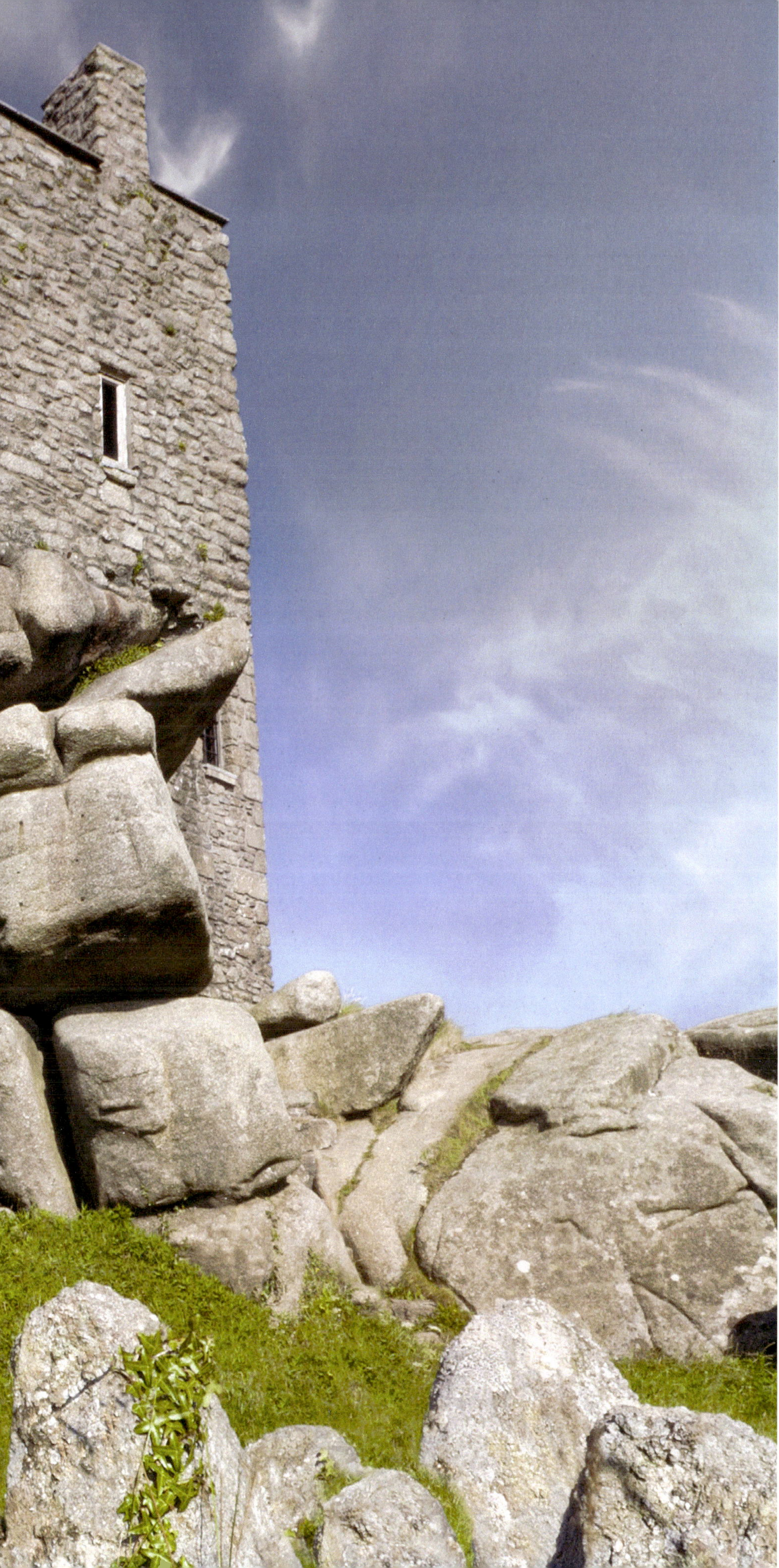

Carn Brea Castle, Cornwall, England
Carn Brea Castle in Redruth, Cornwall, was built in 1379 within an Iron Age fortification that was itself on the site of a Neolithic settlement. There is some evidence that the structure may have originally been built as a chapel. It was repurposed and reconstructed, undergoing wholescale changes in the 18th century to become a hunting lodge.

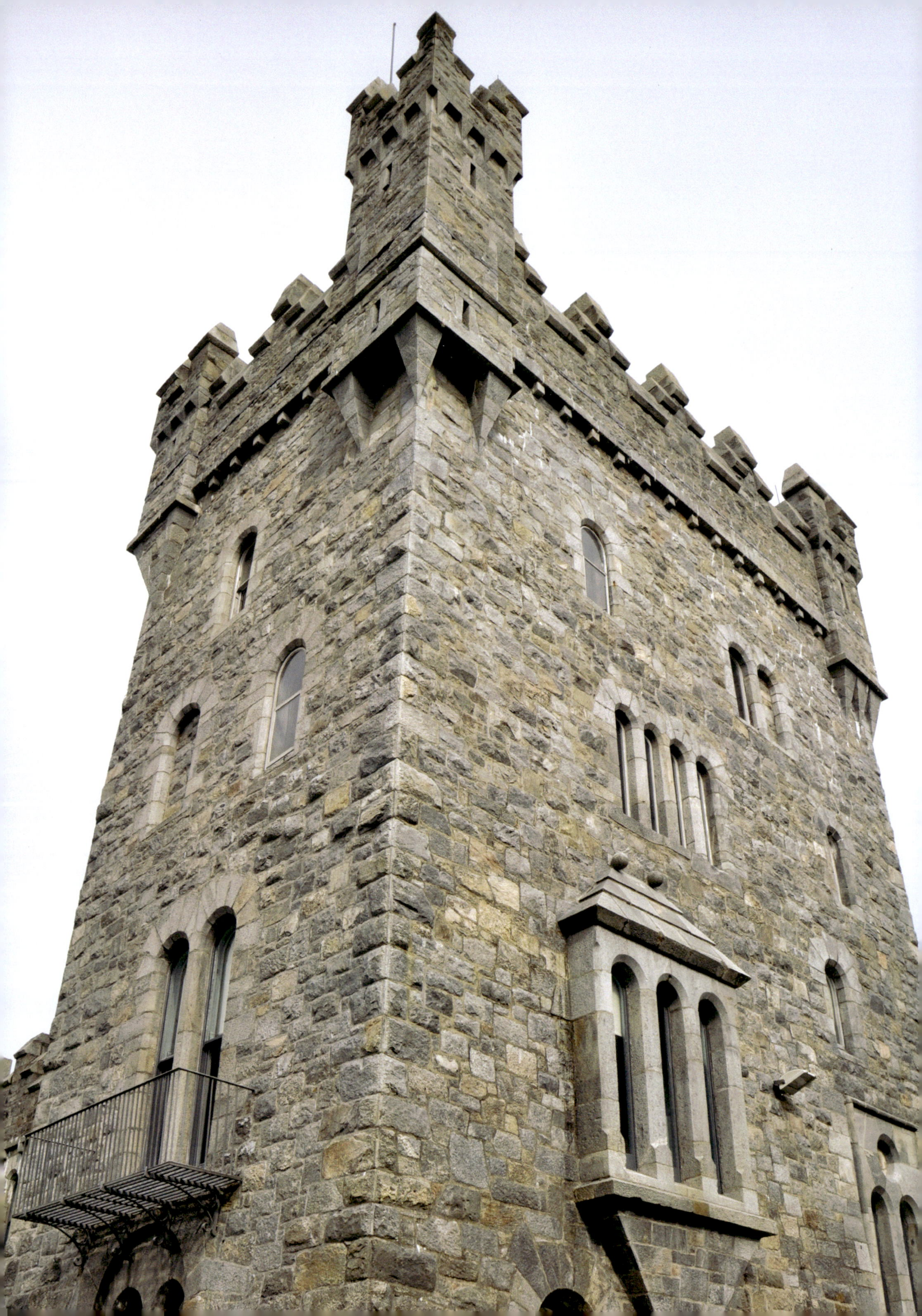

Modern Times

The proliferation of gunpowder artillery made the imposing stone castle obsolete. Defence was achieved by digging in rather than building upward, and the roles of home and fortress were increasingly separated. This was in part a social movement; the rise of the modern nation-state brought to an end an era of powerful families with their own castles and private armies.

Often, castles were abandoned or used as sources of stone for the construction of comfortable mansions nearby, or were so extensively rebuilt that they ceased to be castles in anything but name. Some, however, adapted and continued. Edinburgh Castle, for example, managed to function as a military barracks and grand bastion of history at the same time. Other castles evolved into traditional royal residences and somehow remained relevant in greatly changed times.

Often these surviving functioning castles were remodelled in fanciful style or given a deliberately archaic appearance intended to be evocative of their ancient heritage. This can be confusing to many visitors, who may not realize they are seeing features added in modern times to castles that never had them when they were medieval fortresses. There is no reason why these castles will not continue to evolve and be remodelled in the future.

LEFT:
Glenveagh Castle, County Donegal, Ireland
Glenveagh Castle is a mansion house built in the style of a Scottish castle. It was constructed in the 1870s by Captain John Adair, who made money in America before returning to buy land in Donegal. Adair was a harsh landlord, harking back to times when an overlord needed a fortified home to protect him from his tenants.

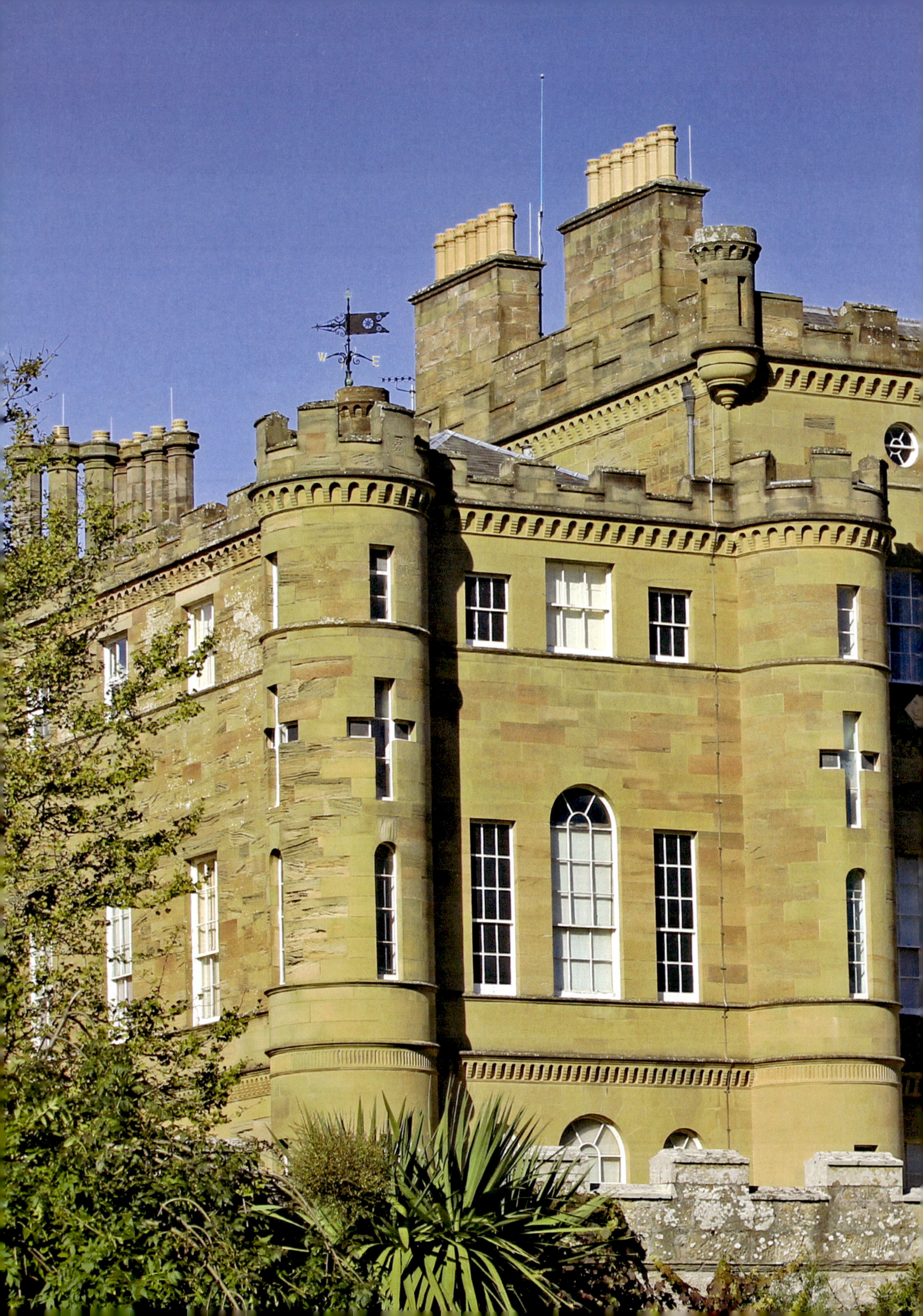
W
E

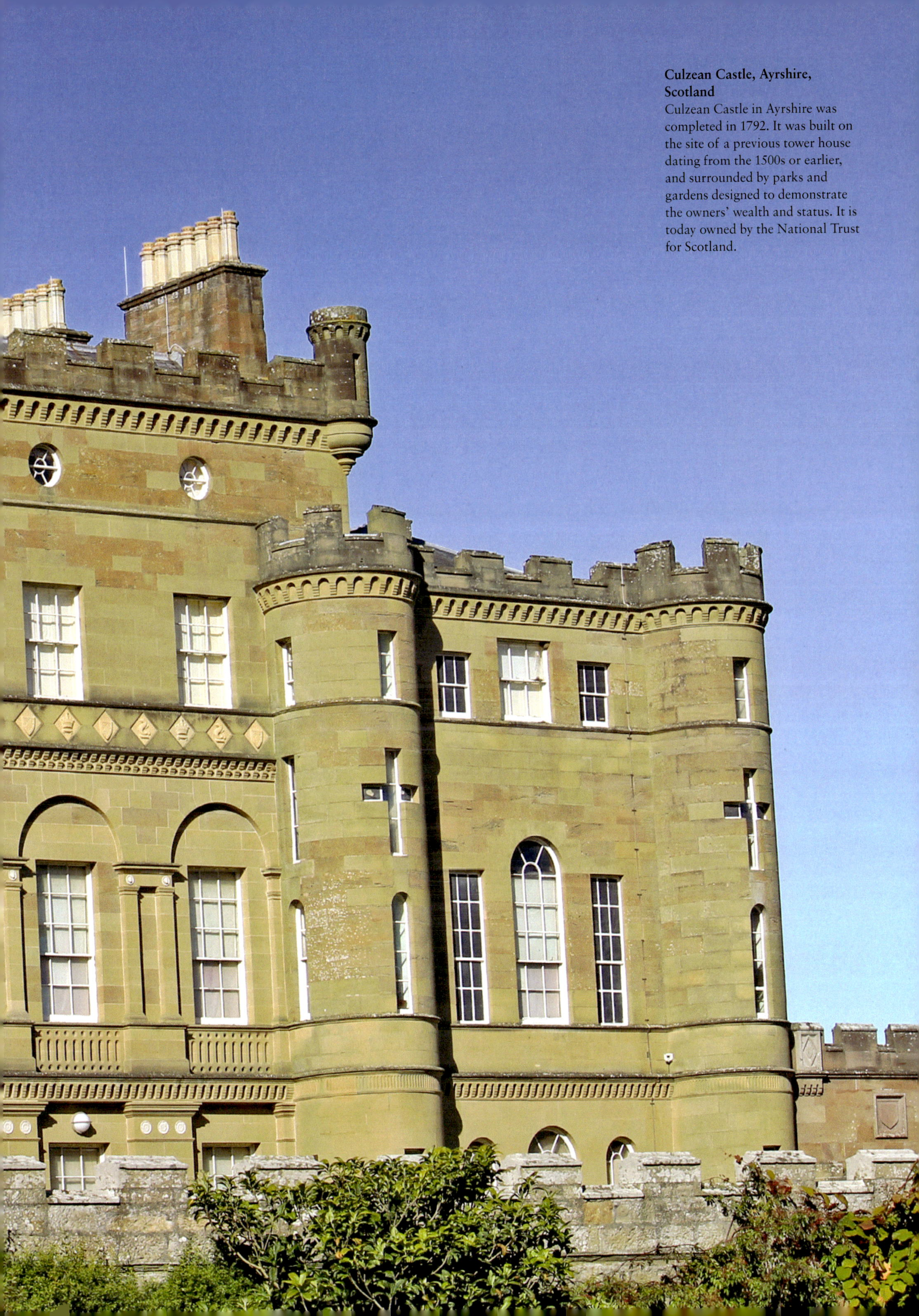

Culzean Castle, Ayrshire, Scotland

Culzean Castle in Ayrshire was completed in 1792. It was built on the site of a previous tower house dating from the 1500s or earlier, and surrounded by parks and gardens designed to demonstrate the owners' wealth and status. It is today owned by the National Trust for Scotland.

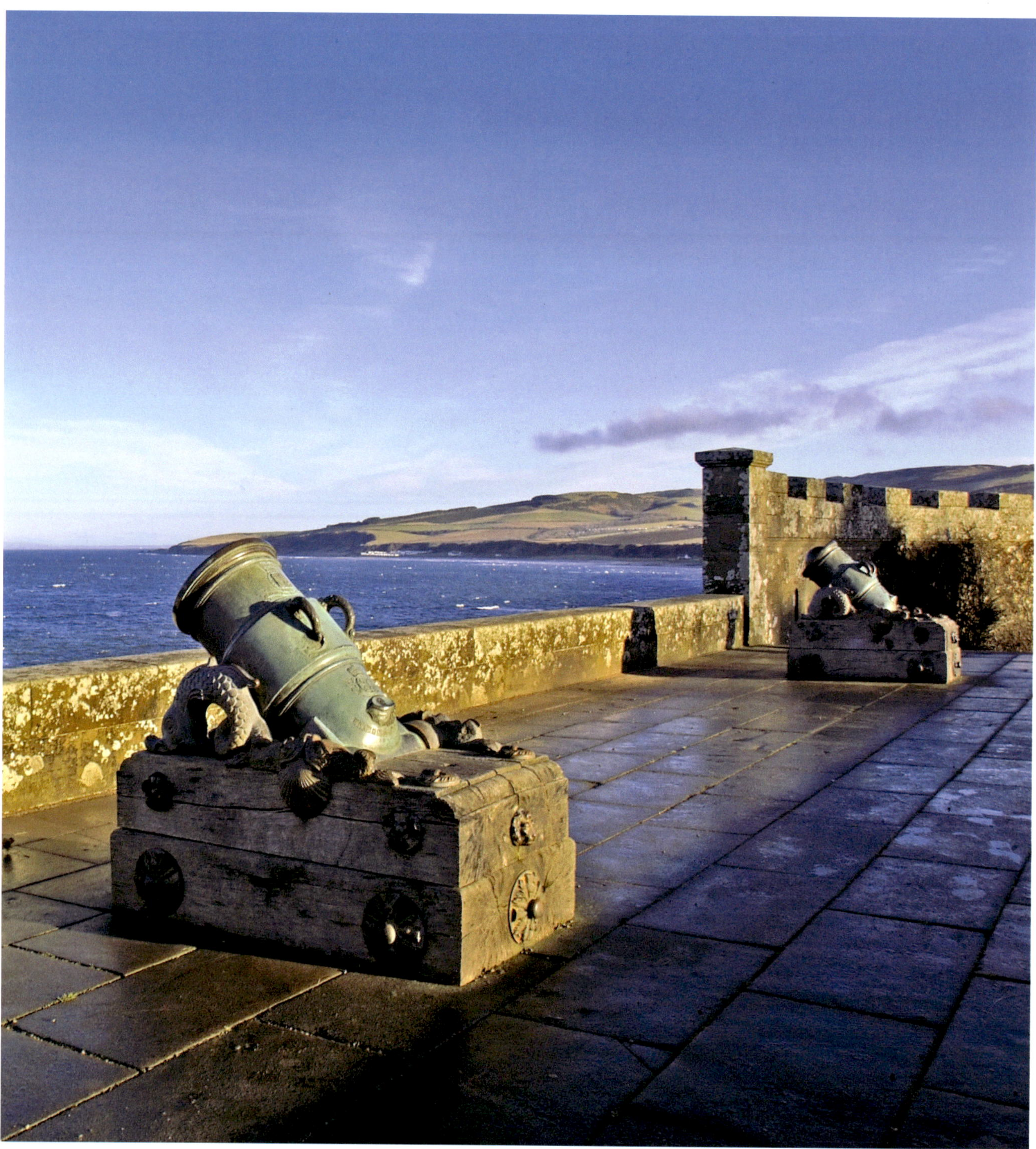

ABOVE:

Culzean Castle, Ayrshire, Scotland

It is common to find archaic artillery weapons on display at historic castles, whether or not they have any genuine connection to the site. These mortars on the battlements of Culzean Castle are from the same era as the castle's construction, though whether such weapons were deployed there is open to question.

RIGHT:

Eglinton Castle, Ayrshire, Scotland

Eglinton Castle was built around the beginning of the 19th century. The keep and four towers were constructed in a gothic style reminiscent of the 12th to 16th centuries, which was popular at the time. The castle was abandoned for lack of funds; all that remains is a tower and sections of wall.

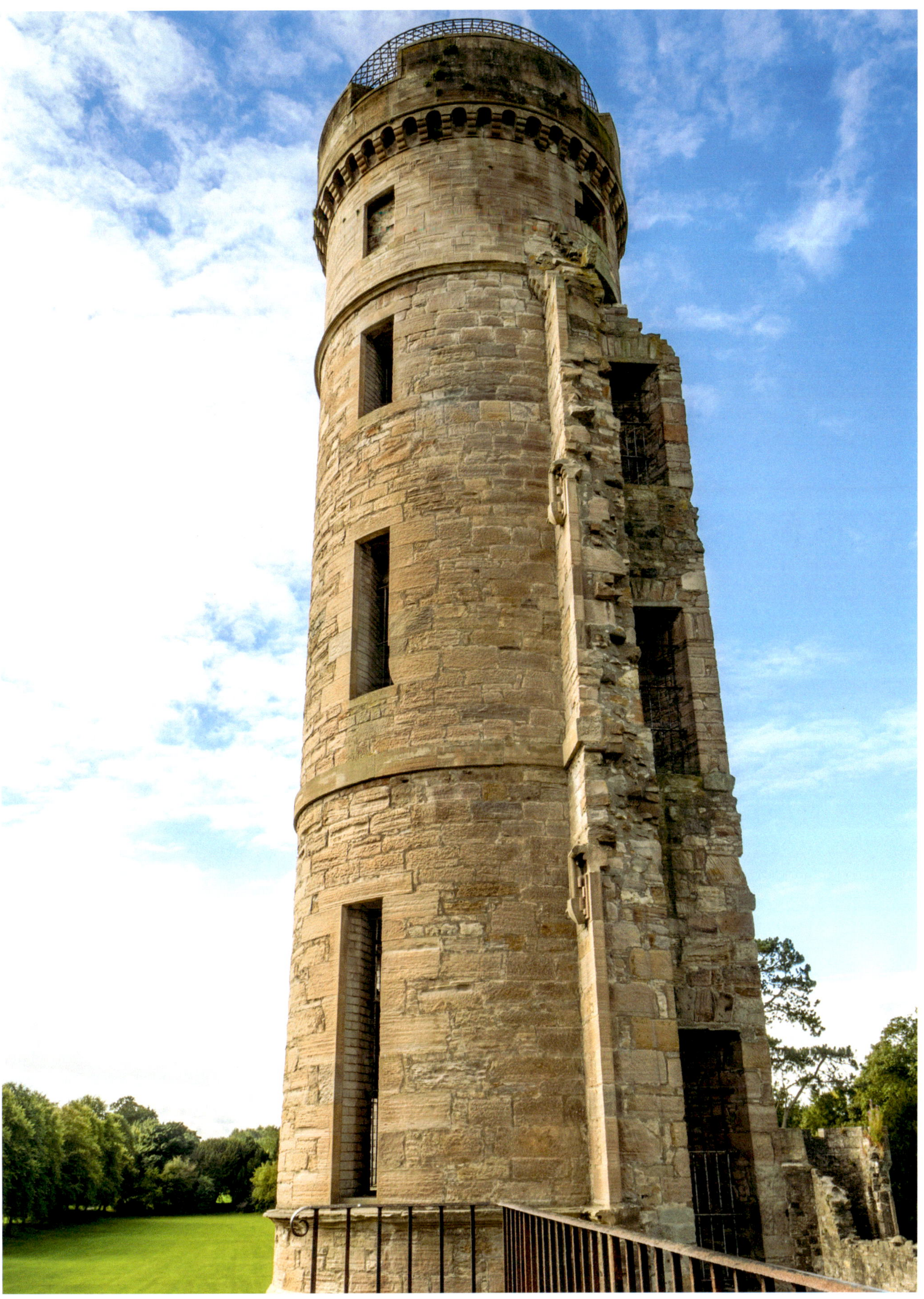

RIGHT:

Lismore Castle, County Waterford, Ireland

Lismore Castle has its origins in the 12th century, and was later owned by Sir Walter Raleigh. The castle was extensively rebuilt in the early 1800s, gaining ornamental gardens and crenellated towers. Today part of the castle houses an art gallery.

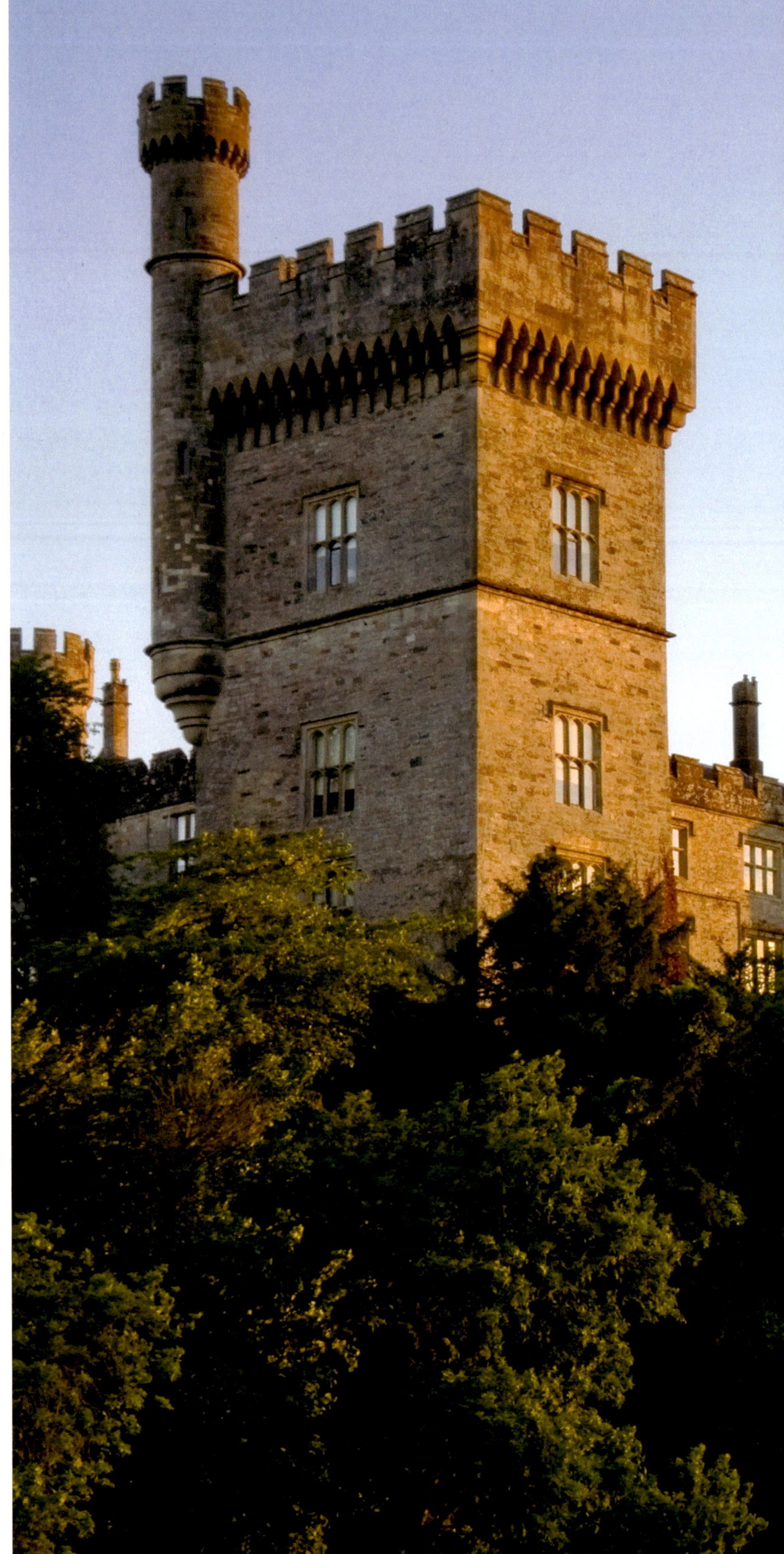

OVERLEAF:

Penrhyn Castle, Gwynedd, Wales

Penrhyn Castle in North Wales was reconstructed in the early 1800s. The original building dated from the mid-1400s, though little remains of it today. The redesigned castle retained a deliberately Normanesque style, and is a popular tourist attraction.

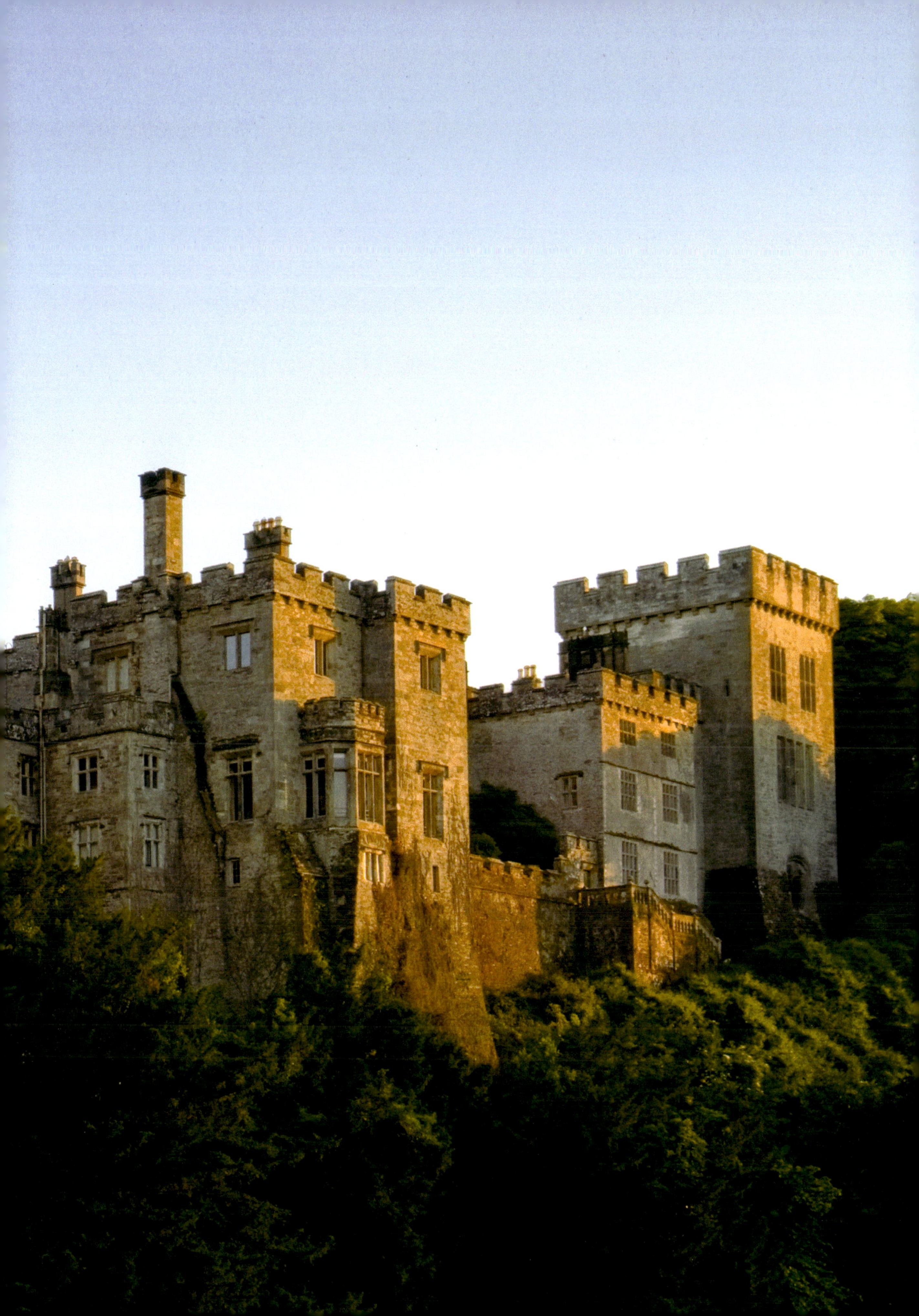

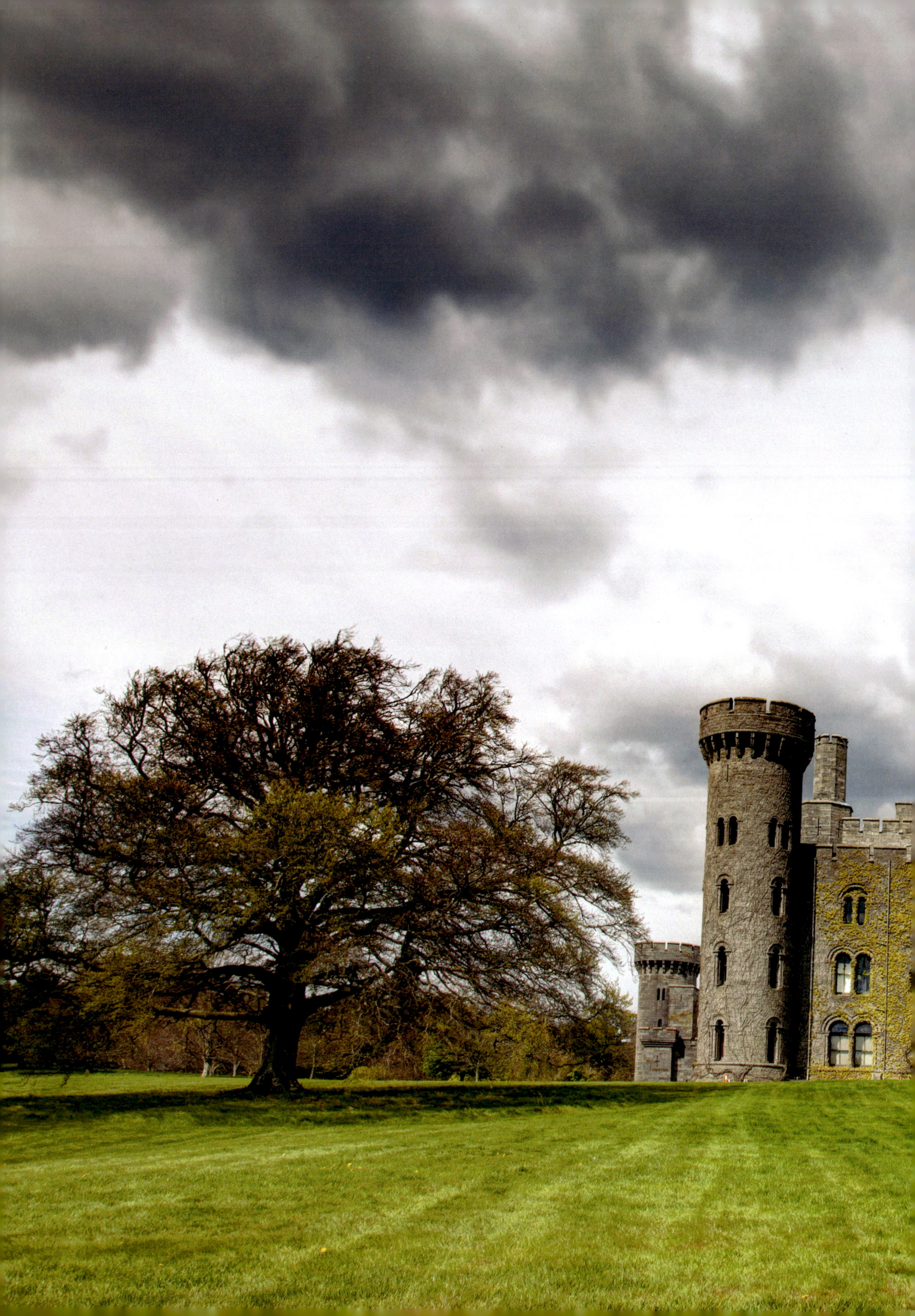

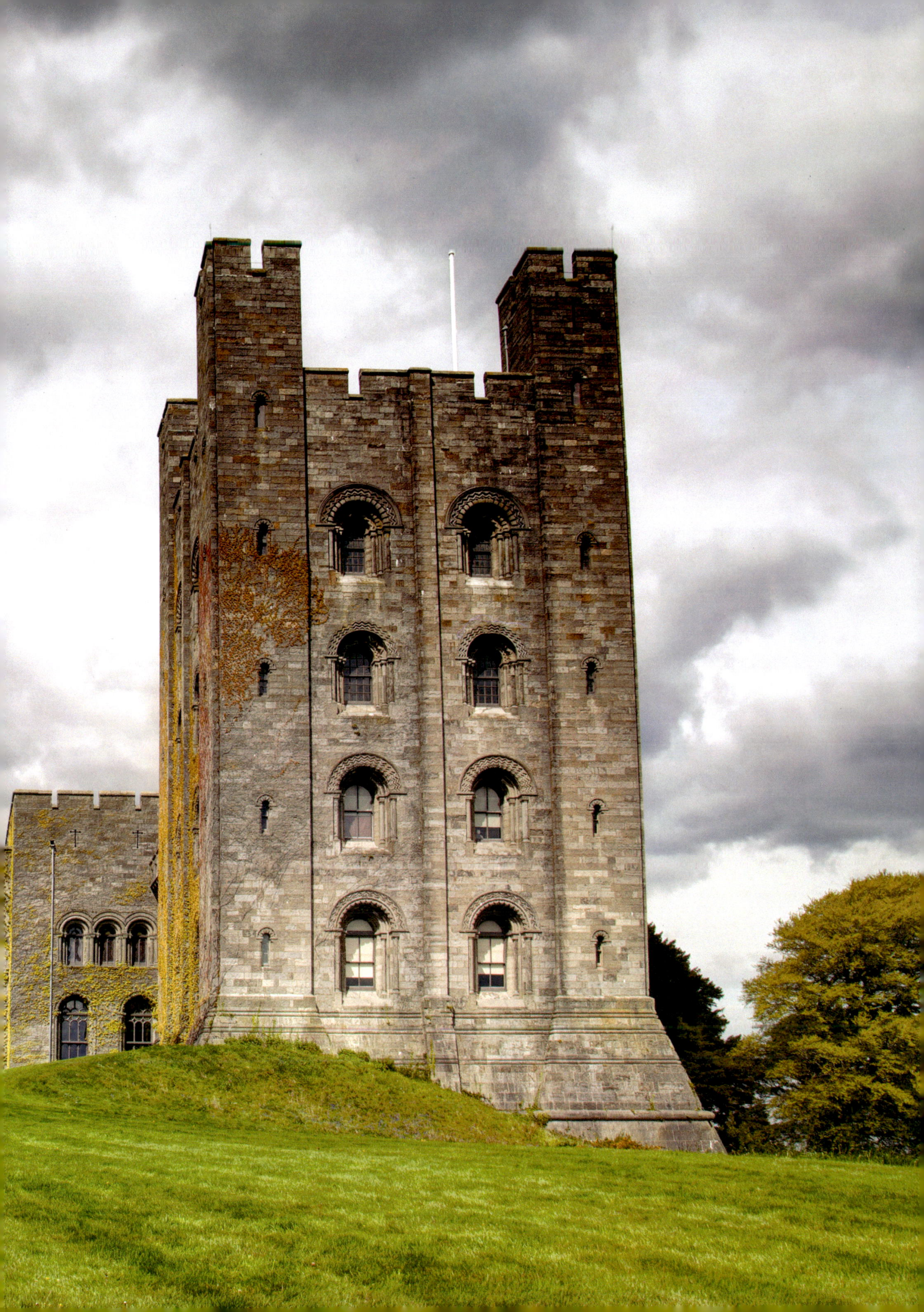

Tower of Refuge, Douglas Bay, Isle of Man

The Tower of Refuge was built as a refuge for sailors whose vessels struck the rocks in Douglas harbour. Built in 1832, the structure was given the form of a mock castle for no reason other than because it was aesthetically pleasing.

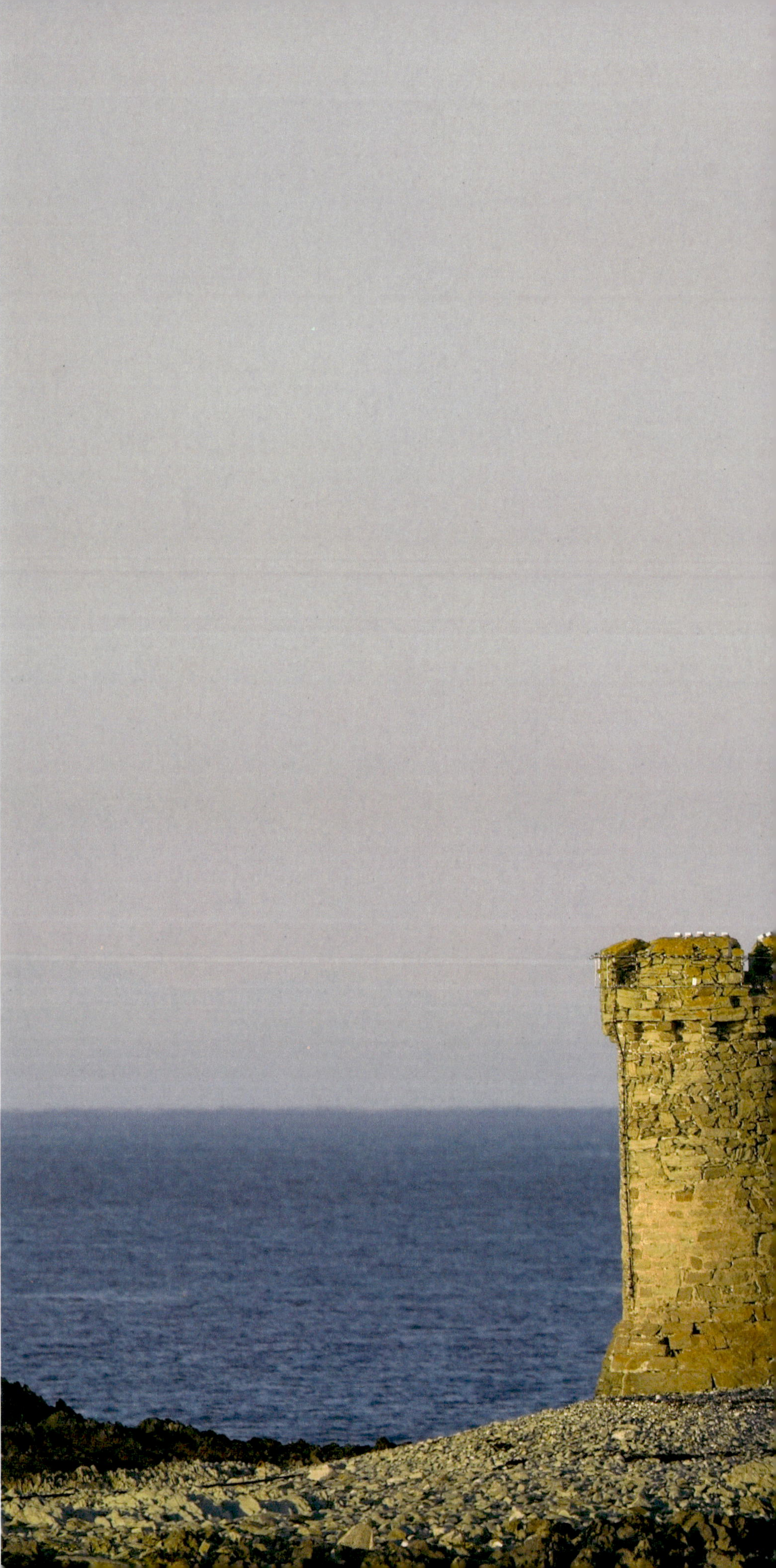

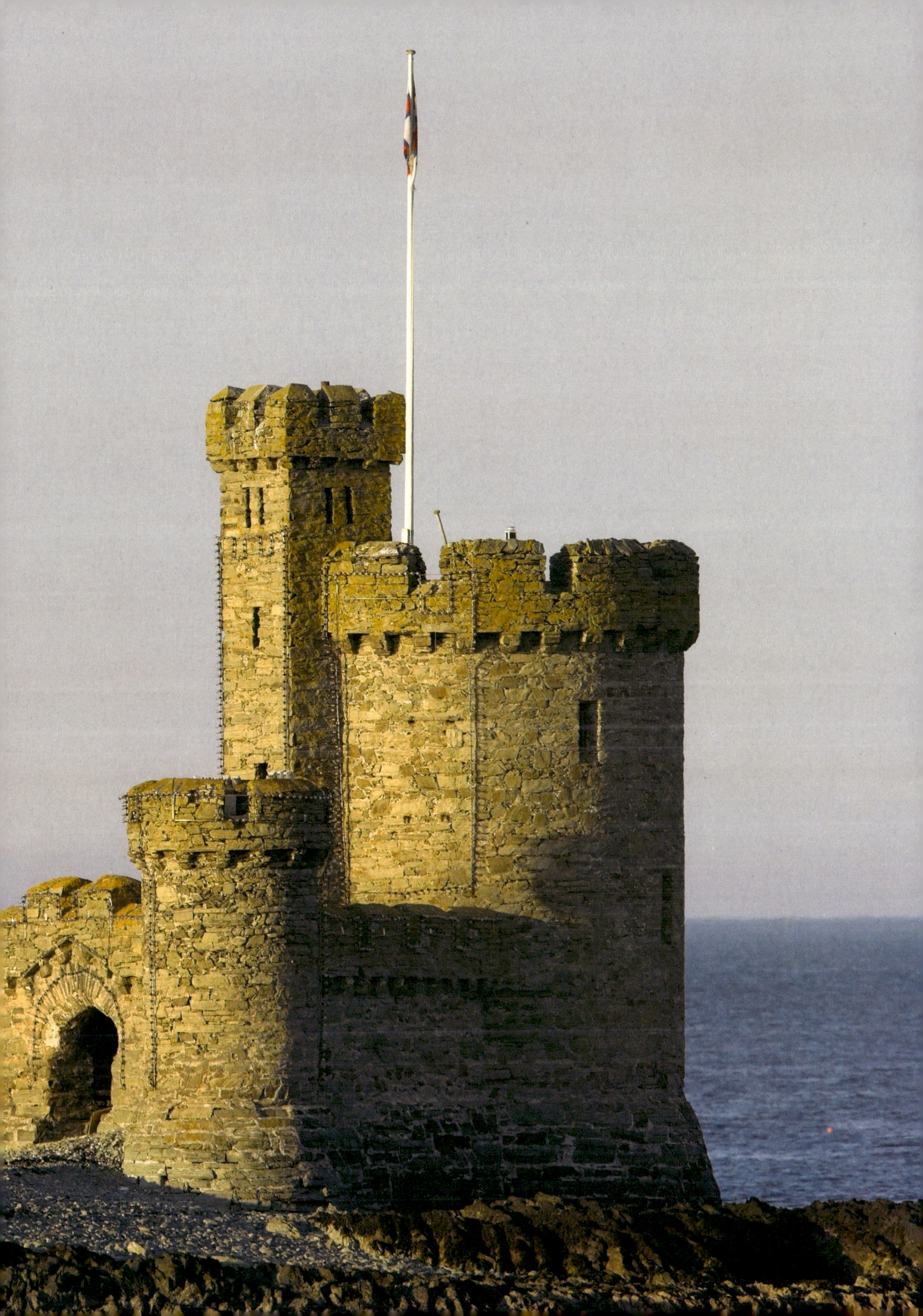

Inverness Castle, Inverness, Scotland

Inverness Castle was built on the site of several previous fortifications, all of which were destroyed or blown up by their enemies. (The castle was the site of at least seven significant sieges between 1429 and 1746.) The present castle was built in 1836, with only small sections of the earlier structures remaining.

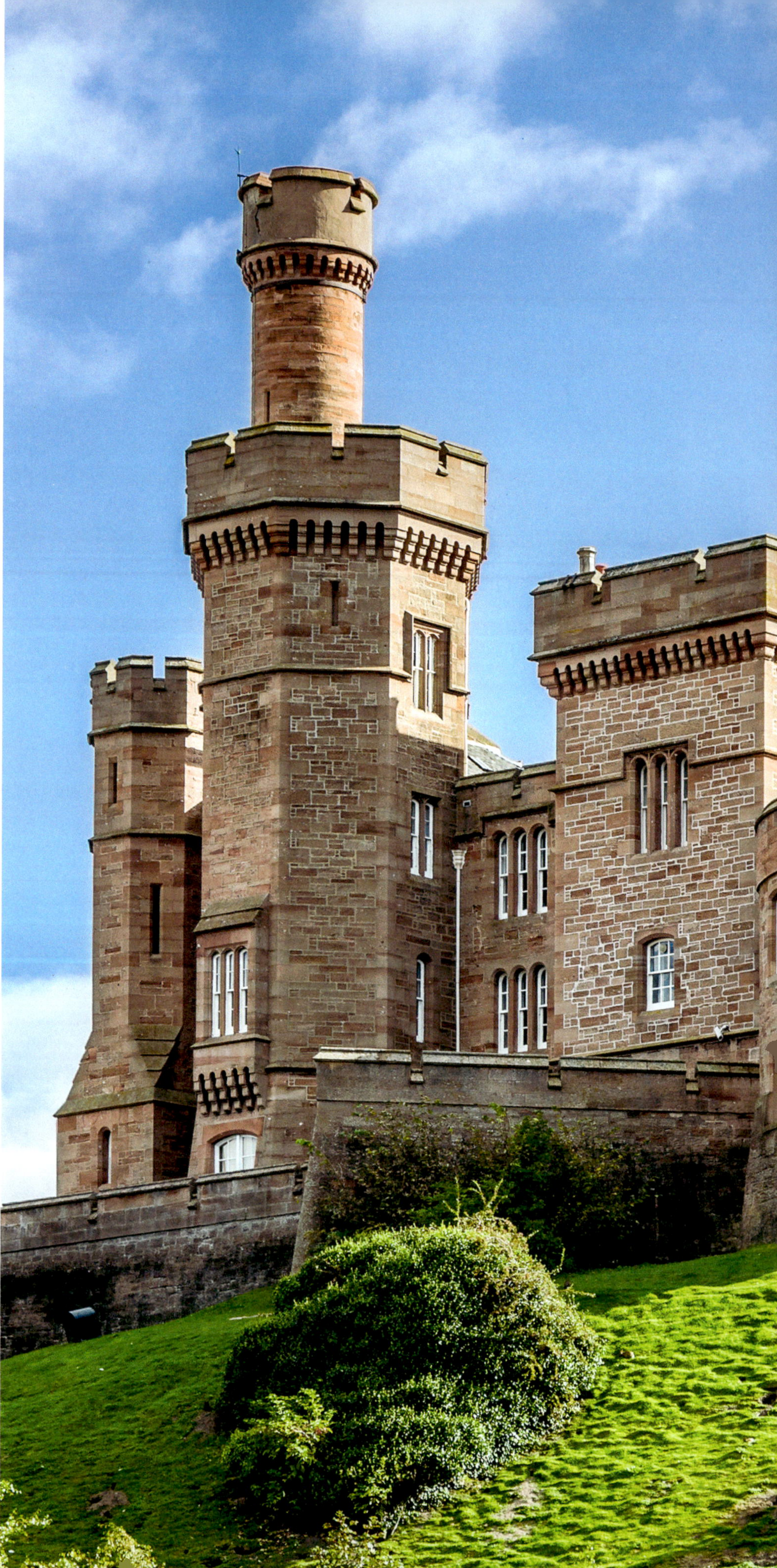

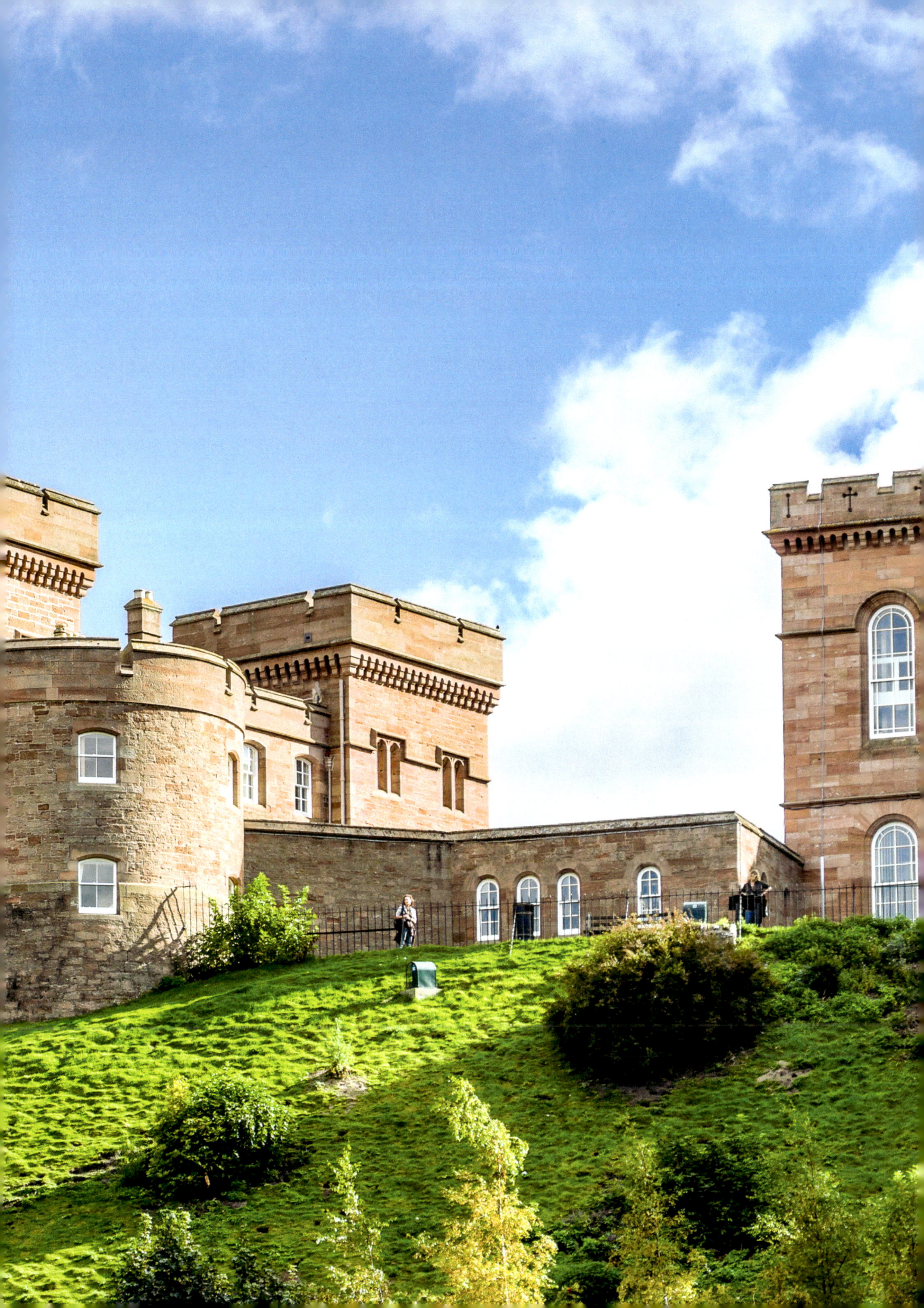

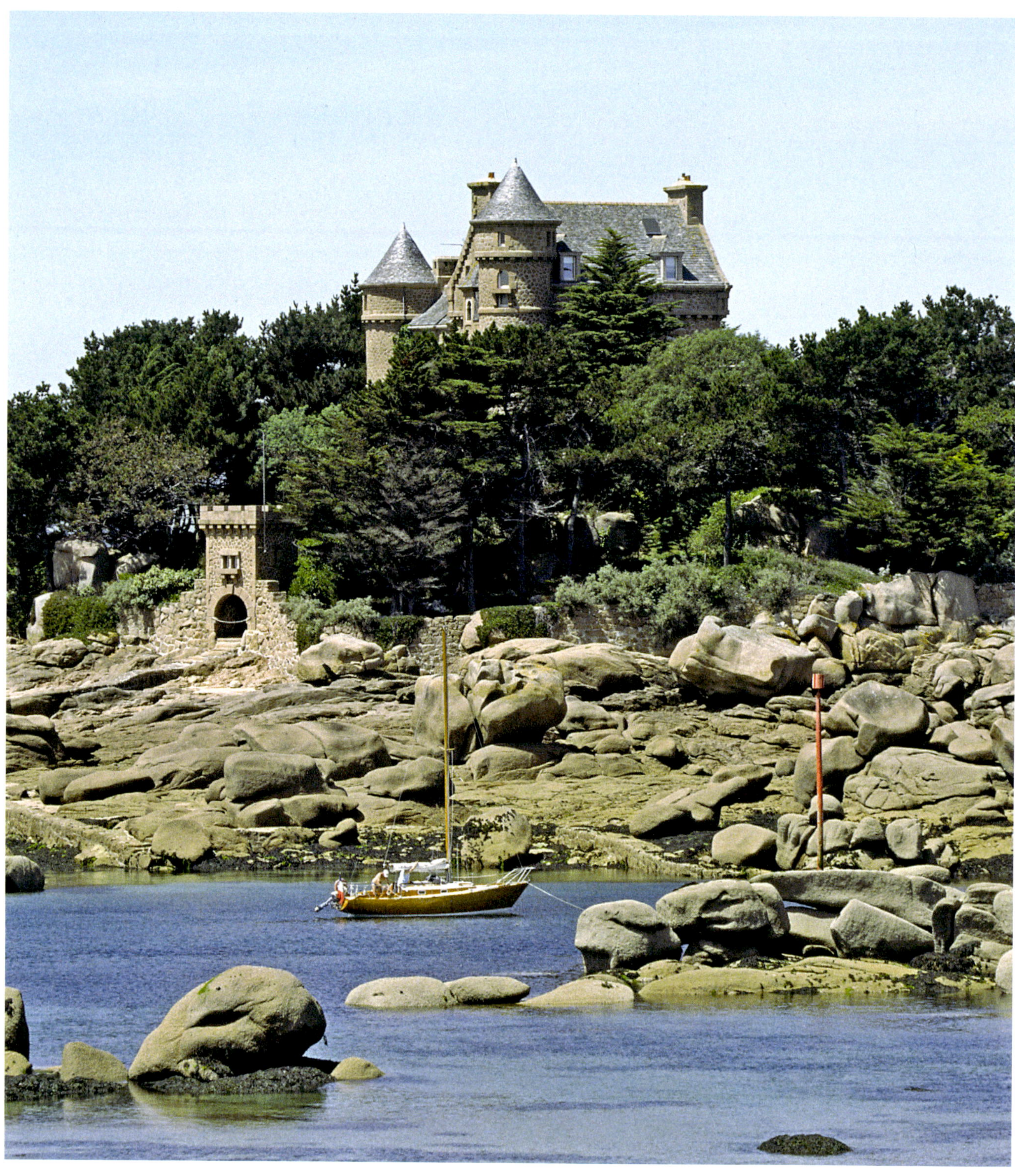

ABOVE:

Château Costaérès, Côtes-d'Armor, Brittany, France

Situated on an island off the north coast of Brittany, Château Costaérès was built in 1885 from pink granite from local quarries. It was renovated in the 1980s and now functions as a luxury tourist destination for private rental.

RIGHT AND OVERLEAF:

Balmoral Castle, Aberdeenshire, Scotland

Balmoral estate was purchased by the royal family in 1852. A castle did exist on the estate, but it was decided to build the present structure and demolish the old one as it was not suitable for its new purpose. As a private purchase, Balmoral is owned by the royal family rather than the crown.

Balmoral Castle is built in the Scottish baronial style, influenced by traditional Scottish castles and continental chateaux. It stands in a large estate containing many other buildings, some of them featuring very different architectural styles.

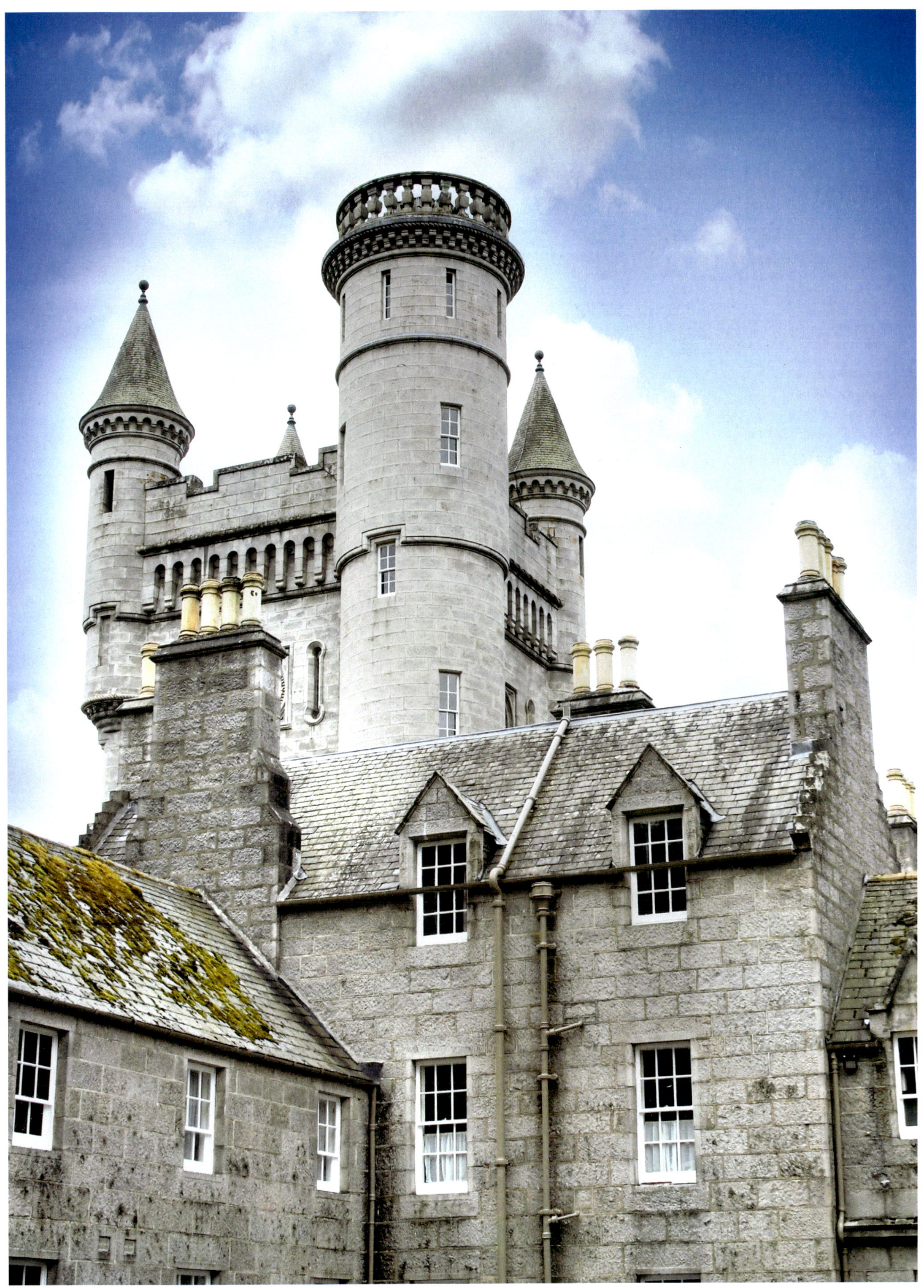

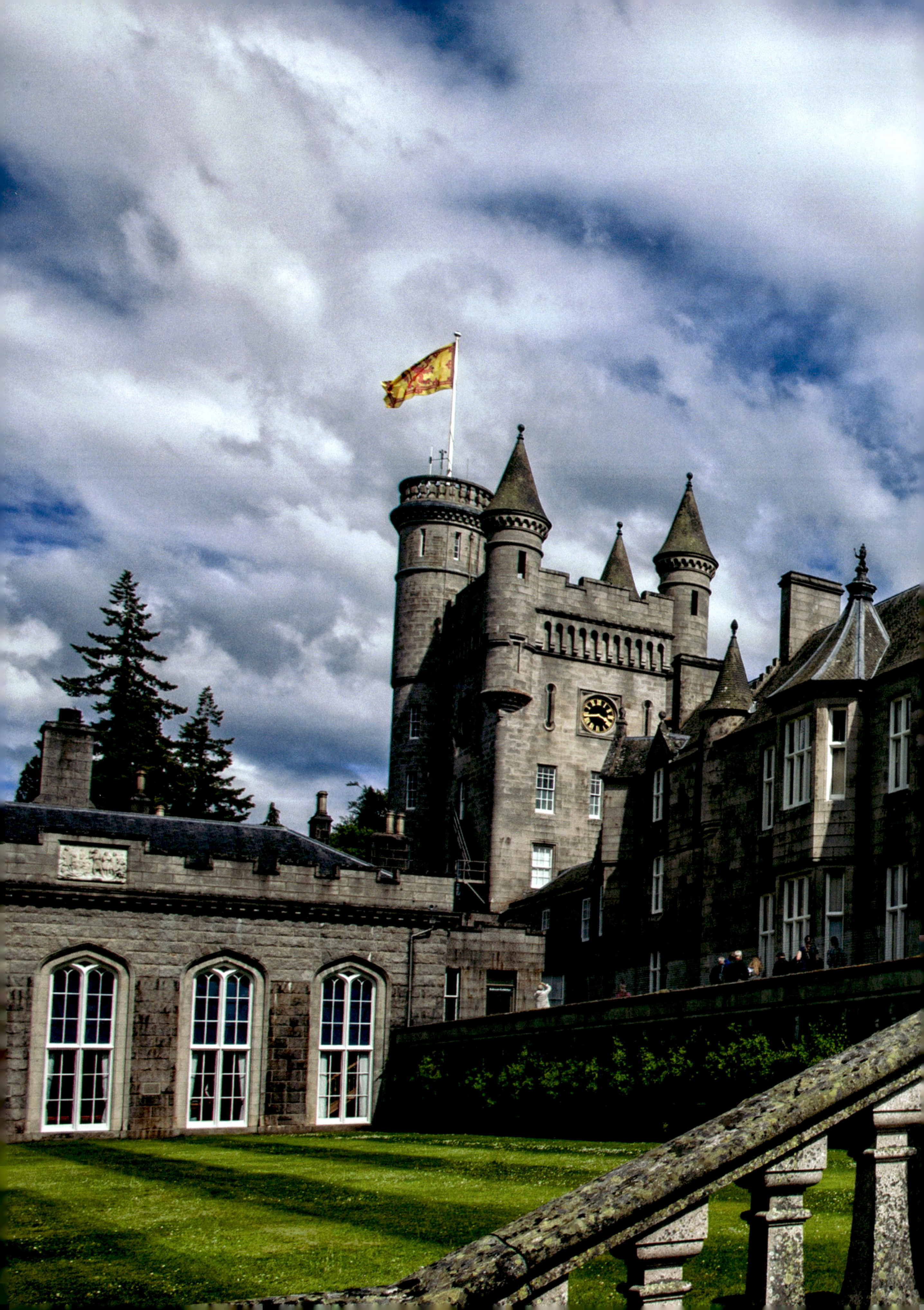

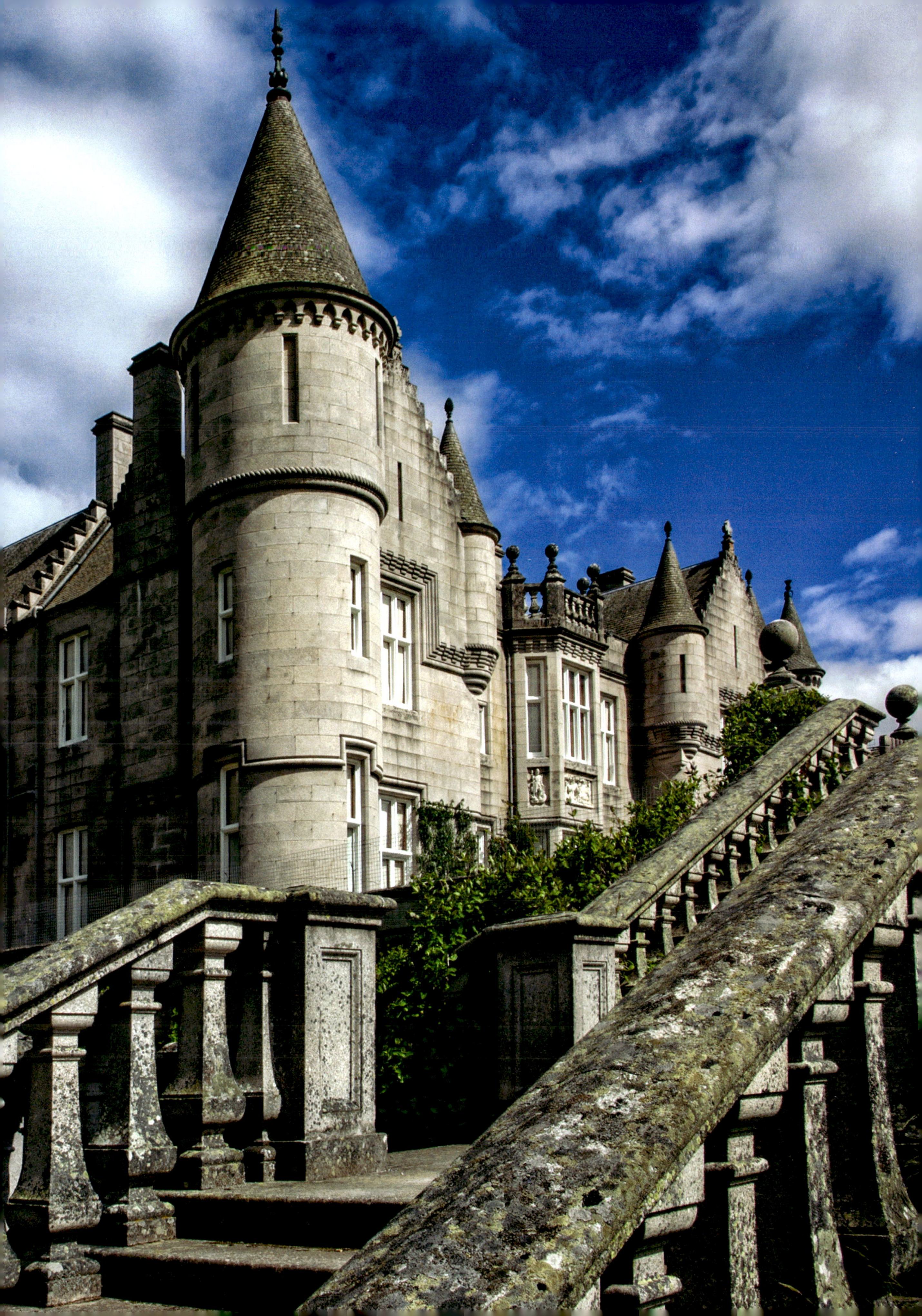

Castell Coch, Tongwynlais, Wales
Castell Coch in South Wales is built on the site of a Norman motte-and-bailey castle and a later stone fortification that was destroyed some time in the early 1300s. The modern castle was built in the late 1800s, in a continental style. It is known as 'the red castle' for its use of red sandstone.

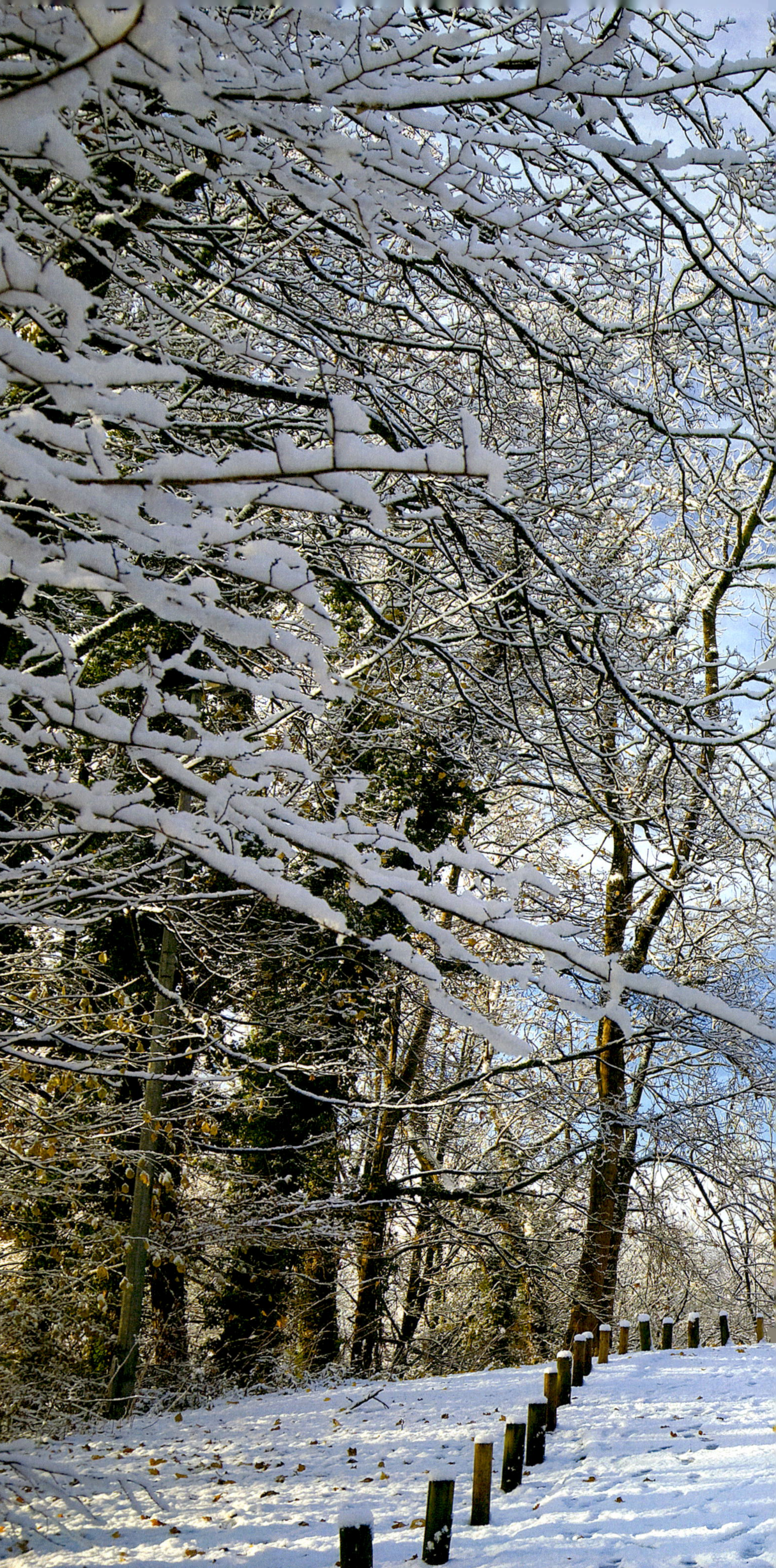

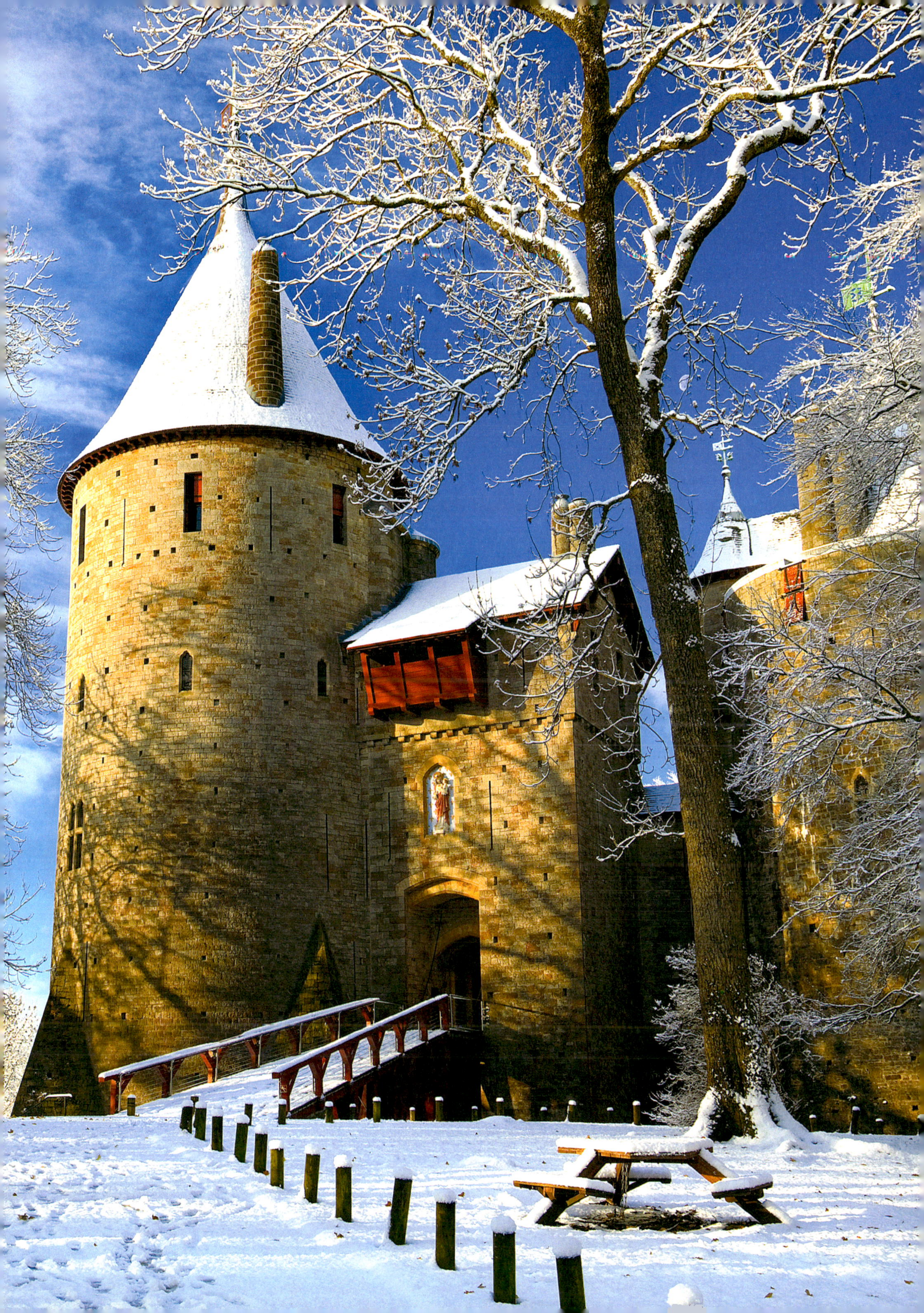

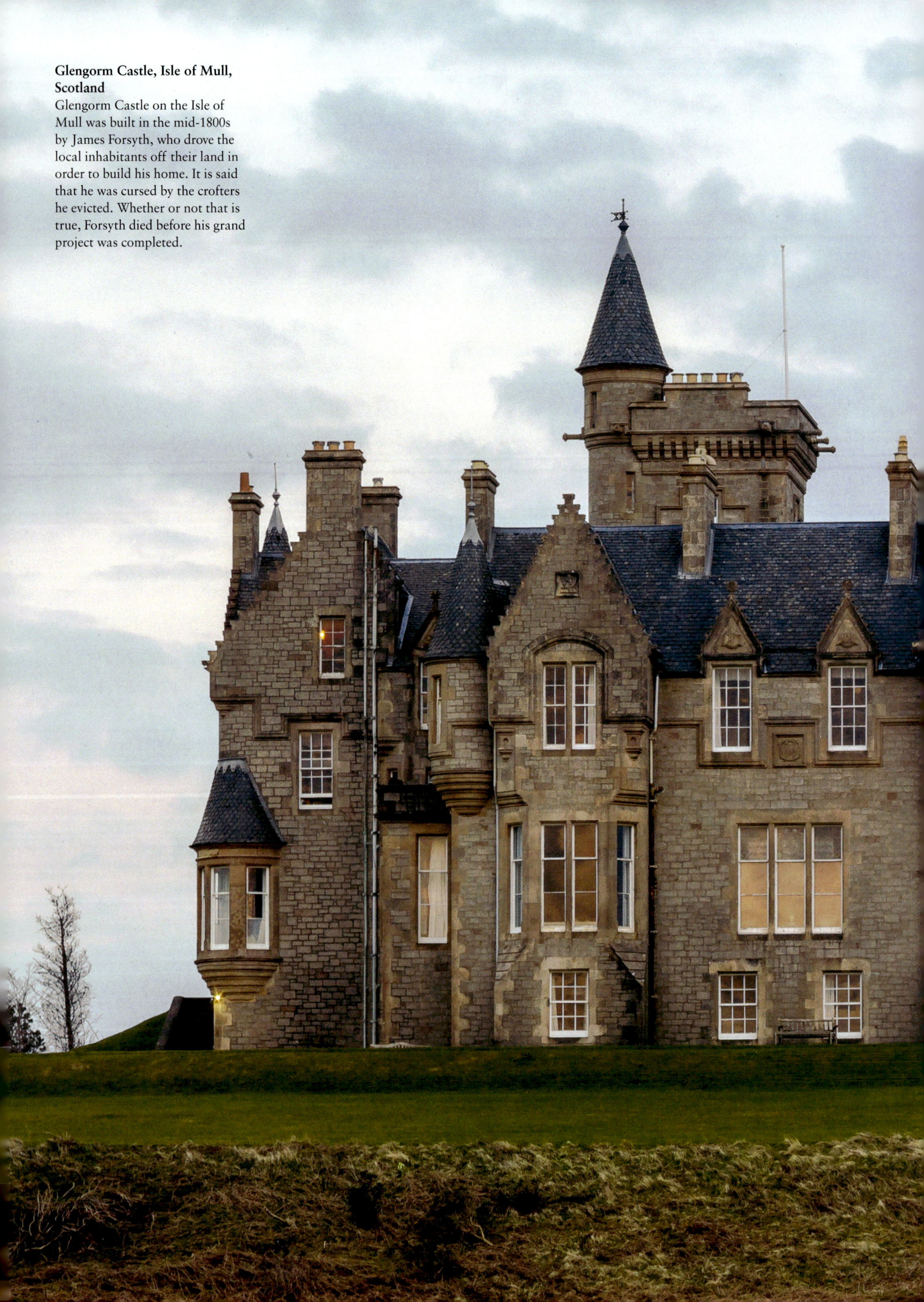

Glengorm Castle, Isle of Mull, Scotland
Glengorm Castle on the Isle of Mull was built in the mid-1800s by James Forsyth, who drove the local inhabitants off their land in order to build his home. It is said that he was cursed by the crofters he evicted. Whether or not that is true, Forsyth died before his grand project was completed.

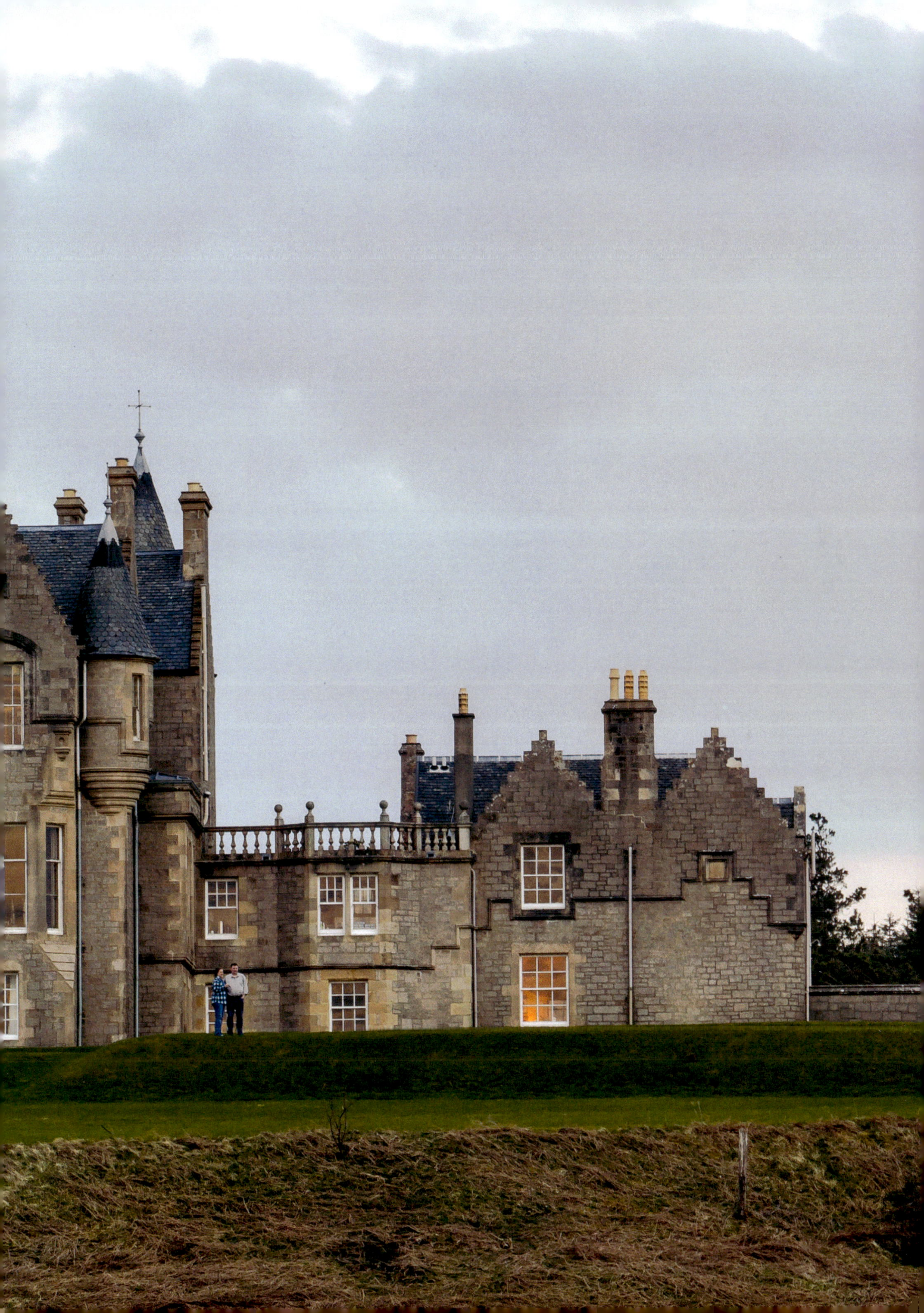

Picture Credits

Alamy: 74 (Arterra Picture Library/Clement Philippe), 75 (Archipix), 98/99 (Robert Harding/Patrick Dieudonne), 135 (Arch White), 147 (Mark Ferguson)

Depositphotos: 95 (Samot)

Dreamstime: 60/61 (Pajda 83), 64/65 (Bobbyrostron), 84/85 (FGCanada), 110 (Daliu80), 111 (Tetyana Kochneva), 162/163 (Danolsen), 176/177 (Paul Brady), 216 (Naturefriend)

Shutterstock: 6 (Gabriel Insuratelu), 7 (Ceri Breeze), 8 (Paul Nash), 10/11 (UAV 4), 12 (Panglossian), 13 (Joe Dunckley), 14/15 (Glyn Swanson), 16/17 (Littlenystock), 18/19 (Fearghal0), 20 (Sosnowska), 22/23 (Richard Faragher), 24/25 (Jim Wearne), 26-29 all (Billy Stock), 30/31 (AerocamUK), 32/33 (Byunau Konstantin), 34/35 (Steve Scribner), 36/37 (Lukasz Pajor), 38/39 top (Gigashots), 38/39 bottom (Walshphotos), 40/41 (Gail Johnson), 42/43 (Anna Phillips), 44/45 (Colin Dewar), 46 top (Cedric Weber), 46 bottom (Prakish Treetasayuth), 47 (Marner 3), 48/49 (Samot), 50/51 (Kisov Boris), 52 top (Elena Gwynne), 52 bottom (Spumador), 53 (Spectrumblue), 54/55 (Gimas), 56/57 (Lauradibi), 58/59 (Stefano Valeri), 62/63 top (Rombo Studio), 62/63 bottom (Andre van de Sande), 66/67 (Radek Sturgolewski), 68/69 (Mark Godden), 70/71 (Valery Egorov), 72/73 (Jolanta Kostecka), 76/77 (Nicola Pulham), 78 (Brian A Jackson), 79 (Ceri Breeze), 80/81 (Marina Kryukova), 82 both (Billy Stock), 83 (Targn Pleiades), 86/87 (Peresanz), 88 top (Swen Stroop), 88 bottom (Bahadir Yeniceri), 89 (Pecold), 90/91 (hipproductions), 92/93 (Swen Stroop), 94 top (Paul Butchard), 94 bottom (Peresanz), 96 (Mattia Querci), 100/101 (Roy Henderson), 102/103 (Treasure Galore), 104/105 (Jan Holm), 106/107 (Leighton Collins), 108/109 (Colin Dewar), 112/113 (Stockescapes), 114/115 (Jericho Cortez), 116/117 (Billy Stock), 118/119 (Steff Bennett), 120/121 (Jaroslav Sekeres), 122 (Heartland Arts), 123 & 124/125 (Steve Scribner), 126/127 (Migdarson), 128/129 (Nick Fox), 130 (Tony Zaccarini), 131 (Treasure Galore), 132/133 (L Daly), 134 (Del Boy), 136/137 (James McKay), 138/139 (Piotr Machowczyk), 140/141 (UTBP), 142/143 (Marek Kotelon), 144/145 (Bill McKelvie), 146 (Heartland Arts), 148/149 (Billy Stock), 150/151 (Rob Crandall), 152 (Jan Holm), 154/155 (Don Fink), 156/157 (Rjmusto), 158/159 & 160/161 (Patryk Kosmider), 164/165 (Honey Cloverz), 166/167 (Spumador), 168/169 (Allan Napier), 170/171 (Hugh O'Connor), 172/173 (Karel Cemy), 174/175 (Jan Holm), 178 (Swen Stroop), 179 (John Braid), 180/181 (Stoyan Marinov Stoyanov), 182/183 (D K Grove), 184 (Helioscribe), 185 (Kwiatek7), 186 (Helioscribe), 187 (Bob Crandall), 188/189 (Gabriela Insuratelu), 190 (Kelleher Photography), 191 (Jaroslav Sekeres), 192/193 (Mara Ze), 194/195 (Ewan Chesser), 196/197 (Tony Zaccarini), 198 (Carole McDonald), 199 both (Patryk Kosmider), 200/201 (Lee Morriss), 202/203 (Noradoa), 204/205 (David Falconer), 206 (Rubiphoto), 207 (James MacDowall), 208/2089 (Walshphotos), 210/211 (Gail Johnson), 212/213 (Graham Taylor), 214/215 (Lowsun), 217 (Silky), 218/219 (Bildagentur Zoonar GmbH), 220/221 (Billy Stock), 222/223 (Luca Cuadrio)